Prague Panoramas

PITT SERIES IN RUSSIAN AND EAST EUROPEAN STUDIES

Jonathan Harris, *Editor*

PRAGUE
PANORAMAS

National Memory
and Sacred Space in the
Twentieth Century

Cynthia Paces

UNIVERSITY OF PITTSBURGH PRESS

Published by the University of Pittsburgh Press, Pittsburgh, Pa., 15260
Copyright © 2009, University of Pittsburgh Press
All rights reserved
Manufactured in the United States of America
Printed on acid-free paper
10 9 8 7 6 5 4 3 2 1

Library of Congress Cataloging-in-Publication Data

Paces, Cynthia.
  Prague panoramas : national memory and sacred space in the twentieth century
/ Cynthia Paces.
     p. cm. — (Pitt series in Russian and East European studies)
  Includes bibliographical references and index.
  ISBN-13: 978-0-8229-6035-5 (paper : alk. paper)
  ISBN-10: 0-8229-6035-4 (paper : alk. paper)
  ISBN-13: 978-0-8229-4375-4 (cloth : alk. paper)
  ISBN-10: 0-8229-4375-1 (cloth : alk. paper)
  1. National monuments—Czech Republic—Prague—History—20th century.
2. Sacred space—Czech Republic—Prague—History—20th century. 3. Church
buildings—Czech Republic—Prague—History—20th century. 4. Collective
memory—Czech Republic—Prague—History—20th century. 5. Nationalism—
Czech Republic—Prague—History—20th century. 6. Political culture—Czech
Republic—Prague—History—20th century. 7. Historic preservation—Czech
Republic—Prague—History—20th century. 8. Prague (Czech Republic) —Buildings, structures, etc. 9. Prague (Czech Republic) —Politics and government—
20th century. 10. Prague (Czech Republic) —Religion—20th century. I. Title.
  DB2632.P33 2009   363.6'909437120904—dc22
  2009014286

For my grandfather, Karel Pačes, 1911–1999
You shared with me your krasné město.

Contents

Illustrations

x

Preface

In 1990, my father's first cousin Miluška Voclová brought me to the street where my father was born. I was the first of my family to return to Czechoslovakia after the fall of Communism, and I was embraced by an extended family I hardly knew existed. Never did I guess that, five years later, I would return to the little row house in Prague 10, to live in the home my grandparents had built more than a half-century earlier. I have stayed in that home many times—on my own, with my husband and daughter, with my parents, with my sister, with many friends, and with my grandfather. Living there brought me closer to history and to the power of place, and helped make this book what it is.

I am grateful to the many people and institutions that contributed to this project. Financially, I received generous support from Columbia University, the U.S. Department of Education (which provided a Fulbright-Hays Doctoral Dissertation Abroad fellowship), the International Research Exchange Board (IREX), the Andrew W. Mellon Foundation, the American Council of Learned Societies, the National Endowment for the Humanities, the Woodrow Wilson International Center for Scholars, and The College of New Jersey (through its Support for Scholarly Activities, Mini Grant, and Sabbatical Leave awards).

Some works in this volume appeared previously in other venues, and I appreciate the permission of these presses and journals to use revised forms of these publications. A version of chapter six appeared as "'The Czech Nation must be Catholic!' An Alternative Version of Czech Nationalism during the First Republic," *Nationalities Papers* 27. A version of chapter seven appeared as "Religious Heroes for a Secular State: Commemorating Jan Hus and Saint Wenceslas in 1920s Czechoslovakia," in Nancy Wingfield and Maria Bucur, *Staging the Past: Commemorations in the Habsburg Lands*. Material in chapters five, twelve, and thirteen previously appeared in "The Fall and Rise of Prague's Marian Column," *Radical History Review* 79 (reprinted in Daniel J. Walkowitz and Lisa Maya Knauer, *Memory and the Impact of Political Transformation on Public Space*). I have also drawn on my articles "Rotating Spheres: Gendered Commemorative Practice at the 1903 Jan Hus Memorial Festival in Prague," *Nationalities Papers* 28; "The Battle for Prague's Old Town Square: Symbolic

Space and the Birth of the Republic," in Blair Ruble and John Czaplicka, *Composing Urban History and the Constitution of Civic Identities*; and "The Sacred and the Profane: Religion and Nationalism in the Bohemian Lands, 1890–1920," (cowritten with Nancy M. Wingfield) in Pieter Judson and Marsha Rozenblitt, *Constructing Identities in East Central Europe.*

My work has benefited from the advice and support of many scholars, friends, and colleagues. At the University of Richmond, John Rilling, Martin Ryle, Bob Nelson, and John Treadway believed in my potential. At Columbia University, István Deák challenged me to rethink my assumptions about nationalism and the nation-state. Atina Grossmann and Victoria de Grazia were role models for women scholars. Richard Wortman helped me to think about memory and commemoration as an essential part of history, and Isser Wolloch shared with me that working in archives was "better than drugs." Special thanks go to Eagle Glassheim, Wendy Urban-Mead, Eliza Johnson Ablovatski, David Frey, Robert Nemes, Dan Unowsky, and Alon Rachimimov for stimulating conversations and unmatched collegiality.

I have been fortunate to be welcomed into a community of scholars who have generously shared resources and ideas. Claire Nolte has supported my career since its earliest days. Blair Ruble, John Czaplicka, and fellow members of the Woodrow Wilson Center and Central European University (Prague branch) urban history workshop enthusiastically encouraged the new directions in which I was taking my work. Jindřich Toman organized Czech cultural studies workshops through the University of Michigan Slavic department, creating an interdisciplinary community that advanced the work of younger scholars. I experienced the ideal model of friendly scholarly exchange with the "Kennebunkport Circle": Melissa Feinberg, Paul Hanebrink and Eagle Glassheim. Later, Melissa Feinberg reread the final manuscript and gave me exceptional feedback. I would also like to thank Brad Abrams, Hugh Agnew, Jonathan Bolton, Maria Bucur, Peter Bugge, Alice Freifeld, Pieter Judson, Jeremy King, Lisa Kirschenbaum, and Matthew Witkovsky.

In 1995, Nancy M. Wingfield sent me a Franz Kafka postcard from Prague, excitedly telling me that we held similar research interests. Since then, she has shared sources, editing skills, and friendship. She read the entire manuscript of this volume several times, providing sharp and thorough advice. Few scholars share her attention to detail and her generosity of spirit. At the University of Pittsburgh Press, Peter Kracht and Deborah Meade provided excellent advice in preparing and revising the manuscript.

In the Czech Republic, I received immeasurable help from the staffs of the National Archives, the Prague City Archives, the Archive of the Presidential Chancellery, and the National Library. Scholars Jiří Musil, Jiří Skalník, and the late Jan Havránek provided resources and advice. Jan Bradna, the sculptor of the new Marian Column, generously supplied me with information and illustrations for this volume. My Czech teacher and dear friend Alice Podobová helped me with translations and grammar.

At The College of New Jersey, my colleagues and students have taught me the joys of being a teacher–scholar. Jo-Ann Gross has been a giving mentor; she read parts of the manuscript with a keen eye and shared her love and knowledge of sacred space. Dan Crofts, Stuart McCook, Tom Allsen, Derek Peterson, Felicia Steele, and Matt Bender read parts of my work, discussed my ideas, and gave advice on the manuscript. Students in my courses and my 2003 Study Tour to Prague shared my passion for the people and places of East Central Europe: special thanks to Stephanie Smith, Elizabeth Johnson, Alexis Becker, and Sara Tomczuk for their enthusiasm. On a plane home from Prague, Jesse Bucher asked perceptive questions about the role of the Communist Party in commemoration and nationalism; his curiosity and insight convinced me to expand my manuscript to cover the end of the twentieth century.

I cherish the memories of Prague wanderings with Jim and Susan Carter, Juli and Rob Wilson-Black, Yi-Li Wu and Michael Thouless, Ellen Paul, J. D. Phillips, Kevin Deagan-Krause, and the "Wilburtha East" gang of Sarah Darrow, Pamela V'Combe, Bill Walto, and Jeanne Malloy.

I could not have completed this project without the support of family and friends. I was welcomed by Czech extended family in Kostelec nad Černými lesy and the surrounding area. My parents, Milo and Dorothy Paces, took photographs and combed the shelves of Prague bookstores for me. My father passed to me his love of history and enabled me to live in his family home during my research trips. My sister, Diane Pačes-Wiles, gave professional guidance on the book's illustrations, and offered unfailing love and support for my endeavors. Her family—John, Evan, and Elena—shared a memorable Prague family reunion in 2007. Thanks also to Jennifer Gohlke, Karen Deaver, Kit Grindstaff, and Danielle McClellan for encouraging me to write.

My husband, James Carter, a gifted historian and writer, read the entire manuscript and believed in this project and in me. He shares a passion for travel, stories, and *české pivo*. I thank him with all my heart. Mariel helped me see Prague with fresh eyes. At age five, she told me that Prague was almost as good as Disney World, because "the Charles Bridge is kind of a ride." She makes life a joyous ride. Charlotte, named for her great-grandfather and a bridge, has brought new joys.

I will always treasure the memories of being in the Czech Republic with my grandfather, Karel Paces, and grieve that my grandmother Marie did not live to return with us. I walked with my grandfather on Prague streets and visited the church in Kostelec where he was baptized. These moments were often difficult and emotional, but they revealed the essence of history—the continual dialogue of the past and the present. When I learned he had passed away in upstate New York, I was again in Prague. I threw a rose in the Vltava River, the heart of the city he called the most beautiful on earth. His sacrifices made my life and this book possible, and I dedicate it to him.

Note on Language

Writing about places in Prague is particularly complex, as each landmark has a Czech and German name, as well as an English translation. Further, names of streets and squares changed during different political eras. Because this study focuses on the Czech national movements, I use the common Czech names, with English translations. If a place name has a standard English usage, such as Prague, Pilsen, or Old Town Square, I use that version. Only where the German name is more well-known (as in the case of a concentration camp) do I also provide the German.

For most of the narrative, I use the term Bohemian Lands to refer to the provinces of Bohemia, Moravia, and Austrian Silesia. The term Czech Lands does not acknowledge the mixed ethnicity of the region before the Second World War, but can be an appropriate usage in regard to the postwar era.

For personal names, I am using the Czech spelling for historical figures, except where the English name is well known, as with St. Wenceslas or Emperor Francis Joseph.

St. Vitus Cathedral
and Prague Castle ■

Josefov/
Jewish Quarter

■ Franz Kafka Statue

National Memorial on Vitkov Hill
and Jan Žižka Monument ■

■ Tyn Cathedral and New Marian Column
Old Town Square with Jan Hus
Memorial and Site of Marian Column

■ Strahov
Monastery

Charles
Bridge

Bethlehem Chapel

Memorial to the Victims ■
of Communism

■ National Theater

Wenceslas Square and
■ St. Wenceslas Memorial

Sacred Heart Church ■

■ Sts. Cyril and Methodius Church/Memorial
to the Victims of the Heydrich Terror

■ František Palacký Memorial

Map of Prague

Prague Panoramas

Prague—Panoramas of History

O N A November day in 1995, I walked through Old Town Square
(Staroměstké náměstí) to the City Archives, then housed in the baroque Clam-Gallas Palace. The weather was discouraging. A proverb
in the morning newspaper warned that St. Martin rides into town on a white
horse on November 11 and brings snow every day for the rest of the winter.
St. Martin's day was still a week away, but it had been snowing—a wet, heavy
snow—for days. Not the magical dusting captured in black-and-white photographs of Prague, but thick splashes that melted into mud.

The cobblestones on the square felt slippery, so I walked carefully, looking
down. Had it not been for the precipitation, I might have missed the makeshift site of memory on the south side of the square. Among the cobblestones,
in a heavily trafficked section of the square, was a marble plaque with writing difficult to decipher. Flowers and nubs of burnt down candles lay upon
the wet circular center of the plaque, but the four triangular corner slabs remained visible. Some of the words on the small memorial had been chiseled
out and cemented over, but with effort I made out the inscriptions. Each of
the four corner pieces declared—in Czech, German, English, and Latin—the
prophetic words, "Here did stand and will stand again the Marian Column of
Old Town Square."

This site of memory embodies the main arguments of this book. A group of
Czech Catholics had recently placed the plaque in Old Town Square, at the spot
where in 1918 Czech nationalists and others pulled down a baroque column
and statue of the Virgin Mary. Soon after the plaque appeared, an unknown
group or individual scratched and cemented over the words "will stand again."
Prague Catholics then returned to the site and laid flowers and candles, once
again marking the cobblestones as their own. The Prague media took up the
question of whether a replica of the baroque monument should again stand
in Old Town Square: a wide range of opinions emerged, revealing divisions
among the population about how public places in the capital city should be

Site of the Marian Column, 1995. Photo by author.

represented. This controversy echoed the debates about public spaces in Prague that resounded throughout the twentieth century.

The definitions of what it meant to be part of the Czech nation or its capital city have never been fully agreed upon, and debates on this have often played out in Prague's public spaces, through temporary commemorations, such as parades and protests, or through permanent sites of memory: statues, monuments, or buildings. Historiography has often emphasized conflicts between Czechs and outside groups or political entities: Slovaks, ethnic Germans, the Habsburg Monarchy, Nazi Germany, the Soviet Union. These conflicts have been crucial in understanding the history of the Czechs, but they have often obscured the contestations within the community of those trying to assert a strong Czech identity. Looking closely at attempts throughout the twentieth century to mark the landscape of Prague with "sacred spaces," intended to form emotional bonds between citizens and "the nation," reveals the impossibility of locating a single definition of the Czech nation.

The complex religious history of Prague and Bohemia dominated Prague's newly created sacred spaces during the twentieth century; in particular, a history of conflict between an early Protestant movement and the domination of Catholic Austria played out on the cobblestones, monuments, and parade routes of the capital city. Although Prague became an increasingly secular city, its leaders still turned to its religious history for the themes of national commemorations. This choice can appear strange or ill advised. In the early part of the twentieth century, rather than search for neutral national symbols, leaders chose Protestant heroes from the national past, angering Czech Catholics; later in the century, even atheist Communists held onto the powerful national narrative of religious independence, lauding Christian figures from the medieval era. Why were these controversial choices made? One answer lies in the power of the sacred in human societies. Religion relies upon emotion and faith. Past stories of martyrdom and sacrifice fit well into a developing national narrative emphasizing independence and defiance against authority. Further, religion and nationalism both inscribe codes of moral behavior for their constituents. As Paul Hanebrink suggests, many twentieth-century European leaders believed that religion "could also be a modern world view, a set of moral absolutes that guided an individual to act publicly in a hostile world."[1] To convey these principles, national leaders introduced religious rhetoric and iconography into the public sphere.

The use of public space has a strong religious dimension. As authors of a recent volume on sacred space have explained, "Space and place inscribe communities of faith and practice in specific locations."[2] Nationalists in Prague sought to inscribe Czech identity into the multinational landscape in a similar way. In urban settings, physical monuments or buildings were built to gather people for a specific reason, and fell into three categories: civic, religious, or commercial. In many public spaces, the civic and the religious were united, thus attracting more people and adding to the power of the places. The religious imagery in the civic sites helped forge the emotional bond between the Czech community and the city.

These debates about national and religious identity, arising in the nineteenth century, remained present throughout the twentieth century. Czech historiography has often marked the annexation of Bohemia and Moravia–Silesia by Nazi Germany as the end of the national narrative. From that moment until 1989, the Czech(-oslovak) state was marked by occupation and political domination by outside forces. Yet the Second World War and Communist eras did not stamp out the national discourse; the same debates reemerged in surprising and fascinating ways. Both dissidents and government leaders sought meaning and legitimacy for their movements through these religious–national debates.

As the capital city and the seat of government, Prague was at the heart of the debates of what it meant to be Czech in the twentieth century.[3] From the urban elite of the Habsburg era, to the leaders of the First Republic, to the Nazi Protectorate, and the Communist and post-Communist governments of the late twentieth century, leaders had a strong stake in demonstrating that the capital city was a Czech city and the arbiter of what the nation represented. Further, the city's singular beauty, architectural diversity, and relative wealth fostered an emotional, almost sacred bond prized by national leaders. Last, political decisions made in Prague, as the capital city—decisions such as legislation on state holidays or responses to unrest in the provinces—affected the entire state.

The City of Memory

Many accounts of the early days of the Czechoslovak Republic, in autumn 1918, mention briefly that a mob tore down the Marian Column, a treasured baroque monument. Yet, few studies have thoroughly explored the conflicting *mentalités* and collective memories of Prague citizens that created such passions, both angry and loving, for a public sculpture. Three quarters of a century after the Marian Column was felled—years of world war, revolution, and authoritarian rule—there were still citizens who cared enough to chisel out words of a plaque declaring a plan to resurrect the fallen memorial, or to light candles and lay flowers to claim this public space for their beliefs. As scholars of religion have shown, "religion and memory are connected . . . to place and to violence."[4] In the case of the Marian Column site, Prague citizens remember a century of religious violence—the destruction of the column itself but also Nazi, Communist, and even Republican violence against religious communities, practices, and sites throughout the century. Roger Friedland and Richard Hecht have argued that "Central places, holy places, sacred places, memory places are those in which time is concentrated, thickened."[5] When Prague residents today lay flowers at the Marian Column site they are only in part commemorating the 1918 destruction of a baroque monument; the site has absorbed a broader meaning and range of time.

Prague's public spaces helped define the culture of a country and capital city. A city is more than a physical location; the Latin root, *civitas,* connotes citizenship, the political and cultural connection between people and the place where they dwell. Therefore, to understand the history of twentieth-century Prague is to delve into the mentalités (the conflicting attitudes, beliefs, and memories) of the inhabitants. Authors have frequently remarked on the attachment of Prague residents to their city. Prague German-Jewish writer Franz Kafka's sentiment about his city, which nearly every study on Prague cites, explains, "Prague does not let go, either of you or of me. This old mother has claws. There is nothing for it but to give in."[6] In this atmosphere—where citizens foster emotional relationships with religiously coded objects like the Marian Column, Jan Hus Memorial, or St. Wenceslas Monument on Wenceslas Square—place, memory, and the sense of sacredness contributed to citizens' self-perception. In turn, the city's denizens created new places to transmit their ideals.

Architectural critic Christian Norberg-Schulz considers Prague a prime example of a place that successfully fuses physical markers and social characteristics in a genius loci (spirit of place). He points out the linguistic relationship between space and events, citing that occurrences are said to "take place" and "In fact it is meaningless to imagine any happening without reference to a locality."[7] Indeed, political events in Prague are intrinsically linked in collective memory to specific "sacred" places: Klement Gottwald, first Communist president, declaring the 1948 Communist victory from a balcony overlooking the Hus Memorial on Old Town Square, or Charles University student Jan Palach immolating himself in 1969 before the Wenceslas Memorial to protest continued Soviet military presence in Prague.

Place, indeed, infuses events with meaning. Yet, writing a history of places poses particular challenges for the historian. The importance of historical actors in creating and interacting with public space cannot be overstated, but often studies of memory focus more on the objects remembered than on the subjects who are remembering. Further, Alon Confino, a prominent scholar of historical memory, warns that studies of collective memory often become overly insular, noting that "the history of memory is useful and interesting not only for thinking about how the past is represented in, say, a museum, but also about, more extensively, the historical mentality of people in the past, about the commingled beliefs, practices, and symbolic representations that make up people's perception of the past."[8]

Prague's physical markers are vehicles for understanding the values, often conflicting, of a range of citizens. Naturally, political leaders and intellectuals play roles in determining how the past should be commemorated. But, it is the common people who pull down statues, attend festivals, and cross Charles Bridge over the Vltava (Moldau) River each day, "past the statues of saints with their faint glimmer of light."[9]

. Prague's manifold statues of saints, described by Norberg-Schulz, convey an overarching theme. Religion—not usually formal institutions, but symbolic gestures and beliefs—emerged as a common and controversial subject of debates and discussions about collective memory, and thus public space, in Prague. Although the famous religious landmarks of Prague—Gothic St. Vitus looming over the river, baroque St. Nicholas guarding the Little Quarter, dozens of saints lining Charles Bridge—obviously date to earlier eras, religious motifs nevertheless dominated twentieth-century debates about the city's ever-shifting identity. Religious Catholics and Protestants did participate in these discussions but, surprisingly, freethinking liberals of the first half of the century and Communist leaders of the second half were the leaders of movements to create spiritual sites of memory. Religious imagery was powerful for both the faithful and the secular. There were certainly nonreligious sites erected in Prague, but they often reflected the external conflicts in which the Czechs engaged: for example, Czechs and Germans in Prague competed by building separate theaters or by attacking or protecting Habsburg statues.[10] The religious dimension exposes, rather, the internal fissures within the Czech national movement of the Czechoslovak state.

Scholars have created a rich historiography of national memory, invented traditions, and national monuments. Pierre Nora, noted French scholar, popularized the idea of *lieux de memoire* ("sites of memory"), which proposed that physical markers and public spaces are the sites where collective memory resides, making it possible for people to engage with and contest ideas about the past.[11] Scholars of East and Central Europe are particularly engaged in the ongoing conversations about history and memory, beginning, two decades after Communism's demise in the region, to understand how the Cold War era represented both rupture and continuity with the past. After years of state control over historiography, Czech scholars have started to investigate the impact of totalitarian rule on the country's collective national memories; historians and semioticians such as Jiří Rak, Vladimír Macura, Zdeněk Hojda, and Jiří Pokorný have sought to understand the impact of the nation's past on modern mentalités.[12]

The City of Change

Within one hundred years, Prague citizens witnessed seven major political transformations. The fall of the Habsburg Monarchy and its Austro-Hungarian Empire in 1918 ushered in a national democracy led by scholar turned politician Tomáš G. Masaryk. After years of dissatisfaction by ethnic minorities who felt underrepresented in a nation-state that privileged "Czechoslovak" ethnicity, this democracy unraveled when the 1938 Munich Pact, negotiated among Germany, Italy, Britain, and France, ceded the Sudetenland, the predominantly German-inhabited borderlands, and other territories to Nazi Germany. The short-lived, authoritarian Second Republic was established when President Edvard Beneš abdicated and formed a London-based government in exile. Within six months Bohemia and Moravia had been incorporated into the German Third Reich, and Slovakia was created as an independent puppet state. The country—absent Subcarpathian Ruthenia—reunited under Beneš after the war, and three years later many Prague residents eagerly welcomed the Communist Party to power, only to be repressed by an undemocratic, authoritarian regime. In 1989 crowds on Wenceslas Square called for the end of Communist rule and embraced playwright Václav Havel as president. Then in 1993 their city was capital no longer of Czechoslovakia but of the Czech Republic, as the Czech Republic and Slovakia peacefully parted in the so-called Velvet Divorce.

As a result of these political upheavals, the population of the city—and of Czechoslovakia as a whole—became increasingly homogenized. In the late Habsburg period and during the interwar years, many Prague Germans assimilated into the now dominant Czech linguistic community. But during the years of the Second World War the diversity of Prague and of Czechoslovakia was violently ended. Most Prague Jews were exterminated in the Holocaust, and German speakers were expelled collectively by vengeful Czechs immediately after the war's end. From a vibrant multiethnic urban culture, Prague has become a Czech city, albeit full of foreign tourists and expatriots from all corners of the earth.

Nevertheless, during the tumultuous twentieth century, Prague's landscape remained remarkably stable. Unlike most major cities in Central and Eastern Europe, Prague's panorama was left virtually unscathed by the Second World War, and the Communist Party did not interfere with the architectural heritage of the city. Prague Castle, perched above the Vltava River, has been the seat of government since 1918, and the city has retained its moniker of the "city of one hundred spires."

Yet, even as the overall look of the city remained constant, many new monuments appeared in Prague during the twentieth century. Many groups within Prague's Czech society—nationalists, conservative landholders, historical preservationists, modern artists, feminists, socialists, Communists, Catholics, Jews and Protestants—debated about monuments that would properly represent the capital and, thus, the Czech nation. And in particular, Czech leaders attempted to adorn parts of the city with monuments and buildings that would reflect a national, rather than a multiethnic, culture.

The City of Panoramas

In the craft kiosks on Old Town Square and in stalls on the Charles Bridge, tourists can find panoramic photographs and sketches of Prague. The long, rectangular scenes carry the viewer through time as a single image takes in a thousand years of architecture: Romanesque, Gothic, renaissance, baroque, neoclassical, and modern. The Roman Catholic heritage of the city is readily apparent: it would be difficult to buy a panorama that did not display a Catholic cathedral, church, or religious statues.

Before the age of photography, the term panorama implied a long painting, such as a Chinese scroll painting, that is rolled out for the viewer. Usually the subject of the painting is a landscape, aspects of which are revealed to the spec-

Panoramic view of St. Vitus Cathedral from Charles Bridge, with baroque statues in foreground. Postcard from the author's collection.

tator slowly: if the observer gazes at an unfurled panorama, he or she inevitably misses details, but by focusing on one segment at a time, the observer may discover special features of the place. In the present book, each featured statue, church, or memorial is examined in great detail—from the expressions on a figure's face to the tilt of a head, from the faded frescoes on a wall to the wooden beams buttressing a roof—each is described "thickly" (using Clifford Geertz's method) to uncover the meanings and the conflicts ingrained in marble, granite, or brick. Similarly, thick descriptions of commemorative events (such as national festivals) elucidate ways that citizens have related and responded to public space. A panorama requires tactile interaction, just as public monuments and architecture demand human contact.

Architectural historian M. Christine Boyer has called the twentieth-century city a panorama. Although her description of a modern city of skyscrapers does not fit Prague, she reminds us that all twentieth-century cities housed "fragmented and paradoxical views. . . . Space itself became a focus of social concern and object of fascination."[13] The panoramic city can be viewed from above—from an airplane or the top of a tall building—or from a tramcar or automobile. Something once viewed as stationary has become for modern urban dwellers a constantly moving image. According to Boyer, these shifting perspectives have allowed viewers to experience space from many angles and therefore to realize that supposedly static objects continually change in appearance and meaning.

Indeed, early twentieth-century cubist painters experimented with the meta- ∿
phoric and tangible fracturing of space, and Prague was the center of cubist 9
architecture, as architects like Josef Gočár and Pavel Janák took Picasso and
Braque's ideas and transferred them to a third dimension. Buildings such as
Our Lady of the Black Madonna and the Legiobanka building challenged traditional architectural forms with series of broken lines and planes.

This modern way of seeing encouraged a multiplicity of viewpoints about
space itself. Citizens began to view their environment as malleable, and invested time and resources in its representation. In Prague, the accession of a Czech
middle class enabled active citizens to use their newfound economic power
to influence their surroundings. The turn of the twentieth century witnessed
an explosion of voluntary organizations that raised funds for new memorials,
churches, and cultural institutions. Naturally, these associations did not always find common ground, and engaged in a war of words over both theme
and design of their competing national representations. Later in the century,
the Communist Party reasserted an imperial approach to monument building, imposing structures and symbols onto the city landscape. By then citizens
had grown accustomed to their involvement in such projects, and the new era's
symbols faced cynicism and scorn. Still, as Václav Havel has written, the communist imposition of symbols and slogans onto the landscape "form part of the
panorama of everyday life. . . . This panorama . . . has a subliminal meaning as
well: it reminds people where they are living and what is expected of them."[14]

Yet the message of what was expected was often blurred and confused.
Ironically for a modern, secular era, many new monuments addressed the
conflicted religious history of the city. This theme was not embraced only, or
even particularly, by religious citizens or clergy, but by secular nationalists who
described themselves as freethinkers and later the Communist Party, which
preached atheism.

The Spiritual City

That religion became such a popular theme in the collective memory of
Prague dates back to the late medieval history of the city, when Catholic priest
and Prague University rector Jan Hus began to preach for church reform. For
his efforts, he was burned at the stake on July 6, 1415. Erupting into civil war
following Hus's death, the Bohemian Lands were among the earliest Protestant
regions in Europe, but the Austrian-sponsored counter-reformation of the seventeenth century forcibly reconverted the population to Roman Catholicism.
In the nineteenth century, Czech patriots created a national revival, claiming
Prague as a Czech city and Bohemia, Moravia, and Austrian Silesia as Czech
lands. Historical research and writing of the period generated a nationalist

history characterized by centuries of conflict between Germans and Czechs; further, the rediscovery of Hus's proto-Protestant ideas led to a historical interpretation that delegitimized Austrian Catholic power over Bohemia. Honoring Jan Hus became a way for Czechs to create a national narrative that distanced Czech history from Austrian rule.

Thus nineteenth-century nationalists revived the figure of Jan Hus as an avatar of the modern Czech nation: because Hus advocated the use of the Czech vernacular and criticized the hierarchy of the Church, his image could evoke the contemporary quest for a national identity separate from the enforced Catholic and German culture of Imperial Austria. Yet, in a region nominally over 90 percent Catholic, the choice of a condemned heretic as the unifying symbol of the nation enraged many, who protested the use of the Hus icon and proposed their own religious heroes, such as national (and Catholic) saints Wenceslas and Jan Nepomucký (John of Nepomuk), as the true symbols of the Czech historic past. The tension between the Protestant and Catholic symbols in Prague is particularly complicated by the fact that few nationalists who revered Hus and Žižka were religious reformers. They were raised in a Roman Catholic environment and substituted Protestant characters into a Catholic landscape of saints and elaborate churches. Scholars of sacred space have pointed out that Protestantism is the least spatially oriented contemporary religion;[15] still, in Prague, a city filled with markers of Roman Catholicism, Protestant and Catholic figures competed for public spaces.

 Focusing on the now-defunct multinational nation-state of Czechoslovakia, scholars have often drawn a distinct line between the secular Czechs and the devoutly Catholic Slovaks. Yet it is necessary to question the traditional interpretation of religion in Czechoslovakia and to reassesses the dichotomy of the religious and the secular. By focusing on the Czech community in the capital city, we may avoid such historiographical tendency to pit Protestant/secular Czechs against Catholic/clerical Slovaks. The inclination to focus on such a Czech–Slovak dichotomy presupposes that there were two, clear-cut positions on national identity, but in fact the debate was multifaceted and ongoing both among Czechs and between Czechs and Slovaks.

As Catholics and Hus supporters feuded over the meaning of Bohemian history, Prague's Jewish community remained on the margins of debates over national identity. Because most Prague Jews were German speakers, Czech nationalists rarely considered them part of the Czech community. The smaller population of Czech-speaking Jews, however, was sometimes recruited by early twentieth-century Czech nationalists to demonstrate widespread support of the "Hus Cult" even by non-Christians.

Yet Jewish citizens were ignored or mistreated when their presence conflicted with nationalist goals. As late-nineteenth-century Czech nationalists sought to modernize the city they finally controlled politically and economically, the city council approved the razing of much of the Old Jewish Quarter. This project, extensively researched and analyzed by historian Cathleen Giustino, coincided with the movement to place a Jan Hus Memorial on Old Town Square, which bordered the Jewish Quarter.[16] Many Czech nationalists celebrated the replacement of the narrow alleys of Josefov with Paris Boulevard, a wide elegant avenue that provided better access to the square and the memorial. When the Czechoslovak Republic held its first census in 1921, "Jewish" was considered a distinct ethnic category; Czechs and Slovaks were not listed separately, so a citizen could be Czechoslovak, German, Polish, Hungarian, Ruthenian, Jewish, or other. So, from the beginning of the Czechoslovak state, there was an implication that Jews stood apart. The anti-Semitic culture that ostracized the Jews from the nation continued even after the Nazi genocide of European Jews, when the Communist Party purged and executed many of its most prominent Jewish leaders.

In general, though, the most common approach to the Jewish question was silence. Over the centuries, Prague Jews made important contributions to the commercial and literary advances of the city. Prague's Jewish community gave rise to many of the city's stories and collective memories, such as that of the Golem, a creature said to have been brought to life by the sixteenth-century mystic Rabbi Judah Loew to protect the Jewish quarter from anti-Semitic attacks. However, in debates in twentieth-century Prague about new monuments, the Jewish contribution to the city's history was generally ignored. As the national question in the late nineteenth and entire twentieth century centered on the Bohemian reformation, the Jews were rarely considered.

The National City

Contemplating conflicts among Czech nationalists—not between Czech speakers and German speakers, or between Czechs citizens and Austrian leaders—uncovers a continuum of opinion on national identity and the role played in it by religion. Many studies have discussed the city's German and Jewish communities. Gary Cohen's classic *The Politics of Ethnic Survival: Germans in Prague, 1861–1914*, and Scott Spector's more recent *Prague Territories: National Conflict and Cultural Innovation in Franz Kafka's Fin de Siècle* tell the stories of how German speakers (including German-speaking Jews) preserved culture within a sea of Czech nationalists.[17] Few scholarly studies attempt to characterize the diversity of Czech nationalists in Prague itself, but to focus on Prague Czechs enables a deeper reading of the multiple efforts to create a singularly Czech capital in the twentieth century. Further, understanding the process by which Czechs fought over an increasingly narrow definition of "the nation"

12 enables us a better understanding of the dissatisfaction of Czechoslovakia's minorities, some 30 percent of the country's prewar population, who did not often see themselves reflected in their capital's narrow definition of the nation.

Historians of Bohemia and Czechoslovakia have often turned to a famous son of Prague, Ernest Gellner, for understanding nationalism in Central Europe. This Bohemian Jewish philosopher and sociologist, who spent most of his academic career in Britain, demonstrated the importance of national symbols and language for creating the sense of community essential for the development of national consciousness. He wrote, "Two men are of the same nation if and only if they share the same culture, where culture in turn means a system of ideas and signs and associations and ways of behaving and communicating."[18] For Gellner, nationalism constituted the means by which people came to share that culture, to understand themselves and to recognize others as belonging to a group called a nation. Newer scholarship characterizes the nation as more fluid and shifting, rather than fixed. Historian Prasenjit Duara has theorized that "nationalism is rarely the nationalism of *the nation,* but rather marks the site where different representations of the nation contest and negotiate with each other."[19] Although Duara uses "site" metaphorically, Prague, like many modern capitals, became an actual site, a physical space, where nationalists created tangible signs of an intangible concept. Indeed, urban history allows us to witness how citizens navigated through public space that presented them with multiple meanings of the nation.

A nation exists somewhere between the "imagined community" described by Benedict Anderson and the real category of identity depicted by Gellner.[20] For nationalists certainly accept the nation as something real, and develop institutions (cultural, political, religious, and military) around that concept. Scholars such as Rogers Brubaker and Jeremy King have argued that studies of nationalism have to illustrate the process of reification by which people come to see and act upon the abstract nation as something material, institutional, and real.[21] Tracing, in this volume, the continual redefining of public space seeks to locate these interstices between the "imagined" and the "real."

Urban history enables us to examine objects constructed for the purpose of making something abstract into a tangible set of symbols and images. Building monuments is an effective way to physically transform the imagined to the real. Eric J. Hobsbawm identified the "invention of traditions" as development of: "a set of practices normally governed by overtly or tacitly accepted rules and of a ritual or symbolic nature, which seek to inculcate certain values and norms of behavior by repetition, which automatically implies continuity with the past. In fact, where possible, they normally attempt to establish continuity with a suitable historic past."[22]

The continual search for a national memory, a shared interpretation of a nation's past, was striking in nineteenth- and twentieth-century Prague. Czechs sought the unifying power of collective memory as they struggled through polit-

ical uncertainties, such as their minority status in the Habsburg Monarchy, their newly independent state, or the aftermath of world wars and authoritarian rule. As John Gillis has stated, "National memory is shared by people who have never seen or heard of one another, yet who regard themselves as having a common history."[23] Indeed, an array of groups that defined themselves as nationalist—from feminists to educated Czech-speaking Jews, from liberals to Communists—sought to show how their modern movement had its roots with Jan Hus. In contrast, those who could not tie themselves to Hus (namely, Roman Catholics) sought to delegitimize this view of national history and invent a different set of symbols that would prove that their religious heritage was not incompatible with patriotism. The idea of the nation carried a tremendous emotional weight that mimicked religious fervor, for many nineteenth- and twentieth-century citizens. Philosopher Ernst Renan wrote in the late nineteenth century that "the nation" was replacing religion as the primary place of belonging and of identity for Europeans.[24] Although he was correct that nationalism became a powerful ideology, this change was not a true replacement: not all Europeans abandoned their religious beliefs or practices in favor of the nation; instead, the two forces often became intertwined, with nationalists reaching for the tools of religion to create emotional bonds, sacred spaces, or senses of community.

Czechs, who declared Prague the capital for their nation, had never reached a definitive consensus about the meaning of Czech nationalism. The struggle became even more contentious with the creation of the Czechoslovak state in 1918: Czechs, Slovaks, Germans, Hungarians, Poles, and Ruthenes were brought together under the rubric of a Wilsonian nation-state, but one that had no clear national majority. For minority groups seeking equality in Czechoslovakia, the location of the capital in Prague, the city that Czech nationalists viewed as the heart of Czech history, was an obstacle. The contentious redefining of "nation" in this single city offers insights into a troubling trend in East Central Europe during the twentieth century: the question of who should occupy particular cities and regions became based upon reified and ever-narrowing concepts of national identity.

The Gendered City

Feminist scholars have built on the scholarship of national memory and urban history to analyze the manipulation of gendered imagery within national movements. In an issue of *Gender and History* devoted to the intersections of gender and nation, Beth Baron explains: "The idea of nationalism was disseminated through oral expression, rituals, and symbols. . . . Gender played an important role in this process. Through the use of the metaphor of the nation as a family, popular notions about family honour and female sexual purity were elevated to a national ideal. . . . Yet women were often not 'imagined' as part of the nation. Rather, they were used as subjects and symbols around which to rally male support."[25]

Nationalism in Prague exemplifies Baron's thesis. The mythical founder of the city was Libuše, a wise princess who foretold the creation of a "great city." Moreover, the Czech word for Prague, *Praha*, is a feminine noun. The beauty of the city and its feminine grammatical identity inspired generations of Prague writers to write love poems to this beloved city. Lawrence Wechsberg, the author of *Prague: The Mystical City* opens his book, "Prague is a feminine city. Not a glamorous young woman, like Paris, but *matička* (little mother) to her troubadours."[26] The only Czech writer to receive a Nobel Prize in literature, Jaroslav Seifert wrote that, although Prague was "often scorched by the flames of war, . . . we still like to find in this city a certain feminine charm, the smiles and gentleness of woman."[27] In Czech literature, Prague can be a maiden to protect and to fight for, a sage, or a fierce warrior, themes that appeared in the public spaces created during the twentieth century. Princess Libuše established the Czech capital with her consort, a peasant turned king, Přemysl; another myth tells of Šarka, who led women into battle against their demanding husbands; another speaks of a woman who courageously defended Prague during the Hussite Wars. Praha, in short, is at once delicate and invincible.

Even though abstract feminine symbols are abundant, male historical heroes dominate the town squares and hilltops of Prague. The symbolic female and the historical male represent their nation and city as a stable and legitimate family. Although Czech nationalists often took progressive stands on women's rights, traditional ideals about gender and family influenced the way Prague artists portrayed their national subjects. In the earlier part of the twentieth century, balancing masculine and feminine symbols was key to the design of art nouveau monuments. Under Communism, the masculine heroic image prevailed, but the national mother did not disappear from the landscape. These gendered symbols were one way nationalist movements used art and symbolism to create strong bonds to the national community and Prague's sacred spaces.

The City in Time

In the waning years of the Habsburg Monarchy, which historians Zdeněk Hojda and Jiří Pokorný have dubbed Prague's "era of monument fever," Czech nationalists, having wrested control of the city government from German speakers, imbued the city with markers of a "Czech identity."[28] The nationalists' dream to create a monument to their national hero, Jan Hus, inspired many Czechs to empty their pockets for the sculpture, but the city's active Catholics protested vehemently.

The artistic movements that contributed to the new monuments ranged from classic monumental form to art nouveau, which became popular among Prague artists after Rodin showed his 1902 exhibit throughout Bohemia and Moravia. As modern artists became more eager to express themselves, rather than merely to reproduce their commissioners' visions, conflicts again arose about whose view of the nation was more correct. In the midst of World War I, Prague leaders silently unveiled their Hus Memorial on the five hundredth anniversary of his death, while many of their colleagues were imprisoned or exiled for anti-Austrian activity.

During the First Czechoslovak Republic, the era between the World Wars, Prague served as the capital of a fledgling multinational nation-state. The Czechoslovak First Republic's birth was celebrated by an angry mob that tore down the most prominent Catholic, Austrian symbol in the city, the ill-fated Marian Column of 1650.

In the ensuing years, festivals and new church architecture fused religious memory with the new nation's identity. In 1925, the government compensated for the subdued 1915 ceremony to unveil the Hus Memorial by staging a lavish national celebration, which ended with the Papal Nuncio breaking diplomatic ties with the fledgling state. Four years later, the state appeased the Catholics with a millennium celebration for Saint Wenceslas. The Prague Catholic archdiocese and individual parishes also contributed to Prague's interwar environment, with new architecture and a lavish outdoor mass for Czechoslovakia's multiple "nations" in Wenceslas Square. With the coming of the Second World War, Nazi occupation of the city became the dominant influence on national culture.

The rise of the Czechoslovak Communist Party did not signal an end to discussions of religion and national identity. Rather, the Party joined the debate and took up the cause of Jan Hus and his followers, as a means to establish its legitimate connection to the historic nation, while still assailing the Roman Catholic Church, a traditional enemy. During the 1950s, the Party, even as it destroyed the lives of innocent citizens in show trials, rebuilt Jan Hus's Bethlehem Chapel and completed the monument to Hussite General Jan Žižka on Vítkov Hill, site of a fifteenth-century victory by Protestant forces. Anti-Communist dissidents, both religious and secular, joined the debate in their poetry and prose; the Marian Column rose again in this literature as a symbol for lost freedoms under Communism. In the post-Communist era, existing sites of memory were reexamined for new meaning, and new monuments reflected the emptiness felt by many Prague citizens.

The City and Place

Prague's tramway No. 22 crosses the Vltava River and offers a stunning panorama of Prague Castle and St. Vitus Cathedral. A history professor at Charles University once remarked that passengers instinctively look up toward the castle: "No matter how long we live here, and what we live through, we love our city." To acknowledge the beauty of the city, though, is not to idealize or glorify it. Another son of Prague, literary scholar Peter Demetz, a German-speaking Jew who lost his mother in the Holocaust, has convincingly argued that the popular image of Prague as a magical, mystical place obscures the difficult questions that Prague citizens—as well as visitors—must ask themselves.[29] Did Czechoslovakia truly succeed as a democracy between the wars? Why was the Czech resistance so weak during the Second World War? Has Prague come to terms with its treatment of its Jewish residents? Heda Margolius Kovaly, a Holocaust survivor, whose husband was wrongly accused and executed for treason in the anti-Semitic Communist Party purges of 1952, warned her readers that the city's beauty offered a false sense of security and perhaps even engendered complacency. Yet, Kovaly admitted her unwavering ardor for Prague.[30] This paradox contributes, too, to Prague's *mentalités*.

The fervor with which Prague citizens involved themselves in debates about their city's monuments surprises many. Yet it is Prague's *genius loci*, its spirit of place, that provoked angry letters to newspapers about a national memorial, melancholy poetry about a statue, feuds with the Pope over a national festival, and chiseled-out words that once promised the return of a monument. For the past in Prague is ever present. When Italo Calvino described his fictional city of Zaira in *Invisible Cities,* he could have been writing about Prague, which also "soaks up [memories] like a sponge."[31] As Calvino wrote about his city of memory:

> The city, however, does not tell its past, but contains it like the lines of a hand, written in the corners of the streets, the gratings of the windows, the banisters of the steps, the antennae of the lightning rods, the poles of the flags, every segment marked in turn with scratches, indentations, scrolls.[32]

Chapter 1

Preserving the National Past for the Future

*In Slavic Prague a dignified monument will be built to one
of the foremost sons of our dear country, and this monument will be built by the Czech people!*

Jan Podlipný, Young Czech Party politician

Iｎ November 1889, Prince Karl IV Schwarzenberg stood on the floor of
the Bohemian Diet and exclaimed, "We see in the Hussites not celebrated
heroes, but a band of bandits and arsonists. Communists from the fifteenth
century!"[1] A leading member of the nobility, a conservative Catholic, and a
wealthy landowner from Southern Bohemia, Schwarzenberg angrily decried
a decision to place a plaque to the memory of Hus in the entryway of the National Museum in Prague. Representing the pro-Habsburg elite in the Austrian
region of Bohemia, Schwarzenberg found the culture of local Czech nationalists distasteful and disrespectful.[2]

Days later, Czech nationalists fought back. At a Prague municipal government meeting, Jan Podlipný, an influential Prague lawyer and nationalist politician, declared the dream of Prague's Czech-speaking bourgeoisie: to build a
great memorial to Jan Hus. Middle-class intellectuals and Czech nationalists
believed a national memorial could evoke nationalist passion among Bohemia's
Czech speakers. No longer would their movement be satisfied with a plaque in
the museum; a grand monument to Jan Hus would stand in the Czech capital.

A Changing City

The conflict over representing Jan Hus's memory reflected demographic
and political changes in Prague during the nineteenth century. Czech nationalists began to dominate Prague's political and economic institutions, but conser-

vative landowners, like Schwarzenberg, led the Bohemian Diet, which oversaw regional affairs. Czech-speaking liberals had only entered the Diet in 1878. The restrictive curial system during the monarchy assured that the conservative landowners retained control of the Bohemian Diet and Austrian Reichsrat. By 1889, seats in the Diet were fairly evenly divided between Czechs and Germans, but German alliances with landowners and political Catholics stifled Czech influence. Yet a growing Czech elite had, in the preceding decades, asserted their political will in the capital city.

Leaders of the expanding Czech national movement sought to broaden the appeal of nationalism by financing public artworks to arouse national zeal and mark Prague with symbols of modernity. This phenomenon was, of course, not unique to Prague. Alois Riegl, the prominent Viennese art historian, wrote in the 1890s of the "modern cult of monuments," and Stanislav Sucharda, a Prague sculptor, insisted that, to maintain a "full life in art," the Czechs should emulate the French, Germans, and Italians by building great monuments.[3] Much of belle époque Europe experienced an outpouring of nationalist fervor that had been quieted after 1848 and rose again following Italian and German unification and the French loss and German victory in the Franco-Prussian war.

By the late nineteenth century, the demographic and political shifts in the Bohemian Lands divided the capital among those claiming Czech heritage and those claiming German heritage. A Jewish population, heavily Germanized but with pockets of Czech-identified Jews, represented 7 percent of Prague residents. The Christian population was 95 percent Roman Catholic.[4]

During the second half of the nineteenth century, Czech nationalists sought to make Prague "Czech." Until the political upheavals throughout Europe in 1848, most residents of Prague considered themselves Bohemian, using regional, not national, designations. The Germanization of the Austrian bureaucracy began in the late-eighteenth-century reign of Joseph II; from that point, government and commercial business was conducted primarily in German, and higher education took place almost exclusively in German. However, Czech was also commonly spoken on the streets of Prague. Even though Prague's elite (aristocrats, state officials, army officers, higher clergy, professionals, wealthy merchants, and manufacturers) were overwhelmingly German-speaking, only the very highest social strata of German speakers learned no Czech at all.[5]

The political and economic tensions that rose after Austria's quick defeat of the 1848 uprising in Prague led many Czech speakers to strengthen the position of their people in the city. Czech-speaking artisans, for example, tended to be poorer than their German-speaking counterparts, since those who could use German most fluently could conduct trade throughout Central Europe, not only locally. In the 1850s and 1860s, therefore, Czech nationalists founded chambers of commerce and aid societies to assist Czech craftspeople. Czech nationalism also found support from prosperous farmers in Central Bohemia, who conducted business in Prague.

Statistics regarding the numbers of Czechs and Germans living in Prague during the mid-nineteenth century are difficult to analyze: the few studies that were done used differing, and often suspect, methods. Gary Cohen has explained that, because most Prague citizens were bilingual, ethnic identity was very fluid, and residents who wanted to join the increasingly influential Czech community could assimilate in a matter of a few years. Large numbers of Czech-speaking peasants moved into Prague, as the city industrialized in the latter half of the nineteenth century. The city's population doubled from 204,488 in 1869 to 442,017 in 1910. In 1900, 60 percent of Prague citizens had been born outside the city. As more Czech speakers moved into the city, and Czech speakers strengthened their political and economic networks, Prague began to a shift from a bilingual city in which German was the language of public affairs to a city that used Czech in both the private and public realms. In 1880, only 15.3 percent of Prague residents declared their everyday language as German, yet that number had further decreased to 7 percent in 1910.[6]

Middle-class Czechs gained control of Prague municipal politics in the second half of the nineteenth century. They passed laws that required all municipal services to be offered in Czech and German, and switched the primary language of instruction in elementary schools from German to Czech (except in schools with a clear German majority, where both languages would be taught). The Czech nationalist grip on Prague municipal politics was so profound that the German parties ceased putting candidates forward for elections to the Board of Aldermen. Only one German, for example, was elected in 1883, and in 1888 the term of Ludwig Bendiener, a German Jewish community leader and the last German speaker to sit on the Board of Aldermen in the era before World War I, ended.

Czech nationalists looked to the city government to promote cultural endeavors. Prague's abundant baroque architecture embarrassed some civic leaders, as it evoked the Czech losses in the seventeenth-century Thirty Years War and counter-reformation. In addition to forcing Bohemians to convert to Catholicism, the Austrians had built Catholic churches and monuments throughout the city and region. Catholic architecture and art became intrinsic to Prague's landscape; it was at this period that the city became known as the "city of one hundred spires."

Bohemia's Protestant legacy enabled nineteenth-century Czech nationalists to assert a unique heritage within Austria. Ironically, few Czech speakers actually converted, and the Catholic population in Bohemia remained well over 90 percent. Still, esteeming Hus enabled nationalists to demonstrate anti-Austrian sentiment and Czech pride; religion was inserted into the discussion about nationalism, even though the debate was more about culture than creed. Although civic leaders insisted that the Hus legacy was not about religion, choosing to emphasize the Czech's Hussite heritage nevertheless ostracized Prague's Czech-speaking devout Catholics, many of whom had enormous pride in their city's architectural beauty. And focusing on an individual still branded a heretic excluded a large segment of the population from fully participating in national gatherings, commemorations, and fund-raising efforts.

In addition to the cultural disagreements about representing the nation's past, the political repercussions of Schwarzenberg's 1889 anti-Hus remarks were profound. The politically dominant Old Czech Party did not condemn Schwarzenberg's statement since the party needed to maintain political ties with the conservative, wealthy, noble landowners. But, the Young Czechs, the liberal, democratic political party on the rise in the Czech Lands, reacted strongly against the prejudicial statements about their hero Hus. Immediately following Schwarzenberg's remarks, the new elite of Prague—professionals, businessmen, and intellectuals, many of then involved in the Young Czech movement—decided to sponsor a Jan Hus monument in central Prague.

Two of the most prominent leaders of Prague's Czech nationalist society, Vojta Náprstek and Jan Podlipný, led the campaign. Náprstek was an ethnographer and a sophisticated world traveler who had founded an ethnographic museum in Prague and who sought to preserve Czech culture through ethnography. Podlipný, a Prague lawyer, rose to prominence in the Young Czech Party and the Bohemian Sokol patriotic gymnastics organization. This ardent nationalist held several government posts over his career, becoming mayor of Prague, a representative to the Prague City Council, and a representative to the Austrian Diet. At a city council meeting less than a week after Schwarzenberg's speech, Náprstek decried the noble's statements. He argued that the city government had donated the land for the National Museum and that the Bohemian Diet and Schwarzenberg had no authority over Prague municipal affairs. The next day, at a meeting of the Prague Board of Aldermen, Podlipný submitted a formal proposal for a Prague monument to Jan Hus on land provided by the city. In his speech to the council, Podlipný emphasized that Prague was, as he put it, a Slavic city, and that the Czech people would undertake the project of financing and building the memorial.

Calling Prague a Slavic city was central to the approach of the Club for the Building of the Jan Hus Memorial. In the 1880s, Prague's Czech nationalists undertook a massive campaign to assert the Czech and Slavic nature of this city where German had long been the primary language. In 1882, for example, the Board of Aldermen resolved to change the bilingual street signs throughout the city to exclusively Czech signs.

The day after Podlipný's speech, Czech nationalist newspapers, sponsored by the Young Czech party, ran a passionate announcement: "Czech people! Tremble with indignation and with wrath! Your country's father, your family, your glory, your sacrifice, which you laid on the altar of humanity, has been insulted. The name of your greatest son, to whom the Slavic family far and wide—indeed the whole educated world—bows with respect . . . our martyr Master Jan Hus, has been abandoned."[7] Not only were liberal nationalist Young Czechs reacting against Schwarzenberg's remarks, but they were also asserting the ineffectual leadership of the conservative Old Czechs. Young Czechs were furious that the Austrian state recognized only Old Czechs as the legitimate leaders of the Czech nation; the campaign for a Jan Hus Memorial was a strike against the Old Czechs, who frequently compromised with Austria on political matters.

A year later, in 1890, the Young Czechs were excluded from negotiations in Vienna about extending minority language rights in the Austrian half of the Empire. When the Old Czech František Rieger made a major concession to the Germans, during the talks, in exchange for a rather modest gain for the Czechs, Young Czechs protested vehemently and used the issue in their campaign for the 1891 elections to the Austrian Reichsrat.[8] The Young Czechs triumphed in the 1891 elections by appealing to a broader constituency than previously and by calling for the extension of suffrage to lower curia, namely enfranchised farmers and small businessmen. Committed to instill a Czech culture in Bohemia, Young Czechs even used the idea for a Jan Hus Memorial as a campaign platform, decrying the indifference of old Czechs to the project.

Jan Hus and the Modern Czech Nation

No campaign for a Czech nationalist cultural project incited as much fervor or rage as the proposed statue of Jan Hus in Prague. The monument site became the most contested public space in the city, and the square that housed it was the setting of protests, civic festivals, and acts of violence.

Born between 1369 and 1373, late in the reign of the Bohemian King and Holy Roman Emperor Charles IV (1316–1378), Jan Hus began life at a time of profound change. In 1348, Charles IV bestowed on Prague the first university in Central Europe. He rebuilt Prague into a cosmopolitan city, and he stabilized the Holy Roman Empire by terminating the agreement that the pope must approve the emperor's election. Soon to be Holy Roman Emperor Charles I, he marked Hus's era with a sense of independence from Rome. Nonetheless, the Church was strong in the Bohemian crownlands, "In Prague alone there existed forty-four parochial churches, twenty-seven chapels, three cathedral chapters, sixteen monasteries, and seven cloisters."[9] Charles also attempted to reform the excesses of the Bohemian Church, bringing Augustinian Canon Conrad Wald-hauser to Prague to preach against the clergy's ostentatious wealth and society's loose morals. He died right before the Great Schism (the Western schism of 1378–1417 that resulted in the election of two popes and discord within the church). His son and successor, Wenceslas IV, was, at seventeen, an immature leader constantly in conflict with Bohemian nobles, German princes, and the kings of Hungary.

Although he came from a poor family in Southern Bohemia, Jan Hus en-tered Prague University in 1390, and there he met Prague's religious dissent-ers and read the reformist theology of Englishman John Wycliff. Ordained a priest, Hus became rector of Prague University. He led the congregation at Old Town's Bethlehem Chapel, the only place where worshippers might hear Czech-language sermons. The passionate, articulate Hus asserted, "All power comes from God," a criticism of the earthly power of the papacy.[10] He criticized ex-communication and the selling of indulgences, and insisted that lay Christians, not only priests, should receive bread and wine at Mass.

In the chaotic period of the Schism, Hus's tremendous popularity and his association with Wycliffism frightened the Church, which distorted Hus's teachings. Hus was accused of supporting Wycliff's arguments against transub-stantiation, though Hus denied this to his death. As Paul De Vooght has noted, Hus's "spirit was catholic, although his heart was with Wycliff."[11] Hus's trial at Constance was presided over by future Holy Roman Emperor King Sigismund of Luxemburg and Hungary, younger brother of Wenceslas IV. The heresy trial had deep political connotations as Central Europe's monarchs quarreled over regional control. Hus became a scapegoat for the era's political upheavals; the Church excommunicated and immolated him on July 6, 1415. Two decades of regional warfare broke out following his death, and his legacy lasted for two centuries, during which most Bohemians converted to some form of Protes-tantism. But, following the 1618 Battle of White Mountain, where Bohemian nobles were defeated by Habsburg allied armies, the counter-reformation took hold. Jesuit priests sought to stamp out Hus's influence by forcing conversions to Catholicism, creating new regional heroes, and marking Prague and Bohe-mia with opulent baroque art and architecture.

In the late eighteenth century, the era of emerging nationalism throughout Europe, Bohemian scholars began to write regional histories. Intellectuals be-gan "imagining communities" based on language and common heritage.[12] Josef

Dobrovský, a forefather of Czech linguistic nationalism, conducted historical studies of Czech oral and written literature that became the foundation of the nineteenth-century national movement.[13] Jan Hus was a central figure in the early linguistic studies. He had translated prayers, written his sermons in Czech, and created an orthographic system with diacritical marks still used today. Hus wrote, "it is the duty of princes to aid and support the Czech language 'that it may not perish,'" and supported Charles IV's command that Prague inhabitants "teach their children Czech and at the City Hall . . . that they speak and deal with their complaints in Czech." According to Hus, "the Czech disgrace" involved the mutation of the Czech language into a bastardized combination of German and Czech; those Praguers who spoke the hybrid were "worthy of being beaten."[14] Hus's strong invectives inspired nineteenth-century Czech nationalists, who campaigned tirelessly to preserve their national language within Austria; they were also following Johann Gottfried von Herder's admonishment that Slavic peoples preserve their mother tongues: "And does any people (*Volk*), even an uncultivated one, have anything more dear than the language of its fathers? Its entire intellectual wealth of tradition, history, religion, and principles of life lives in it, its entire heart and soul."[15]

Further, nineteenth-century nationalists viewed Hus's defiance of papal authority as a precursor to the contemporary Czech struggle against the Roman Catholic Habsburgs. Historian František Palacký pointed to the Hussite era as the apogee of Bohemian history, which he defined as an ongoing struggle between Czechs and Germans.

University professor Tomáš Garrigue Masaryk, who in 1918 would become Czechoslovakia's first president, wrote and lectured extensively on the resonance of Hus's teachings for the modern Czech. Raised a Catholic, Masaryk converted to Protestantism during his university studies in Vienna. Religious thought was important in the development of Masaryk's political philosophy, as stressed by Roman Szporluk in his influential study on Masaryk. Following Herder, Masaryk believed that each nation had a predestined providential mission; studying the past would help nationalists grasp their sacred calling. Masaryk's study of Palacký's history and the nationalist literature of Jan Kollár and Karel Havlíček convinced him that "all Czech history had pointed to the great era of the Czech Reformation in the fourteenth century and thus to freedom of conscience."[16] He anachronistically interpreted the Czech reformation as a nationalist movement, explaining, "The entire Czech nation, as one single body, defied Rome; this is the special significance of the movement. . . . We see in the Czech Reformation a deeper manifestation of the Czech soul and of our national character."[17] As René Wellek explained, "The Czech revival is seen then by Masaryk as a rebirth, not only of the language and of national consciousness

... but also ... of what to him is the specific glory of Czech history: its Protestantism, which Masaryk interprets not in the theological or polemical terms of the Hussite Reformation but as an assertion of intellectual freedom, of the right for the search for truth against any authority."[18]

The Club for the Building of the Jan Hus Memorial in Prague

Prague's Czech nationalist community reacted enthusiastically to plans for a Hus memorial. Within eight days of the initial announcement in the Prague newspapers, the club had collected ten thousand crowns in donations. By April 1890, the amount had risen to fifty thousand crowns, and the club included three hundred individual or corporate members, each of whom had contributed over one thousand crowns. Donors included the town councils of the districts and suburbs of Prague, corporations, and individuals. Club records also proudly announced that constituencies less represented in the political sphere became leaders in the fund-raising drive: "Students and women vied for the palm of victory in the collection of contributions."[19] Although the club was proud to advertise its other constituents, the Young Czech Party dominated discussions in the early 1890s.

Two hundred citizens attended the first official meeting of the club on May 31, 1890. Professor Masaryk spoke of Hus as a symbol of the past greatness of Czech history. Artists and architects Quido Bělský, E. Liška, Jan Zeyer, and Václav Bílek also provided the creative vision for the monument; and writers and journalists Josef Anýž, Josef Svoboda, and Svatopluk Čech used their literary skills to garner public support for the Jan Hus monument. Politicians, university professors, journalists, lawyers, doctors, manufacturers, entrepreneurs, bankers, and wealthy farmers also served on the steering committee, in effect the elite of Prague's growing bourgeoisie. Prominent figures included Jan Podlipný, Karel Pippich, Gabriel Blažek, Václav Brežnovský, Emanuel Engel, Jan Kaftan, and František Tilšer. Vojta Náprstek was unanimously elected president of the club. In his acceptance speech, he explained that honoring Hus was not "an attack against the Catholic Church but against the extravagances of the hierarchy."[20]

Nonetheless, Catholic Czechs did not approve of building a monument to a heretic. Prague's Roman Catholic leadership accused the club of purposely provoking the Church through this choice of a national hero. At a meeting of the Prague City Council, Canon M. Karlach announced the Catholic opposition to the Hus Memorial: "Vojta Náprstek's viewpoint toward the Catholic Church is well known. This statue will stand as a disgrace and insult to the Catholic Church and its people, humiliating this Catholic city."[21] Not only did

Catholic leaders reject as a national symbol a man who had questioned the Church's practices, but they also resented the emphasis on Hus's martyrdom at the hands of a deeply divided medieval Church. Members of the Church hierarchy noted that, in other eras, the Roman Catholic Church had contributed profoundly to Prague's culture, with Jesuit missionaries founding libraries and schools and beautifying the city with its now-characteristic baroque elements. Such reminders to the public that Prague was a "Catholic city" with a majority Catholic population and elegant Gothic and baroque architecture was a tactic Czech Catholic leaders would continue during the next fifty years.

Finding a Site for the Memorial

The club for the building of a Jan Hus Memorial sought not merely a statue that commemorated an important historical individual, but a memorial to engage Czechs with their Hussite past, challenge the dominant Catholic aesthetic, and forge a bond between citizens and city. The site of the memorial, therefore, was tremendously significant; club leaders insisted that it be placed on a well-traversed, historically significant square within Prague.

The club commissioned a team of prominent Prague academics, sculptors, and architects to study potential locations. Early in the process, the Prague City Council chose Malé náměstí (Small Square) in Old Town as the future site. Yet, many club leaders opposed the choice and continued to assert other potential locations. The club agreed that Malé náměstí was in a lively and well traversed section, quite near one of the city's most important squares, Staroměstské náměstí (Old Town Square). However, they resented the name of the "small" square, and also noted its historical insignificance.

Although the city council had designated a location, the club continued to fight for a more central, more significant site. In the official history of the memorial, the club characterized this search for a site as a fight or struggle. It was a struggle that pitted pro-Hus nationalists against Catholics, but also divided club members among themselves. A significant number of committee members favored Václavské náměstí (Wenceslas Square), already a sacred space for the nation, and housing the National Museum and a baroque equestrian statue of patron Saint Wenceslas (Václav). The commercial center of Prague, the enormous and sloping Wenceslas Square was by far the most traversed area of Prague. The steady rise of the square created a dramatic vista of the museum and the Wenceslas statue. But with this grand view already taken, the club feared a Hus memorial would always retain a secondary place in the nation's imagination. The club declared, "If the monument is to awaken Hussitism within us, the entire area" must be devoted to that cause.[22]

For this very reason, intellectuals tended to favor Bethlehem Square. The square was the former site of the chapel where Hus had preached. Hus had lived in an adjacent home, and several club members believed that the memorial should stand where Hus had lived and worked. The chapel had been gradually demolished over the centuries, and Jesuit missionaries had replaced the chapel with a Catholic College; when the order was disbanded the entire site fell into disrepair. Those who favored the Bethlehem Square location argued that the memorial would reinstitute the Hussite legacy upon the once sacred square. Tomáš Masaryk led the Bethlehem Chapel faction, penning a series of articles arguing for this location in *Naše doba* (Our Era) and *Čas* (Time), the Prague periodicals associated with Masaryk's "realist" wing of the Young Czechs (this wing would later break away from the Party altogether). In his columns, Masaryk not only pointed to the historical importance of the square, but suggested that this location might spare the feelings of Prague Catholics: Bethlehem Square, tucked into a corner of the Old Town, did not house any significant Catholic landmark with which the memorial would compete. Other club leaders resented Masaryk's attempts to appease Czech Catholics. *Narodní listy* (National News), the more radical nationalist daily newspaper, lambasted Masaryk's opinions and stepped up its support for locating the memorial on Old Town Square.

Although this square was among the most important public squares in Prague, heavily traversed and aesthetically distinct, the club did not propose the site in the early negotiations with the Prague City Council. By the end of the decade, though, the club leadership lobbied strongly for Old Town Square, and for the same reason they originally had not considered it: Old Town Square's centerpiece was one of the most significant baroque Catholic landmarks in Prague, the Marian Column erected in 1650 to commemorate the Habsburg defeat of Sweden in the Thirty Years War. By 1896, when the club began to push for this location, Czech nationalist politics, having further radicalized, sought to challenge Catholic landmarks more directly, and Catholic leaders responded harshly to this proposal to the city council on the location of the memorial: "The Catholic Czech nation will not permit Old Town Square—which is reigned over by our Marian Column, the monument which represents our return to glory—to contain a Hus Memorial, that symbol of insult, heresy, and rebellion against the Catholic Church and faith!"[23]

The club's leadership insisted that honoring Hus did not equal defiling the Roman Catholic Church, and labeled Catholic leaders who claimed otherwise "fanatics" and "clerics." Václav Březnovský, at a meeting of the Prague Board of Aldermen, claimed "The Hus concept is not a religious idea." Still, throughout 1897 and 1898 Catholic organizations such as the Marian Nation, Catholic men's and women's clubs, and Catholic workers' organizations staged demonstrations on Old Town Square to protest the proposal to place the memorial so near the Marian Column. In June 1898, a procession to honor the Marian Column and oppose the memorial gathered over four thousand participants on Old Town Square.[24] Nonetheless, on January 16, 1899, the Prague Board of Aldermen approved the proposal by a vote of forty-four to thirty-nine. For the next two decades the square would be a battleground for competing visions of the Czech nation.

A Gathering for "Every Czech"

In early 1902, Dr. Jan Podlipný petitioned the Prague City Council to finance the "Festival for the Laying of the Jan Hus Memorial Foundation Stone" at Old Town Square in July 1903. Podlipný, the former Prague mayor and current president of the Czech Sokol Union, had assumed the Hus Memorial Club's presidency after Náprstek's death in 1894. Podlipný chose "a memorable day for every Czech," as the theme for the festival; he believed the celebration would indeed be a unifying moment.[25] Podlipný hoped to use the festival to demonstrate the inclusiveness of the Czech nation; distressed by the Czech-German conflicts that marred the turn of the century, and by the continued bitterness of Catholics that Old Town Square had been selected, he planned a celebratory, uncontroversial gathering. Further, Podlipný was a stalwart member of the Young Czech Party, whose significance had waned over the preceding decade. He simultaneously sought to embrace some of the new Czech political parties and to assert the inclusiveness and supremacy of the Young Czechs.

Meanwhile, ethnic tensions between Germans and Czechs in turn of the century Prague kept rising. In 1897, Austrian Prime Minister Count Kasimir Badeni issued a language ordinance that placed Czech on par with German in imperial administrative services throughout Bohemia. Riots broke out in Prague when Germans protested the new law. A year later, the language ordinances were repealed, and radical Young Czechs replied with a wave of anti-German riots in the city. These violent events occurred during Podlipný's reign as Prague's Young Czech mayor, and Podlipný blamed German university professors and students for provoking the disorder. Yet, in 1903, festival organizers sought a more conciliatory strategy. They deemphasized those aspects of Hus's legacy that aroused the most fervent passion among nationalists: his anticlericalism and his warnings against German domination. In fact, Hus Committee publications insisted that Hus was a viable hero for Prague Germans, citing Martin Luther's statement that he was "a Hussite." This argument would appeal to few German speakers in Bohemia, an overwhelmingly Catholic population, yet the committee proposed Hus as a unifying symbol through an emphasis on morality, education, democracy, and equality.

Josef Anýž, a Young Czech representative in the Austrian Reichsrat and editor of the influential nationalist newspaper *Národní listy*, ran several news articles each month to inform the public about the upcoming festival and to solicit donations.[26] The response to Anýž's articles—and to letters sent by the club to organizations and city councils throughout Bohemia and Moravia— was tremendous. Monetary donations came in from Czech cultural and economic organizations, including Sokol gymnastic clubs, reading clubs, singing groups, trade associations, baker and butchers' unions, workers' organizations, women's clubs, religious (including Jewish and Protestant) organizations, student groups, Young Czech and National Socialist regional committees, charity associations, and town governments outside Prague.[27]

The Czech Sokol took a leading role in the festivities. Founded in 1862 by Miroslav Tyrš, Sokol gymnastic organizations were among the most patriotic voluntary associations in Bohemia, and had strong ties with the Young Czech Party. Sokol leaders and Young Czechs were at the forefront of the Hus Memorial movement. On annual trips to attend meets in France with the French Society of Gymnasts, Sokol members made pilgrimages to Constance, where Hus was immolated in 1415.[28] Regional Sokol gymnastics societies from Bohemia and Moravia sent representatives to the Prague celebrations and held local ceremonies to honor Hus.[29] Yet many Sokol leaders looked more to the military tradition of Hus's followers, especially the blind military genius General Jan Žižka, than to Hus's intellectual and spiritual legacy. The Sokol followed a military model and viewed itself as a potential standing army.[30] Czech Jewish associations also enthusiastically accepted the invitations to join the Hus celebrations, despite Hus's leadership of a Christian movement. The Central committee of the National Union of Czech Jews in Prague, the Circle of Czech Jewish Youth in Prague, and the Association of Czech Academic Jews in Prague all thanked the club for inviting their organizations to participate, sent small donations (between one hundred and two hundred crowns), and agreed to send representatives to the festival.[31] The Association of Czech Academic Jews, founded in 1876 "to promote greater integration of Jews into Czech society,"[32] noted that it would send not just one but three dozen (or more) delegates to participate in the festival and march in the parade, as a means of emphasizing support for this monument to the national (albeit Christian) hero.[33]

That Jews willingly, and even enthusiastically, participated in this nationalist festival does not demonstrate a widespread Jewish assimilation into Czech culture, either in Prague or in the provinces; in fact, there were many more German Jewish than Czech Jewish organizations in the Bohemian Lands. Nevertheless, the participation does show that the Jan Hus Memorial Festival organizers made efforts to invite Czech Jewish organizations willing to overlook Christian symbolism. A Hus Committee publication cited a Jewish civic leader, a Dr. Zucker, who argued that Hus represented religious tolerance and freedom rather than a particular creed or the Christian doctrine.[34]

This citation is particularly striking, for Czech nationalism had become increasingly anti-German and anti-Semitic at the turn of the century. Gary Cohen has suggested that the weakened position of the Young Czechs as well as the increased economic competition among Czechs, Germans, and Jews led radical nationalists to develop a more xenophobic nationalism. The Club for the Building of the Jan Hus Memorial was not immune to such tendencies. For example, Václav Březnovský, an officer in the Club for the Building of the Jan Hus Memorial, was among the radical nationalist leaders who, according to Cohen, "engaged in unrestrained anti-German and anti-Semitic demagoguery."[35]

Nationally oriented women's groups also enthusiastically participated in the festival. Since 1848, women's organizations had rallied behind the nationalist movement, and they used nationalist rhetoric to promote their causes, especially the advancement of educational opportunities for women and girls.[36] Women's journals such as *Ženské listy* (Women's News) and *Ženský obzor* (Women's Horizon) dedicated their pages to the argument that women's access to higher education would lead to a stronger Czech nation. Since mothers taught the national language to future generations of Czechs, well-educated women could raise intelligent, nationalist children.[37] Hus was an obvious choice as a role model for these educated, nationalist women, since he had promoted (although for different reasons) increased access to the Czech language.

Participating women's organizations included the American Club of Ladies, a Czech women's association founded by Vojta Náprstek upon his return from the United States, and the Central Association of Czech women, an umbrella organization of Czech women's groups, founded in 1897. Both organizations promoted Czech women's participation in nationalist activities. The editor of *Ženský obzor* promised to donate 120 crowns toward the festival with the proceeds made by selling Hussite banners to organizations planning to march in the festival parade.[38] Although politically active, Czech women's groups emphasized their domestic skills, such as sewing banners and decorating halls, as their key contribution to the national movement.[39] Two women served on the festival committee, and the Central Association of Czech Women sponsored academic lectures and meetings for progressive women at the festival. Women were to play prominent roles throughout the festivities, and would be linked symbolically with the Hus legacy in speeches and rituals during the celebrations.

Workers groups were also called upon, as the steering committee attempted to gather "every Czech" to the festival. At the turn of the century, following the addition of a fifth electoral curia of all men over age twenty-four, Young Czech dominance gave way to the blossoming of mass parties in Bohemia. Two political movements, Social Democracy and National Socialism, competed for the allegiance of Czech workers. Attitudes toward nationalism formed the key difference between them. Marxism's internationalist philosophy made nationalist-leaning workers wary of the Austrian Social Democracy movement. National Socialism, a newcomer to the political scene, was able to capitalize on the growing dissatisfaction toward Social Democracy among Czech workers. Founded in 1897 by an assembly of Czech workers and tradespersons, the National Socialist Party combined socialism's emphasis on social justice and economic reform with Young Czech nationalism. In fact, as Czech politics yielded to democracy-oriented mass parties at the turn of the century, the National Socialists captured the second-largest share of the original Young Czech constituency, competing with the Czech Agrarian Party for the votes of the third and fourth electoral curia.[40]

National Socialist Party leaders developed strong ties with the Club for the Building of the Jan Hus Memorial. Alois Simonides would later become the secretary of the club.[41] Simonides had been raised in a devoted Catholic family, but, as an adult who promoted working-class welfare, he began to view the Catholic Church as an oppressive and unjust institution. His fascination with Czech national history led him to embark on a private study of Jan Hus, and to amass a large personal library of books by and about Hus. Although many club members ignored Hus's religious philosophy and focused only on his importance as a heroic figure in national history, Simonides absorbed Hus's spiritual and moral teachings, and considered himself a Hussite.[42] As editor of the National Socialist paper, *Český dělník* (Czech Worker), he, like Josef Anýž, published articles and advertisements for the club's fund-raising campaign.

The National Socialist party was an ideal constituency for the club, which wanted to reach beyond its traditional Young Czech bourgeois liberal supporters. The new members had rejected the ideology of Austrian Social Democracy, seeing it as having pro-German bias whereas the philosophy of National Socialism emphasized Czech nationalism and Slavic unity as well as improvements in the lives of industrial and trade workers.[43] Jan Hus was an appealing hero for the National Socialist Movement, which frequently declared itself "the truest representation of the Czech nation." National Socialists admired Hus's use of the vernacular to spread God's word to the uneducated lower classes, and they

characterized Hussite religious communities, in which members shared property and work, as early utopian socialist societies. Further, National Socialism's
emphasis on the "politics of the streets" coincided with one goal of the Club for
the Building of the Hus Memorial: to attract the Czech citizenry through public
festivals and rallies.[44]

Even as the club strove to gather every Czech to the Foundation Stone
Festival, Social Democrats were not represented. This did not mean that the
Social Democrats did not seek to appropriate Jan Hus for their own political
needs. Like many other political movements, the Social Democrats capitalized
on the popularity of Hus among Czechs. They portrayed Hus's followers as the
first socialists, since they advocated communal property and social equality,
and used Hus's image to add national connotation to their movement. In turn,
they criticized the bourgeois emphasis on higher education and language reform in liberal propaganda about Hus. The Social Democrats' differing use of
Hus challenged middle-class liberal propriety of national imagery at the turn
of the century.

The Festival for Laying the Foundation Stone
for the Jan Hus Memorial

The nationalist festivities that took place throughout Prague on July 4, 5,
and 6, 1903, sought to educate and inspire Prague Czechs through cultural and
intellectual events. The festival was among the largest gatherings of nationalist
Czechs to have occurred. Members of voluntary organizations, political parties,
religious associations, trade and student unions, town and village councils, and
women's clubs marched behind Hussite banners and Czech flags to celebrate
the creation of the monument. Pamphlets, songbooks, and decorations were
available.

Throughout the weekend, participating associations sponsored meetings,
lectures, exhibits, and performances in various Prague venues. A huge parade
from Wenceslas Square to Old Town Square on the warm, sunny Sunday morning of July 5, 1903, gathered representatives from many voluntary associations
and regional town governments. As George Mosse has written, national festivals of the time "were all infused with a feeling of historical continuity, a sense
of being part of an organic whole."[45] Although the club continued to assert a
nonreligious identity, the parade felt like a religious procession. Participants
assembled near Wenceslas Square behind red and white Hussite banners and
Czech national flags. Emblazoned on the Hussite banners was the quintessen-
tial symbol of Jan Hus, the Eucharistic chalice, signifying the preacher's advocacy of Utraquism: that all congregation members, regardless of social status,

be permitted to receive both the body and blood of Christ during the mass. Although the chalice was clearly a religious symbol, Czech socialists had given it the secular meaning of a symbol of social equality, considering Hus thus an advocate for the lower classes.

Festival organizers also implied that it was not a contradiction to assert Czech national symbols while still respecting the Monarchy. The morning parade, therefore, achieved two goals: it identified the Czechs as a historical and political unit within the larger framework of Austria, and it imparted to the Czech people a passionate desire to belong to a vibrant historical nation. The laying of the foundation stone was carried out in the name of Francis Joseph, Emperor of Austria and King of Bohemia, Prague mayor Vladimír Srb, Czech representatives of the Austrian Reichsrat, and city council members.[46]

After the parade, representatives of Czech and Slavic society ceremonially laid the foundation stone. The delegates were: Vladimír Srb, representing the entire Prague community; Professor Jan Horbaczewski from the Czech branch of Charles-Ferdinand University; Josef Herold of the Czech National Council; Jan Podlipný, from the Club for the Building of the Hus Memorial; and Josefina Náprstková, "on behalf of the Czech women."[47] In addition, "to represent Slavic brotherhood," a Russian visitor and a Polish guest helped to lay the stone. Each representative stepped onto the podium and the crowd of thousands observed a moment of silence. Then the seven delegates knocked on the stone with their fists. This symbolic act was followed by speeches by Podlipný as well as by the famed Young Czech orator Edvard Grégr, who told the crowd that "true Czechs" kept Hus in their hearts.[48]

The National Mother at the 1903 Celebrations

The parade was but one way the festival committee sought to portray the Czechs as a unified and inclusive nation. Another was to give key segments of Czech society prominent roles in the speeches and ceremonies that made up the festival. Although there were no women on the club's steering committee, women were prominent at the 1903 festival. In the festival, gendered representation was used to portray the Czechs as both modern and family centered. Hus was a particularly potent symbol for Czech women, and the image of Czech women and mothers was an integral part of the Hussite myth.

Many historians have demonstrated that European and colonial nationalists used feminine imagery to create a familial image of the nation. According to Samita Sen, "The idealisation of womanhood as the repository of tradition [was] based on a general valorisation of motherhood: as the creator and protector of the sanctuary of the home, as the good and chaste wife, and as the iconic representation of the nation."[49] Some male nationalists even supported feminism to demonstrate the progressiveness of their movement. For example, in turn of the century Iran, "female emancipation was simultaneously symbolic of the modern progressive potential of the state to strengthen and reform itself and society and 'proof' that such states were not backward or reactionary."[50] As Eleni Varikas has shown for this period in Greece, "Situated within the logic of nationalism, feminists gained an unexpected audience and became for more than two decades an important component of the public sphere."[51]

Speakers emphasized the centrality of the Czech language to Hus's ministry, and lauded Czech women for maintaining the "mother tongue" at home, when German had supplanted it in public discourse. Podlipný began his speech by remarking that Hus loved the "maternal language" of his people, and he reminded the crowd that the memorial would soon "face the Mother of Christ, for whom Hus had infinite respect."[52] Podlipný insisted that the Marian Column could symbolize Hus's love and respect for motherhood rather than represent Habsburg domination.

The keynote academic lecture, "On the Meaning of Jan Hus for Czech Women," was sponsored by the Association of Czech Women, a prominent organization of nationalist feminists. The speaker, A. J. Šnajdaufová-Čadová, from the association's educational division in Pilsen (Plzeň), placed women at the center of the national cult of Hus, announcing, "We [Czech Women] are the latter-day Hussites!"[53] Šnajdaufová-Čadová's lecture centered on connections among motherhood, the national language, and the collective memory of Hus, and praised modern Czech women as the heirs of the collective memory of all Czech mothers, beginning with Hus's own mother. Very little is known about Hus's early life, and Šnajdaufová-Čadová's characterization of his mother stems from the romantic nationalism of the speaker's own day rather than from any historical accuracy. Citing a poem praising Hus's mother, Šnajdaufová-Čadová explained that this mother must have recognized "the little saint" in Hus even when he was still "enjoying the outdoors." Further, she envisioned Hus's mother's role in preparing him for his life of education: "We imagine, in Hus's childhood, him reading the Bible with his mother."[54] (This, of course, would have been highly unlikely in the fourteenth century.)

In particular, Šnajdaufová-Čadová believed that women contributed through their role as mothers. Just as Hus's legacy to the nation included his moral and linguistic teachings, mothers were the ones who carried the burden of remembering that legacy. "Instilling morality into the children's tender souls is primarily the work of our women, mothers." Prague mothers should work harder not to disappoint Hus. "I don't know, I don't know dear ladies, what he would say to us today . . . [to] you honorable Czech mothers, mothers of the nation's youth."[55] Czech mothers, that is, must strive to keep the national memory alive through language and morality.

Like many of her contemporary feminists throughout Europe, Šnajdaufová-Čadová, envisioned a broader definition of motherhood, one that included social work such as medicine, teaching, and charity: "Of course for our women this is a new era full of new responsibilities, new worries, new urgent problems, new serious work, but as always the Czech nation has a great need for a moral character, which would join Hussite morality with the national and the cultural work."[56] Feminists of this generation used the promise of social motherhood to push for educational opportunities in their societies. Czech women had recently opened the first gymnasium for girls in Prague, and education remained central to the women's goals; remembering the participation of educated women in the medieval Hussite movement strengthened this goal. Indeed, Czech female activists capitalized on the opportunity to link their own political goals to the public commemoration. Šnajdaufová-Čadová told her audience, "Some of the most educated women of [Hus's] era, sat with their nearest neighbors at Bethlehem Chapel."[57]

At the end of her speech, Šnajdaufová-Čadová quoted Hus's essay "Daughter": "Come daughter, listen and bend your ears: respect the dignity of your soul" and paraphrased it for her modern women followers, "Come mother, listen and bend your ears: respect the dignity of the Czech soul!"[58] In the national memory publicly commemorated in 1903, the Czech mother was the Czech soul.

However, a more masculine assertion of the Hussite legacy was gaining popularity, too, in 1903. Whereas Hus represented the linguistic and cultural nation, Jan Žižka had come to represent the Czech fighting spirit. This masculine Hussite warrior legacy was not completely ignored at the festival, although its representation was carried out at private, indoor events. At the National Theater, the audience could relive moments from the Hussite mid-fifteenth-century wars. The National Theater Company presented the historical play *Žižka,* by Alois Jirásek, a beloved nationalist writer and future club officer. The five-act play celebrated the Hussite general Žižka's military achievements, including attacks on Catholic institutions such as monasteries. Žižka was already an enormously popular figure among Czech nationalists, such as Young Czechs and Sokol members, who had evoked his memory at state rights demonstrations of the 1860s and 1870s.[59]

The performance at the National Theater began with the recitation of the epic poem "Hus," by Svatopluk Čech, esteemed poet and Hus Club steering committee member. Like the play *Žižka,* the poem accented Hussite militarism. Čech wrote that, after Hus's death, the whole nation "rose up with their maces and flails" to defend the martyr's beliefs.[60]

The more violent, masculine, warrior legacy favored by the new socialist parties contrasted sharply with the conciliatory strategy sought by the Young

Czechs who still led the Club for the Building of the Jan Hus Memorial. The club's attempt to appease Catholics, as well as Germans and Jews, backfired as vehement nationalists insisted that the festival did not indeed represent "every Czech."⁶¹

Reactions to the Hus Festival

Surprisingly, the Catholic press declared itself, "totally satisfied" with the celebrations since the Jan Hus festivities did not offend Czech Catholics.⁶² Clearly, Podlipný had achieved one of his goals—to create an atmosphere of inclusion, not rivalry. Yet pleasing the Catholics automatically incensed other groups. Some nationalists were dismayed at the overtly religious symbols, such as the chalice; others believed the speakers too conciliatory toward Roman Catholics. The Social Democratic press was especially vitriolic in their criticism. "A Hus Festival against Hus!" proclaimed the headline of Social Democratic daily newspaper *Právo lidu* (The Right of the People).⁶³ In this scathing criticism, the Social Democratic paper claimed that the festival actually violated the memory of Hus by appeasing Catholics, and decried the festival's "clerical characteristics" (such as the chalice symbol). For Podlipný to acknowledge the Marian Column was to betray Hus and to make peace with Hus's murderers, who were also class oppressors. *Právo lidu* announced that future socialist Hus festivals would invoke the spirit of "anticlerical agitation" and would not embrace "clerics and also chalices."⁶⁴ *Právo lidu* further bemoaned the festival's "fully national character" and criticized the celebration's "Young Czech flavor."⁶⁵

But festival participants also expressed dissatisfaction with the festival. The nationalist women's journal, *Ženský obzor*, attacked the festivities' clerical mood. *Ženský obzor* warned that clerics "live in the lap of luxury and hunt . . . for sheep for their churches. . . . To us Hus is simply a representative of the great struggle for free thought, and he is to us merely a model of perseverance and bravery."⁶⁶ The leaders of *Ženský obzor* warned that, in the future, "our women would only participate in those Hus festivals, which are completely devoid of clericalism of any kind."⁶⁷

The Sokol organization vehemently attacked its leader Podlipný for honoring the Virgin Mary at the cornerstone ceremony. Nicknamed "King of the Sokol," Podlipný had now lost favor with the organization. Denounced for his pro-Catholic "clericalism," he defended his speech in the Sokol journal. He began his short response by explaining why he remarked that the festival was "in defiance of no one." Reminding his fellow Sokols that many members of Prague society were determined that the Hus monument never be built, Podlipný noted the pragmatism of "a little concession, a little diplomacy."⁶⁸

Podlipný termed the Marian Column a memorial of victory over the

Swedes in the in the seventeenth century, not a reminder of Bohemia's defeat by Habsburg-sponsored armies at White Mountain. Czechs must use history cautiously and truthfully, explained Podlipný, so that misplaced hostility did not interfere with national goals. Puzzled that nationalists criticized him for remarking that Hus respected Christ's mother, Podlipný asked, "Is it necessary to explain even that?" Podlipný defended his dramatic conclusion to his cornerstone speech in which he called out "In the name of the Father, the Son, and the Holy Spirit" as a way to defy "clerics" who called the religious Hus a heretic.

Although known as a radical nationalist in the 1880s and 1890s, Podlipný was also admired in Czech politics for skillfully compromising with the opposition. In 1897, when Prague Germans had rioted over the proposed Badeni language ordinances giving Czechs increased right to use their mother language in the public sphere, Podlipný had implored Czechs "not to lose their heads" by responding to the violence, and had also negotiated with the German leadership to try to quell their anger. Fellow club steering committee member Josef Anýž had joined him in the latter endeavor. By chastising the Germans for provoking the violence that erupted throughout 1897, Podlipný maintained his reputation as a committed Czech nationalist, yet by 1903, with the explosion of mass politics, the increased use of demonstrations and rallies as political weapons, and the demise of Young Czech supremacy, Podlipný could not keep up with the new radicalization of politics. His use of "clerical" language and his appeasement of Czech Catholics served to alienate both socialists and nationalists, and only made Catholic groups happy for a few days—until they realized that Podlipný's audience did not agree with him.

The 1903 Festival for the Laying of the Foundation Stone of the Jan Hus Memorial began as a dream to unite every Czech under Hussite banners and Czech flags. This dream could never have been more than an illusion. Czech society had become too fragmented to expect that a festival could please every Czech. As soon as Podlipný and his committee tried to placate Czech Catholics, socialists and liberals felt excluded. Similarly, socialists and liberals were growing further apart, and chose to honor Hus in separate ceremonies. As Claire Nolte has pointed out, the earlier goal of "national inclusiveness" in Czech politics had given way to "overtones of racial exclusivity and national intolerance."[69] As Czech nationalist parties splintered, it was no longer enough to embrace the Hus legacy; different constituencies held wide-ranging and conflicting views about what the medieval hero represented and how he should be commemorated.

Chapter 2

Art Meets Politics

"Hus has lived in my soul since childhood."

Ladislav Šaloun, sculptor of the Jan Hus Memorial

ADISLAV ŠALOUN, a prominent Prague sculptor, frequently wrote of the deep and personal meaning Jan Hus had held for him since youth. Šaloun wrote that Hus's soul was "full of life," yet simultaneously represented the dark and tragic national past and the uncertain abyss of the future.[1] When the art jury of the Club for the Building of the Jan Hus Memorial in Prague selected Šaloun to design and sculpt the monument to the martyred national hero, the sculptor had achieved one of his intimate and artistic goals. Through a modernist rendering of Hus, Šaloun could convey his emotions about the tragic struggles of humanity and the Czech people. A leading figure in Prague secessionist art circles, Šaloun believed that the modern artist served as a medium for the creative forces of the cosmos, and that powerful artistic subjects such as Hus revealed a higher truth about the human spirit.[2]

However, the Club for the Building of the Jan Hus Memorial in Prague had a different vision for Šaloun's sculpture: Prague's leading liberal nationalists wanted to convey the modernity and competence of the Czech nation, and building a memorial to a national hero was another step toward establishing the Czechs as a historical nation with the right to autonomy within the Empire. Thomas Nipperdey has written that national monuments are the "self-representations of a democratically controlled nation, objectifying the ideals for which the nation is supposed to stand."[3] Obviously, nondemocratic societies have also erected historical and patriotic memorials, but, as George Mosse demonstrates in his study of Germany, by the nineteenth century even monuments hailing nondemocratic traditions often were created democratically, since poets, artists, business persons, and politicians all contributed to their creation. The Club for the Building of the Jan Hus Memorial represented Prague's Czech-speaking elite, who were determined to render an idealized portrait of their nation. The conflicting visions for the Hus Memorial reflected the politicization of art within the national movement: modern artists sought to free themselves of the constraints of nineteenth-century historicism, and liberal nationalists commissioned nationalistic work conforming to an idealized standard. Criticism of other Prague monuments remained primarily within artistic circles, but conflicts over Hus, the most important subject for new public monuments in the city, also involved politicians, academics, journalists, and art preservationists.

Original Visions for the Prague Memorial

Debates over the appearance of the monument spanned the entire quarter century during which the club worked toward the 1915 unveiling. When, in 1891, the city council chose Malé náměstí (Small Square) in Old Town as the site of the memorial, the club sponsored a contest open to Czech sculptors and judged by a group of French and Czech artists, writers, and historians. The judges chose the design of Prague artist Vilém Amort, a traditional realist sculptor. Amort titled his winning design "From love to art, country, and nation," and the sculpture featured a Corinthian column on a pedestal, with Jan Hus standing at the top and an angel floating above his head. This portrayal of Hus was strikingly like artistic renditions of Christ, arms outstretched, preaching to the people. Also on the pedestal were two seated figures, a commoner and a king, representing Hus's appeal to Czechs of all backgrounds.

When, in July 1899, the city government changed the monument site, approving Old Town Square, the club announced a new contest for the memorial. Club leaders, dissatisfied with Amort's design, believed the competition had been too rushed and the contest rules perhaps not followed to the letter. Underlying these rationalizations, however, was the club's developing philosophy regarding the memorial's purpose. Tomáš Masaryk often stressed that a statue of the Czech national martyr should convey the whole history of the Czech people, since Hus was not a simple historical figure but a moral representative of the struggles of the Czechs throughout their history.[4] Further, radical new concepts of art marked the 1890s. Although the club remained committed to a historical memorial, they recognized that Amort's design had become outdated.

In 1893, a plan by Prague's Czech leaders to modernize the city's Old Town was approved, despite the vehement protests of many local residents. In particular, the Josefov neighborhood, home to much of Prague's German Jewish population, was slated for destruction. Victorious proponents of the plan argued that the old buildings were decrepit and dangerous, but it was difficult to mask the anti-German and anti-Semitic sentiment that underlay the plan. Despite these implications, the renovation of Old Town, and the building of new boulevards and bridges, led to a building frenzy that continued into the twentieth century.

This project, according to Cathleen Giustino, was "one of the most ambitious urban-modernization programs to appear in nineteenth-century Europe."[5] The building projects gave new craftspeople unprecedented opportunity to decorate the city with secessionist sculptures, murals, furniture, and architecture. Institutions such as banks, hotels, and apartment buildings reflected the art nouveau style that was sweeping Europe. The style—also known as secessionism—emphasized emotion and symbolism over strict realism, and incorporated organic forms. The human figure, often nude or draped in loose cloth, featured prominently in secession art, making it a viable choice for Prague's monument designers hoping to employ new ways to commemorate the past. On Old Town Square, adjacent to the Jewish Quarter, narrow alleys soon gave way to Pařížská ulice (Paris Street). This wide avenue provided easier access to the square and would enable viewers to view the projected Hus Memorial from multiple angles, a fact that allowed artists to create more ambitious, complex designs that could embrace Masaryk's vision of the monument's larger purpose.

In 1900, the second art jury of the club announced the results of the new contest. Out of twenty-four entries, the art nouveau design of prominent Prague sculptor Ladislav Šaloun received first prize. Šaloun often commented that Hus's life and death had foreshadowed the fate of the Czechs, and his original model went beyond a mere depiction of Hus's martyrdom. The winning design for the contest depicted the devastating impact of Hus's death upon the Czech nation. Šaloun's model placed the martyr atop a traditional pedestal inscribed with the dedication "To Master Jan Hus, in the name of the nation."[6] Wearing a martyr's cap, Hus stood with his arms bound to a stake behind his back. His downturned and bearded face showed little expression as it hung silently toward the flowing robes of his clerical vestments. Reflecting traditional representations of the crucified Christ, Šaloun's early version of the Hus statue conveyed the tragic sacrifice a Czech hero had made for his people.

Below the main pedestal holding the figure of Hus, Šaloun created a large, rectangular platform upon which he placed statues of Hussite warriors looking exhausted yet still brandishing swords and standing proudly behind a shield emblazoned with the Hussite chalice signifying Hus's vision of spiritual equality. The ten warriors on the platform created a triangular formation on Hus's left side, with the highest figure reaching the height of Hus's foot. At the top of the triangle, a sculpted priest raised a chalice with his outstretched hand, symbolizing that Hus's spiritual legacy would live on beyond the martyr's death.

On the bottom of the triangular formation, in front of the other soldiers, a sculpture of a female warrior was seated next to a small child.[7] Although she appeared weary, the woman soldier held her sword high. Including a woman and a child, as well as young and old male soldiers and priests in the formation of Hussite followers, enabled Šaloun to convey the message that the entire Czech nation stood by the memory of Jan Hus. In this 1899 model of his Hus memorial, Šaloun adopted the methods of the naturalist movement in art and literature. Following the philosophy of French art critic and writer Émile Zola, Czech modern artists sought what they saw as a higher purpose than the idealization of the past popular with historicist artists.[8] In contrast, these modern, naturalist artists attempted to depict the harshness of the human condition, and saw art's value as lying in its ability to communicate injustice and suffering. Although Šaloun experimented with naturalist methods, he also retained traditional historicist techniques. The use of classical elements like the pedestal was common in nineteenth-century nationalist art since it linked the nation to a "sacred" tradition of history and culture, and the geometric and static structure of the monument also suggested the strength and stability of the nation.[9] Yet, as Šaloun became more influenced by European trends in art, he decided to move further from historicism and to push the boundaries of the naturalist movement.[10] Art nouveau had become almost a religion for Šaloun, who held séances in his studio with other artists in the hope of harnessing that "basic force of the cosmos" of which the artist was the medium.[11]

Šaloun's design thus portrayed a historical subject in an art nouveau style. This phenomenon separated the Prague secession from its manifestations in centers such as Paris and Vienna. Whereas many European proponents of the new art movements disdained nationalist art, Czech secessionists tried to embrace both nationalism and modernism. As the Czech secessionist art journal *Volné směry* (Free Directions) explained: "On one side, there is historicism; on the other, its negation (absolute if possible) that is modernism. And between the two there is this kind of happy medium that some people have found to safeguard patriotism in art."[12]

A 1902 Prague exhibition of the works of Auguste Rodin, which Rodin accompanied, convinced the leading group of Prague sculptors to reevaluate their artistic purpose. Moved by the emotion present in Rodin's work, artists like Šaloun committed themselves to capturing the complex psychology of the human condition.[13] In 1903, Šaloun reworked his design in two new sketches.[14] He must have known that he would face opposition for at least some of his new ideas. Even when he had won the design contest in 1900, he had found his concept not unanimously supported. The historian on the art jury, Dr. J. Želakovský, opposed Šaloun's original depiction of Hus for its historical inaccuracy.[15] Šaloun's model portrayed Hus as tall and thin, whereas, the historian argued, contemporary writings had characterized the priest as short, broad-shouldered, and stocky.[16] Although this objection did not change the jury's decision, it foreshadowed future controversies between the artist and the organization overseeing his work. Amid the conflicts over details of the sculpture lay a deeper debate about the purpose of national monuments.

Conflicting Visions of the Jan Hus Memorial

As Šaloun reworked his early model, his primary concern was to enhance the emotional content of the sculpture. Following the example of Rodin, Šaloun and his contemporary artists in the Mánes Association of Fine Artists promoted the theme of "inner contemplation with [a] distinctive elegiac accent" in their art.[17] Although his original model depicted Hus's martyrdom, Šaloun did not believe that the sculpture had captured the depth of tragic emotions that it must.

Following the secessionist rejection of historicism, Šaloun removed the baroque pedestal. The martyr retained his place in the center of the monument, but he would no longer be elevated and set apart from the rest of the sculpture. By removing the pedestal and incorporating the statue of Hus more directly into the sculpture, Šaloun's new model conveyed Hus's centrality within the entire Czech historical epic. The sculptor replaced the static platform and pedestal with a massive circular granite base that gave the piece weight and a sense of permanence. He carved into the stone base with heavy, uneven strokes, creating the effect of human figures standing on top of an angry, swirling sea, thus emphasizing Hus's unjust death.[18]

Instead of grouping the auxiliary figures in a single geometric formation, as in his original design, Šaloun spread the components around the central figure of Hus. The monument was thus to be considered from all angles, since the sculpted figures clung on all sides of the seemingly undulating base. Placing his figures around a circular foundation enabled Šaloun to illustrate his vision of "the eternal spirit of Czech history."[19] He also added new elements to the design to demonstrate Hus's relevance to future chapters of Czech history. The small group of Hussite warriors to Hus's left symbolized the triumph of Hus's teachings immediately after his death, on Hus's right was a larger group, representing the later Czech Protestant exiles who fled Bohemia after the Battle of White Mountain in the seventeenth century.

Šaloun wrote that his new design better conveyed the deep tragedy of Czech history.[20] The statues of the exiles clung to one another helplessly as they gazed into an unknown future in a foreign land. Their clothes tattered and their hair knotted, the refugees displayed unmistakable pain and anguish. In the back of his model, Šaloun included a sculpture of a young woman fleeing her homeland with her infant child, her expression simultaneously evoking grief and terror. Crouched low to protect her child, the future of the Czech nation, against her breast, the mother appeared to be fleeing her pursuers. Šaloun separated the young woman from the group of exiles yet portrayed her as running to catch up with them, further creating the motion of history around the perimeter of the monument. By replacing the defiant female Hussite warrior from his original design with a young, desperate mother escaping her native country, Šaloun emphasized the defeats in Czech history rather than the triumphs.

More subtle changes altered the figure of Jan Hus. In his revised model, Šaloun retained the portrayal of the hero in his final moments of life, being put to death after his heresy trial in Constance. Yet, the sculptor attempted to carve a more expressive face into his main subject, conveying a deeper sense of Hus's physical and emotional suffering and pain. Šaloun hoped, too, that the massive and vital new foundation beneath Hus's lifeless body would express the anger the Czech nation felt over the injustice of the martyr's death.[21]

Šaloun believed that his new designs for the monument better conveyed the richness and complexity of Czech history than had his original entry. Through mystical séances and meditations at his workshop, Šaloun believed that he had become one with his creation, had developed an inner understanding of Hus through the senses rather than through the intellect,[22] and could capture the life force of Hus and Czech history in his sculpture.[23] Enraptured by currents in psychology and philosophy, Šaloun practiced Nietzsche's concept of Dionysian Art, in which the artist achieves drunkenness so as to lose all inhibitions and find the psychic essence of his creative work.

Since the Hus memorial project had become a spiritual quest for Šaloun, he found it emotionally painful when the steering committee and the art jury of the Club for the Building of the Jan Hus Memorial in Prague disparaged the monument's new tone. Even though the original winning design had depicted Hus's immolation and death, the large group of his followers beside him had symbolized the triumph of his ideas. Now that Šaloun had significantly reduced the size of this component in favor of the defeated exiles and fleeing woman, the entire monument spoke more of the tragedy of Czech history than of the triumph of the Czech spirit. The committee demanded that the figure of Hus convey the martyr's strength, not his victimization, and instructed that Šaloun sculpt Hus with an upturned head, not tied to a stake with his head hung low.

Šaloun concluded that he had been hired as a public servant, not a freely commissioned artist. He accepted the ruling of the art jury, since he could not risk losing the commission. Nonetheless, he remained unhappy with the sculpture and continued to rework the design. Deciding that it was absurd to portray a dying man looking strong and triumphant, he abandoned the concept of Hus at his execution. Šaloun published his new ideas in a pamphlet, which contained photographs of his new designs and an essay by the artist. In both new designs, Hus stood alone, slightly elevated on the granite foundation. Characters from Czech history surrounded Hus, several of them looking upward toward him with longing. Although the committee insisted that Hus be more prominent in the sculpture, Šaloun would not remove the auxiliary sculptures of the exiles, priests, and warriors, which conveyed Hus's centrality in national history. The exiles and the Hussite warriors appeared weary, Hus strong and triumphant.

Šaloun's bitter essay accused the club of usurping his artistic authority by dictating the proper tone for his sculpture. He felt constrained by the demand that Hus's head be turned upward, and condemned the art jury for dictating creative aspects of his work. "Willing or unwilling, I had to be satisfied with . . . an upturned face on the statue, with omissions of necessary, substantial details from my studies." Nonetheless, the sculptor hoped that his new version of Hus depicted him as "powerful" and filled with "sacred majesty and grandiose dignity." Šaloun explained that there was a great deal of conflict among those who revered Hus as to how the national hero should be viewed: some saw "in Hus only a historical figure," whereas others emphasized the "religious or national shades" of his legacy. Šaloun realized that he could not fully satisfy his entire audience because of the "differences of views and the diversity of conceptions of Hus and his meaning." According to Šaloun, artists desired to remove themselves from political conflicts in their society, yet, as he had learned, when creating a public monument an artist was not free to create an "artistic expression of a given idea," but had to negotiate the new creation among the conflicting "ideas and opinions of political, religious or social parties," all of whom had to "give their blessings" to the sculpture.[24]

Šaloun's negotiations with the club did not end with his concessions regarding the position of Hus's head. Over the next several years, the art jury appointed by the club oversaw Šaloun's work to ensure that the monument properly reflected the club's vision of Hus. In 1905, the club negotiated a new contract with Šaloun, which included very specific regulations about the size and height of each element of the memorial.[25] The club thought that the figure of Hus did not stand out enough against the other components of the monument. Once Šaloun had removed the baroque-style pedestal, Hus's figure became more incorporated into the design, and the art jury, though allowing this change, wanted assurance that the focus would still be Hus, and not a more general vision of some eternal "wheel of Czech history."[26] Šaloun's contract specified that Hus must be the "dominant" figure, approximately six meters high, with the other figures ranging from two-and-one-half meters to four meters tall.[27]

Šaloun's work was also under scrutiny by the press and Prague voluntary organizations. An editorial in the nationalist newspaper *Národní listy* (National News) criticized some of his concepts. Since Josef Anýž, the editor, sat on the steering committee of the Club for the Building of the Jan Hus Memorial, it is fair to assume that this column reflected the opinion of many committee members. Expressing rigid opinions about the purpose of a historical monument, columnist Ninus Karo wrote, "The celebrated statue on the memorial must be a portrait that is a picture of [Hus's] personality, representing his physical and psychic individuality, nothing more and nothing less." Karo argued that Šaloun's early design portraying the immolation at Constance had been an inappropriate idea. It misrepresented Hus by depicting only a "piece of history. . . . Hus on the monument should not be represented as a preacher (speaking), nor in front of a judge, nor in prison, nor at the stake," because these portrayals each conveyed only a limited sense of the man's multidimensional character.[28]

Other critics joined Karo in denouncing Šaloun's portrayal of a weak, defeated Hus. In the journal *Zvon* (Bell), an editorial bemoaned the absence of the "true" Hus, "our Hus, the great Czech, the liberator of the nation's spirit and power."[29] Nationalist journalists wondered what the point would be of a monument that did not glorify Hus's strength. Karo supported Šaloun's revision in which Hus's head turned upward, but criticized Šaloun's liberties with Hus's appearance. To be a legitimate national memorial, Karo argued, a statue should be historically accurate, not merely a symbol of a particular character trait.

The conflicts over the design reflected the wider debate at the turn of the century regarding the purpose of public monuments. Contemporary Viennese art historian Alois Riegl decried the lack of artistry in the "modern cult of monuments," whereas Karo's reference to the "celebrated statue" implied that monuments existed to glorify national history. Secessionist artists, on the other hand, wished to depict historical subjects to portray universal emotions and human conditions. The pathos in Šaloun's work conflicted with the liberals' glorification of the past, yet it was the liberal nationalists who had dismissed Amort's traditional sculpture for a modern design.

Female Imagery on the Memorial

The nationalist constituencies were primarily concerned with the portrayal of Hus. Therefore Šaloun had more freedom to experiment with other elements of the memorial. The component that underwent the most radical changes, over

SVĚTOZOR

ČÍSLO 20.　　　　ROČNÍK XV.

K DOKONČENÍ HUSOVA POMNÍKU.

Při práci na pomníku.

Šaloun with female model. Reprinted with permission of the Archiv hlavního města Prahy.

the course of the decade in which the sculptor worked toward a final design, was the female figure. That Šaloun devoted so much time and reflection to the woman on the memorial indicates how essential he believed her role to be. The female figure also intrigued (or perhaps titillated) Prague society. As Šaloun worked on the monument, pictorial magazines covered his progress. *Světozor* (Horizon), for example, carried a cover photograph of Šaloun posing his nude model. Several other art journals and popular magazines also commented on the inclusion of a female nude on a nationalist monument.

This female figure went through several manifestations. Initially, she was in the foreground of the large grouping of Hussite warriors, rather than as a distinct element, and thus symbolized the strength and cohesiveness of the entire community. Further, the most radical branch of the Hussites had lived communally and was famous for female participation in battles and in spiritual life. After the Czech national revival, when memories of the Hussite era were revived, nationalist feminists would often cite women's actions during the Hussite period, when arguing for full acceptance into the national community. Nationalist men, too, used women's participation in the Hussite movement to prove that the Czech nation had long stood for progress.

Stories of the heroic deeds of female warriors in several battles of the Hussite Wars that followed Hus's death became legendary during the national revival. Lauding heroic medieval women was, of course, popular throughout nineteenth-century Europe. From Joan of Arc in France to Katica Dobos in Hungary, female warriors had demonstrated what nationalists considered the ultimate courage: defying woman's "true" peaceful nature to fight for their country. During the Hussite wars, women had not only taken on such auxiliary military roles as nursing, but had built defensive structures, led attacks on Prague monasteries such as St. Catherine's Convent, and fought in other battles. In fact, the chief chronicler of the Hussite wars, Lawrence of Březová, considered a female soldier the most heroic warrior at the Battle of Vítkov, during the siege of Prague in 1420. As King Sigismund's Royalist army—composed of anti-Hussite troops from Meissen, Thuringia, Silesia, and Hungary—approached the fortifications on Vítkov Hill, two women, one girl, and twenty-six men, having neither arrows nor guns, defended their bulwark by hurling stones and lances. Of this battle, Lawrence of Březová reported, "And one of the two women, though she was without armor, surpassed in spirit all men, as she did not want to yield one step."[30] By creating the figure of the female soldier and placing her in front of the group of male soldiers, Šaloun recalled and honored this beloved story of Czech heroism. The female soldier sat next to a small child, one arm around the child's shoulder, the other holding a long sword across her lap, a "national mother" ready to protect her child against any danger.

Šaloun's revised models from 1903 modified the female image. One version ☙
retained the woman in the grouping of Hussite soldiers, but no longer carry- 47
ing a weapon and now with two children to protect; physically shielding the
children with her body, this mother sheltered future generations. The second
new model pictured the mother as an exile, running while protecting her baby,
symbolizing the danger faced by Czech culture throughout history.

In the end, however, Šaloun abandoned his representations of women from
the imagined Czech past, and created instead the image of an anonymous
woman who could have lived in any era. The final version separated the female
figure from all other components of the monument. Only visible from behind
the memorial, this woman sits solidly on the foundation, not appearing to be in
motion, as are the figures of the exiles and warriors. Two children sit with her,
one suckling at her breast, the other leaning against her for protection. This figure of the nursing mother, this ahistorical, symbolic woman, transformed the
Hus Memorial from historical monument to art nouveau allegory. Each previous model had included a figure of a mother, yet none had emphasized her nurturing function as did the final form. Unlike earlier sketches where the female
statue was cloaked in historical costume, this final version showed the mother
nude, with wide, fleshy hips and full breasts. Her breast milk sustained the
nation's youth; her appearance conveyed fertility and sturdiness, and signified
to onlookers that the Czech nation endured. In the midst of chaotic historical
events—the Hussite wars, the Battle of the White Mountain, the counter-
reformation and exile of the Protestants—this national mother continued to
give nourishment, both physically and culturally. And this nourishment was
understood to include language: Czech men were compelled to use the German
language in their public and professional lives, but Czech women imparted the
mother tongue to the nation's youth.

Breastfeeding as a national duty was a popular belief in nationalist movements throughout Europe. Following Jean-Jacques Rousseau's admonition to
women to abandon reliance on wet-nurses and nurture their children with their
own milk to impart moral and national knowledge directly to new generations,
European nationalists began to view motherhood as women's primary contribution to nation building. Feminist nationalists frequently cited their maternal
activity as their patriotic contribution, a contribution that should earn them
increased rights.

The inclusion of a female body on the Hus monument also enabled Šaloun
to compete with the sculpture and feminine image already on Old Town Square:
the baroque Marian Column and, high atop it, the Virgin Mary, depicted as
Maria Regina, Queen of Heaven, who symbolized regal power. This representation of Mary was immensely popular with the Jesuits during the counter-

Maternal imagery on early Jan Hus Memorial models, 1903.

reformation, serving as a reminder of both terrestrial and heavenly monarchical power.[31] On the pedestal of the column, pristine warrior angels slew grotesque creatures, and many Czech nationalists interpreted these images as celebrating the defeat of Hussite culture at the hands of the Roman Catholic Church.

Šaloun acknowledged that he had to respond to the Marian Column. Although he speculated that future generations might consider moving the column, he knew he must work under the assumption that the two monuments would share the square. He commented, in a newspaper interview, that he purposely designed his monument to be massive and horizontally oriented to rival the towering verticality of the baroque pillar.[32] The image of a nursing mother also challenged the maternal figure of Mary. Šaloun's earthy, nude mother nourished her children, the future of the nation, while the pure, robed Virgin was removed from day-to-day life on the square. This contrasting of secular and Catholic feminine imagery was not uncommon in nationalist and revolutionary movements. Most notably, French revolutionaries contrasted the feminine icon, Marianne or Liberty, with the Virgin Mary, even renaming Notre Dame

Photographs from author's collection.

Cathedral: the Temple of Liberty. The "anticlerical" Hus statue also replicated Catholic Marian imagery. Julia Kristeva has noted that the Jesuit articulation of the Marian image had tremendous influence even upon those who decried the Church's power; Kristeva even "wonders if [the emergence of feminism] is not also due to Protestantism's lacking some necessary element of the Maternal, which in Catholicism has been elaborated with the utmost sophistication by the Jesuits (and which again makes Catholicism very difficult to analyze)."[33]

Šaloun used male figures to portray historical events; his female imagery functioned symbolically. His constant modification of the female figure on the memorial reflected the complexity of feminine iconography. The original feminine image, the woman warrior, signified modernity; the final version used the female figure to evoke the stability of Czech culture. Nationalism was itself a paradoxical construct: the desire to create culturally uniform nation-states was thought to be an essential step toward the modernization of the world, yet the burden of nationalism was to demonstrate national legitimacy by showing the nation's movement through history. Šaloun emphasized Czech motherhood in

Final manifestation of female image on Jan Hus Memorial. Photo by author.

order to assure his audience that (family) stability would remain in a society rapidly journeying toward modernity.[34]

Final Look of the Hus Memorial

Although Šaloun altered the design of the Hus Monument several times, he settled on a design, around 1907, that satisfied both himself and the steering committee of the Club for the Building of the Jan Hus Memorial. In 1907, the municipal government sponsored the exhibition of a small-scale version of the monument on Old Town Square; popular pictorial magazines, such as *Světozor* and *Život*, published photographs of citizens viewing the mock-up. Šaloun maintained his concept of a "wheel of Czech history" that would convey to spectators the interconnectedness of events from the nation's past. The circular shape of the monument imparted, further, a feeling of eternity, a sense that the nation endures through hardships.

Soon after Šaloun won the design contest, art critic Karel Mádl had attacked the original proposal's "dead space" at the back of the monument. All the figures on the memorial faced forward, and did not, he said, form a complex and intriguing composition.[35] Šaloun's wheel responded to this criticism and allowed the monument to be viewed from different angles around the square, which had been newly opened in the urban modernization project. Further, each of the elements, cast in bronze, stood upon a granite base that further emphasized humanity's struggles. Since Šaloun could not portray Hus as a tragic figure facing his death, as the sculptor originally intended, the rocky, craggy, curving granite foundation had to speak to the insecurity and danger a nation must face.

The four principal groupings on the memorial conveyed Šaloun's message that the nation's body and soul endure. Two of the four elements—Jan Hus and the mother with her children—appear stationary. Hus stands triumphant, his gaze one of spirituality, inner strength, and peacefulness; as the spiritual leader of Czech nationalist history, he represents the permanence of the nation's soul. And Jan Hus is the principle feature of the monument: he stands taller than any other figures and his position at the front center of the base is meant to persuade onlookers of his centrality to the nation's history and national movement. Behind Hus, facing the south side of Old Town Square, sits the mother nursing her infant; in her unmoving solidity, she assures the nation of its physical survival.

These two elements of the memorial represent iconography common in cultures throughout the world: Father Spirit cares for his people's souls, and Mother Earth protects her children's bodies.

The other groups on the memorial reflect the chaos within Czech history. These compositions, Hussite warriors and priests on Hus's left side and religious exiles on his right side, each convey motion and confusion. The Hussite soldiers and priests protect the symbol of Hussitism, the chalice; the exiles cling to each other, run from pursuers, and appear haggard and worn. These melodramatic depictions of scenes from the nation's past demonstrate the courage as well as the suffering of the nation's ancestors. Šaloun hoped to convey that they never lost sight of the ideals of steadfastness and stability expressed by Hus and the mother figure.

The Club for the Building of the Jan Hus Memorial portrayed itself as representing true Czech nationalism. Yet, as Šaloun developed his ideas, it became increasingly clear that his memorial was not popular with all those citizens who called themselves Czech nationalists. In particular, Klub za starou Prahu (Club on Behalf of Old Prague) rallied against the placement of his piece on Old Town Square. Although the Club for the Building of the Jan Hus Memorial in Prague claimed that any opposition to the memorial was antinationalist, the Club on Behalf of Old Prague naturally argued that their position grew out of nationalist sentiment as well.

The Club on Behalf of Old Prague was a volunteer organization of art and historical preservationists that sought to protect older Prague landmarks and works of art as Prague swiftly modernized. Organized at the turn of the century,

Jan Hus Memorial with Hus and warriors. Photo by author.

the organization began publishing a monthly journal in 1910. The organization considered the beauty and genius of Prague a national treasure, distinguishing the Czech nation from both its friends and enemies, and argued that the Czech nation was at a historical crossroads when the development of a "unified national culture" centered in Prague would give the entire nation material and spiritual strength.[36]

The first major project of the Club on Behalf of Old Prague was to petition the Prague municipal government against the placement of the Hus Memorial on Old Town Square.[37] Emphasizing that this opposition was based not on political philosophy but on scientific and aesthetic judgments, the organization launched a campaign in the press and the city government to save Old Town Square from "true catastrophe."[38]

The organization launched a study on the potential effect of Šaloun's memorial. When, in March 1911, the Hus Memorial Club displayed Šaloun's plaster model on Old Town Square, the preservationists' organization employed professional photographers and printers to create a pamphlet demonstrating the huge memorial's symmetrical disruption and division of the square. Engineers and architects provided the Prague City Council with diagrams and mathematical equations proving the detrimental effects the large horizontally aligned monument would have on the relationships among the buildings and

alleys in Old Town. Views across the square would be obstructed, according ⚜
to the pamphlet, and traffic on the square would be blocked. The organization
also contended that the relatively small (nine-hundred-square-meter) square
should be kept clear of a massive monument, which by its size would limit
the number of participants at nationalist gatherings such as Sokol festivals and
demonstrations. Further, the group argued, the architectural uniformity of Old
Town would be destroyed. The vertical relationship between the Marian Column and the towers of the Gothic City Hall and Týn Church would be thrown
off by the massive horizontal structure, which would dominate the delicate architectural space.

Beyond objections to the architectural effects on Old Town Square, argued
the Club on Behalf of Old Prague, the artistic style of the monument did not suit
the baroque and renaissance plaza. The group's journal characterized Šaloun's
piece not as a monument but as a "living picture." The contemporary naturalist
monument was "agitated, undulating"; the "main figure was pushed out too far
from the center of gravity"; and the entire piece "expressed symbolic pathos."
According to the club, these characteristics did not suit the tone of Old Town
Square, which "preserved the familiarity of historical inheritance and the peace
of a bygone era."[39] Demonstrating that it had no objections to the memorial's
subject, the organization also studied the possibility of placing it in a different location, recommending Karlovo náměstí (Charles Square) in Nové město
(New Town), spacious enough to allow better viewing of the complex sculpture
and to provide, for popular celebrations in honor of Hus, a large and open space
where many participants could gather. Further, the group noted, the proposed
spot was the former site of the Romanesque Chapel of the Body of Christ, a
church used by Hus's followers in the fourteenth century.[40]

Opposition to the placement of the Hus Memorial on Old Town Square extended to other organizations. For example, the nationalist organ of the State's
Rights Progressive Party, *Samostatnost* (Independence), printed an editorial in
January 1911 objecting to the location of the monument. The editorial argued
that the Club for the Building of the Jan Hus Memorial in Prague had actually
done a disservice to the memory of Hus by insisting that the sculpture stand on
the square: "It is indisputable that the placement of the Hus Memorial on Old
Town Square was originally greatly motivated by a sense of revenge against the
Marian Column." The editors agreed that the Marian Column was a "disgrace
against the Czech nation," but suggested that Šaloun had sacrificed the memorial's aesthetic value so that it could compete with the column, and that it would
be an insult to Hus to place his memorial in an unsuitable location.[41]

The efforts of the Club on Behalf of Old Prague and other groups to change
the memorial site were in vain.[42] On April 11, 1911, the Prague City Council

Marian Column and Church of Our Lady before Týn, c. 1900. Courtesy of Jan Bradna and the Society for the Rebuilding of the Marian Column.

reviewed the 1899 ordinance approving the placement of the Hus Memorial on Old Town Square. A motion to affirm the earlier decision passed with a vote of seventeen to five.[43] As in 1899, the Club for the Building of the Jan Hus Memorial had successfully argued that a statue of the nation's most important historical figure must be located in the most important public space in the old city.[44]

The artistic design of a statue dedicated to Jan Hus could stir so much passion and so much anger in Prague society because conflicts over the nationalist statue reflected disagreements among the Czechs not only about religious matters but also over the nature of modernity and progress at the turn of the century. As scholars have long argued, rapid industrialization during the late nineteenth century influenced Europeans to cling to traditions in art and culture, even while vying for success in the modernizing world. The Hus Memorial symbolized this paradox. Nationalists concurrently sought to prove their modernity through economic success, as well as contemporary architecture and art, while still proving their historical legitimacy. Representing a medieval hero like Jan Hus with an art nouveau sculpture, though this seemed anachronistic to some, could cleverly show that the Czech people could, like Janus, look to a vibrant past as well as a prosperous future.

Chapter 3

Generational Approaches
to National Monuments

"Our art began with the life of the Nation."

Stanislav Sucharda, sculptor of the
František Palacký Memorial in Prague

W HILE controversy swirled around the Jan Hus Memorial design and
festival, other associations of Prague's Czech nationalists prepared
additional monument projects to mark the city with a national narrative. In Prague, the Czech civic leaders focused on the Hus Memorial but
also supported statues planned to commemorate patron saint Wenceslas, national historian František Palacký, and Hussite general Jan Žižka. Monuments
to these historical figures did not carry the emotional weight of the Hus project,
but they were part of a larger effort by Czech civic leaders to create national sacred spaces throughout Prague during the "era of monument fever,"[1] when the
extension of voting rights for the lower classes persuaded the middle classes to
reaffirm their political and cultural leadership by "mass-producing traditions."[2]
In Prague, these building projects would assert the Czechs' primacy over the
city's Germans and German Jews, who had dominated Prague culture until
the late nineteenth century. The projects would also reinforce the power of the
middle-class elite, as working-class and student groups began to assert their
own separate versions of Czech nationalism.

Like so much of the Czech cultural movement, each monument shared an
important link connecting Czech nationalism to Bohemia's complicated religious past. However, the monuments' thematic similarities were not reflected
in their artistic styles. Even though the Wenceslas, Palacký, and Žižka projects
were planned at the same time, they represented three distinct generations of
Prague's art community. The Wenceslas Memorial was sculpted by Josef Václav

Myslbek, father of Czech nationalist sculpture, the Palacký Monument was created by his foremost student, Stanislav Sucharda, and another Myslbek student,
Jan Štursa, who was fourteen years younger than Sucharda, submitted one of
the two leading designs for the Žižka Memorial (a winner for that contest was
never chosen). The Wenceslas Memorial, the Palacký Monument, and the designs submitted for the Žižka contest represent the period's rapid shift from
neoclassicist historicism to art nouveau to modernism.

As Katherine David-Fox has demonstrated, exploring different forms of
European modernism was another way for Prague writers and artists to discern what it meant to be Czech.[3] Prague's artistic dynamism at the turn of the
century made it a leading European creative center. Prague artists sought inspiration from other such centers of modernism—Paris, Munich, Berlin, and
Vienna—where creative leaders often rejected nationalist politics or subjects
for their work. In Prague, though, modern artists sought to marry these divergent trends, embracing new artistic styles for their nationalist commissions and
creating unique, modern styles to commemorate the nation's past.

Replacing a Memorial to Saint Wenceslas

In 1891, the Emperor Francis Joseph Bohemian Academy of Arts, Humanities, and Sciences in Prague undertook a project to erect a Saint Wenceslas
statue on Wenceslas Square. Wenceslas, the patron saint of Bohemia and Moravia, had long been a popular figure in Czech national mythology. Although
his popularity in the nineteenth and early twentieth centuries was eclipsed by
Jan Hus's, Wenceslas remained present in national iconography throughout the
Czech national movement. The Bohemian Academy raised funds primarily
from the Prague city government and the Zemská Banka, one of the wealthiest
banks in Bohemia and the foremost promoter of nationalist art.[4] The bank and
city each gave fifteen thousand crowns, which covered most of the monument's
cost.[5] Other voluntary associations contributed smaller amounts. In encouraging organizations to donate, the academy emphasized that the meaning of
Wenceslas was "not only a regional question, or solely a religious question, or
purely a question of patriotism, or only Czech." Instead, a statue on the important square would carry multiple meanings and speak to "the entire Prague
community."[6]

Wenceslas was a key symbol for the legitimacy of a Bohemian political nation. He was the "Good King" of the English Christmas carol, itself an adapta-
tion by J. M. Neale from a nineteenth-century poem written in German by
Czech national revivalist Václav Alois Svoboda (1791–1849). The tenth-century
King Wenceslas was the son of the Bohemian rulers Duke Rastislav and Duch-

ess Drahomíra, daughter of the chief of the Veletians, a northern Slavic tribe. Rastislav's parents, the previous Bohemian rulers Duke Bořivoj and Duchess Ludmila, converted to Christianity during their reign; however, most of their subjects did not convert and many powerful Bohemian families strongly opposed the new religion. Ludmila arranged to raise her grandson, Wenceslas, and teach him the Christian faith. Her personal chaplain, Paul, was a disciple of that St. Methodius who, with St. Cyril, brought Christianity to the Slavs. Paul baptized young Wenceslas and educated him in the Christian faith, as well as in Latin, Greek, and Church Slavonic. Wenceslas grew to become quite pious, and legends maintain that he wore a hair shirt and cultivated grapes and corn to make sacramental wine and bread.

Sometime around 920, Wenceslas's father, Rastislav, was killed fighting the Magyars. His mother Drahomíra, a pagan, assumed her husband's reign and began to pursue an anti-Christian or secularist state policy. When her mother-in-law, Ludmila, encouraged Wenceslas to depose his mother and establish a Christian kingdom, Drahomíra had the older woman murdered. Nonetheless, the noble estates supported Wenceslas over Drahomíra, and he assumed power in 922. Wenceslas immediately proclaimed that his kingdom would support the Christian law and church. Promising to rule with justice and mercy, he pardoned his mother for murdering Ludmila and welcomed her back to the court. According to legend, he was known for his high education, his suppression of the nobles' abuses of the peasantry, his compassion for the poor, and his combination of strict punishment of murderers and disapproval of the death penalty. He was also an excellent warrior. Encouraging but not enforcing Christianity, Wenceslas influenced many Bohemians to convert during his short reign. In 929 (some sources say 936), Wenceslas's brother Boleslav—perhaps motivated by the birth of a nephew who would have removed him from direct inheritance of the throne—associated with an opposition party of nobles, whose grievances included the clergy's influence in Wenceslas's court and the king's suppression of the nobles' powers over peasants. While Wenceslas was walking to mass at a religious festival in Stará Boleslav, Boleslav and his followers attacked and killed him.

Immediately, according to the legends, Wenceslas's people venerated him as a martyr.

Another aspect of Wenceslas's fame, however, made him less palatable to Czech nationalists: his political policy involved cultivating friendly relations with nearby German groups. By acknowledging the German king, Henry I, as his overlord and rightful successor to Charlemagne's Holy Roman Empire, Wenceslas was able to preserve the unity of the whole region later known as the Crownlands of Saint Wenceslas, whose boundaries were used as late as 1919 when Czechoslovakia was carved out of Austria-Hungary. Although national-ists appreciated his unification of the kingdom, many questioned his apparent affinity for the Germans. In particular, Palacký argued that Wenceslas com-promised with the Germans and allowed his nation to be exploited.[7] In fact, Palacký claimed, Wenceslas agreed to pay an annual tribute to Emperor Henry of 500 silver talents and 120 oxen. Early-twentieth-century historian and Cath-olic Josef Pekař, who disputed Palacký's romantic version of national history, asserted that there was no evidence for Palacký's claim and that Wenceslas must be credited with fashioning Bohemia as a "full member of the community of Western nations."[8]

Despite Palacký's criticism, the powerful stories of Wenceslas's faith, reign, and martyrdom remained within the realm of national mythmaking, and Czech nationalists used the story of Saint Wenceslas to assert their political legitimacy in Bohemia. The saint's powerful though short reign reasserted the primacy of the Přemyslid dynasty during a period of clan conflicts; further, it tied Bohemia to European Christendom by providing the nation with a royal martyr and patron.

Wenceslas legends were used to foster enthusiasm for nationalist enter-prises. Fundraising literature for the Wenceslas Memorial retold the legend that Saint Wenceslas and his knights lived on within Mount Blaník in Eastern Bohemia, ever ready to emerge and rescue those Czechs who remained true to their nation.[9] Wenceslas was one of the few national heroes who appealed to Catholics and anticlerics alike. Seventeenth-century counter-reformers cre-ated a cult of Saint Wenceslas, but the Hussites had also venerated the man. They sang the "St. Wenceslas Chorale" at the Battle of Lipany and admired his martyrdom, the Wenceslas myth adding to the power and imagery of Hussite legends. Catholics could adopt Wenceslas as a hero since his reign predated the era of church reform and schism in Bohemia.

Palacký had written, about the Czechs, "We were here before Austria, and we will be here after it is gone."[10] A monument to Wenceslas would acknowl-edge the presence of a Bohemian dynasty well before the Habsburg rise to power. According to the Bohemian Academy, the statue would also remind the Prague public that Wenceslas was soon to emerge from Blaník to support the nation's autonomy within Austria.

Unlike most of Prague's nationalist monuments, the Wenceslas project was not entirely new. It would stand on a site that had featured a Wenceslas Statue for two centuries. An equestrian statue of Wenceslas had stood there from 1678 to 1879, when it was removed because of weather damage; this original sculp-ture was by baroque master Jan Jiří Bendl, creator of the Marian Column in Old Town Square. However, although the seventeenth-century Wenceslas sculpture had been sponsored by Jesuit leaders seeking to make Catholicism attractive to Prague residents, the nineteenth-century statue would represent the saint's national and religious contributions.

The location of the monument was significant beyond its replacement of the Bendl statue. Built in 1348, Wenceslas Square was the centerpiece of Nové město (New Town), the modernization project developed by King Charles IV (the Holy Roman Empire's Charles I) for Prague. Shaped like a long boulevard measuring 170 by 60 meters, the square had become Prague's nineteenth-century commercial center. Named the Horse Market for its original function, the square featured key landmarks of Czech nationalism. In particular, the square was the site of the beginning of the 1848 insurrection in Prague. In June 1848, nationalist students held a Catholic mass in honor of Saint Wenceslas and, when the celebration turned into an angry protest, Austrian soldiers fired on the students. The students responded by building barricades on the square, and six days of fighting ensued. Although the Czechs were defeated, 1848 remained a symbolic turning point in the national struggle. After the uprising, Czech residents renamed the square in honor of Wenceslas.

The square's most prominent building was the National Museum, a landmark to Bohemian regional patriotism and Czech nationalism. Members of the landed aristocracy, most notably Count Kašpar Sternberg, a German speaker who nonetheless believed in reviving Czech language and culture, chartered the museum in 1818. In 1827 historian František Palacký became the editor of the museum's Czech-language journal. The museum sits atop the hill formed by Wenceslas Square as it slopes upward toward the south. Its building, an impressive neorenaissance domed structure, opened to great fanfare on May 18, 1891. Until then, the museum's collections had been housed in small palaces throughout Prague. Today the museum houses collections of the natural history of Bohemia, as well as a pantheon focused on Czech nationalism and featuring busts of prominent figures in Czech history. Demonstrating the relationship between nationalism and sacred space, National Museum literature calls this pantheon a "secular cathedral" where public functions have occurred since the museum's opening.[11]

Two months after that opening, the Bohemian Academy of Science, Humanities, and Art in Prague announced that it would sponsor a new statue of Wenceslas on the square, below the museum's grand staircase. When the academy decided on this sponsorship, it employed the prominent Josef Václav Myslbek, a professor at the School of Applied Arts in Prague, to create the statue. Myslbek was a highly respected nationalist sculptor whose work hearkened back to classical and renaissance traditions. One of the first Czech artists with significant contacts outside the Habsburg Lands, Myslbek had traveled to Paris in 1878, examining French monumentalism, then at its peak in the wake of the Franco-Prussian War. Just as French artists and politicians sought grand monuments to revive the nation's spirit after their crushing defeat, so Myslbek believed that sculpture could inspire Czech nationalists disheartened by Hungary's having achieved new autonomy in the empire at the same time that the Czechs had won few political rights. Upon returning to Prague, Myslbek had thus become a spokesperson for French neoclassicism.

Myslbek impressed art critics and nationalists through his series of sculptures of Jan Žižka and his statues for the National Theater. His romantic nationalist generation relied for thematic inspiration on the Královodvorský and Zelenohorský Manuscripts, the forged Slavic epics supposedly discovered earlier in the nineteenth century.[12] Myslbek's sculptures on Prague's Palacký Bridge featured legendary heroes from the forged epics, including Libuše and Přemysl, the seventh-century founding couple of Prague, Záboj and Slavoj, the Bohemian leaders who defeated the attacking Franks in 805, and such notables as Lumír, Ctírad, and Šarka.

Even though Myslbek continued to receive commissions for important monument projects like the bridge and the (1891) Wenceslas Memorial, his career was beginning to suffer even by the mid-1880s. In 1886, Professors Jan Gebauer and Tomáš Masaryk exposed the Královodvorský and Zelenohorský Manuscripts as forgeries: rather than dating from the early medieval period, the manuscripts had actually been written in the early nineteenth century by romantic poet Václav Hanka. Gebauer and Masaryk's accusation caused tremendous controversy in the nationalist movement, as Myslbek's generation and the editorial staff of nationalist newspaper *Národní listy* defended the manuscripts and Prague's younger generation supported Gebauer and Masaryk. Soon after the manuscript crisis began, Masaryk and his associates founded the Realist Party, which decried the romantic nationalism of both the Old Czechs and the Young Czechs.[13]

Myslbek's crisis, however, was not only thematic and political but also stylistic. His work was prominently featured in the 1891 Prague Jubilee, an exposition of art and industry—which became a Czech nationalist showpiece after most German contributors pulled out. However, he was beginning to lose support from the artistic and nationalist communities. Progressive students, writers, and artists had become infatuated with French symbolism, the precursor to art nouveau, and other Bohemian artists—often fluent in German and Czech—studied in Vienna and Munich, where they experimented with Central European modernism.[14] With the 1887 foundation of the Mánes Association of Fine Artists and the 1894 inauguration of the progressive art journal *Moderní revue* (Modern Review), young artists were demanding new approaches;

the faculty of the Prague School of Applied Arts also had begun emphasizing the new "secession" style (as it was called in Vienna and Prague). Myslbek and another nationalist artist, František Zeníšek, left the Prague School of Applied Arts to join, in 1896, the faculty of the nationalized School of Fine Arts, which maintained a more conservative approach to art.

Myslbek did experiment with the new style in some of his more personal work, such as a symbolic sculpture of Music, depicted as a woman. Yet he refused to change his approach to public monuments. Instead, he actually accentuated the monumental style of his work, "particularly through the use of large amounts of drapery";[15] his work also exaggerated physical features and distorted proportion to make his subjects appear more powerful. The Palacký Bridge sculptures, unveiled throughout the 1890s, received considerable criticism in the press and from fellow artists; the man who had only recently been the most influential and popular sculptor in the Czech Lands was vilified by the new generation of artists, many his former pupils.

Nonetheless, Myslbek continued his work on the Saint Wenceslas monument, and retained its original plan for a traditional historicist statue. This plan reflected his renowned attention to detail, a key feature of neoclassical sculpture. For example, Myslbek borrowed an authentic chain mail suit as a model to create a costume for the king, did considerable historical and archeological research on his subject, and also studied Bendl's original equestrian statue. Cast in bronze, Myslbek's sculpture featured Wenceslas in full armor, sitting proudly on his horse, and flanked by four statues of the Bohemian saints Ivan, Anežka, Ludmila, and Prokop. On the base of the statue was a line from the "St. Wenceslas Chorale", "May we and our descendants not perish."

Myslbek's equestrian statue was unveiled in June 1912, but the work never received the attention given other patriotic sculptures in Prague. By the second decade of the twentieth century, Myslbek's style was outmoded. Contemporary artists called the work mundane, and the statue's supporters never sought the publicity of the nationalist press that the Club for the Building of Jan Hus Memorial used so effectively to rally public emotion over Hus's memory. Further, the historical figure of Wenceslas did not inspire the passion that other monument projects did, perhaps because Wenceslas had not confronted Austrian power, as had Palacký, or Catholic clericalism, as had Hus.

The František Palacký Memorial

Although plans for a Hus memorial raised tremendous controversy and the Wenceslas statue attracted artistic criticism, another monument was widely celebrated: for František Palacký, renowned for his work as a historian and

Myslbek statue of St. Wenceslas in front of National Museum. Postcard from author's collection.

political leader of the Old Czech Party, and a principal voice of the Slavs in the Austrian parliament. In 1880, only two years after his death, Prague leaders began to discuss erecting a memorial to honor him. Even though Palacký represented the more conservative, earlier stage of Czech nationalism, Prague's Young Czech leaders viewed him as their beloved predecessor.

Even a monument to this relatively recent and seemingly secular figure conveyed religious connotations. Positivist historiography was an important step in the Czech nationalist movement in the nineteenth century: following the model of German historian Leopold von Ranke, František Palacký researched his six-volume study, *Dějiny národu českého v Čechách a na Moravě* (History of the Czech Nation in Bohemia and Moravia). Palacký's contribution to knowledge of Czech history earned him the epithet "father of the nation," and Hus became a central figure of his study. Palacký's interpretation of Hus was rather anachronistic; for Palacký, raised a committed Protestant by his minister father, Hus became a hero. Palacký, like many of his fellow nationalists, presupposed a national consciousness during the medieval period, when regional identity actually prevailed (Hus's promotion of the vernacular local Slavic language owed more to a religious conviction to reach more followers than to a nationalist conviction). Yet many of Hus's statements about the period's regional conflicts fed Palacký's interpretation of the Czechs' place in the Austrian Empire. Palacký's thesis was that the Czech nation had struggled, throughout its history, in a cycle of conflicts with the German nation; understanding the long history of German domination over the oppressed yet defiant Czechs would enable the latter to regain their former greatness.

In his work, Palacký defined the era of Hus and his followers as the apogee of Czech history. When, in 1401, Bavarian and Meissen troops invaded Bohemia, the latter reaching as far as Prague, Palacký noted, Hus reproached Bohemian nobles for lack of resistance: "The Czechs are in this matter more wretched than dogs and snakes, for they do not defend their country, although their cause is just. Similarly, I say that the Czechs in Bohemia, according to laws, both the divine law and the natural instinct, should be first in offices of the kingdom of Bohemia, as are the French in the kingdom of France and the Germans in their own lands, so that the Czechs should rule their subjects and the Germans theirs."[16]

Thus, Palacký viewed Hus as a hero for the so-called Czech revival. Inspired by Palacký, other intellectuals began to create literature, histories, plays, art, and music about Hus and his movement. Masaryk was a great admirer of Palacký and believed it his moral obligation to follow in the historian's footsteps. Through Palacký's scholarship, Masaryk became convinced of Hus's primary place in the Czech pantheon; Masaryk believed that a scholarly study of Hus's teachings and Palacký's histories was essential for any Czech nationalist. Honoring Palacký with a monument, therefore, celebrated Hus as well.

The monument to Palacký was to sit on the Vltava River embankment, near the National Theater and looking out toward the Palacký Bridge. Although less central than the Hus and Wenceslas Memorials, the chosen location did create a sense that Palacký guarded the river that flowed through Prague. A contest for a Czech sculptor for this memorial was announced in 1897, six years after Myslbek was chosen for the Wenceslas statue. That half decade had remarkably altered the landscape of Prague as well as artistic trends within Czech nationalism and the Prague community.

One of the leading masters of the Prague secession style was the sculptor Stanislav Sucharda, who had studied in Vienna and under Myslbek at the Prague School of Applied Arts. Sucharda had won a celebrated reputation in Prague through his decorations for many of its new buildings, particularly the Zemská Banka. In 1899, he was appointed a professor at his Prague alma mater, and two years later he received word that, out of fourteen submissions, his was the winning design for the Palacký Memorial.[17] Sucharda was the president of the Mánes Association, whose artists used ahistorical symbols to "give weight to the 'inner eye' of imagination and fantasy," while still idealizing figures from the new Czech national pantheon.[18] They sought inspiration from France and

the pan-Slavism emanating from Russia; they also fused designs found in nature with scientific principles of geometry.

As president of the Mánes Association, Sucharda was instrumental in
bringing the Rodin Exhibition (influential on Šaloun's design for the Hus
monument) to Bohemia. Rodin's work seemed such a departure from Czech
sculpture that the conservative press accused the association of staging the influential exhibition to eclipse the popularity of national sculptor Myslbek. The
1902 exhibition and visit by Rodin had such a profound influence on Sucharda that he reworked his entire plan for the Palacký Memorial (as Šaloun had
reworked his for the Hus statue) to reflect these new views of art. Even before
the Rodin show, Sucharda's column in the Mánes Association's journal, *Volné
směry,* had praised Rodin for capturing human emotions "of love and suffering,
hope and despair, abnegation and contempt."[19] Indeed, Sucharda hired Josef
Mařatka, a Czech sculptor who had studied with Rodin in Paris, to assist with
the new memorial, so that Sucharda could learn to capture the emotions and
psychology of his subject.

Sucharda was primarily concerned with capturing the *meaning* of Palacký
for future generations. While earlier sculptors, like Myslbek, had researched
the physical appearance and appropriate costumes of their subjects, Sucharda
committed to capturing Palacký's "essence, his innermost existence."[20] Sucharda emphasized the link between the national body and its spirit. The secessionist monuments in Prague, particularly the Hus and Palacký memorials, were
not designed to instruct on history but rather to create a "sacred" bond between spectators and the nation's history. The inscription on the Palacký Monument—"To our awakener and leader of the resurrected nation!"—celebrated
the dynamic relationship between the national past and its future.[21]

Sucharda extensively read Palacký's histories and articles in the journal of
the National Museum. In turn, the sculptor wrote prolifically on the symbolism
he hoped to convey. He used Bohemian granite to connect Palacký with the
nation's natural world, he noted. A realistic rendering of Palacký, he said, constituted "the heart of the whole monument," but the historian was not merely "a
man of meat and blood." Sucharda chose instead to "unite him with something
deeper, bringing a different truth to light."[22] Sucharda's memorial combined a
portrait of Palacký, sitting sternly in the center gazing toward the Vltava River
and the bridge that bears his name, with symbolic human figures that "grow
from the pain of the Czech people's wretched spiritual condition, as a result of
the ferocious Germanization."

Sucharda's Palacký Monument used gendered symbols, prevalent in the secessionist movement, to express strong emotion. The dominant cultural conception associated women with nature and the irrational, men with culture and

Stanislav Sucharda's Palacký Memorial. Photo by author.

the intellect. The masculine central figure, famed for his cultural and intellectual contributions balanced with the fervor for the nation expressed by the female imagery. Sucharda chose to include a range of feminine symbols familiar to his contemporary audience: the violated, the procreative, the beautiful, and the threatening. Male symbols represented fatherhood and strength as well as oppression and danger.

In the center of the monument, overseeing his city, Palacký himself clearly represents the *otec národa* (father of the nation), as he is called in the commemorative pamphlet for the statue's unveiling.[23] Palacký is the only historical character; the sculptural groupings surrounding him are allegorical figures representing the struggles and triumphs of the nation. The sculptures on Palacký's right feature two separate groupings, one male and one female. The sculpture "Oppression," which represents the victims of Austrian political and cultural domination, appears as two angry and deeply tormented men lying beneath an abstract arch of earth and stone; they struggle to push away the source of their oppression, revealing strong and virile muscles. Male figures also dominate the sections of the memorial called "History Tells the Story" and "The Awakener," which represent Palacký's historiographical and intellectual contributions.

Female figures create the emotional impact of Sucharda's work. A nude woman clings to the floor of the monument; painfully thin, she weeps in anguish and tightly clenches her legs together, as though she has been raped. Sucharda called this violated female "White Mountain" to express the nationalists' view that Czech culture and spirituality was desecrated at the 1620 Battle of White Mountain, where the predominantly Protestant Bohemian nobility met total defeat at the hands of Austrian and allied forces, ushering in the counter-reformation and Habsburg hereditary rights in Bohemia. It has been said that within secessionist art, "gestures of submission . . . denote a realm of masculine dominance,"[24] and Sucharda's White Mountain figure represented such a spiritual violation of the nation by imperial powers.

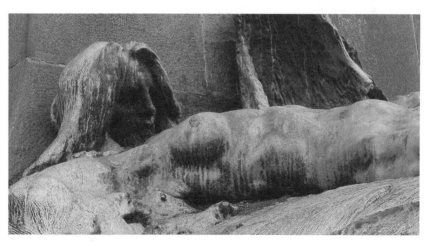

"White Mountain" sculpture on Palacký Memorial. Photo by author.

Another female image, described by Sucharda as the "witch" or a "hundred-year-old hag," represents the forces that oppressed Czech national awakeners. Sucharda wrote, "Alarmingly enormous, powerful through her terrible beauty, the Witch soars up between heaven and earth" and "hates every awakener." She terrorizes the nation's youth, who thus "daydream" rather than build the nation.[25]

Although these and other female images convey the Czech national tragedy, a sculptural grouping of women at the top of the monument tells the story of victory and triumph. This group spirals up the pillar behind Palacký and culminates in a beautiful robed woman, her left arm triumphantly raised. Another young woman, who Sucharda describes as personifying "softness and humility," stands above the witch. Although this young woman catches her garment and is thus poised between the nation's future and the hag's past, a young man stands ready to catch her. "The man, her companion, . . . touches her arm, aspiring for something more—where he has a strong foreboding of a clear future." This couple represents the hope for the new nation. As Sucharda explains, "In them shoots are already sprouting."[26]

The figure of "Victory" rises atop the monument. Sucharda implies that she is the offspring of the young couple. Her arms, he writes, emerge from the man's eyes and the woman's full breast. This "ascending woman, almost still a child, [is] the new woman, awakening through a new spring." The New Woman (Sucharda capitalized this name throughout his narrative) appears "jubilant," as her "soul flies high through the country, with thirsty longing." She is the "resurrected soul of the nation the soul that strove for existence," and she stands in "powerful reverence," lifting her shoulder to reveal her simple and pure "Slavic heart." Sucharda announced at the end of his essay that his New Woman "gives from her heroic body, the kiss of the sun blazing as it sets over White Mountain."[27] The Czech nation has triumphed.

The "new woman" was a powerful symbol at the turn of the century, as feminism gained ground and women took their places in the public sphere. In art, Sucharda's "New Woman" conveyed contradictory meaning to its audience: women participated in the national movement but did not overturn traditional gender roles. As a symbol in art nouveau, the "new woman" conveyed communal strength but simultaneously inspired male "anxieties over this proactive female."[28] Sucharda's national "New Woman" simultaneously sent a victorious celebratory message to the nation and emphasized that the battle had not yet been won. Czech society's identity was still uncertain.

The Palacký Monument was unveiled in 1912 as part of the enormous Sokol Slet (Sokol Festival), an international gathering of that patriotic gymnastics organization. One key theme of the Sokol Festival was to show off Prague, "the jewel and mother of Czech cities and the pride of the Czech nation."[29] The contrast between the Wenceslas statue's quiet unveiling in June and the lavish festival only weeks later, on July 1, was palpable. The Sokol commemorative pamphlet from the unveiling ceremony emphasized the participation of delegates and journalists from Slovakia, the United States, France, England, Russia, Poland, Slovenia, Serbia, Bulgaria, Macedonia, Georgia, and Croatia. In particular, the Sokol emphasized the Slavic character of the event, highlighting the eight hundred Russian visitors and over one thousand Serb participants.[30] Like the Hus cornerstone ceremony, the Palacký unveiling ceremony included participants from other Prague political and voluntary organizations, such as the National Council, Association of Czech Women, and Mánes Association, as well as from educational institutions.

A Sokol member and local celebrity, Sucharda, dressed in top hat and tails, proudly presented his monument to the public. Underlying the stylized gymnastic performances, the Czech national costumes and music, and the celebratory unveiling of the Palacký Memorial, a militaristic tone suggested to the international community that the Czechs would be ready for battle if necessary. Claire Nolte has demonstrated that in the years preceding the Great War, Czech nationalism and the Sokol movement in particular asserted a radical, martial character.[31] Like Sucharda's victorious "New Woman," the Sokol Slet and the Palacký Memorial unveiling of 1912 formed a show of strength in the face of rising international tensions in Europe.

The Žižka Monument Competition

Another monument project from this era more pointedly portrayed a strong and militaristic image of the nation. Jan Žižka had been a popular figure with radical nationalists, particularly from the working class, since the mid-nineteenth century. However, Žižka's military connotations made Habsburg authorities apprehensive about approving commemorations to him; the medieval general had led the radical Taborite Army to victory against Emperor Sigismund, then king of Hungary. Crucial to that victory, the famed Battle of Vítkov, on the outskirts of Prague, was one of the few military victories Czechs could celebrate. Placed alongside martyrs Hus, Wenceslas, and the victims of the 1620 battle of White Mountain, Žižka stands out as a thoroughly masculine, triumphant hero.

As with other heroes from Bohemia's past, religious connotations made Žižka a controversial idol—the Taborites had been the most radical sect of Hussites, and their extreme anticlericalism and communal lifestyle had contrasted with the views of the more moderate Utraquists. Nonetheless, Žižka's often socialist nineteenth- and twentieth-century followers insisted that the religious ideas inspiring the general had metamorphosed over the centuries into faith in the nation.[32] In 1877, Vítkov residents, largely from the industrial working class, renamed the Prague suburb Žižkov to honor their hero. Žižkov was one of the independent cities—along with Karlín, Smíchov, and Vinohrady—that many Czech nationalists wanted to incorporate into a Greater Prague to bolster the city's Czech-speaking population. German speakers still lived primarily in central Prague, yet the working class of Žižkov and Smíchov was becoming increasingly radicalized, and Young Czechs feared the political competition. Žižkov's leaders desired the respect and support of Prague but also wanted to assert a separate identity. A monument to Žižka, on the site of the Battle of Vítkov, would legitimate Žižkov's independent identity, yet link the suburb to Prague's "cult of monuments."[33]

Although the Society for Building a Žižka Memorial in Žižkov was founded in 1883, it was not until 1913 that the voluntary organization had the resources and political backing to sponsor a monument competition. The Žižka monument society by that point had garnered tremendous support from the local community, collecting over ninety thousand crowns by 1907—three times more than was contributed to the Wenceslas Monument.[34] Residents were frustrated with the society, though, for continually delaying the project. In 1903, Žižkov residents watched the laying of the Hus memorial's cornerstone, and angrily questioned whether their own city's monument would ever rise.[35]

When the Žižka contest finally took place, in 1913, Prague's artistic community responded enthusiastically. In early 1914, the fifty-seven submissions to the monument competition were displayed at the Palace of Industry, an art nouveau building at the Prague Exhibition Grounds. The majority of models were hackneyed designs, which avant garde painter Josef Čapek likened to plaster statues found in local pubs.[36] However, a handful of designs for the Žižka monument were so innovative that they attracted considerable attention from the daily press and from art journals. Following the European trend of insisting that modern style infuse all forms of creativity, the competition invited sculptural and architectural design or a combination of forms. Prague architects and sculptors paired to explore some of the most modern styles emanating from France, particularly cubism. Although cubism in Western Europe remained a preoccupation of an artistic elite, the movement attracted a wide array of young Bohemian and Moravian artists, who creatively employed the style in not only sculpture and architecture but even theater. Prague's avant garde believed it could use cubism, with its emphasis on dissecting and opening preconceived forms, to discredit the historicism still popular among the

Czech bourgeoisie. Ironically, these young artists, unlike their West European contemporaries, did not automatically snub monumental projects and public art. Just as art nouveau was infused by nationalism in such regions as Bohemia, Hungary, and Scandinavia, where the national question dominated public discourse, Czech cubists did not automatically dismiss national subjects for their work.[37]

The radical submissions to the Žižka competition illuminated a new generation of artists, in their twenties and early thirties in 1913. The only competitive submission from a slightly older sculptor, forty-one-year-old symbolist František Bílek, represented a bridge between the secession style and more radical modernism. In the 1890s, the man considered Prague's foremost cultural leader, the literary critic František Xavěr Šalda, had called for a new synthetism in art, a "concrete symbolism" fusing the artist's physical observations with an inner, spiritual essence;[38] for the 1913 competition, Bílek, a spiritual seeker who left Catholicism to explore the Hussite tradition, proposed an attenuated figure of Žižka surrounded by twenty abstract boulders, a grouping symbolizing the whole Hussite era. However, the jury rejected the overt religious tone of Bílek's design, which disregarded Žižka's military contributions; contemporary nationalists were insisting on secularizing the Hussite message, particularly through Žižka's warrior manifestation.

An equestrian statue by Jan Štursa better served the military image. Eight years younger than Bílek, Štursa also embraced synthetism. Štursa, a prolific sculptor who studied under Myslbek and contributed decorative sculptures to numerous Prague architectural projects, also experimented, unlike the older generation of decorative sculptors, with cubism. His fruitful partnership with the father of Prague modern architecture, Jan Kotěra, led to a powerful joint submission to the Žižka competition: Štursa and Kotěra's proposal featured a huge, somewhat abstract Žižka on horseback, flanked by soldiers wielding swords; the sculpture fragmented Žižka's commanding silhouette and broke the lines of his huge shield. The massive monument could only be viewed at a distance, becoming more abstract as the viewer neared it; this force and weight of the monument, however, led critics to call it Germanic and inappropriate for a Czech nationalist sculpture.[39]

Although Bílek and Štursa's synthetic contributions still embodied some realist principles, other, young artists experimented with truly abstract forms. Czech cubism grew out of Šalda's earlier calls for a synthetism of art and life: in the second decade of the twentieth century, young artists indeed fused the French cubist model of Picasso and Braque with Šalda's synthetism. Czech cubo-expressionists used cubist fragmentation to express changes of mood and inner spiritual and intellectual activity. The radical direction of these youth led to tremendous controversies in Prague's art community; generational conflict, and diverging concepts of abstraction in art, led fifteen artists to leave the powerful Mánes Association to form the Group of Plastic Artists. Even Šalda, though he still supported the young artists' radical experiments, began to criticize the "drastic abstraction" for becoming more "formulae and diagrams [than] works of art."[40]

In spite of the censure of the older generation, however, the Group of Plastic Artists reenergized Prague art in the years surrounding the Žižka competition. The most radical proposal of the monument contest was that of twenty-three-year-old sculptor and painter Otto Gutfreund, a member of the Group of Plastic Artists, who had studied cubism in France. With thirty-one-year-old modern architect Pavel Janák, Gutfreund proposed a cubist monument that appeared revolutionary, seeming infused with movement, in contrast to the more traditional sculpture that Gutfreund disparaged as inert. The architect Josef Gočár, a fellow Plastic Artist member, also submitted an innovative cubist design— and Gočár, who had recently unveiled the House of the Black Madonna, his cubist café and gallery in central Prague, helped to bring yet more attention to the competition, through his newfound fame. Vlastislav Hofman, Ladislav Machoň, Čeněk Vořech, Vladimír Fultner, and Bedřich Feuerstein also submitted cubist designs.[41]

Although the competition attracted a wide array of proposals, the much delayed Žižkov monument continued to face disappointments. Intellectuals' negative response to the commonplace traditional designs, coupled with the public's intolerance for avant garde abstractions of a beloved hero, led the competition jury to avoid choosing a winner. Soon war engulfed Europe, and all new monument projects were postponed. A finished Žižka statue would not be unveiled until 1950. Yet, in spite of its failure to produce a tangible outcome, the 1913 competition revealed innovations in synthetism and cubism that would influence the rapid development of Prague modernism. The generation that revolutionized concepts of public art and monuments during the Žižka contest would lead independent Czechoslovakia's contributions to European modernism in the years to come.

Modernism and Nationalism

Although the monuments to Wenceslas and to Palacký, and the model submissions for a Žižka memorial, were unveiled within a one-and-a-half-year period, they epitomized vastly different artistic styles. Although linked by the belief, common among Prague's artists, that art rendered public spaces sacred, the sculptors nonetheless engaged differing approaches in marking urban space with modern spirituality.

Myslbek's Saint Wenceslas statue is Prague's last great nineteenth-century monument. In it, the fledgling national movement sought to capture and glorify Bohemian history to lend legitimacy to the contemporary Czech struggle. The realism of the work imposed an uncomplicated picture of the past onto the contemporary world.

Sucharda's Palacký represented the uncertainty of the fin-de-siècle. Artists struggled to unite realistic historicism with inner spiritual and psychological essences of identity. Where Myslbek's message was unambiguous and celebratory, Sucharda's statue might be read on multiple levels. An onlooker had to engage intellectually and emotionally with the memorial and its subject, thus encouraging a spiritual connection between present and past. No longer only triumphant, national art could acknowledge struggle and suffering as well. Public art had become less didactic and more subjective, as the national movement had broadened and matured.

The cubist submissions to the Žižka contest asked what public art's purpose was to be in the twentieth century, and the art jury's inability to choose a sculptor suggested that Prague's nationalist community was not yet ready to answer.

Prague's avant garde believed that art must acknowledge the human struggle against individual and social chaos: whether on public squares, on hills overlooking the city, or in obscure journals or galleries, art must pull apart human experience to arrive at inner truth. Nationalist leaders, on the other hand, asserted that art should honor the past and inspire contemporary citizens to support the movement's political goals. Only a few persons were willing to accept a new modernist credo, that the Czechs could find a middle ground between historicism and abstraction. On the eve of the Great War, the possibility of completely reconceptualizing the modern national monument was not yet fully realized.

Chapter 4

World War I and the Jan Hus Jubilee

"Silent Day for the Great Jubilee"

Headline of *Večerník Práva lidu,* July 6, 1915

THE five-hundredth anniversary of Jan Hus's death passed in the Czech capital with none of the fanfare and fireworks that nationalists had planned for twenty-five years. When war broke out in Europe in June 1914, the members of the Steering Committee of the Club for the Building of the Jan Hus Memorial in Prague were confident, like so many Europeans, that the fighting would be short. The members continued to plan an extravagant international celebration for the unveiling of Šaloun's celebrated sculpture, an event scheduled for July of the following year on the momentous anniversary of Hus's trial and immolation in Constance. Yet by March 1915 it had become evident that the war would continue beyond the summer and that an international festival would be impossible to plan; thus the committee agreed to postpone the lavish festivities "for a more suitable time."[1]

During the war, relations between Czech nationalists and the Austrian state were particularly strained, and many Czechs felt conflicted between their loyalties to their ethnic nation and to the state for which their sons and brothers fought. Therefore, those nationalists still willing to be involved in the Jan Hus 1915 jubilee knew that they would have to be careful not to send a blatantly nationalistic and hostile message. Yet few who had spent twenty-five years planning for the unveiling of a great monument to Hus were willing to ignore this anniversary.

Prague's streets were quiet on the warm summer Tuesday of July 6, as residents of the city walked to and from work and shopped in the market. There were few outlets for nationalist Czechs to express publicly their emotions about the jubilee, but the day did not pass unmarked. All major Prague, and several provincial, newspapers carried front-page articles detailing the private meeting of the Club for the Building of the Jan Hus Memorial.[2] Many also printed editorials emphasizing Jan Hus's historical significance for modern Czechs.[3] The base of the Jan Hus Memorial, quietly unveiled on Old Town Square in the morning, had soon been covered with red and white flowers and wreaths, signaling to the local press that hundreds of citizens had visited "in quiet respect."[4]

Politics during the Great War

National mythology during the First Republic emphasized the strong Czech opposition to the First World War. This opposition was especially manifest in the glorification of the Czech legionnaires who deserted the Austro-Hungarian army to fight on the Russian front. Contemporary British scholar (and associate of Masaryk) Robert Seton-Watson commented that, unlike in Vienna and Budapest, "in Prague there was not a trace of warlike enthusiasm."[5] Yet, recent historians have remarked upon the hesitancy of most Czech politicians to take a strong stand against the Austrian war effort. With the exception of Karel Kramář, who believed that the war would realign the Czechs with their Slavic Russian brothers, most Young Czechs did not want to give up their concilia-

Visitors to the Jan Hus Memorial, c. 1920. Postcard from author's collection.

tory stand toward Austria. The Social Democrats reaffirmed their commitment to Austria, and the agrarian press proclaimed the war "right and just."[6] The Czech Catholic parties, longtime imperial allies, naturally remained loyal to Vienna. Even the radical National Socialists and State Rights Progressive Party cautiously reserved judgment, as seen in their party newspapers. Further—and much to the surprise of the Austrian authorities, who mistrusted Czech nationalist sentiment—the Austrian army's first mobilization effort in Bohemia easily succeeded.

Despite the subdued mood in Prague, the Austrian authorities were suspicious of potentially subversive politicians in the Bohemian lands. In the months following the outbreak of war, Austrian wartime censorship restrictions closed down the National Socialist newspaper, *České slovo* (Czech Word), and the State Rights Progressive Party organ, *Samostatnost* (Independence). The Austrian authorities also sought to suppress the National Socialist movement in general, and arrested its leader, Václav Klofáč, in September 1914. Nevertheless, the initial support—or at least passivity—of the Czech people for the war effort swiftly died down as the Austro-Hungarian military experienced early misfortunes and losses on the battlefields. Czechs soon questioned the sense of fighting against their Slavic brothers, the Serbs and the Russians, and wondered if it were prudent to support an Austrian war effort that seemed doomed to quick defeat. Yet this change in attitude did not give rise to a surge of political resistance; most Czechs feared reprisals from the Austrian government should they resist, and political life in 1914 "ground almost to a halt."[7]

By 1915, however, Czech politicians began to form into an opposition movement. Encouraged by Tomáš Masaryk, in exile in Western Europe, leaders of several Czech political parties and organizations—Young Czechs, Realists, State Rights Progressives, Social Democrats, and the Sokol—formed a loose coalition, in the spring of 1915, known as the Czech Maffia.[8] The group maintained a communication network with the Czech leadership abroad, and plotted to use the Sokol as a National Guard to back Russia in case of a Russian invasion.

When military fortunes turned in favor of Austria-Hungary in 1915, the Austrian authorities used the opportunity to suppress the activities of Czech politicians. On May 21, members of the Maffia, the Young Czech Karel Kramář, and Sokol leader Josef Scheiner were imprisoned. Fear descended upon Czech nationalists, the Maffia retreated underground, and anti-Austrian activism in the Czech lands again died down. Further, after the Bohemian governor, Prince Thun, died in early 1915, he was replaced by Count Karl Coudenhouve, who was under considerably greater influence from the military authorities. For the first time during the war, Czech politicians were effectively silenced. As C. A.

Macartney has contended, "by the summer of 1915 it really looked as though the centripetal forces in the Monarchy had triumphed fairly decisively over the centrifugal."[9]

Preparations for the Jan Hus Jubilee

The summer of 1915 was certainly an inauspicious time to be planning a celebration of a martyred anticlerical and nationalist hero. With the recent arrests of leading politicians, even the most ardent supporters of Jan Hus commemorations feared participating in an event that must appear anti-Austrian. Josef Scheiner's arrest, in particular, frightened those involved in the jubilee. Scheiner had served on the Club for the Building of the Jan Hus Memorial since 1904.[10] He was also a committee member of the 1903 festival that had laid the memorial's cornerstone on Old Town Square. As head of the Sokol, he worked closely with the club's fund-raising efforts and on related projects, such as renovation of Hus's childhood home in Husinec and the five-hundredth anniversary celebrations of the 1409 Kutná Hora Decree, which gave the Czech nation a leading position at Prague University under Hus's rectorship.[11] Therefore, Austrian attempts to repress the Sokol resonated deeply with those involved in the club.

By the time of Scheiner's arrest, the Club for the Building of the Jan Hus Memorial had already decided to hold a smaller event. The first of the authorities to suggest the celebrations be canceled had been Moravian governor Bleyleben, and in January 1915, the regional administrator of Bohemia banned the Hus celebrations planned for that summer.[12] The steering committee of the Hus Memorial club thus had to decide if and how to uphold the rulings of Bohemian and Moravian imperial authorities. In a March 1915 meeting of the steering committee, club leaders decided to proceed with the unveiling on July 6 but make the celebrations of "lesser scope" than originally intended.[13] Instead of an outdoor public celebration, there would be a private meeting, open only to a select group of club members and invited guests representing organizations that had financially supported the building of the memorial. (Originally, the club had planned to host foreign dignitaries from throughout Europe and America, as well as representatives from Czech religious, political, and social organizations.)

The club received permission from the city government to hold its meeting in the Meeting Hall of the Old Town Hall, on Old Town Square; subsequently, the group decided to transfer ownership of the Hus Memorial to the Royal City of Prague. An article in the independent journal *Národní politika* (National Politics) explained that placing the monument under the "protection of the

Prague municipality" would safeguard the new national treasure "in our stormy era, which made it impossible for representatives of this cultured nation to celebrate" the jubilee.[14] Although the club limited invitations to the July 6 private meeting, it did invite delegates from many prominent Czech national organizations. However, unlike the enthusiastic response of voluntary organizations to invitations to the 1903 Jan Hus festival, this time many groups declined. Several of the regrets failed to explain the reasons for declining, and merely apologized, but the Sokol in Holešov, Moravia, admitted that it would be "impossible for us to participate during this current precarious era."[15] Similarly, the Sokol in Kostelec n. Orlem referred to the "difficult era" when it replied that no representative could attend. Other Sokols, such as those in Černovice, Pacov, Přívoz, and Mor. Ostravský Český Lip, also declined, as did several of the Bohemian and Moravian town councils invited, including those of Plzec, Sušice, and Hus's birthplace, Husinec.[16] The letters of regret were plaintive. The Sokol in Mor. Ostravský wrote that members would be at the unveiling "in their hearts," and the Sokol in Kostelec n. Orlem praised Hus for his "purity [and] freedom of conscience."[17] Rather than distancing themselves completely from the memory of Jan Hus, those who sent regrets praised the club's efforts and the memory of the national martyr. Their fears of reprisals outweighed their patriotic sentiments, however.

The city government in Prague, which was to host the proceedings at the Old Town Hall, also worried: in a letter to the club's steering committee about the July 6 meeting, city officials noted, "In regard to the issue of safety, we ask that the number of participants be restricted and that only those with official tickets be permitted entry."[18] The official published program for the celebration included the warning "Entry for members only."[19] Despite the apprehensive mood that had descended, however, there were nationalist organizations that eagerly awaited the culmination of the dream to honor Hus with a Prague monument. The Sokol in working-class, radical Žižkov responded that its representatives would "joyfully greet the statue."[20] The Czech Sokol Union, which oversaw the activities of the local branches of Sokol, committed to sending participants to the ceremony.

Other organizations acknowledged the difficulties of commemorating the Jan Hus jubilee during the war. The Central Association of Czech Women, prominent in the 1903 Festival for the Laying of the Foundation Stone of the Jan Hus Memorial, wrote in its journal, "We cannot say that the women's clubs are preparing for the Hus jubilee in a way that is suitable [in] this wartime era." This nationalist women's organization assured its readership that, although apprehensive about displaying sentiment toward Hus at this time, their "hearts and souls overflowed." Despite such fears, the women's association did decide to "make a humble contribution to the Hus jubilee,"[21] sponsoring a series of lectures by Anna Císařová-Kolářová, who had recently published a history of women in the Hussite movement.[22] Topics included "women in Hus's teachings," "women in the United Brethren Church," and "women in Hus's sermons."

Nevertheless, the women's association stated in its journal that it "would withdraw this year [1915] from any kind of Hus festival," because "[our] hearts and souls were filled with all the worries of the wartime era."[23] Thus, even those organizations that had stood at the forefront of Czech liberal nationalism in the nineteenth and early twentieth centuries believed it either inappropriate or dangerous to stand with Hus against Austria during the Great War.

The Jan Hus Festival of 1915

In the early morning of July 6, employees of the Prague city government removed the scaffolding and drapes of Šaloun's memorial to Hus. The unveiling on Old Town Square occurred without pomp or ceremony; any other commemorations that day took place indoors, away from potential public view. Czech nationalists, who had created a culture of lavish national festivals that engaged the public, had to contend with a quiet nonspectacle on this day that was to have been their most important celebration of nationhood.

At ten that morning, the small group that had accepted invitations to the commemoration gathered in Old Town Hall's meeting room, where Václav Brožík's famed painting *The Condemnation of Jan Hus* hung.[24] Attending the ceremony were the steering committee of the Club for the Building of the Jan Hus Memorial, Prague mayor Stanislav Groš, and Prague Bank president Karel Mattuš, whose institution managed the finances of the club. That such prominent politicians and business leaders participated in the pared-down ceremonies indicates that leading members of Czech society realized that Austrian authorities had more pressing concerns than to interrupt a meeting at Old Town Hall. And in fact, once it became clear that the Hus commemoration would be a short, subdued ceremony, the Austrian authorities did little to control the day's events. The meeting proceeded peacefully inside, while a few Imperial guards stood on Old Town Square to prevent potential demonstrations. It is possible that the Imperial authorities realized it had an ally in Mayor Groš; a year earlier, on the eve of the Great War, Groš had stood against the extreme nationalists on Prague's Board of Aldermen, who had passed a proposal to name a bridge near the Rudolphinum Concert Hall after Hus. Instead, Groš had sided with the Bohemian governor, Count Thun, who supported naming the bridge after Francis Ferdinand, heir to the Habsburg throne. Groš had convinced the aldermen to back his proposal as a show of loyalty to Austria, at a time when Europe was caught amid a tense political situation. It was at the beginning of 1914—ironically only months before the crown prince's assassination—that Groš secured this unanimous vote to name the bridge after the future emperor and Bohemian king; the most radical nationalists abstained rather than vote against a proposal favoring Francis Ferdinand's name, which suggests that already even the most extreme nationalists did not want to isolate themselves from Austrian favor. (At first, Francis Ferdinand had little interest in having a bridge named for him in the Czech capital, but when Count Thun assured him it was the only way to prevent the name going to a "Czech heretic," the prince and heir agreed.)[25]

Thus the commemoration of Jan Hus's five-hundredth jubilee took the form of an annual club business meeting, such as took place every July since the club's founding in 1890. The president, Karel Baxa, made opening remarks, and the secretary, Alois Simonides, presented the report of club activities of the previous year, as well as a brief club history. The floor was then opened for suggestions and comments from members and guests regarding the transfer of the statue into the safeguard of the Prague city government.[26] Club members discussed the possibility of creating a perpetual fund for the monument's upkeep, and Groš proclaimed the memorial's importance for the city and promised that the city would always care for and guard it. Prague Bank president Mattuš thanked club leaders, living and dead, for their dedication to the dream and for holding a quiet yet dignified ceremony for the Hus monument's unveiling. With these comments and the singing of the Czech national chorale, the meeting ended.[27]

This meeting's chairperson, Karel Baxa, had been president of the club since the death, the year before, of longtime club leader Jan Podlipný. Had it not been for the war, Baxa might have moved the club in a more radically nationalist direction. Podlipný had been known throughout his political career as a moderate compromiser, but Baxa was an ardent nationalist with extreme political views. He had gained fame as the lead attorney for the defense of nationalist students during the Omladina trial of 1893, and was one of the founders of the State Rights Progressive Party, which split from the Young Czechs in 1898. The following year, he had prosecuted a Jewish man, Leopold Hilsner, accused of "ritual murder" in a disturbing anti-Semitic trial that Tomáš Masaryk quickly decried. During the war, the State Rights Progressives took the strongest stand of any nationalist political party against Austria and the war. Indeed, a few months after the Hus celebrations, the State Rights Progressives would withdraw from negotiations with the Young Czechs, Agrarians, and Social Democrats to create a Czech national party, because the other parties remained loyal to the Austrian state.

Baxa's keynote address at the 1915 meeting, meanwhile, offered his audi-

ence an approach to understanding Jan Hus's meaning that reflected the international situation of the pan-European war. His remarks marked a shift from
using Hus as a symbol for the sufferings of a small nation at the hands of a
greedy, powerful empire to viewing Hus as a sign of the split in Europe between
anachronism and modernity. Shifting the meaning of Hus in this way allowed
Baxa to express discontent about the conditions of his people without directly
attacking Austria–Hungary. While protecting himself from the wrath of Austrian authorities by not attacking specific policies, he still cautiously criticized
the anachronisms of the monarchy. Baxa began his speech by expressing what
the festival should have been had it not been for the war: "Prague wanted to
invite representatives from all the *cultured* nations" to a lavish international
festival. Throughout, Baxa emphasized the Czechs' place among these cultured
nations, and, although he never specified which nations qualified as cultured, it
became quickly evident that he was not making a distinction between Western
civilization and the rest of the world, but was instead dividing Europe between
the enlightened modern nations and the anachronistic Old World.

Baxa argued that, through Hus, the Czech nation had become the vehicle for
carrying Europe into the modern era. This emphasis on modernism of course
differed from the artistic explorations of the concept before the war. Whereas
modern art had decried overtly nationalistic interpretations of culture, Baxa's
concept of modernity valued the nation above other political and social categories. This philosophy of progressivism interpreted history as a series of challenges against authority, and envisioned a Europe progressing toward national
self-rule. Baxa thus emphasized Hus's stand against the "most powerful authority" in the world, a stand that provided the impetus for the reformation movement in the most advanced of the European nations. In turn, Hus's "spiritual
movement influenced the general cultural progress of humanity": the reformation gave way to the Enlightenment, and Hus's scholarly contributions to
European thought "inspired the development of education and the progress of
a new age." These achievements of the Czechs' "national son" earned the nation
"a place in the community of cultured European nations."[28]

Baxa never attacked Austria for repressing Czech culture, nor did he declare
outright that Austria was not among the enlightened cultures of Europe. Yet his
definition of the cultured nations as those that supported freedom of thought
and conscience was meant to exclude Austria, which still identified with what
Baxa viewed as Roman Catholic clericalism and outdated political structures.
Baxa's address used Hus as a metaphor for the war. He claimed that that war
"pitted modernity and progress against anachronism"; the Czechs stood on the
side of progress and the modernizing revolution begun by Hus five hundred
years before. Thus the commemoration of Hus's death enabled Baxa to dem-

onstrate that the Czechs belonged among the "enlightened, cultured, modern nations," not within an oppressive anachronistic empire. He had to use metaphor because of the increased oppression of Czech nationalists (including the imprisonment of one club leader) by Austrian authorities during the war, yet he did acknowledge disappointment that his message was prevented by the war from being spread to the civilized world; he ended his speech by looking forward to a "better future for his great country."[29]

Although the Imperial authorities had prevented a large public commemoration, there remained outlets through which Czechs could express nationalist sentiment. The National Theater staged Bedřich Smetana's patriotic opera, *Libuše,* which celebrated the foundation of the city of Prague and the Bohemian Kingdom. The Czech division of Charles-Ferdinand University in Prague, officially divided into German and Czech universities since 1882, commemorated Hus's death with a lecture, "Rector of the Prague University, Master Jan Hus in History." Like the meeting of the Club for the Building of the Jan Hus Memorial, these university celebrations took place behind closed doors.[30] The university's Czech rector, Dr. Václav Novotný, commented on the contributions of his predecessor Hus, implying, as had Baxa, that the lessons of the Czech historical past could inspire fresh directions for the nation. Hus's death, explained Novotný, "opened new paths, paths to freedom."[31] Novotný too was careful not to antagonize the authorities by directly referencing the national movement, yet his emphasis on Hus's fight for freedom and independence clearly evoked nationalist sentiment.

Many other Prague residents found ways individually to commemorate Hus. The most tangible sign of the citizenry's enthusiasm was the display of flowers and wreaths around the Hus monument's base. On July 7, *Národní listy* reported, "The completed Hus Monument on Old Town Square became yesterday the site of a pilgrimage of thousands of Praguers and country dwellers, who hastened to place fresh flowers on the lower part of the monument." Prague clubs contributed floral wreaths and individual flowers, and a group of working-class children decorated the base with a ring of roses. The Prague press expressed pride in these individual commemorations: "All throughout yesterday there was life, festive life around the Master's monument." These small remembrances were characterized as demonstrating the strength of character of the Czech people in the face of recent political crackdowns. "This the police could not prevent!"[32] Yet, clearly, the police did not try to prevent these personal commemorations; guards stationed at the memorial that day were present to prevent violence, not the laying of wreaths.

The "Struggle Abroad"

Although nationalists at home had to be cautious when invoking Jan Hus's memory for political purposes, Czech wartime exiles and their supporters, leaders of the so-called "struggle abroad," used this anniversary of Hus's martyrdom to garner international support for the Czech cause. On the morning of July 6, Tomáš Masaryk, staged an international meeting of European Protestants, Czech émigrés, and his own political supporters in the Hall of the Reformation in Geneva, Switzerland.

Masaryk's French colleague, Ernst Denis, joined him at the podium. A historian and professor in Paris, Denis was also a French Protestant who had taken a scholarly interest in Czech and Slovak history, especially the Hussite period. He had founded the Paris journal *La Nation Tchéque* in May 1915, and, during the war, Masaryk met often with him to discuss scholarly issues of Czech history. Masaryk made it clear in his memoirs of the war, however, that Denis was not of great political value to him, since French authorities distrusted Denis's liberalism and Protestantism; in fact, Masaryk wrote, Denis was "politically at a disadvantage—exactly as he would have been in Bohemia!"[33]

In the Hall of the Reformation, Denis began with a historical lecture on Hus. Then Masaryk, who had recently decided that the time had come "to take public action against Austria,"[34] spoke about the political significance of the five-hundredth anniversary commemoration. In April the 28th Prague Regiment had joined the Russian side at the Dukla Pass; in May Italy had declared war on Austria; more recently, Masaryk, receiving news of intensifying political tensions in Prague and learning that Kramář and Rašín had been arrested, had decided to work more forcibly on two fronts: to gain the support of the British and French governments and to step up his "educational propaganda" to sway Czech communities abroad and the Western powers to support the Czech national struggle.

After Denis finished his address to the Geneva gathering, Masaryk made his political speech, "In the Name of Hus for the Freedom of the Nation." He noted, "in the spirit of our Hussite ancestors, we were fighting for a moral as well as for a political purpose." Although both the fifteenth-century Hussites and the nineteenth-century Czech nationalists had emphasized political or economic benefits in their struggles, contemporary idealistic politicians like Masaryk colored both struggles as moral conflicts—as virtuous and holy campaigns.

Like Baxa, Masaryk also discussed the contradictions between the Hussite view of progress and Austrian anachronisms. Yet, Masaryk did not need to rely upon such veiled metaphors as did his fellow nationalists in Prague. He spoke directly about the conflict between the Czechs and Austria: "Every Czech must decide to be for reformation or against reformation, for the Czech model or for the Austrian model, an organ of European Counter-Reformation and reaction."[35] Austria regarded Masaryk's address as a direct provocation; in fact, the Vienna newspaper, *Neue Freie Presse,* proclaimed the Geneva meeting "the first Czech declaration of war against Austria."[36] Newspapers in Britain and France also carried the story of Masaryk's Geneva Manifesto, and many viewed July 6, 1915, as marking a shift in the goals of the Czech nation from more autonomy to complete independence from Austria-Hungary.

Jan Hus, 1918, and the Czech Nation's Future

The two Hus commemorations of 1915 came to symbolize the split between the Czech struggles at home and abroad during the First World War. The Prague celebrations had been intended to show the world the advanced culture and intellect of the Czech people through celebration of the nation's Hussite heritage; however, the war forced the Czechs at home to pare down the festival in order to appease the Austrian authorities, who had become wary of Czech wartime political maneuvers. Therefore attention had shifted abroad, where Masaryk's strong words on a day carefully selected to symbolize the moral and political heritage of the Czech nation demonstrated to Vienna that Austria-Hungary perhaps had more to fear from the Czech émigré community than from Prague. Soon after Masaryk began his campaign of educational propaganda, which used the Hussite heritage to distinguish the Czech nation from Roman Catholic Austria, the Austrian authorities in Prague arrested his daughter, Alice Masaryková, as well as the wife of his associate Edvard Beneš. Further, attempts were made, Masaryk believed, on his life in Switzerland and later in Britain.

By October 1918, it was clear that Austria-Hungary could not continue in its prewar form. Traveling in America toward the end of the war, Masaryk (joined by Czech and Slovak immigrants) issued, in Pittsburgh, a Czechoslovak declaration of independence, and subsequently won Woodrow Wilson's support for a new state.

However, it was neither the Slavs nor the Allies who ultimately dissolved the Monarchy. Once the German-Austrian deputies in the Reichsrat left their positions in the assembly and declared themselves the provisional assembly of a new Austrian-German state, the government in Vienna asked Wilson to proceed with an armistice.

When news of these developments reached Prague on October 28, 1918, the Prague National Committee declared an independent Czechoslovak state,

and soon chose Masaryk as the first president of the new parliamentary democracy. Declaring a state was only the first step of a long process of creating
a Czechoslovak Republic, however. Although founded on Woodrow Wilson's
principle of national self-determination, the new country was multinational.
Czechs represented approximately half of the state's 13.5 million inhabitants,
the Slovaks only 15 percent. Yet, these two groups were officially counted as
one Czechoslovak nation in the 1921 and subsequent censuses, giving them
a two-thirds majority in the state. There were 3 million German-speaking citizens, representing 23 percent of the total population, and smaller numbers
of Hungarians (5.6 percent), Poles (0.5 percent), and Russians and Ukraini-
ans (counted together at 3.5 percent). Jews, also considered a separate ethnic
group, made up 1.35 percent.[37] Czechoslovaks had, in addition to ethnic and
linguistic distinctions, a range of economic, social, and cultural characteristics:
for example, in Bohemia and Moravia, more than half of the population lived in
towns, whereas in Slovakia the population was over 75 percent rural;[38] further,
although there were religious Bohemians, Roman Catholicism was considerably stronger in Moravia and Slovakia.

The Czech-dominated Hussite legacy lived on in the foundation of the
new Czechoslovak Republic, three years after Masaryk's Geneva declaration.
When Masaryk returned from his travels abroad to the newly declared national
capital of Prague in December 1918, he began his first speech as president to
the Czechoslovak National Assembly with words from the inscription on the
Jan Hus Memorial: "The government of your affairs returns to you, people."[39]
(The quote, though often attributed to Hus, was actually from an exile from the
Battle of the White Mountain era, the Enlightenment philosopher Jan Amos
Komenský [Comenius], last bishop of the Church of United Brethren, which
followed Hus's teachings.) For his presidential seal and flag, Masaryk chose another quotation attributed to Hus and inscribed on the Hus Memorial: "*Pravda
vítězí* (The truth prevails)." Masaryk saw himself, as this choice makes clear, as
an heir of Hus and Komenský, his vision of moral leadership growing out of
his spiritual convictions. As Vladimír Macura has written, "Through its relation to Masaryk and its transferal to the presidential flag, this phrase [*Pravda
vítězí*] became officially statist . . . and joined the ranks of relics of nation and
state."[40] The Hus legacy that had inspired Czech nationalists in the Habsburg
era to oppose Austrian hegemony would now represent a diverse, multiethnic
populace.

Prague was the obvious choice for the national capital. It was the most cosmopolitan city in the new country and had been the seat of the medieval Bohemian Kingdom as well as the provincial capital of Bohemia under the monarchy.
Filled with Gothic and baroque reminders of Catholic heritage, this "city of one

hundred spires" was now also marked with its Hussite legacy. The monument to Jan Hus stood across from the column to the Virgin Mary as if the two were dueling for the national memory of the new citizenry. Prague suddenly had a new responsibility: to represent all its citizenry, to house a Czechoslovak identity. Yet the legacy of the nineteenth-century *Czech* nationalism lived on in the city's new monuments: the national theater, the Palacký and Wenceslas monuments, and the massive sculpture of Hus and his followers.

In the first years of the new republic, Prague changed geographically and demographically. In 1922, a 1920 law took effect that drew into the city four previously independent cities, including Žižkov, tripling the population to 676,700. A major reason for this change was to bolster the Czech population of Prague in relation to the Germans, who tended to live in the city center. As Derek Sayer has written, Prague "was demographically remarkably unrepresentative of those whom it now aspired to represent symbolically. It remained emphatically a Czech capital."[41] Nationalist leaders who had been anti-Austrians before the war took leadership in the new government (Baxa as the first mayor of the new capital, Masaryk as first president of the country), insisting that this capital *was* Hus's city. The choice of the dissenter Hus as national hero, which had provoked antinationalists before the war, now distanced large segments of the population from the new state.

Chapter 5

Toppling Columns, Building a Capital

"You are the National Council; we are the Nation!"

František Sauer-Kysela, defending the toppling of
Prague's Marian Column

"DOWN with it, down!"[1] The frenzied mob that crowded Prague's Old Town Square cheered and shouted on the cold November evening. There was much reason for celebrating: less than a week earlier, on October 28, 1918, the National Council had proclaimed Czechoslovakia an independent nation-state and peacefully taken power from the protesting governor, Count Karl Coudenhove, and Austria-Hungary's General Kestránek. Rejoicing crowds had gathered in Prague's Wenceslas and Old Town squares throughout the following days, but leaders of the crowd on November 3, 1918, had a specific purpose in mind.

"Down with it," the crowd insisted. Finally, above the shouts, there came a loud crack, and then a crash, and the Marian Column came tumbling down. The seventeenth-century baroque column broke into three large chunks; the delicate marble statue of the Virgin Mary shattered into pieces onto the cobblestones. A group of the most radical nationalists in Prague had finally achieved their goal: the destruction of a blatant reminder of Habsburg dominion. Announcing themselves as heirs to the medieval Hussite warriors, these nationalists claimed to have purified this public space for the Czech national tradition; finally Jan Hus stood alone, overlooking Prague's most important historic square.

This drastic act reflected Prague's revolutionary mood in Czechoslovakia's early days. The first few years of the Czechoslovak Republic witnessed many battles over the new state's symbols, even as the government secured the country's new borders by engaging in combat with Poland and Hungary. Some Czechs were determined not only to create their own state symbols, but also to rid their country of reminders of the Habsburg past. Statues of Austrian leaders (such as Field Marshall Joseph Radetzky and Emperor Francis II), as well as the ubiquitous Habsburg double-headed eagle emblem, disappeared from Prague's landscape. In the so-called Sudeten border region, inhabited by nearly three million German speakers, numerous statues of Emperor Joseph II met their demise.[2] Those seeking to create a Czechoslovak political culture no longer tolerated such references to a former regime.

However, throughout Bohemia, and particularly in Prague, religious statues were meeting the same fate as statues of now foreign emperors. Roman Catholic icons, dedicated to the Virgin Mary and Czech patron saint Jan Nepomucký, became signs of political oppression. In his influential 1903 essay "The Modern Cult of Monuments," Austrian art historian Alois Riegl had distinguished between intentional and unintentional monuments. Intentional monuments, products of a society's egoism, "retain[ed] value only as long as the conditions that brought them into being prevail";[3] unintentional monuments would be valued for their age and beauty, and their preservation would be an act of society's altruism. Whether baroque statues and architecture might be considered intentional or unintentional monuments was unclear; sponsored by Jesuit leaders of the counter-reformation, the ornate art was designed to attract followers to Catholicism, a religion forced upon largely Protestant Bohemia. Although Catholics claimed the statues were primarily objects of religious devotion, others argued that they embodied the Austrians' intentional political messages, and, tracing a gradual politicization of religious art, historians Zdeněk Hojda and Jiří Pokorný called baroque statues "monuments, against their own will."[4]

Whether to destroy, remove, or preserve Austrian monuments became a key question for Prague's leaders and citizens. They were deciding the new capital's identity, whether it was still the center of Czech nationalism (Hus's city) or, alternatively, would embody the diverse history of a multinational nation-state. Also in question was the city's role in the new state bureaucracy.

In the state's first two years, Prague shifted from revolutionary city to administrative capital of a diverse populace. In September 1919, the Treaty of St. Germain formally recognized Czechoslovakia, comprising Bohemia, Morovia, Czech Silesia, and Slovakia; Subcarpathian Ruthenia was added through the Treaty of Trianon in June 1920. The political environment of the new capital reflected the complexity of the population. As Daniel Miller remarked, "The plethora of parties in Czechoslovakia reflected the sorts of social, economic, national, and confessional divisions evident in society."[5] Several political movements, such as the Catholic or People's parties and the socialist parties, com-

bined a national affiliation with an ideological stance. For example, there were
five separate socialist parties in interwar Czechoslovakia, three of these representing minority ethnic groups; there were three agrarian parties and four
Catholic parties, also with distinct national affiliations. With such a diverse
and complex political spectrum, national politicians learned quickly the art of
compromise. Most German parties took an activist stance; until the crises of
the late 1930s they willingly participated in coalition governments. Further,
the centrist prime minister, Antonín Švehla of the Republican Party of Farmers
and Peasants (Agrarians), who served through much of the First Republic, recognized the importance of working with German, Slovak, and Catholic parties.
Thus, nationalist cultural politics could never be as straightforward as before
independence, when politicians could separate into loyalist or anti-Austrian
groups, and nationalists could demonstrate their identity through anticlerical
rhetoric. During the early First Republic, many Catholics considered themselves patriots, and many Germans considered themselves loyal. The attacks on
Roman Catholic and Austrian icons, in the early days of the republic, reflected
a style of agitation and confrontation that some Czech nationalists had adopted
at the turn of the century but that was becoming swiftly outmoded in the early
moments of independent Czechoslovakia.

Rise and Fall of the Marian Column

Sunday, November 3, 1918, was the first full day off from work since the
proclamation of independent Czechoslovakia, and radical nationalists were
celebrating their newfound freedom. Gathering at Letohrádek Hvězda (Star
Chateau) on Bílá hora (White Mountain) in the outskirts of Prague, radical
nationalists and socialists commemorated the defeat of the Czech estates by
Habsburg imperial troops there on November 8, 1620.[6] Since its nineteenth-
century national revival, the Battle of the White Mountain had come to symbolize every hardship that had ever befallen the Czech people.[7] Historians, such
as R. J. W. Evans have commented on the "absurdity" of the battle, "an hour-
and-a-half skirmish with makeshift armies on a featureless plateau just west
of Prague."[8] Although the battle came to be seen by later Czech nationalists as
a Protestant–Catholic conflict, religion did not at the time necessarily determine one's side in the clash. About 16 percent of those nobles who rose against
the Habsburgs were Catholics, and some Protestant nobles sided against the
Czechs or remained neutral. Further, the conflict was not purely national. Many
Czechs did not solidly back the position of the estates; Bohemian towns such
as Pilsen and Budweis (now České Budějovice), with majority German populations, opposed the Czech nobles. Despite the complex history of the conflict,

however, no event carried so much weight in the collective memory of Czech nationalists. František Palacký and his followers argued that the defeat of the Czech estates at this early battle of the Thirty Years War halted the golden era of the Hussites and their Protestant descendants and ushered in a period of *temno* (darkness). Subsequent artistic manifestations of White Mountain (such as the violated female figure on the Palacký Memorial) conveyed the suffering of Czech people and culture at the hands of Habsburg monarchs and the Roman Catholic Church.

Those nationalists who gathered, then, at White Mountain in November 1918 were reviving a tradition quelled only during the Great War. Czech students and workers marked November 8, 1892, as a national day of mourning, and commemorating White Mountain had become an annual event among nationalist politicians, especially among National Socialists who advocated a public display of revolutionary politics. In 1908, on November 8, in the midst of violent clashes between German students and radical Czech nationalists, the National Socialist Party had organized a *tábor lidu* (gathering of the people) at White Mountain.[9] The term *tábor,* which means camp, also referred to the Southern Bohemian town where Žižka's army and religious followers had lived in community, and in 1908 more than ten thousand Czechs commemorated this tradition, singing patriotic songs and Hussite hymns and carrying national and Hussite banners as they marched from Prague Castle to White Mountain.

In 1918, nationalists sought to reclaim Prague on the anniversary of the infamous battle. From White Mountain, a crowd of several hundred marched into Old Town Square and met another group of nationalists and socialists who had set up camp at the Hus Memorial after securing the Marian Column with harnesses and ropes. A band of firemen tugged at the ropes as the rest of the crowd cheered.[10]

A delegation from the National Council (the provisional government), which included František Soukup, a Social Democrat and secretary of the National Committee, and Vavro Šrobar, a Slovak politician and associate of Masaryk, arrived at the square to prevent the destruction of the Marian Column. Soukup read a prepared statement, condemning the plan to destroy this most valuable example of baroque sculpture in Central Europe, designed by the famed Bohemian artist Jan Jiří Bendl, who also had created the original Wenceslas Memorial on Wenceslas Square.[11] But the gathered people did not heed the pleas of the professional politicians; instead, František Sauer-Kysela, the crowd's leader, exclaimed, "You are the National Council; we are the Nation!"[12]

Quickly, the politicians returned to their vehicles and drove out of Old Town Square, and minutes later the Žižkov firemen, who had tied a noose around the neck of the Virgin Mary, pulled down the column, in the direction of Our Lady

before Týn Church. Sauer-Kysela had planned to fell the column toward the
Hus Memorial, so it would lie at Hus's feet, but for safety reasons the plan was
changed. The symbolic effect remained: the Marian Column had succumbed to
Hus's memory. Never again would the most vexing emblems of the Habsburg
Monarchy tower over the symbols of the Czechs.[13]

Although Sauer-Kysela later wrote that his group's action served every
Czech, only the radical wings of the nationalist and socialist constituency advocated it. The former National Socialist Party (which had changed its name to
the Czech Socialist Party in April 1918, and would become the Czechoslovak
Socialist Party in January 1919) had long advocated a confrontational, public
political style; as Mills Kelly has shown, this party considered "the streets . . .
the place of revolution."[14] Only by engaging the public, the National Socialists
had believed, could the Czech nation defend itself against its primary enemies,
Roman Catholic "clerics" and Germans. During the war and the consequent
economic crises, the National Socialists radicalized, in both the nationalist and
socialist realms of their philosophy,[15] but it is important to note that the party
never embraced fascism and never affiliated with the German movement that
coincidentally shared its moniker.

The crowd's leader was not a National Socialist, however. František Sauer-
Kysela spent his days drinking in the pubs of working-class Žižkov with *The
Good Soldier Švejk's* author Jaroslav Hašek. Described by the Catholic press as
a "sugar smuggler, writer, dry-goods dealer, and who knows what else," Sauer-
Kysela had alliances with anarchists and socialists throughout Prague.[16] Like
Hašek's, Sauer-Kysela's politics were hard to discern. Sympathetic to the Russian Revolution, profoundly anti-Catholic, both men also saw trouble-making
as part of their public personas. Sauer-Kysela had some nationalist sentiment;
his pen name included the translation into Czech of his Germanic surname
(Sauer and Kysela both translate in English as "sour"), hinting at the complex
identity of Prague's residents.

Although Sauer-Kysela wanted the column's destruction to appear an act of
spontaneous popular action, he had informed Social Democrats and National
Socialists of his plan only days after Czechoslovakia's declaration of independence. On October 31, leading Social Democrat Jan Skála advised caution, telling Sauer-Kysela that the Marian Column would eventually be taken down.
Sauer-Kysela furiously retorted that the workers would topple the column,
instead of waiting for the passive "chicken-hearted cowards" in the new government to act upon their promise. According to Sauer-Kysela, he had also
informed Václav Klofáč, leader of the Czech (National) Socialists, and politician Karel Kramář, who headed the National Democrats (formerly the Young
Czechs), of his plans and his need for ropes and ladders.

Most of the participants in the destruction were factory workers who frequented Žižkov pubs with Sauer-Kysela and Hašek. After a 1917 Prague workers' uprising, these men had been handcuffed and sent to the front to fight for Austria-Hungary (which Sauer-Kysela referred to as "the clerics"). The men had returned home on October 28 ready to claim the new state for the Czechoslovak nation. The Austro-Hungarian Army's conscription of Czech workers seemed Sauer-Kysela's main reason why the Marian Column had to come down: these workers had been forced to fight for an unjust government in an unjust war. Further, the clerics, supposedly fellows and compatriots of these downtrodden worker-soldiers, had acted hand in hand with the Austro-Hungarian state to promote the war; in addition, not one writer for the Czech Catholic press had condemned the war, and priests had used their pulpits to pray for Habsburg victory, not for an end to the fighting.[17]

Sauer-Kysela argued that Czech workers were the direct heirs to the Hussite warriors and the Czechs who had fought at White Mountain, and the Marian Column commemorated the victory over these men and the humiliation of the entire Czech nation. Acknowledging that the column memorialized victory over the Swedes, Sauer-Kysela nevertheless warned his audience not to be fooled by the illogical argument that this fact rendered the monument harmless: any memorial to the Thirty Years War represented the defeat of Czech culture and, more important, political and religious liberty.

The column, he argued, was a political symbol, not a religious one. Yet the language in his account of the monument's destruction emphasized mistrust of clerical leaders more than defiance of the already defeated Austria. True Catholics followed Christ, he wrote, rather than the international political clerical movement, whose "central committee" sat in Rome. In fact, Sauer-Kysela sympathized with an old woman who lay down on the cobblestones, apparently willing to let the column crush her if this sacrifice could preserve it. Calling her a "fine lady," he believed that she did not understand the distinction between the column as a symbol of political clericalism, and her personal, Catholic religious beliefs. Yet in describing other old women who followed her lead, Sauer-Kysela called them "candle-lighting hags," who lacked the first woman's pure intentions and were representative of the blind support given to the clerics.[18]

Reactions to the Destruction

In the daily press in 1918, journalists were understandably more concerned with the final days of the war and the establishment of a new Czechoslovak state than with the attack on the Marian Column. *Národní listy,* the major nationalist paper, covered the event in a single paragraph in its small "Daily News"

A crowd gathers on Old Town Square near the destroyed Marian Column, 1918. Photo courtesy of Jan Bradna and the Club for the Rebuilding of the Marian Column.

section.[19] Since many of the leaders of the recently formed National Committee had affiliations with *Národní listy*, the column made it clear that the new Czechoslovak government condemned the action. Even the Catholic paper, *Lidové listy*, did not report the column's removal on its front page, though its article was naturally more emotional.[20]

Shortly after independent Czechoslovakia was declared, Catholic politician Moric Hruban had remarked: "In Prague one observed the appearance of two main trends of thought: the social revolutionary and the anti-Catholic. The casual observer could not recognize the real situation because everything around was hidden under flags and flowers and covered by a mood of rejoicing for the newly won state and national independence."[21] Although this statement was made days before the events in Old Town Square, it uncannily predicted what occurred. A writer and sometimes actor with a flair for the dramatic, Sauer-Kysela had carefully orchestrated the vandalism as a national festival, a joyous procession of workers and former soldiers marching through the streets, singing nationalist hymns and waving Czech flags, in the midst of which he, with the other leaders, planned a stunning political act. Not only did Sauer-Kysela hope to provoke rereadings of Bohemian historical mythology, but he also wanted to tie the Czechs to European and American traditions of revolutionary vandalism, from the Boston Tea Party to the storming of the Winter Palace. Most important of these was the link to the French Revolution, when crowds destroyed Catholic icons throughout Paris. Paul Connerton has argued that those who study commemorative practice focus too closely on the content of rituals, rather than on the form.[22] Sauer-Kysela's event was not unique—featuring historical battle hymns, a military-style procession, and a dramatic destructive act, it had a form purposely borrowed from key historic commemorations.

The destruction of the Marian Column was nonetheless a creative act. Sauer-Kysela wanted to make Prague a truly new capital city, free from the icons of the former regime. Although anticlerical in motivation, the act had much in common with religious ceremonies, which simultaneously reenact destruction and rebirth. The Jewish wedding ceremony features the breaking of a glass; a Catholic baptism uses funeral chrism. New life also involves death. The peaceful, even anticlimactic Czechoslovak independence movement lacked the cathartic bloodshed Sauer-Kysela admired from his French and Russian revolutionary heroes; thus, he symbolically invented the destruction and rebirth of Prague. "Objects speak," during festivals and rituals, according to Victor Turner.[23] Sauer-Kysela gave no address in Old Town Square, but let the monuments send his message. Fallen and shattered, the Marian Column said that political Catholicism would no longer be tolerated; it was of the old world, and its fragments belonged in a museum. Towering now over the square alone, the Jan Hus Memorial, emblem of the Hussite movement long admired by Czech socialists for its tolerance and egalitarianism, proclaimed the message of the social revolutionaries.

Beyond such broad links to political and spiritual ceremonies, Sauer-Kysela had a specific political goal: to challenge the new government's seeming willingness to work with Czechoslovak Catholics. It was clear in November 1918 that political Catholicism was not dead, though weakened by its association with pro-Austrian policy. After all, in the last days of the war, a progressive wing of the Czech political Catholic movement, led by the Moravian priest Msgr. Jan Šrámek, had replaced the old, conservative pro-Austrian camp and declared a pro-Czechoslovak, anti-Habsburg stance. Although this strategy came late, on September 21, 1918, it nonetheless displayed Czech Catholic politicians' willingness to work toward the new state.

Catholic parties held four of twenty-nine seats on the Czechoslovak National Committee, the provisional government formed on July 13, 1918; representation on this council had been based on the results of the 1911 parliamentary elections.[24] Šrámek also secured a cabinet post for a Catholic politician on the National Committee. His quiet yet insistent manner prevailed over the demands of many socialist and liberal politicians to exclude Catholic politicians from all high posts. Šrámek was a highly visible politician from the first day of the new Czechoslovak state. With Antonín Švehla, a leader in the Agrarian Party and the president of the National Council, he wrote the Czechoslovak declaration of independence; he then joined the delegation of politicians sent to meet with General Edward Zanatoni, commander of the Prague garrison, to negotiate a peaceful surrender of the Austro-Hungarian company in the Czechoslovak capital. Šrámek personally addressed the soldiers, and received some credit for assuring a peaceful transfer of military power.

Nonetheless, no Catholic politician was invited to sign the proclamation of the new state. This double standard reflects the ambivalence with which the established nationally oriented politicians regarded the entry of Catholic politicians on the Czechoslovak political scene.

That Catholic politicians were joining the new government signaled to radical nationalist and socialist Czechs that the leadership of the state was willing to unite with conservative forces.[25] This was not welcome news to a workers' movement that was moving to the Left. During the war, food shortages and poor working conditions had radicalized a sector of Czech socialists. Therefore, the revelry at the destruction of the Marian Column carried with it a contemporary political message. The radical leaders, led by Sauer-Kysela, were warning against concessions already being made toward conservative and moderate elements. Sauer-Kysela's memoir especially scorns the social democratic "cowards," such as Bechyně and Soukup, who had joined forces with the reactionary National Council.[26] Displeased with this apparent shift to the Right in Czechoslovak politics, members of the radical Left thus staged the symbolic demonstration (literally, a demonstration against a symbol) to suggest that the Left would not tolerate reactionism.

The official statement of the National Council remarked on the gravity of the Left's action, which had destroyed an art treasure through a "historical misunderstanding" about the column's original purpose. The provisional government was particularly concerned with the reaction of the Czechs' new compatriots, the Slovaks: "The principle of freedom excludes every violent act, especially during this era of developing relations with Slovakia, when we are developing a way for the whole nation to be happy."[27] For the first time in history, then, Czech nationalists had to consider the effect their anticlerical language or actions could have on the very stability of their state. Joining forces with the predominantly Catholic Slovaks meant a need to abandon some of the "Hussite" principles on which Czech nationalism had been based;[28] events in Prague would have repercussions throughout the entire state. Yet, the statement of the National Council also reflected the attitude among many politicians that true Czechs were not Roman Catholic, though over 90 percent of the Czech population was baptized in the Catholic Church. According to the National Council, Sauer-Kysela's group destroyed the Marian Column without regard to the delicate relationship that Czechs and Slovaks had entered into. Further, that members of the mob were not prosecuted raised doubts of the sincerity of the council's condemnation. The Czechoslovak government did not at this time consider Sauer-Kysela's act the "criminal damaging of foreign property," since it took place in the "era of revolution," and when, in February 1919, Sauer-Kysela was examined for violating Criminal Code 305, a misdemeanor, he was released because the statute of limitations had run out. Another leader of the Marian Column action, Ferdinand Šťastný (a senator by the time of his prosecution), was granted parliamentary immunity.[29]

Those who destroyed the Marian Column, and those who perhaps condoned its destruction, believed that Prague's landscape should reflect the values of the new state, regardless of the artistic importance of a particular historical monument. Much of Prague's art community called this position "pseudopatriotic," arguing that the religious art and architecture that made Prague renowned was indeed a national treasure. The Club on Behalf of Old Prague sponsored a lecture series at Old Town Hall in May 1919 to recommend a law protecting religious art. Dismayed by the Marian Column's demise, several art and architectural associations described the Czech contribution to baroque fine art. The organizations reminded citizens that the emotional and illogical attacks on baroque art ran counter to national interests, Czechoslovakia having attracted the negative attention of the foreign press from the Marian Column's destruction. A memorandum to Masaryk, signed by the Club on Behalf of Old Prague, the Czech Charles-Ferdinand University, the Mánes Association, and twenty other cultural organizations pleaded for state preservation of monuments, particularly of church art and architecture. However, within the Prague municipal government, anticlericalism enjoyed popularity, and politicians had little interest in legislating protection of religious art; the national government determined the issue divisive and refused to engage the debate.[30]

Yet, though anticlerical radicals had removed the Marian Column from Old Town Square, they could not erase its three-hundred-year history completely. The new capital would continue to house the memory of conflicting versions of Prague history. Minutes from the first City Council meeting after the declaration of Czechoslovakia's existence ordered that the column's pieces be cleared from the square.[31] The city government sent the fragments to the Lapidarium of the National Museum at Prague's exhibition grounds, where they were soon joined by statues of Austrian emperors and generals, and where they remain today.

Attacking Jan Nepomucký in the Name of Jan Hus

The violence against the Marian Column set off a chain reaction of attacks on Catholic symbols. A common victim of this wave of political vandalism was Saint Jan Nepomucký. Statues of this saint were abundant throughout Bohemia and Moravia, and, like the Marian Column, these memorials dated from the seventeenth century counter-reformation. Nineteenth- and twentieth-century Czech nationalists viewed Nepomucký as the avatar of Habsburg cultural domination in the Czech Lands. During the counter-reformation, Jesuits sought to find a new spiritual figure that could replace the martyr Jan Hus as a hero for the Czechs. Nepomucký emerged as a perfect choice: he too was a Prague resident, a martyr, and a priest who stood up to royal authority. Some historians have disputed whether this figure even existed; others insist that his story actually combines the lives of two contemporary figures. Nonetheless, as Vít Vlnas points out in his study of the Saint Jan legend from the fourteenth through the twentieth centuries, the important issues are not the myths' accuracy, but that they successfully created a powerful cult.[32]

One version of the legend, promoted and memorialized by the Jesuits, is a medieval morality play reminiscent of the tales of King Arthur and Camelot. According to Jesuit mythology, Jan Nepomucký was a priest and religious advisor in the court of Wenceslas IV, irrational son of Charles IV (and a descendant of the tenth-century "Good King Wenceslas"). One evening, under the shroud of secrecy, Father Jan heard the confession of the queen. When the eternally jealous Wenceslas IV discovered that his wife had confessed to the priest, the king demanded that Father Jan disclose her sins. For refusing to break his vow of silence, Nepomucký paid with his life.

The more accepted version of the Saint Jan legend recounts that Nepomucký, an advisor to the king, refused to approve a royal appointment to the court.

In either case, King Wenceslas IV ordered his guards to take the priest to the Charles Bridge and throw him into Prague's frigid Vltava River. Nepomucký drowned that night in 1393, and, according to the legends, the river lit up with stars upon his death. This first miracle became a part of the iconography of the saint, always depicted with a five-star halo, and often shown holding a crucifix. Almost immediately after his death, Nepomucký attracted a small cult of followers, and Archbishop Jan of Jenštejn handed charges against the king to the papal curia in Rome, though little more than a reprimand resulted. Promptly, the vicar of St. Vitus Cathedral at Prague Castle permitted the reinterment there of Jan Nepomucký's remains. During the Thirty Years war in 1619, a Calvinist assembly attacked St. Vitus Cathedral, damaging the tomb, in an event similar to ones that would occur in the capital three centuries later. The Prague archbishop declared Nepomucký his patron and submitted his name for beatification. In 1683, a baroque statue by Master Jan Brokof was erected on the Charles Bridge in Prague. The cult of Nepomucký continued to grow, and reached its pinnacle in 1719, when the martyr's body was exhumed; inside the skull, it was said, Jan Nepomucký's pink tongue remained. The symbol of the tongue was added to the iconography of the silent martyr, and the pope immediately beatified the priest. In 1729, Nepomucký was canonized, and an enormous silver sarcophagus, with statues of angels and depictions of tongues, was built to house the saint's remains within St. Vitus Cathedral.

Nineteenth-century Czech nationalists vilified Nepomucký for replacing the memory of Hus in the so-called era of *temno* (darkness). Artistic depictions of the two Jans were uncannily similar. Both figures had thin bearded faces and sad eyes that seemed to gaze peacefully upward into a better world to come. Dressed in medieval clerical robes and often praying, the Jans seem only distinguishable by the halo of five stars that enveloped Nepomucký's head and the cross that he held.

A cartoonist for the satirical journal *Šibeničky* reflected on the symbolic rivalry between the two Jans, in the early years of the First Republic. In "Fire and water do not get along," the cartoonist depicted a beleaguered Jan Nepomucký, stooped over and dripping with water, being comforted by the vibrant-looking Jan Hus, who, surrounded by flames but otherwise healthy-looking, explains to the decrepit Nepomucký, "Friend, it can't be any other way. The nation has to choose between us."[33] Although both heroes appear with the agents of their martyrdom, fire and water, it is clear that Nepomucký will finally succumb to his symbolic death, while Hus will survive and be chosen by the nation.

After Sauer-Kysela toppled the Marian Column, anger against Nepomucký was unleashed, with part of the mob marching to the nearby Charles Bridge to destroy the 1683 statue of the saint. However, the statue was left unharmed, and a Catholic legend about this maintains that a non-Catholic Czech legionnaire, just returned from the war, blocked the crowd from tossing the statue into the river like the man it represented. The Club on Behalf of Old Prague urged the Czechoslovak state to install a commemorative metal plaque acknowledging the statue's historic date and artistic value, but the government did not comply; nevertheless, the statue survived.

Not all statues of Saint Jan were so lucky. In Prague, the statue of Nepomucký in front of Charles-Ferdinand University Faculty of Law was beheaded in the middle of the night.[34] During the first two years of independence, in Bohemian and Moravian towns such as Kladno, Dobrovice, Slaný, Vinoř, Krušovice, Štáhlavy, and Koloděje, Nepomucký statues were vandalized, some secretly at night, others publicly.[35] Catholic symbols such as crosses and Ma- donnas were also attacked, but wrath was most often directed at Saint Jan, since he was directly associated with the counter-reformation in Bohemia.[36]

Violence against Nepomucký's memory peaked again in May 1919. At a mass celebrating the eve of the saint's feast day, for example, a mob assault- ed a priest at the altar of Our Lady before Týn Church on Old Town Square. The next morning anti-clerical protestors gathered at the Nepomucký statue on Charles Bridge. As with Sauer-Kysela's warnings in November 1918 against the influence of Catholic politicians, the May 1919 attacks had direct political connotations. Nepomucký's feast day coincided with the parliamentary debates on a new liberal marriage law, which the Catholic parties attempted to block. Although the Catholics did not have the votes in parliament to defeat the leg- islation, many nationalists and socialists decried the Catholic opposition to the bill, which legalized civil marriages and loosened divorce regulations. Those as- sailing Nepomucký at public demonstrations and in newspaper columns linked his symbol directly to Catholic conservative political views, which they argued did not befit the progressive new republic.[37] By the early 1920s, anticlerical pas- sions had died down, but Prague Catholics did not forget the indignity suffered by their monuments.

Chapter 6

Catholic Czech Nationalism in the Early 1920s

"The Czech nation must be Catholic!"

Jaroslav Durych, Catholic poet and essayist,
in *Lidové listy*, May 10, 1923

I N May 1923, five years after the proclamation of the Czechoslovak Republic, the Catholic press boldly entered the war over national symbols by publishing in the Czechoslovak People's Party newspaper, *Lidové listy* (People's
News), a scathing commentary on the Hussite symbols that had come to represent the fledgling democracy. For five years, as the party gradually strengthened under the cautious leadership of Monsignor Jan Šrámek, Czech Catholic
political leaders had quietly endured attacks on religious statues, as well as personal insults by fellow members of Parliament (for example, socialists taunting
Šrámek in the Constitutional Assembly, calling him a "black devil" and accus-
ing him of having murdered Hus). Yet by 1923 the Czechoslovak People's Party,
which was founded in January 1919 and represented the Catholic political constituency in Bohemia and Moravia, had gained enough political strength to
take an offensive position on the national question. The Czechoslovak People's
Party had become one of the five most important Czechoslovak political parties, along with the Social Democrats, the Czechoslovak Socialists (formerly
the National Socialists), the Republican Party of Agrarians and Smallholders
(Agrarians), and the National Democrats (formerly the Young Czechs).

Whereas during those first five years, Catholic leaders were mostly concerned to quell anti-Catholic nationalist rhetoric and prevent the destruction
of Catholic monuments, their newfound political strength in the 1920s allowed
them to promote Catholic-inspired national symbols for the new republic, with

Czech Catholics promoting alternative symbols to the immensely popular Hus.
Although there were tensions between Roman Catholic Slovaks and secular
or pro-Hus Czechs, politically oriented Catholics in Bohemia, particularly in
Prague, also decried the monolithic Bohemian Hussite identity advocated by
self-proclaimed nationalists.

Political Catholicism in Czechoslovakia

As the Czechoslovak political spectrum continued to develop in the early
years of the republic, the Czechoslovak People's Party was able to situate itself
as a legitimate and moderate political movement. The 1920 constitution established a parliamentary system and representative democracy, allowing for
the participation of an array of political parties. Party leader Šrámek, a shrewd
politician and a man with intense national feelings, felt that the best way to
establish the party was to associate himself with the national government and
the *Hrad* (the "Castle Group") of President Masaryk and his closest political allies. His goal was to create a moderate Catholic political movement uniting the
petty bourgeoisie and small farmers around social and economic reform. The
Czechoslovak People's Party combined this "Christian socialism" with Roman
Catholic morality, but opposed any direct influence of the Catholic hierarchy
in state politics.[1]

The Czechoslovak People's Party formed when the nineteenth-century
Bohemian and Moravian Catholic parties merged on January 26, 1919. The
deputies unanimously chose Šrámek as the party chair and picked the name
"Czechoslovak" for its appeal to citizens throughout the country. However, Slovakia also had its own Catholic political organization, the "Ľudáks" (Slovak
Christian People's Party), which had been established in 1913 when the clerical
wing of the Slovak National Party broke away to form its own organization. Its
activity was suspended during the First World War, until Fr. Andrej Hlinka, a
fiery Slovak nationalist orator, helped reestablish it in December 1919.

In the first years of the First Republic, the two Catholic parties, the Czechoslovak People's Party and the Slovak Christian People's Party, worked together
but tended to run candidates in their own regions only.

Political Catholicism had suffered during the wave of anticlerical nationalism after the war. The Czechoslovak People's Party fared badly in the 1919 local
elections, gaining only 5.9 percent percent of the vote in Bohemia; 19.6 percent
percent in Moravia; and 18.1 percent percent in Silesia. Within a year, however,
Šrámek had established the party as moderates, resulting in a significant increase in constituents. In the first parliamentary elections held under the new
constitution, in April 1920, the Czechoslovak People's Party, which ran candi-

dates in the Czech Lands, gained 8.6 percent in Bohemia and 27.1 percent in Moravia and Silesia for seats in the House of Representatives. For the Senate elections, the result was even better; the Populists gained 9.1 percent of Czech votes in Bohemia and 29.8 percent in Moravia.[2] In Slovakia, the Ľudáks were disappointed, winning17.8 percent of the Slovak vote (twelve senate seats) and placing third, after the Social Democrats and Agrarians.[3] The Slovak Christian People's Party immediately sought ways to bolster their position, and joined a parliamentary bloc with the Czechoslovak People's Party.

Although the Czechoslovak Peoples' Party made significant gains in Bohemia, Moravia, and Silesia in 1920 compared to their results for the 1919 local elections, they actually held no more seats than before the war: 21. In fact, the parliamentary elections of 1920 marked a shift to the Left. The Czechoslovak Social Democratic Party became the largest party in the National Assembly, with 25.7 percent of the vote (74 out of 281 seats). Adding to that the gain of the Czechoslovak (National) Socialists, as well as the vote for the German and Hungarian Social Democrats, socialist parties held 136 out of 281 contested seats.[4] Therefore, the parties known for anticlerical attitudes represented a plurality in the newly constituted legislature.

After the 1920 parliamentary elections and the implementation of the constitution, Šrámek focused on associating with the national branch of the government as much as possible. Although the majority of party supporters lived in Moravia, much party activity centered in Prague. Šrámek was determined to demonstrate to Masaryk and to Edvard Beneš, Masaryk's closest associate, that he and his followers were true democrats and nationalists. As Miloš Trapl, the foremost expert in the history of Czechoslovak political Catholicism, has written, "Nationalism was very characteristic of the Czechoslovak People's Party policy because the leaders wanted to conceal the Austrophile attitudes of Czech political Catholicism as soon as possible."[5] Šrámek rode this political tide as early as October 1918, when he helped draft the Czechoslovak declaration of independence and stood with National Council members to proclaim the republic. However, many Czechoslovak nationalists and socialists mistrusted Šrámek's intentions, since Habsburg-era political Catholicism had sided with Vienna against Czech nationalism.

In 1921, a tumultuous split between the Communists and Socialists led politicians to fear the radicalization of politics, and the government sought support from the political Right and center. In November 1921, Prime Minister Beneš invited the Czechoslovak People's Party to join his coalition government and appointed Šrámek Minister of Railroads. Although many Socialists disapproved of Beneš's acceptance of the Czechoslovak People's Party as a government party, they could do little to prevent its entrance into the political mainstream. In fact after 1921, the Czechoslovak People's Party held a spot in every coalition cabinet of the First Republic.

In 1922, the new prime minister, Antonín Švehla of the Agrarian Party, offered another olive branch to the Czechoslovak People's Party. Not only did he retain the Czechoslovak People's Party in his coalition government and on the *pětka,* the five-man, extralegal political body that directed the agenda for the government's executive and legislative branches and held most of the real power in the state, but he also transferred Šrámek to the post of minister of public health, an office that suited the priest's abilities and political goals much more than the Ministry of Railroads had.[6] By earning a seat on the *pětka,* Šrámek arguably became one of the most influential and important politicians in Prague.[7]

Šrámek's association in the national government put him at odds with Hlinka, the radical leader of the Slovak wing of the Czech and Slovak Catholic Parliamentary Club, which was disbanded in 1921. Hlinka was a Roman Catholic priest of peasant origin, educated in strict Catholic tradition. A vocal advocate of Slovak-Catholic nationalism, he had been imprisoned by the Hungarians during the Habsburg period. After the declaration in 1918 of the unified Czech–Slovak state, Hlinka surreptitiously journeyed to the Paris Peace Conference, where he appealed for internationally recognized Slovak autonomy within Czechoslovakia.[8] The French turned him over to Czech authorities, who imprisoned him until April 1920. This cemented Hlinka's distrust of the Czechs, and the rest of his career would be dedicated to radical Slovak nationalism. His extreme tactics were so different from Šrámek's cautious moderation that the two men's political relationship was short-lived. The Slovak People's Party left the national government in 1921.

Politically oriented Catholics in Bohemia did not universally support Šrámek, either. The conservative church hierarchy represented by the Prague journal *Čech* (The Czech) also criticized Šrámek's moderation, especially his willingness to work with the socialist and so-called anticlerical parties within the government coalitions. Writers for *Čech,* most notably Jaroslav Durych and Rudolf I. Malý, constantly attacked Šrámek for his policy of political restraint and compromise.

Despite opposition from the other Catholic camps, though, the Czechoslovak People's Party enjoyed growing popularity with the citizenry and increased respect within the government. Beneš, realizing that Šrámek's cooperation in the governing coalitions had become essential to a functioning, moderate democracy, publicly condemned anticlerical violence and forbade continuation of the "religious struggle."[9]

Attacking Jan Hus

As political Catholicism gained strength, leaders began to speak out against the Hussite imagery prevalent in Prague and in government discourse. In 1923, Durych, the conservative Catholic poet, demanded that the symbol of Jan Hus no longer represent Czechoslovakia: "The Czech nation is not Hussite and never will be. The Czech nation is Catholic."[10] Although Durych often opposed the moderation of the Catholic People's Party, he served as an ideological spokesman for political Catholicism. He wrote for the conservative Catholic *Čech* as well as for the populist *Lidové listy,* the organ of the Czechoslovak People's Party. In his regular column in *Lidové listy*, he wrote, "Hus was a heretic, and his homilies are lifeless and empty." Further, the author declared, modern Hussitism was "the most hypocritical of ideas," because so many "professors, bureaucrats, writers and politicians" invoked Hussite rhetoric "like some magical formula" without regard to its historical meaning. Durych suggested that these elites manipulated a mediocre historical figure into a symbol of modern political and cultural power.[11]

Although he belittled so many Hussite symbols, Durych saved his most virulent attacks for the monument to Jan Hus on Prague's Old Town Square: "This bad monument of a bad preacher by a bad sculptor badly erected offends, through its bombastic and comical form, the sensibilities of every person," Durych wrote; "It cannot for long terrorize the most beautiful and historic place in the heart of the Czech lands!"[12] Unlike earlier debate about the artistic merit and suitability of the sculpture, carried out in the refined and subtle language of academics, Durych's unapologetically belligerent tone shifted the conflict to an emotional debate, played out in the highly politicized daily press for public consumption.

Durych's column also harshly condemned the Hus commemorations that annually filled Prague's Old Town Square: "So many vulgar faces put on airs, so many disgusting speeches oozed out"; such events were the "greatest disgrace of Czech life." Durych emphasized that the Hus statue and festivities incorrectly represented the mostly Catholic Czech nation, and his article's headline, "The Czech nation must be Catholic," suggested that the Catholic political movement, not the pro-Hussites, could create proper symbols for the nation. Rather than reject the idea of Czechoslovak nationalism, Durych claimed that Hussite nationalism was a manipulative tool of the progressive elite, one that never represented the interests of the majority Catholic Czechoslovaks. His stand marked a shift from prewar conservative Catholic politicians, who had attacked nationalism in favor of loyalty to Vienna. Indeed, once the First Republic began, most Catholics shifted their allegiance to the new state.[13]

Durych's scathing critique of "Hussite" culture did not go unanswered.[14] Reactions against his editorial were strong. "The 'people's' party is making preparations for a new cultural war,"[15] proclaimed *Večer* (Evening), the evening paper of the Republican Party of Agrarians and Smallholders. This moderate party counted many Catholics among its supporters, and its leader, Prime Minister Antonín Švehla, identified himself as Roman Catholic. Yet, as Daniel Miller has shown, the party embraced a range of political and social goals—including nationalism, bourgeois liberalism, and social reform—to appeal to its broad constituency. Švehla and other party leaders participated in Hus commemorations and defended the martyr's meaning as national rather than religious, so as to display the party's patriotism. After Durych's inflammatory article, the Agrarian Party newspaper, which after all represented the ruling party of the government coalition, reprinted Durych's column with commentary, emphasizing that Durych's extreme comments had appeared in a "Šrámek political organ." Although Šrámek had long distanced himself from Durych's radical commentaries, the Agrarian press held the entire Czechoslovak People's Party responsible.[16] *Večer* further remarked that the Czechoslovak People's Party had demanded the Hus Memorial be taken down, though Durych's column never went that far.

The nationally oriented Czechoslovak Socialist movement continued to challenge political Catholicism, as it had in the republic's first days. The nationalist journal *Socialista* carried the headline: "Arrogant insult to the Czech nation! Master Jan Hus disgraced."[17] Socialist journals, like the Agrarian Party newspaper, used Durych's piece as an example, to expose the dangers of Czech "clericalism."

Among the anticlerical and militaristic imagery pervading the Prague press were depictions of Czech legionnaires gathering around the Hus Memorial. These Czech legionnaires were the esteemed group of Czech deserters who had fought alongside the Russians against the Austro-Hungarian army during the First World War. After the war, activists in the legionnaire movement had become among the fiercest supporters of radical nationalist politics. Jan Hus "became to [legionnaires] a symbol of our independence and freedom." The anticlerical press questioned Catholic loyalty to Czechoslovakia: "Of course the clerics as late as October 1918 negotiated in Vienna with the Habsburgs against the independence of the Czechoslovak nation. They despise the memorial not only because of hatred for Master Jan Hus, but also because it came to symbolize our liberation."[18] Habsburg resurgence was hardly a threat by 1923, but anticlerical politicians now warned that Catholics might use their international connections to dismantle the secular democracy from within. Durych's inflammatory article was all the evidence these wary politicians needed to argue that Šrámek's moderate politics were a sham. A party that did not support Hus could not possibly support national goals, argued one editorial: "Up until now the government socialists sit with Father Šrámek in the government. . . . Due to clerical impudence, this must come to an end."[19] The socialist parties had lobbied since the birth of the republic against the inclusion of Czechoslovak People's Party in the government, and Durych's threatening tone furthered their argument that Šrámek's club posed an internal threat to Czechoslovakia. The Czechoslovak Socialists implored their readers to "speak out" against the "clerical menace." They advised their followers to "Read all the words of the clerics, so that you will know the danger, so that you can fill yourself with anger, so that you will go to war against the black, as you did in the past."[20]

Šrámek distanced himself from the interparty conflicts and busied himself with government projects, particularly the continuing process of land reform. Although he did not make a public comment about the press war, it is likely that he was disappointed with the scathing tone of Durych's article. As leader of the liberal wing of the Czechoslovak People's Party, Šrámek kept an eye on the party organ, *Lidové listy,* to prevent the conservative branch of the party from unduly influencing the editors; usually he did not have to worry about this, since rightist and high-church factions instead gathered around the second Catholic daily paper, *Čech.*[21]

Although Šrámek remained silent about the recent articles in the daily press, other Catholic papers defended Durych's stand. *Pražský večerník* (Prague Evening), a late edition of *Lidové listy,* argued that the reference to the legionnaires at the Hus Monument subtly honored a group that had participated in toppling the Marian Column and had displayed "devilish joy" over the destruction of that Catholic icon. *Pražský večerník* emphasized some party's accomplishments for the lower classes, such as setting up a welfare fund for young and poor citizens, arguing that the Hus supporters represented, rather, an elite. "The hard-fought entry of the Catholic force will last! For the interest of the nation, it must last."[22]

Resurrecting Mary

Clearly, the Catholic press was unwilling to back down once it had made its first offensive in the battle over national symbols. Having scathed the Hus Memorial, the Catholic press made its next demand; it would resurrect the monument that truly represented the populace, the Marian Column. This monument, in the "most beautiful spot" in the Czech Lands, should reflect the character of the Czech people, not the fantasies of a few elite politicians and professors who promoted the symbol of Hus. Even though a main argument for using Catholic symbols in the new state was to appeal to Slovaks as well as Czechs, the Catholic press still used the terms "Czech nation," "Czech Lands," and "Czech people"; thus, Slovak nationalists continued to feel distanced even from fellow Catholics.

Calling upon citizens to join his effort to rebuild the Marian Column, Durych proclaimed, "The old column was an independent gift of Emperor Ferdinand III. The new column will be a gift of the entire nation."[23] Durych, like other participants in the battle for national symbols, never specified who belonged to this "entire nation." As more players entered the public discussion of symbols, it became increasingly clear that there were as many definitions of Czechoslovak national identity as there were debaters.

Over the summer months of 1923, the press war settled down, only to be resumed with more vitriol with the approach of the fifth anniversary of the Marian Column's demise. In late October, *Čech* printed an article that bemoaned the column's destruction on, according to the author, November 8, 1918, proclaiming that the Jesuit fathers spilled tears after the crime.[24] Unable to stand the unbridled emotion and misinformation in this article, Sauer-Kysela reemerged. In a series of short columns in the Communist Party paper, *Rudé právo*, Sauer-Kysela revealed himself as the leader of the Marian Column attack and provided facts about the event. He was particularly concerned that those who wrote about his group's actions report the correct date, November 3. (November 8, the anniversary of the Battle of the White Mountain, was commonly assumed to the date of the column's fall, but Sauer-Kysela, having orchestrated a historical event, albeit one of minor significance, insisted on setting the facts straight.)

As Sauer-Kysela would reflect in his memoirs, he was shocked that this minor event in the five-year history of the Republic had become such a divisive issue. The fledgling national government dropped all criminal charges within days of the vandalism, and the National Council issued only a mild statement of disapproval. So little had been made of the crime in 1918 that few remembered who had facilitated the destruction of the column.[25] Throughout October 1923, the Catholic press printed speculations, until finally Sauer-Kysela came forward with his story.

Soon the colorful leader became a popular figure in the daily press. *Lidové listy* printed a caricature of him and analyzed his family background for clues about his character, concluding, "Sauer's mother was a faithful Catholic; he alone is without a confession."[26] Calling him a "cowardly" and "sorry hero,"[27] the Catholic newspapers called upon the minister of justice and the police to renew charges against him. After he was questioned in his apartment by the police, Sauer-Kysela printed yet another article in *Rudé právo*, chastising the government for its "holy inquisition."[28] Even after this second questioning, no charges were filed, but that the minister of justice took the right-wing Catholics' demands seriously demonstrated the new strength of the Catholic movement.

Sauer-Kysela bemoaned that political strength, and castigated the Masaryk government that supposedly embodied "our Hussite nation."[29] He argued that the government's commitment to Hus was only a symbolic illusion; by allowing the Czechoslovak People's Party to enter the coalition government, the state had abandoned Hus and turned power over to the clerics. Just as he had shouted to the governmental leaders in 1918, "You are the National Committee, we are the Nation," he continued to write that the state's policy of compromise with the Catholics violated the wishes of the Czech nation.

With the passing of the fifth anniversary, the debate about the column began to subside. Proposals in the press to build or move a Marian Column back onto Old Town Square appeared frequently in the Catholic press in November 1923, but the appeal of such articles fizzled. Art historian and devoted Catholic Antonín Šorm printed a list in *Pražský večerník* of Marian columns in small Bohemian towns that could be moved to Prague, but no government channels would consider such a proposal.[30] Although the Catholic press failed to garner real support for rebuilding the column, still less for removing the Hus memorial, it did accomplish its underlying goal. The strong stand of the Catholic press sent a message to the government that Roman Catholics (or at least their spokespersons) would not tolerate anti-Catholic behavior by the state and its leaders.

Jan Nepomucký

Activist Catholics hoped to do more than prevent institutionalized prejudice in the new Czechoslovakia. Determined to promote a Catholic vision of the nation, these groups adopted many of the approaches of liberal and socialist nationalists. In addition to utilizing the political daily press to engage in public debate, Catholic organizations began to sponsor public festivals blending Catholic and national symbolism in a Catholic version of a Czechoslovak historical narrative.

Nepomucký, the medieval martyr whose memory had been a victim of postwar anticlerical vandalism, could serve as a perfect antidote to Hus. With their newfound political strength, the populists thus determined to rescue Nepomucký's reputation and assert him as a national symbol; in 1923 they staged an elaborate celebration in Prague of his feast day. The anticlerical parties lamented this new attempt of the Catholic politicians to assert their national vision. The Social Democratic, Czechoslovak Socialist, and Communist newspapers bemoaned the atmosphere in the capital city on May 16, 1923, the feast day: "In the Czechoslovak Republic, May 16 is, for progressive people, the most painful of all days," proclaimed the evening edition of the Communist Party paper.[31] But in this very year that the Catholic press had revived the Marian Column debate, Czech Catholics continued to seek means to claim public space for their heroes and symbols.

The Nepomucký celebrations of 1923 combined religious ceremonies with elaborate public festivities. The events took place throughout the city, over the course of two days, and were heavily advertised in the Catholic newspapers.[32] By utilizing some of the most important public spaces in Prague, rather than restricting their celebrations to Catholic church buildings, the organizers gave the celebrations a national and inclusive flavor, aimed to engage the entire community.

The boldness of the Catholics in 1923 continued to incense the anticlerical parties, who believed that, in a modern nation-state, any public display of religion, especially Catholic, should be restricted. However, in this case, the Czech Catholic organizations had the law on their side. Legal codes Sections 122 and 303, passed by the National Assembly, stated that the government could not interfere with freedom of religion, and the Catholics cited these in obtaining permission to hold their celebrations.[33] Yet a close reading of the public debate in the daily press reveals that much more than freedom of religion was at stake.[34] Just as the Catholic newspapers had argued that the Marian Column was a more appropriate symbol of the Czech nation than was the Hus Memorial, the Catholic press further asserted that Nepomucký was a truer national figure than Hus.

Hus was no nationalist, the Catholic press maintained, but a precursor to the Germanization of the Czech Lands, because Protestantism was a native German movement. Catholic press articles described a rich Czech Catholic culture but made no mention of the counter-reformation and the forced conversion of the Czechs after the Battle of the White Mountain. Like Czech nationalists, the Catholic press interpreted Czech history through a selective lens. In a column in *Čech*, Rudolf Horský explained that Nepomucký, as a native Czech who had served in the Bohemian Royal Court, stood for Czech defiance of German infiltration: "Every statue of Saint Jan in the most western villages signified not only religion but national consciousness."[35]

The implication that Hus was, for all practical purposes, an agent of German cultural and religious imperialism infuriated pro-Hus Czechs. The anticlerical parties tore apart the argument that Nepomucký, not Hus, represented the zenith of Czech history and culture. For instance, the Social Democratic newspaper *Právo lidu* described him as a symbol of the "unhappy era" of Habsburg and Jesuit rule.[36]

Further, the Socialist press cried out against Catholic organizations that demanded the right to use public spaces for the Nepomucký festivities. Stating that the debate over May 16 was a political, not a religious, question, the Socialist press declared that the festivities promoted the "tyrannical position of a so-called Catholic majority over the minority."[37]

The Communist newspaper admitted that its opponents had won this round of the battle, and headlined the evening edition of *Rudé právo*, "The Victory of Jan Nepomucký in the Fifth Year of the Republic."[38] The fact that the state had permitted the use of the castle grounds where the executive branch of the government was seated, as well as the Charles Bridge and Charles Square, for Nepomucký parades and gatherings rendered the Catholics victorious. According to the Communists, it was unimportant that schools and government offices would remain open on May 16: "It is not about school lessons or working in offices. It is that this is an officially recognized festive day."[39]

The celebrations began on the evening of May 15 on the Charles Bridge, near the statue (which had survived the wrath of an angry mob only five years earlier). The ceremony on the bridge had a religious content of devotional prayer and song, but the organization of the event was reminiscent of earlier nationalist celebrations (such as the 1903 cornerstone ceremony) dedicated to Hus. Participants assembled by voluntary associations and social clubs, standing with fellow members behind the flags and banners of their organizations.[40] A pyrotechnic extravaganza followed the solemn public prayers. Fireworks lit up the Vltava River—much as stars had sparkled in the muddy waters after the saint's violent death. The Catholic press made no pretenses about the reasons for adding this entertainment: "There is no doubt that the great majority of the Prague population will welcome this event with pleasure and will happily support it."[41]

The highlight of the following day was the huge parade. *Čech* proclaimed the success of such public festivities: "Catholic processions in Prague in the last few years have awakened feelings of respect in our enemies and admiration in our fellow countrymen."[42] According to the Catholic press, these processions won over the citizens of Prague by combining religious and patriotic traditions:[43] it was not a contradiction to be a Czech Catholic nationalist.

The Council of Catholics in the Czechoslovak Republic, an umbrella organization of Catholic-oriented voluntary associations, had sponsored and organized the parade. That the paraders marched behind the banners of their private clubs, not with their parish churches, signified that the event was a grassroots endeavor and not directed by the church hierarchy (whom radical socialists and nationalists decried as internationalist clerics). No solemn procession, the Nepomucký parade was lively, filled with music, with young girls interspersed in the crowd bedecked in picturesque, richly colored national costumes.[44] Young gymnasts of the Orel (Eagle) organization, the Catholic equivalent to the

Jan Nepomucký statue on Charles Bridge. Photo by Dorothy Paces.

Sokol (Falcon), marched in step, proudly displaying their colors, and older men wore the uniforms of their Catholic fraternal organizations. Women's groups and youth clubs were well represented, as were workers' organizations, such as the Union of Catholic Ironworkers.[45]

The church hierarchy distanced itself from the parade. In an announcement to the "entire spiritual community of greater Prague," the archbishop's office declared that priests, catechists, religion professors, and others who wore the cloth of the church were not bound to participate in the public procession.[46] Instead, the spiritual leaders of the Catholic community would meet the marchers late that afternoon at the courtyard of Prague Castle, the seat of the Czechoslovak government and site of St. George Church, where a religious ceremony would take place.

By removing church leaders in clerical vestments from the procession, the archbishop's office in effect rendered it secular. Colorful national costumes, not black cassocks, dominated the affair. Just as Monsignor Šrámek, as head of the Czechoslovak People's Party, had distanced himself from the church hierarchy in political matters, so the civilian and religious branches of Czech Catholicism maintained distinct events at the Nepomucký celebrations.

Though the civic aspects of the Jan Nepomucký festivities in Prague were emphasized, they were certainly not devoid of religious content. During the two-day festival, parish churches held masses in honor of Saint Jan, and public prayers were offered at the site of his martyrdom on the Charles Bridge.[47] However, the tone of the most public events, the fireworks display and the parade, was more reminiscent of a national celebration than of a religious holiday. The Czech Catholics were not only honoring a saint's feast day, but were also promoting Nepomucký as national hero. The rhetoric of articles in the Catholic press posited him as a national icon and argued that his followers instinctively loved their Czech country, instinctively erected "thousands and thousands of statues and chapels" to Nepomucký to promote Czech culture.[48] "In the cult of Saint Jan national and patriotic feeling grew from the pure and devoted love of country, whereas in the pseudocult of Jan Hus national sentiment was unimportant." Nationalism, the Catholic press claimed, was inserted into Hussite ideology by liberals who cared more about party politics and enmity toward other political points of view than about Hus's teachings. Catholic organizers declared that, where Hus festivals were not national celebrations but "Party manifestos," Nepomucký festivities were true outpourings of Czech nationalist emotion.[49]

In 1923 Czech life, political Catholics did not posit themselves as alternatives to nationalist politics. Instead, they argued that the Catholic majority in Czechoslovakia should be rendered the arbiters of nationalist symbolism.[50]

Each group that debated nationalist symbols in Czechoslovakia declared that its version of national culture represented "every Czech." Czech Catholics did not claim that their symbol represented an alternate version of Czechoslovak nationalism; rather, they claimed that Nepomucký was a better national symbol than Hus. In short, the manifold nationalists believed that there was no room for compromise in this debate. Five years into the Republic, groups continued to propose their respective true symbol for the Czechoslovak nation, rejecting all others as national heresies.

Martyrs of the Nation

In 1925 the Czechoslovak People's Party again increased its electoral support in Bohemia and Moravia. After the elections, this party became the third strongest in the country, after the Agrarians and the Communists. The Social Democrats fell from first- to fourth-largest party in the state, receiving 8.9 percent of the vote, compared with 25.7 percent in 1920. Victor Mamatey referred to the Czechoslovak People's Party as the real winners in the election, because they went from 7.5 percent of the overall votes in 1920 to 9.7 percent in 1925 and received thirty-one seats in the lower parliamentary house.[51] Moreover, the Czechoslovak People's Party was the strongest party in Moravia, having received 21.3 percent of the votes there.[52]

Political Catholicism's appeal continued to center in Moravia, but the party still focused its efforts on the national question in Prague, where support for Hus was strongest. The city's rich Catholic heritage further appealed to the nationally oriented Catholic leadership.

The success of the Czechoslovak People's Party was unprecedented. Throughout Europe, the great political upheavals, including Bolshevik and socialist revolutions and new state formations, encouraged Catholic leaders to seek innovative methods to become involved in secular politics. As Martin Conway has written, "Catholicism was one of the more surprising beneficiaries of the First World War."[53] In Czechoslovakia, dissatisfaction with Social Democratic leadership led much of its constituency to abandon that party. Radical elements voted Communist; more moderate members of the working class, many having become involved in alternative Catholic trade unions, often cast their ballots for the Catholic parties. Poor country dwellers were unhappy with Social Democracy's lackluster agricultural policy, and divided their votes between the Agrarians and the People's Party. Šrámek's broad-based politics led, according to Frank Hajek, to success. Instead of appealing to a single class-based constituency (as did the Social Democrats, Communists, Agrarians, and the bourgeois National Democrats), the Czechoslovak People's Party melded such varied constituent groups as professionals, petite bourgeoisie, industrial workers, and farmers,[54] and the party's support of a capitalist economic system emphasizing social reform made this party a real alternative on the Czechoslovak political spectrum.

The Catholic press in Prague also helped lead political Catholicism into the nationalist dialogue. Šrámek, as well as more conservative party members, adapted its political vocabulary to reflect the dominant discourse of the period. After nationalism clearly won out as the victorious discourse of the twentieth century, Catholics recast their allegiance to Saint Jan Nepomucký and the Virgin Mary in patriotic terms.

The popularity of figures such as Hus and Nepomucký, and the intensity their images invoked, raise the wider question of the enormous appeal of medieval religious heroes in national movements throughout Europe. Some heroes are easier to comprehend than others. In Hungary, for example, Saint Stephen is seen as not merely a religious leader but also the man credited with the establishment of the Hungarian Crownlands. Yet the changing reputation of Nepomucký had more in common with the legends and myths surrounding the peasant warrior Joan of Arc than with the royal patron saints of many European nations. Like Nepomucký, Joan's reputation ricocheted between servant of the Church and hero of the nation. Like Nepomucký, she was reviled by the most radical nationalist groups (such as the Jacobin revolutionaries) but promoted by later nationalists, such as Napoleon and nineteenth-century Republicans, who staged elaborate festivals dedicated to her during the 1889 celebrations of the Revolution's centennial.[55] A historian of Joan of Arc wrote, "One of the major ironies of history is the tendency of humanity to make icons of rebels and heretics and revolutionary trouble-makers once [they are] safely dead."[56] Similarly, literary critic Robert Pynsent has noted the centrality of martyrs in the Czech national pantheon. Jan Nepomucký and Jan Hus both meet these qualifications, and the romance of their medieval legends continues in the modern era.

Chapter 7

Religious Heroes for a Secular State

"There will be no rolls!"

Prague Bakers Union, declaring
its intent to honor Jan Hus Day

HEADLINES throughout Czechoslovakia on July 7, 1925, announced the strange news that the pope had suddenly recalled his representative from Prague and broken diplomatic relations with the Czechoslovak government. A European state with a majority Catholic population had provoked a rift with the Roman Catholic leadership that would last for three years, and at the heart of the conflict was a Prague festival: the Catholic Church in Rome was protesting the alleged insensitivity of the Czechoslovak state's lavish Jan Hus celebrations.

By 1925, it should have been clear that internal conflicts within Czechoslovakia, and within Prague itself, prevented consensus on how to commemorate the nation's history. Individual citizens, voluntary organizations, and religious groups attacked competing versions of national memory with, literally, clubs and swords, and figuratively, with pens and newsprint. High government officials, however, tried to stay out of the fracas, abiding by President Masaryk's admonition "We have more important business than statues."[1] Foreign Minister Edvard Beneš tried to call off the culture war, and pleaded for tolerance of diverse views of national memory.

Nonetheless, Czechoslovakia could not avoid the necessary rituals, symbols, and festivals that legitimate the very existence of any new polity. Already it had designed currency and postage, but there remained the difficult job of sanctioning national heroes whom citizens could esteem and emulate. In any nation, stories and images of such heroes impart values; they provide context for shared celebrations; they tie diverse individuals to a common historic past. These tasks were especially important for a new state trying to forge its identity.

As Thomas Carlyle had argued in his 1840 lectures, heroes offer a model for imitation but also create history through their strength and wisdom.[2] This historicist interpretation of heroism, later expanded by such German philosophers as Friedrich Nietzsche, influenced nationalists throughout Europe. Jan Hus had obviously served such multiple heroic purposes for nationalists during the Habsburg Era, but he was becoming a divisive rather than a unifying symbol. Nonetheless, his popularity with many of Czechoslovakia's current leaders (not least of all the president) blinded many to the dangers of his two-edged symbolic meaning.

Thus, as leaders tried to retain Hus as a national symbol while appeasing those who despised his memory, much of the 1920s was spent in a cultural tug of war. Battles over national holiday legislation and state-sponsored festivals erupted throughout the decade. As usual, Prague, in its role as the present national capital and historic center of the Czech past, was the principle battleground. As the home of the Czechoslovak Parliament, and as host of lavish festivals, Prague wrestled with how to recognize Hus's role in that past while still representing the new nation's diverse citizenry.

The 1925 Holiday Law

Creating a national calendar was an essential task for the new state, but Czechoslovak legislators delayed enacting a holiday law until seven years into the young republic. Choosing state holidays had economic, political, and cultural repercussions, and have effects on official state ideology. The Habsburg calendar was unsurprisingly heavy on Catholic holidays, and not only were anticlerical nationalists concerned with avoiding any official sanctioning of Catholicism, but commercial interests warned against the economic burdens of adding, rather than replacing, days off from work and trade.

Yet holidays were necessary for the ongoing process of legitimating a new state. Holidays would teach citizens what to celebrate—indeed, that they *should* celebrate their country's existence. A few key decisions about holidays took effect as early as 1919.

Honoring October 28, the date of Czechoslovakia's declaration of independence from Austria-Hungary, was a natural choice. And, in a country with strong workers' parties, privileging May 1 was essential. Removing the official April 11 holiday, which commemorated Hungary's 1848 constitution (bestowed by the Habsburg king), was an easy choice as well: the Slavic cabinet ministers certainly did not want to encourage irredentism among the six hundred thousand Hungarians who lived within the Czechoslovak borders.[3]

Other Habsburg successor states faced difficult choices regarding holidays.

Hungary also discarded April 11, in favor of March 15, the day the 1848 revolution broke out in Pest.[4] Romania struggled throughout the 1920s to settle on an appropriate founding date, since the various regions making up the state had joined on different dates and in different years. Like Czechoslovakia, Romania could not afford to add every important historic date to a calendar mandating workers' days off, nor was the central government willing to relinquish control over commemorative practice to regional entities.[5]

In Czechoslovakia, religious questions, often perceived as tied to regional identity, postponed the completion of the national calendar. In 1919, the cabinet of ministers considered a proposal to remove some Roman Catholic feast days from the list of public holidays. The Ministry of the Interior and the Ministry of Education and National Enlightenment worried that holidays suitable in Prague, the heart of Czech culture, would make little sense in Slovakia and Subcarpathian Ruthenia. The regional administrator of Subcarpathian Ruthenia, in fact, suggested that a new holiday law should only apply in Bohemia, Moravia, and Silesia;[6] however, this proposal, it was felt, would do little to create a uniform national culture in the diverse country.

Despite these controversies, there was a perceived need to consecrate national heroes and create a tradition of Czechs as historical agents. Jan Hus remained the most popular choice among influential Czech politicians, yet in 1920 the Council of Ministers blamed "political complications" for not acting on a Ministry of Education proposal to sanction July 6, the anniversary of Hus's martyrdom.[7] Liberal nationalist circles continued to lobby the government to add Jan Hus Day to the list of civic holidays. Voluntary associations that participated in Hus commemorations during the Habsburg period (the Society for Free Thought, the Union of Czechoslovak Students, the Czechoslovak Community of Workers, the Union of Office Workers, and the Worker's Academy) argued that Hus's movement represented the nation's most significant achievement and had even inspired the national revival. However, the Ministry of Education said that its hands were tied because the government had decided, for the time being, not to repeal any religious laws and to add only one new state holiday, Czechoslovak Independence Day, October 28.

Like the devout Czech Catholics, minority nationalities within the new republic's borders resented Czech nationalist domination over official national symbols, holidays, and ideology, all of which seemed to emanate from Prague. The Ministry of Education and National Enlightenment promised to respect the traditions of citizens in Slovakia and Subcarpathian Ruthenia, as well as the holidays of the Germans living in Bohemia and Moravia, but did not recognize those of other minorities living in Czechoslovakia, such as Hungarians and Poles. Jews in particular remained unacknowledged in the legislation, as all of the religious holidays, and even the supposedly secular Jan Hus Day, were Christian. Only temporarily could government officials appease minority groups, by postponing the inevitable legislation concerning state holidays.

Political parties, voluntary organizations, and local town governments continued to press for a memorial day for Hus. The Czech Socialist press was most vocal in demanding that he be honored with such a state holiday. Declaring the proclamation of July 6 as a state holiday "the will of the nation," *České slovo* argued that the Czech people needed to commemorate Hus's anniversary to reflect on the martyr's moral strength.[8] A 1921 parliamentary bill proposed replacing the Feast of the Assumption of Mary with Jan Hus Day as a summer holiday for workers.[9] As it had with earlier proposals, the parliament refused to act, fearing reprisals from the eastern provinces as well as from local Czech Catholics. But the inaction instead angered nationalist and socialist organizations, which began to take the matter into their own hands.

"There will be no rolls" on Jan Hus's anniversary, declared the bakers' union in 1922.[10] The Czechoslovak Workers' Community called upon members to take off from work on July 6 whether or not the state declared it a public holiday. The Czechoslovak Community of Legionnaires, the Czechoslovak Church, the Central Organization of Czechoslovak Evangelists, the Czechoslovak Teacher's Union, the Central Union of Private and Industrial Builders, and the Society for Free Thought also called for a general strike on the unsanctioned Hus Day. In Prague, where sympathy for Hus was tremendous, the Corporation of Prague Shopkeepers declared that all Prague stores would close. Yet the banks remained open and state offices functioned as usual. The director of the state rail system firmly announced that trains would not follow a holiday schedule, and that tourist express trains to the mountains would not run. Confusion spread within the state bureaucracy, as nationalist journalists encouraged citizens to create, on July 6, 1922, their own Jan Hus Day. Postal workers and factory managers feared attacks by Czechoslovak (National) Socialist workers, particularly in Prague and Bohemia. In Southern Bohemia, the Tábor City Council ignored the decision of the national government and proclaimed July 6 its own "national holiday."[11] The Minister of Post and Telegraphs suggested that, in the future, for reasons of public safety, July 6 must become a state holiday.[12]

The Catholic press disagreed, of course, declaring, "The cult of Hus is dangerous for the free nation and the independent state."[13] While socialist and liberal editorials claimed that rejecting the Hus holiday threatened the independent state, political Catholics, as governing partners in the Czechoslovak state, denied that a citizen must be pro-Hus to be pro-state.

The Czechoslovak parliament debated a new holiday law throughout 1924, as rifts deepened among Czech Catholic, Slovak, German, and Czech liberal and Socialist politicians. Socialists demanded that the state recognize no church feasts as official holidays, while Populists argued that no religious holiday should be abolished. Even secular holidays faced opposition. For example, echoing the Romanian debates, some Slovak politicians argued that the celebration of Czechoslovakia's founding on October 28, 1918, should be shifted to October 30, the day the Slovaks officially accepted the invitation to join the state.[14]

In early 1925, the coalition party leaders finally hammered out a proposal for a holiday law. An earlier draft of the legislation, which would have repealed all church feasts except Christmas, was replaced with a compromise bill that required the Czechoslovak People's Party to accept civic holidays and the Socialist parties to permit holidays with religious connotations.[15] The new law would swap three national holidays for three church feasts; Czechoslovak Independence Day, Labor Day, and Jan Hus Day replaced Easter and Pentecost Mondays and St. Stephen's Day. In addition, the bill added two religiously oriented national holidays, commemorating patron Saints Cyril and Methodius, who introduced Christianity to the Moravian Empire, and Saint Wenceslas, the martyred tenth-century king. Moderate Catholic political leaders, especially Monsignor Šrámek, considered the bill a major victory for Czechoslovak Catholics. Whereas earlier versions of holiday laws would have abolished all festivals with religious connotations, this bill retained almost all of the Catholic feasts celebrated publicly during the Habsburg era: New Year's Day; Feast of the Three Kings; Ascension Day; Corpus Christi; Saint Peter's and Saint Paul's Day; the Assumption of the Virgin Mary; All-Saints Day; the Immaculate Conception of Mary; and Christmas.[16]

Despite the apparent success of the moderate Catholic politicians, the official commemoration of Hus disturbed many conservative and Slovak Catholics. During the Senate debate, Slovak Populist Senator Josef Barinka proposed adding the feast of Saint Jan Nepomucký, May 16, to the official holidays. Just as the Catholic press had argued for the past several years, Barinka insisted that Nepomucký was a more appropriate national figure for the united Czechoslovakia: although citizens celebrated Nepomucký's feast day in every village in Bohemia, Moravia, and Slovakia, Slovak citizens considered Hus a foreigner. Barinka's suggestion met hostility from Socialist and nationalist senators, who believed they had compromised enough in adding the feast of Saints Cyril, Methodius, and Wenceslas to the proposed state holidays.[17]

The Catholic heroes sanctioned by the state combined religious and national memory. Cyril and Methodius had brought Christian thought to the Moravian Kingdom in the ninth century, but had also opened the door to a literate Slavic culture by creating the glagolitic alphabet.[18] And Wenceslas not only had been a Christian martyr but had, as a political ruler of the Bohemian and Moravian lands, represented the long historical tradition of just power that modern Czechs appropriated in their national myths. Czech nationalists would not tolerate Nepomucký, however: his memory was intrinsically tied to the counter-reformation of the Habsburgs and Jesuits.

The Slovak People's Party representatives were not the only senators to decry the addition of Hus Day as a state celebration. On behalf of the German population, Senator Bruno Kafka, of the German Democratic Freedom Party, announced that the German opposition would not accept such a commemoration. Arguing that Hus symbolized the Czech peoples' resistance to the Germans, Kafka focused on this symbol's political, not religious, connotations. Soon, the German and Slovak Catholic parties, in opposing the holiday, left the parliamentary constitutional committee in solidarity with Kafka.

Opposition to a state-sanctioned Jan Hus Day came also from one unlikely source. Some members of the Church of Czech Brethren and of the Union of Czechoslovak Evangelists, who followed the religious teachings of Jan Hus, believed that the legal debates about his commemorations detracted from his power as a religious figure,[19] while other Protestant leaders argued that the national sanctioning of Hus would lead to a wider acceptance of his moral and religious teachings.

Although there was constant debate within the government and in public about the holiday laws, in March 1925 the parliamentary committee announced that it would no longer accept counterproposals, and the coalition parties decided to forward the draft bill to the National Assembly. When the bill came to the floor for a vote, several Czechoslovak People's Party deputies left the Assembly Hall in protest, yet, when the provision for the holiday came up for general vote, both Šrámek and his close associate Dolanský raised their hands in assent.[20] Although most Catholic politicians remained firm in their opposition to Hus, Šrámek continued to support compromise positions that would not estrange the Czechoslovak People's Party from the other members of the coalition government.

After heated debate, the holiday bill passed parliament with a majority vote. From then on, the state would designate Jan Hus as an official national hero. The Catholic bloc in the government had much to be proud of, however. In less than a decade, the Catholic political movement's strong stand on the injustice surrounding the toppled Marian Column, its lavish commemoration of Jan Nepomucký, and its demands for a compromise on the holiday law had established it among the cultural and political leaders of a new Czechoslovakia. Nonetheless, resentment that Prague culture continued to dominate national decisions continued into the first decade of Czechoslovakia's existence.

The 1925 Jan Hus Commemorations in Prague

Even though nationalists had commemorated Jan Hus Day since the mid-nineteenth century, 1925 was the first year the Czechoslovak state could officially honor this hero. Government leaders knew that many Catholics disapproved of the Jan Hus holiday, but they desired a national festival with strong historical content to convey a mood of tradition and stability. Further, the new country had never officially celebrated its break from Austria. Since, in 1915 (the five hundredth anniversary of Jan Hus's death), President Masaryk had delivered the Geneva Manifesto, in which he announced the Czechoslovak quest for independence from Austria-Hungary, a public festival dedicated to Jan Hus would celebrate national history as well as Masaryk's leading role in the Czechoslovak independence movement during the First World War. And Masaryk, a convert to Protestantism and the author of several works about Hus and his legacy, personally supported the Hus celebrations, believing Hus a moral role model for the nation.[21]

Prague was the obvious choice to host the festivities. The 1925 celebration featured events designed to entice citizens of diverse backgrounds to the national capital, yet in fact the organizers did not succeed in attracting citizens not already feeling an affinity with Czech nationalist discourse, and Prague retained its character as a Czech, not a Czechoslovak, city. Not only did many Slovaks, Germans, and Hungarians resent the Czech hero, and Catholics disapprove glorifying a heretic, but others were simply apathetic about the day. Many industrialists, as an article in the Czechoslovak Socialist press bemoaned, even refused to close their factories and give their workers a day off.[22] *České slovo* editorialized that the owners of industry were "in a united front with the clerics" in not honoring the most important holiday on the nation's calendar. And the Ministry of the Interior was concerned about the situation in Slovakia, where Hungarian activists protested Hus Day by keeping their businesses open. Yet these protests were mild and peaceful, and in Bohemia Czech nationalists were eager to celebrate Prague's Hus festival in elaborate style.

Although the government did not succeed in converting all citizens to its Hus cult, the celebrations did attract crowds in Prague. The festivities took place on Sunday, July 5, as well as on Monday, July 6, the actual anniversary of Hus's death. The Prague municipal government held the July 5 events at the Hus Memorial on Old Town Square, in part to compensate for the disappointing commemorations of Hus's five-hundredth anniversary. Now, ten years after that disappointment, these middle-class Prague nationalists, who had once worked tirelessly on the Committee for the Building of a Hus Memorial in Prague, would use the ceremony to rededicate the statue and to commemorate the city's history of defying the Habsburg Monarchy.

Events in 1925 intentionally mirrored the quiet wartime ceremonies. As in 1915, flowers covered the Hus Memorial. On its base lay 160 floral wreaths, with ribbons noting the donors, including Foreign Minister Edvard Beneš, the Czechoslovak Sokol, the Freemasons, and various parliamentary clubs and political parties. Of course, in 1925 the state's leaders welcomed the floral remembrances, and the nationalist press reminded its readers, "Ten years ago this type of public declaration was forbidden."[23] *Národní listy* further emphasized that six Slovak towns also donated wreaths, and city governments and voluntary organizations from throughout Moravia, Silesia, and Těšín, areas where Catholicism was deeply rooted and where sizeable German and Polish minorities resided, also sent flowers. This fact was so important to the newspaper that it followed the statement with an exclamation point, attempting to demonstrate a national consensus. By showing that Slovaks supported the Jan Hus holiday, the Czech nationalists could claim Hus as a secular hero of the nation, not a divisive religious symbol. Significantly, though, no German and Hungarian organizations sent wreaths.[24]

Despite the Prague press's attempt to demonstrate the diversity of Hus's following, the 1925 celebration aimed mainly toward Prague's Czech middle class. At the Sunday ceremonies, Prague children made a "children's proclamation of love and respect for the great teacher of love, truth, and sacrifice,"[25] and children marched to the Hus Memorial behind banners of organizations such as the Sokol, the Czechoslovak Church, and Prague community groups; then, after the short ceremony, the children received pamphlets about Hus's importance to the nation. Meanwhile, "crowds of citizens," according to *Národní listy,* witnessed the event on Old Town Square.

Mayor Josef Rotnágl, elected members of the city council, and representatives of academic institutions attended a private ceremony in Old Town Hall where Prague historian Jaroslav Prokeš recalled the festival of ten years earlier, emphasizing that "Hus's endeavors established our national progressive program." Prokeš's address reinforced the unofficial theme of the 1925 celebrations—that the philosophy of the Hussites and the current direction of Czechoslovak politics were linked—thereby legitimating the fledgling state and its leaders

Rain fell upon Old Town Square and the Hus Memorial as the outdoor ceremony began. Yet the inclement weather, *Národní listy* proudly proclaimed, did not prevent the citizenry from fully participating. The solemn ceremony conveyed the strength of the Czechoslovak nation. Sokol members and Czechoslovak legionnaires from the Great War stood on the monument holding rapiers and rifles; Czechoslovak Army riflemen from throughout the republic formed a circle around the memorial. The soldiers, in their dress uniforms, lit eight flames around the base of the memorial and draped a Hussite banner, with its symbol of the red chalice, over the Old Town Hall balcony.[26]

The Sunday evening portion of the two-day festival commemorated the struggles of the Czech and Slovak people during the First World War. Rather than paying tribute to Hus directly, this ceremony celebrated the nation's bravery during the five-hundredth anniversary commemorations of the martyr ten years earlier. Mayor Rotnágl recalled the difficult times faced by the citizens of Prague in 1915. Rotnágl (a member of the Young Czechs, which became the National Democratic Party, who had worked in nationalist politics during the war) encouraged his fellow citizens to be proud of the nation's triumph over Austria, reminding them how it had attempted to quell Czech national passion during the Great War. Exaggerating Austria's rather mild injunction against the 1915 celebrations, Rotnágl proclaimed, "The rigid military regime attempted to prevent public displays of celebration for the unveiling of Šaloun's Hus Memorial." Rotnágl reminded the crowd that citizens had filled the square in 1915 and covered it with flowers to pay tribute to the national hero; this display of quiet courage, according to the mayor, had set the Czech and Slovak people on the path toward full national independence.

In short, the 1925 Hus festival emphasized the Czech patriotic struggles during the First World War more than the contributions of Hus himself. In Prague's Obecní dům (community house), government officials and Prague citizens celebrated Masaryk's activities in July 1915. After a patriotic musical program, the professor Lev Sychrava spoke about Masaryk's Geneva Manifesto, which proclaimed the Czechoslovak break from Austria-Hungary. Like Rotnágl and others who spoke during the 1925 celebrations, Sychrava had been a leading nationalist politician during the First World War; an important leader in the "struggle abroad," he had fled to Switzerland, where he produced Czechoslovak independence propaganda. His lecture emphasized the importance of Masaryk's manifesto in rallying the Czechoslovak community abroad around the fight for national independence.

The events of Monday, July 6, centered around the elected and appointed leaders of the Czechoslovak government, and emphasized symbolically that Masaryk and his entourage were the legitimate heirs of Hus's intellectual and moral leadership. The ceremony featured Masaryk, who stepped out onto the balcony of Prague's Old Town Hall at precisely eleven in the morning to greet the crowds. The Prague city government hosted the day's ceremony, yet the event had a national, rather than a municipal, character, because the most prominent politicians in the state, including Masaryk and Prime Minister Antonín Švehla formally attended the celebrations. The July 6 ceremony was brief, but the symbolism was powerful. A brass ensemble triumphantly announced the arrival of Masaryk and his entourage. The musical selections hearkened back to Czech nationalist mythology: the fanfare from Smetana's opera "Libuše," which dramatized the Czech national foundation myths, and "Kdož jste boží bojovníci" (Ye, who are God's warriors) the ancient Hussite battle hymn. After this introduction, President Masaryk bowed and waved to the enthusiastic crowds on

Old Town Square. He did not address the crowd, yet he was the focal point, the citizens gathered to celebrate his leadership as much as Hus. An editorial in the Social Democratic daily explained, "Hus threw himself into battle with church authorities and Masaryk with political authorities." Cabinet members Prime Minister Švehla, Foreign Minister Beneš, Minister of Railroads Jiří Stříbrný, and Minister for Unified Laws Ivan Markovic (a Slovak who had overseen the creation of a unified legal code for the Czech Lands and Slovakia) also formally attended the ceremony. Their presence signaled that the executive branch supported the use of Hus as a national symbol. Other government branches, too, sent their most prominent leaders, including Speaker of the Parliament František Tomášek, a leading Social Democrat, and General Mittelhauser of the Czechoslovak Army. Several members of Parliament, leaders of certain institutions of higher learning, and the elected leaders of the Prague city government attended officially. Masaryk's daughter, Olga Revilliod-Masaryková accompanied her widowed father.

The only speech made was a recitation, "Manifesto of the Czechoslovak People." Ferdinand Hrejša, a Protestant theologian and historian at the Hus Evangelical Faculty in Prague, read this, beginning, "By law Hus Day has become a holiday in our reborn state, into whose crest we have inserted Hus's motto, 'The truth will be victorious!'" Hrejša explained that the nation's fathers and brothers, "who gave their lives on foreign battlefields and domestic prisons for a future national independence," emulated Hus's personal sacrifice for "truth and justice." The Hus legacy had set the Czechs on their journey toward democracy and culminated in the modern era; thus, Hus's nation had a moral responsibility to work for democracy not only within but also anyplace in the world where "humans strove to live humanely." To do this, Hrejša declared, the Czechs must follow the ideal that Hus had bravely declared on the eve of his death: to love and defend truth at all costs.[27]

The brief celebration ended at 11:30 a.m., lasting slightly longer than half of an hour. After the national anthem, the dignitaries rode back to the seat of government at Prague Castle, where the Hussite flag, a red chalice on a white field, flew between the state and presidential flags for the two-day festivities. The police report remarked that there were no disturbances during Masaryk's return trip, and that the festival had been relatively peaceful.

The celebrations did afford the Prague police a few minor opportunities, however, to invoke the Law for the Protection of the Republic. The National Assembly had passed this law in March 1923 after the assassination of Minister of Finance Alois Rašín by a young Communist. The law criminalized a variety of actions, both symbolic and violent, against the Czechoslovak state. Although aimed originally at Communists and Fascists, the law was broad enough to be used against national minorities. This law was widely denounced by Communists, national minorities, Slovak autonomists, and some members of the Social Democratic and National Socialist Parties. At the Hus ceremony, police arrested a thirty-nine-year-old German-speaking glass cutter in the Vinohrady section of Prague for "behaving provocatively" and refusing to remove his hat during the national anthem and confronted a nineteen-year-old locksmith for smoking a cigar during the anthem. Yet, the police reported no group protests, violence, or other serious reasons for invoking the "protection" law. The simple, brief ceremony appeared indeed a success.

Therefore, few were prepared for the news that Papal Nuncio Francesco Marmaggi, the Vatican representative in Prague, had left Czechoslovakia in protest. As early as March 1925, when the holiday law passed, the Czechoslovak ambassador to the Vatican, Václav Pallier, met with the Vatican's foreign minister, Cardinal Gasparri, to discuss the implications of a Hus Day for Czechoslovak–Vatican relations. The ambassador assured Cardinal Pietro Gasparri that the Czechoslovak people did not celebrate Hus's religious significance, but focused on his cultural contributions to the nation. Still, the cardinal insisted that Hus was a heretic and that honoring him was an insult to the Catholic Church. However, Gasparri remarked, he might just "swallow the toad." The ambassador was not sure "if the toad signified Hus himself or the fact that we were establishing his memorial day," but he believed the Vatican would accept the celebration. Besides, the holiday law commemorated Catholic saints Cyril and Methodius on the same weekend, which seemed to appease the Church.[28]

Czechoslovak leaders thus believed they had smoothed over relations with the Catholic Church, strained during the first few years of the new republic's existence. But with the Catholic Czechoslovak People's Party, by 1925, having joined the governing coalition and having a representative on the *pětka,* Czechoslovak leaders believed the Vatican satisfied. However, the Vatican took particular offense at President Masaryk's participation in the Hus festivities, as this confirmed to papal officials the president's reputation as anti-Catholic. Czechoslovak Catholic activists also decried his insensitivity. According to the People's Party newspaper, *Lidové listy*: "In regards to the boisterous manifestation of anti-Catholicism, which was organized for the memorial day for Master Jan Hus, and which was held under the protection of President of the Republic T. G. Masaryk and Prime Minister Švehla, the Holy See ordered Papal Nuncio Msgr. Marmaggi to leave Prague, as a meaningful protest for this offense against him and all Czechoslovak Catholics."[29]

The conservative Catholic newspaper, *Čech,* was more extreme: "Because of the indescribable pain driven into the hearts of all Czechoslovak Catholics, when they heard that the highest political representative of our state would officially celebrate the memory of the predecessor to the disintegration of religion in the sixteenth century, the Holy See ordered his representative to leave Prague."[30]

In a later article, "Was the Jan Hus Festival a National or a Religious Act?" *Čech* declared that the celebration was a religious celebration, hence anti-Catholic. The papal representative reportedly had been particularly disturbed that the Hussite flag flew at Prague Castle with the state and presidential flags: "The road from the castle was densely lined with Hussite flags . . . a religious symbol of Hus's disciples and not at all a sign of national citizenship."[31] *Čech* decried the president's official patronage of a festival that supposedly attacked Catholicism. Arguing that Protestantism dominated Prague politics, *Čech* encouraged its Bohemian Catholic readers to strengthen alliances with Moravian and Slovak Catholics.

The Catholic press was disturbed by several affronts: the participation by numerous government officials, Hrejša's national "manifesto" that praised "Hus's reforming endeavors," a young boy at the Hus Memorial selling newspapers headlined "Rome—the Enemy," and a National Theater production about Hussite general Jan Žižka and the Hussite army's attacks on monasteries. Of the play, the newspaper concluded, "Lom's play *Žižka* is a very painful, but moving, picture of the beginning of the Hussite era, yet the present situation is even sadder."[32]

It is understandable that Catholics interpreted the festival as religious. The only speech came from a Protestant theologian who emphasized that Hus's thought informed the president's national program. Still, the calm and brevity of the celebrations left few prepared for the Catholic reactions both within the state and abroad. Militant Slovak Catholics immediately sought to use the controversy to their advantage. Father Andrej Hlinka, the radical head of the Slovak People's Party, issued a statement to the Bratislava Populist newspaper, *Slovak,* in the form of a letter to Nuncio Marmaggi: "We here in Slovakia would give you our most hearty welcome. . . . Vivat Rome! Vivat Nuncio!"[33] However, Šrámek insisted that the offense was minor. Though Šrámek tried to persuade the public that most Czechoslovak Catholics disagreed with the Vatican's stand, sentiment against the pope and his nuncio appeared in the press and on Prague streets.

On the Saturday following the nuncio's exodus from Prague, progressive organizations organized a *tábor lidu* (gathering of the people) to protest the action of the Catholic Church. The independent progressive newspaper *Národní osvobození* (National Liberation) estimated that six thousand participants "from all the political parties" gathered to demand the complete separation of church and state. These protesters also paid homage to Masaryk and sang the national anthem. The newspaper article further commented: "The clerics should . . . realize that the Czech nation will not go with the Pope and Marmaggi, but will go unified, openly and peacefully with Hus and Masaryk."

Judging from the progressive press, Masaryk had succeeded in further associating himself with the Hus legacy. For example, *Národní osvobození* declared, "We saw at the Hus celebrations and at the protest gatherings a unified nation, which gladly sided with its beloved President-Liberator."[34] The evening edition of the Czechoslovak Socialist newspaper wrote, "The Holy See or the papal ambassador do not have the right to insult the giants of history, such as our President Masaryk."[35] Several other newspaper columns elaborated the connections between Hus and Masaryk; one, for instance, stated that Masaryk "stood up for the freedom of the spirit and against the subjugation of his people. His revolutionary concept originated with Hus.[36]

Meanwhile, neither Masaryk nor Švehla issued public statements regarding the nuncio's departure. Instead, they continued to support the state's connection to the Hussite legacy. A few days after the controversial ceremony, Masaryk and the Roman Catholic Švehla attended the opening of Hussite House, a place of worship for the Czechoslovak Church (a sect founded in 1920). This decision was, on the part of the pragmatic, coalition-building prime minister, "an act of defiance," as Daniel Miller notes in his study of Švehla.[37] Czechoslovak politicians may have been making it clear they did not relish the interference of foreigners in the creation and sustenance of national ideology.

Other observers were puzzled by the extreme emotions on both sides of the conflict. The American minister to the Czechoslovak Legation, Lewis Einstein, reported to the U.S. Secretary of State: "The Nuncio's personality, for reasons difficult to comprehend, had aroused the most intense feelings among the Czechs. His previous abrupt departure on Huss [*sic*] Day had been regarded [as] so great a slight toward President Masaryk that some of my own servants, I learned afterward, had at that time expressed the wish themselves to burn him at the stake, as the Church had burned John Huss, if he were ever to return."[38] Indeed, a popular joke in the streets of Prague asked, "Why did Mr. Marmaggi leave? Because he was afraid that he [too] would be burned!"[39]

Aside from the demonstrations, editorials, and political humor engendered by Marmaggi's departure, political maneuvers resulted from the embarrassing rift. Most notably, the Czechoslovak Socialist minister of railroads, Stříbrný, tried to use the situation to oust the Czechoslovak People's Party from the government coalition. However, the majority of the Czechoslovak Socialists rejected Stříbrný's radical politics. The Czechoslovak People's Party itself was divided on how to respond. Members of the more conservative wing of the party suggested that the People's Party voluntarily leave the government coalition, in solidarity with the Vatican. Yet, the moderate Šrámek, who valued membership in the government more than his relationship with Rome, would not hear of it. At a party meeting, he declared, "The People's Party per se is for us far more important than the Vatican. We must decide, not the episcopate." He convinced his party that their strength derived from cooperation with the coalition; to move into the position of opposition party would cost up to three-fourths of their party membership. "Would it make sense to stay forever in the opposition, on the grounds that the party could never enter a government whose cabinet members would attend Jan Hus festivities?"[40]

However, in contrast to the moderate attitude of the Czechoslovak People's Party, whose constituency resided in Bohemia and Moravia, the Slovak People's Party and the German Christian Socialists condemned the government's participation in the celebrations. As a result, Šrámek decided to extend the reach of his the Czechoslovak People's Party into Slovakia and Ruthenia, setting up provincial organizations there. This action angered many in both People's Parties, but Šrámek insisted that the pro-state Czechoslovak People's Party must be an all-state party to be truly successful and influential. Foreign Minister Beneš issued a statement that the Czechoslovak government had no responsibility for the action of the papal nuncio, but that the state was eager to settle domestic and international religious issues.

Commemorations during the Rift with the Vatican

While the leaders of the government worked to heal domestic and international tensions, citizens continued to celebrate Jan Hus's memory, especially in Prague. The Czechoslovak government retained Hus's anniversary as a state holiday but no longer sponsored Hus commemorations or festivals. Nationalists, disgusted at this compromise, took matters into their own hands: in 1926, Prague nationalists sought to recreate the Hus celebrations of the Habsburg period. These festivities revived the urban character of pre-state festivities; organizers wanted to show that Prague was still Hus's city and the heart of the Czech nation. Announcing that the Sokol would sponsor the 1926 Hus celebrations in Prague, *České slovo* proclaimed, "This year's festival for Master Jan Hus will be carried out in the same spirit and in the same scope as last year's celebrations."[41]

The theme of the 1926 celebrations was the triumph of reason over force. The Hus anniversary coincided with the Eighth Sokol Slet, the international gymnastics festival and competition, yet Poles and Italians boycotted the event, and German Catholic bishops encouraged their constituencies not to attend. With little interest in Hus's memory outside Bohemia, the festival catered almost solely to Prague's leading nationalists; nonetheless, the events were well attended. The program was indeed reminiscent of Hus festivals of years past: a parade of children who placed fresh flowers around the Hus Memorial in Old Town Square; performances of patriotic music including the Hussite hymn "Ye, who are God's Warriors" and Smetana's fanfare from "Libuše"; a procession of members from various voluntary organizations; a presentation by Czech legionnaires; and an address about the meaning of Jan Hus for modern Czechoslovaks. Unlike the celebration of the year before, however, President Masaryk did not appear as a modern symbol of the Hussite struggles. Those cabinet ministers present, including Edvard Beneš, did so unofficially and quietly.

The old cast of characters (leaders of the Sokol and the Club for the Building of the Jan Hus Memorial in Prague) reprised their roles as ambassadors of Hus's memory; two former leaders of the club gave keynote addresses. The first was by Josef Scheiner, the current leader of the Czechoslovak Sokol Association, who had been a long-time member of the steering committee of the Hus Memorial Club, and whose arrest and imprisonment in 1915 had led the club to suspend the monument unveiling festivities. Scheiner announced: "We proclaim joyfully and frankly, that there is and will be no power . . . that could muffle our memory of Master Jan."[42] The mayor of Prague, Karel Baxa, leader of the Hus Memorial Committee during the First World War, then remarked that the Czechoslovak nation had come a long way since the war, but subtly criticized the state's submission to international pressure to subdue Hus commemorations. Baxa addressed Hus, promising that, even when it appeared that the state had abandoned him, "Prague will remain a faithful guardian of your moral value to the nation. She will remain the national home of all Slavdom. She still wants to be the protector of the socially weak, just toward all. She will also remain like a mother to all Czech towns and cities, laboring for our independence, which was so difficult to attain and has become today so threatened and endangered."[43]

Baxa's analogy here reflects the gendered, romantic nationalism of the pre-state years, which retained its popularity during the interwar period. Women had gained considerable rights with Czechoslovak independence, including suffrage and a provision in the 1920 constitution (Article 106), stipulating that "privileges of sex, birth and occupation must not be recognized by the law."[44] Further, Masaryk had long advocated women's equality, lecturing and writing on the issue in the early twentieth century. The Czechoslovak citizenry was remarkably supportive of legislation that supported women's rights until (as Melissa Feinberg has shown in her work on women's political equality in the First Republic) feminists began to challenge traditional duties and gender roles. When feminists proposed using Article 106 to revise family law, however,

"Czechs were more ambivalent about the idea of equality than many of them might have wanted to admit."[45]

Baxa's maternal or female imagery was common for European descriptions of beloved cities; Paris was sometimes a lover, sometimes a queen. Prague's coat of arms contained the phrase *Matka měst* (mother of cities). Capital cities, in particular, became mothers and protectresses. But using feminine descriptions for cities carries contradictory messages, offering the possibility of women's participation in urban life but retaining traditional gendered roles, often as the object of a male gaze.[46] Feminine political imagery often serves the dominant (masculine) power, not women.[47] As in 1903, the 1926 Hus festival featured female imagery and women's participation, symbolizing broad participation in the national culture. Newspaper reports emphasized that the parade in which representatives from fifty clubs processed to Old Town Square was especially striking for an "abundance of women." Further, *Tribuna večer* reported that among the overflowing pile of flowers and wreaths on the Hus Memorial "hundreds of cards were dedicated to the Hussite Women" and many more were from women's clubs.[48]

In contrast, newspaper articles about the 1925 festival had not commented on women's participation, and the only woman who officially attended that state celebration was Masaryk's daughter Olga Revilliod-Masaryková, who did so as a surrogate first lady. Indeed, Czechoslovak women had gained suffrage upon state independence, but few held leadership positions in the new government; feminist organizations were frustrated with the widespread perception that the "woman question" had been solved. As political theorists, such as Carol Pateman, have documented, women have generally found easier access to leadership in the less structured settings outside the framework of patriarchal government structures; such was the case in this new republic.[49] Even feminine imagery found a more welcome home in events organized outside the realm of state control. Hence when voluntary organizations organized Hus festivities, women featured prominently, but when the state (even this state with its feminist president) presided, even in 1926 where a superficial women's "participation" was touted, women actually played minor roles.

The 1926 festival's rhetorical emphasis on Prague represented a deliberate distancing from the national government. Baxa's decision to speak on Prague's behalf reflected a widening gap between the city's identity as the capital of a multinational state and Czech nationalism's historical center. Prague intellectuals and civic leaders were unwilling to relinquish their role as safeguarders of national memory; they resented the perceived need to temper Czech national symbols, created and defended in the Habsburg period. This leadership, not significantly changed since the declaration of the Czech Republic, wanted

to protect "their" city's Czech identity, which they had wrestled away from
Habsburg, German, and Jewish culture.

This bold assertion by Prague civil society was short-lived. In 1927, the Prague nationalist community commemorated Hus's martyrdom rather quietly, without the audacity of Baxa's and Scheiner's admonition to the government. As John Sterret Gittings, of the American Legation in Prague, pointed out in his memo to the secretary of state, "The usual demonstrations occurred [but] no epithets were hurled, at least publicly." Gittings further mused that, a year earlier, the quiet mood on July 6, 1927, would have been considered "vassalage to Rome," but by this time the "feelings of others" were of primary concern.[50]

The Wenceslas Millennium

By the late 1920s, Czech nationalist organizations had begun to tone down their anticlerical stand. After 1925, Masaryk's circle realized that it must do a better job appealing to citizens who did not share the Hussite nationalist ideology. Masaryk decided to sacrifice an essential aspect of the nationalists' political program, a constitutional law formally separating church and state, given a public perception of insensitivity to the religious feelings of many citizens. Meanwhile, Foreign Minister Beneš continued to negotiate for better relations with the papacy. In 1928, the international discord ended when Czechoslovakia and the papacy signed a modus vivendi detailing the two states' new relationship. The papacy agreed to realign dioceses and archbishoprics according to new national borders; this was especially important in the Slovak-Hungarian border region. In turn, Czechoslovakia recognized the Catholic Church's authority in some civil matters and compromised on land reform issues.

In sum, from the Marmaggi Affair, Prague learned that national identity could not be imposed merely from above, or contested only within a state's borders; international institutions, too, challenged national histories.

Although the state had settled the domestic and international rifts following the Hus celebrations, Masaryk and Švehla determined to acknowledge the role of Catholicism in creating the new state's national memory. The success of the Czechoslovak People's Party, which became the third-strongest party in Czechoslovakia in the 1925 parliamentary elections, reminded these two men that Bohemian and Moravian Catholics represented a serious electoral challenge. These elections had "shattered the relative consensus that had previously characterized Czechoslovak political culture," as Andrea Orzoff has noted.[51] Further, Slovaks' growing disenchantment with the Czech-dominated national discourse worried the Prague leadership. The state sought to demonstrate to the citizenry as well as the world that Czechoslovakia respected its Catholic as well as its Hussite past. In 1929, Czechoslovakia sponsored a state festival in Prague to mark the millennium of Wenceslas IV, its patron saint; four years later, the government and the Catholic Church worked together to affirm Slovakia's Christian heritage by celebrating the eleven-hundredth anniversary of Nitra Cathedral, the site of the first Catholic church in the region. The two festivals were sincere efforts to balance the Hussite memory that dominated Czechoslovakia's first decade; however, many citizens considered them too little, too late. Creating a consensus on an official, cohesive national memory remained an elusive goal.

In the Marmaggi Affair's aftermath, Masaryk and Švehla pragmatically decided to extend an olive branch to Czechoslovak Catholics. To avoid future domestic and international rifts over religion, and to atone for the anger engendered by the 1925 Hus festival, the government planned an equally extravagant celebration of a Catholic hero. Saint Wenceslas was the obvious choice. The millennium of this Czechoslovak patron saint and martyr, who instituted Christianity in the Bohemian Crown Lands, was conveniently on September 28, 1929; further, unlike other popular saints deeply associated with the Habsburgs and Jesuits, such as Jan Nepomucký and even the Virgin Mary, Saint Wenceslas had a history that did not conflict with the memory of Jan Hus.

Thus, the Czechoslovak government was determined to heal the wounds of religious tensions by ending the decade with an elaborate state celebration that acknowledged the country's Catholic legacy. The Saint Wenceslas Celebrations would be more elaborate than the 1925 Hus festival: the 1925 state ceremony for Hus was brief and simple, but the 1929 Millenium festivities would feature a week of painstakingly staged parades, speeches by state leaders, military displays, and museum exhibitions. Further, the Catholic Church in Czechoslovakia would execute a parallel celebration with processions, speeches, ceremonial masses, and candlelight vigils. Wherever one was in Prague during the week of September 22–28, 1929, one was sure to encounter a commemoration of the "Good King."

Wenceslas's status as a Czech martyr tied him to Hus mythology and to Masaryk's glorification of Czech suffering on the road to liberation.[52] Although Masaryk viewed himself as an heir of Hussite tradition, modern legends also tied Masaryk to the Wenceslas myth. Wenceslas's promise to reemerge from hiding to save the nation became associated with Masaryk's return from exile to establish Czechoslovakia. In fact, during the interwar period, artists often depicted Masaryk wearing Wenceslas attire.[53]

As the state prepared for the Wenceslas celebrations, many contemporary newspapers compared the Hus and Wenceslas legacies. In the Czechoslovak Socialist newspaper, an editorial explained that Hus and Wenceslas stood for similar principles. Both leaders concerned themselves with the preservation and integrity of Czech culture distinct from German civilization; *České slovo* hailed Wenceslas as a precursor to Hus in the "progress toward our national unity." Although Hus would always be the most important national hero, the author explained, "Progressive Czech people have no reason to abstain from honoring Wenceslas's memory" as well.[54]

However, the Catholic press expressed a different perspective. Some progressive Czechs could ignore Wenceslas's Catholic symbolism and focus on his political leadership of a flourishing Czech state in the tenth century, but Roman Catholics could never honor Hus, since he had been designated an excommunicated heretic. *Čech* argued rather convincingly that Wenceslas, not Hus, defined Czech history's success and strength, since Wenceslas's conversion of the Czechs—not Hus's anti-Roman positions—had brought Bohemia into the realm of Western Europe; Wenceslas's favorable relationship with Rome had stabilized the Czech state, but Hus's followers had led the country into civil and then international war. Further, the editorial reminded its readers, Wenceslas's political philosophy of compromising with neighboring states still resonated in the modern era: "Is 'peace with Germany' not the program of our government today?" For Czech Catholics, Wenceslas represented the exemplary Czech past, continued the editorial; "We need positive mottoes as we build the state, . . . not, 'Away from the Catholic Church.' . . . The motto 'Hus' [has] only an empty sound."[55]

Different constituencies emphasized divergent meanings of Wenceslas's legacy. The "Good King" represented, simultaneously, powerful religious faith and strong political will, Roman Catholicism and Czech progressivism, unity with Hus and an alternative to Hus. Wenceslas's legacy was contradictory for the modern Czech, and it was not simple to decide how to celebrate his heritage.

Meanwhile, though Masaryk was eager for the festivities to heal religious tensions, his stubborn belief in complete separation of state and church (that is, the Catholic Church) led him to insist that the state commemorations omit all religious connotations. In his interview with *Život* (*Life*) magazine, he explained, "Immediately following the Hus festival, Švehla and I agreed that this year the government would itself organize a Saint Wenceslas celebration, of a political character, of course"[56]—that is, he insisted that Catholic religious symbolism be downplayed in favor of secular historical themes. He told *Život*, "As Head of State, I am naturally anxious that the fact should be properly publicized that we had a well-organized state even in the late ninth and early tenth century."[57] In his continual effort to justify the existence of the new multinational nation-state, especially in response to the resentment of Hungarians and Germans, he used Wenceslas to demonstrate the long duration of Czech leadership in the region. Wenceslas's reputation as a just, peaceful, compassionate leader further supported Masaryk's quest to link his "liberal, democratic" Czechoslovak state to a long history, of which the so-called "autocratic" Habsburg period was only an exception. Indeed, the Wenceslas commemorations would prove nationalist historian František Palacký's famous dictum, "The Czech nation existed before Austria and will still exist when Austria is gone."

Yet Wenceslas's political heritage contained an ambiguous legacy for the contemporary state: Wenceslas's historical negotiations with neighboring Germanic kingdoms might be taken to imply that compromise had been possible with Austria-Hungary in 1918. Therefore, the state avoided this topic, too, in the millennial celebrations. But by dodging the questions of Wenceslas's religion and his relationship with the Germans, the Czechoslovak state stripped away layer upon layer of Wenceslas's heritage until all that was left to commemorate in 1929 was an empty symbol.

This emasculated symbolism inspired neither the passion nor the anger that Hus commemorations had. Still, some citizens remained disappointed that the state had commemorated a Catholic saint. The Czechoslovak Church leadership (which had broken from Rome in 1918) strongly opposed participating in the celebrations, believing Roman Catholic leaders unjustly prejudiced against their religion. In a letter to the presidential chancellery, the Czechoslovak Church wrote, "Leading Catholic circles tolerate Judaism, Islam, and Protestantism, but do not tolerate members of the Czechoslovak Church."[58] Hrejša, the leading theologian at the Prague Evangelical Faculty (and the keynote speaker from the 1925 Hus jubilee), stubbornly refused his invitation to attend the Wenceslas celebrations, and the Czechoslovak Church leaders warned Masaryk to "ascertain in a round-about way how the Catholics plan to conduct themselves."[59] Masaryk's longtime mistrust of Roman Catholicism led him to similar misgivings, and his advisors in the chancellery debated the president's role in the ceremonies.[60] It was at this point that the government festival committee determined that the celebration would emphasize Wenceslas's creation of an independent political heritage for the region rather than the saint's religious ideas.[61]

The official state activities for the "Jubilee Festival on the Occasion of the Saint Wenceslas Millennium in Prague" began that September 22, with the exhibition of the crown jewels at St. Vitus Cathedral at Prague Castle.[62] The festival emphasized mutual cooperation of government officials, church authorities, and citizens. Minister of Education and National Enlightenment Cyril Merhaut ceremonially unveiled the exhibit; and Interior Minister Karel Novák, Bishop Podlaha of Saint Vitus Cathedral, and Kamil Hilbert, head builder and architect of the cathedral, cochaired the opening ceremony. Podlaha presented a historical address on the crown jewels' significance; Kamil Krofta, assistant minister of foreign affairs, gave the festival address.[63]

Following the speeches, a choir sang the medieval "Saint Wenceslas Chorale" and the national anthem. American Legate Gittings attended the week's events along with many other foreign dignitaries. In his report to Washington, Gittings commented on the link between the Wenceslas and the Hus commemorations in the new state: "The rather weird and impressive hymn of petition, which has survived to this day and which figured in all the recent functions, was also used, according to historians, by the Hussites who, in the confusion of ideas at that time, never ceased regarding Wenceslas as the nation's protector."[64] He then postulated, "The customary final hymn of petition to St. Wenceslas has lately been followed by the Czechoslovak national anthem. If these two airs continue to be used in conjunction, it will serve to bind together the present national feeling of the Czechs with that curiously surviving sentiment of oneness with their early leader; and will thus help identify the Church of today with the beginnings of Czech independence."[65]

As had occurred during the Hus celebrations, Prague children processed in the ceremony, placing flowers from the Prague Castle's gardens on Wenceslas's sarcophagus (which was permanently located in the front of the cathedral).[66]

The display of crown jewels also suited the theme as laid out in Masaryk's *Život* interview, by tangibly affirming the claim of a long, rich Czech state history and attesting to the material and cultural wealth of the nation. The Ministry of the Interior issued numerous documents stressing the jewels' "historical and material value" and the importance of their protection.[67] The cabinet ministers used similar language about these symbols of state sovereignty, as indeed did Masaryk when he spoke of the country's history, which needed protection from outside forces. Throughout the week, for the performances dedicated to Wenceslas in the theaters and concert halls of Prague, the government Cabinet of Ministers carefully divided tickets among themselves, so that the state would be well represented at each venue.[68]

On Friday, September 27, the day before Wenceslas's actual feast day, Masaryk reviewed the Eighth Division, the Saint Wenceslas Cavalry. Speeches by the president and historian Jan Kapras followed an elaborate military display at the Wenceslas statue; Kapras spoke about Wenceslas's progressive judicial philosophy, which he declared well ahead of tenth-century law.[69] Masaryk used the image of King Wenceslas to promote his own political program; in fact, he ended his speech with a reminder of the upcoming parliamentary elections, in which he was a candidate for a second term: "Our forefathers prayed to Saint Wenceslas to protect them from perishing in the future; we must remember that the fate of the state in the republic and in democracy is in all of our hands. . . . Citizens, decide carefully whom you will vote for, so that you and the nation will be well represented in the Parliament. With God's help, we will not perish in the future."[70]

The speech emphasized Wenceslas's political legacy for the modern age of independence: "Saint Wenceslas was a Prince of Peace, but he bravely defended the Přemyslid state. . . . To him the entire nation was one: the martyr felt that in his heart and loved all people."[71] Typical of his romantic style, Masaryk's speech nonetheless emphasized his own political philosophy through Wenceslas's historic example, showing that they shared beliefs in a unified independent nation, compassion for all people, a commitment to peace, yet a willingness to fight for their people. Masaryk, who earlier in his career had urged realism over romantic nationalism, now defended the importance of Wenceslas, despite controversies over the veracity of the legends about him: "And if historians still do not know what is historical fact and what is legend, I would say, that it is the legend that can articulate the ideal of the nation, and to me that is also historical fact."[72]

The events of September 27 were divided into national and church functions. That the Saint Wenceslas week began with a joint celebration of the crown jewels but later broke into segregated activities epitomized the inability of Czechoslovakia to reconcile church–state relations. The eve of the saint's feast day centered on Wenceslas's contributions to the nation. František Udržal (head of the Ministerial Council), Prokůpek, and Baxa addressed the crowd on Wenceslas Square. State dignitaries in attendance included the president, prime minister, and the ministers for foreign affairs, interior, justice, railroads, agriculture, welfare, and unification. At the ceremony's conclusion, the night sky above Myslbek's Wenceslas Monument shone with the glow from lanterns and candles. Bells chimed throughout the city. Later on, the Catholic Church held a nocturnal adoration in St. Vitus Cathedral, at which the Slovak Populist leader Monsignor Andrej Hlinka officiated. Later in the weekend, Hlinka celebrated a high mass at Stará Boleslav, the site of Wenceslas's martyrdom; the Slovak autonomist remained subdued during the celebrations, yet Hlinka's visibility concerned the Ministry of Interior, which watched for divisive radical politics from him during the festive week.[73]

The Wenceslas festivities coincided with the official opening of St. Vitus Cathedral after a major ten-year restoration project. At 1 a.m. on September 28, Prague bishops celebrated a solemn mass in the St. Vitus Cathedral. Later that morning, at nine, the week's "high festival" took place at Prague Castle, commencing in the courtyard outside the cathedral.[74] The ceremony began with the festival fanfare and state hymn and a speech by the minister of education on the meaning of history in state and national philosophy. Kamil Hilbert, who had led the renovation project, lectured on the cathedral's history. While the choir

sang the "Saint Wenceslas Chorale" in the courtyard, guests processed to the
cathedral where Bishop Podlaha symbolically reopened the main doors.

Conspicuously absent from the feast day celebrations at the cathedral were
the three most prominent state leaders: President Masaryk, Prime Minister
Švehla, and Foreign Minister Beneš. In fact, the only official government representatives were the ministers of education and of post and telegraph, both
members of the Catholic People's Party. The presidential chancellery staff debated for a year whether Masaryk should attend Wenceslas events with clear religious connotations. Only a month before the Millennium, Chief of Staff Josef
Schieszl and the president had still not reached a decision. In early September,
a chancellery staff member informed Schieszl that the president had decided
not to attend events in a church but insisted that, "The celebration must be attended by more state ministers, not only Šrámek and Novák."[75] Schieszl worried
"It would cause a sensation, if the President did not attend these activities and
went to see the church independently, on his own time."[76] However, he justified the president's decision, explaining that Masaryk would tour the cathedral
two days beforehand, privately escorted by the bishop and by architect Hilbert.
During the official high ceremony, Schieszl added in justification, "the church
will clearly be filled with citizens, whose presence would hinder the President's
visit."[77] He further explained that the president was to be out of town, in the
Topolčánek resort, during the weeklong Wenceslas celebrations and could only
return for the Oratorio in the Community Theater on September 26 and the
military review and national homage on September 27.

American legate Gittings expressed what many foreigners and citizens alike
felt toward the decision of Masaryk, Beneš, and Švehla to avoid the Saint Vitus
consecration: "I heard some adverse criticism expressed . . . over the failure of

Coin commemorating Wenceslas Millennium, with St. Vitus Cathedral and state seals.
From author's personal collection.

certain Czechoslovak officials to attend the exercises at the re-opening of the cathedral. . . . Neither the President, nor the Prime Minister, nor the Minister for Foreign Affairs was present, although the two latter were in Prague and all three had been to the Homage at the Statue the evening before. The President left town Friday evening directly after the exercises ended. Critics said he might have stayed over until the following morning."[78]

The absence of the three prominent leaders reopened accusations that the Czechoslovak state, especially these three men, were antireligious or anti-Catholic. Gittings seemed puzzled that the usually perceptive politicians would make such a gaffe: "It is true that the Cathedral is a Catholic edifice, but it is also a national historical monument and shrine."[79] Still, he noted: "My personal feeling is that the absence of the Prime Minister and the Foreign Minister responded as much to political reasons as to any personal anti-Catholic feelings, especially in view of the coming general elections, in which both are candidates. . . . They did not wish too close association with what many considered rather a sectarian act."[80]

Like many foreigners and citizens who revered Masaryk, Gittings withheld criticism: "As regards the President, my opinion is that, at his age and with the recent extra burdens of the disaccord in the Government Coalition, he did all that could reasonably be expected of him. . . . I am convinced that had he felt his presence outside the Cathedral to be helpful in binding the very religious Slovaks (and perhaps even some of the clergy) closer to his new State, he most assuredly would have been there. The President is too conscientious a statesman and too great a lover of his people—all of them—to have put personal feelings first."[81]

Yet, Masaryk's belief in total separation of church and state and his personal discomfort with Roman Catholicism, the religion he had abandoned, had political repercussions. Masaryk had adopted the idea of separation of church and state from his American wife and father-in-law, Huguenot Protestants passionate about freedom of religion. In Central Europe, however, there was little familiarity or sympathy for dissociating religion from politics. Leaving Prague immediately following the evening ceremony rather than staying overnight for a one-hour morning ceremony at the cathedral must have been a conscious decision. Rather than healing wounds from the Jan Hus commemorations, Masaryk's absence from the final Wenceslas ceremony reopened them. Slovaks particularly continued to complain that Prague promoted a Czech national ideology that excluded the Catholic majority.

Chapter 8

Modern Churches, Living Cathedrals

*"Will the cross erected on Wenceslas Square
stand higher than the museum?"*

Právo lidu, 1935

T H E Wenceslas Millennium celebrations were the last major attempt by the state to celebrate Prague's Catholic heritage, and the last national festival before the worldwide economic depression. The phenomenal economic growth of the provinces and the relative prosperity of Prague were over. Although Czechoslovakian industry grew 80 percent during the 1920s, the country would suffer a decline of 60 percent in industrial output from 1929 to 1933.[1] Non-Czech citizens, already economically disadvantaged, would particularly suffer during this period. Even during the Depression, industrial employment in Bohemia and Moravia was higher than its 1921 levels, yet in Slovakia, Ruthenia, and the German-populated border regions, the reverse was true. Employment of minority citizens dropped dramatically during the Depression, and Prague became even more symbolic of a capital that represented only the country's majority nationality.

As in earlier eras, the marking of public space through architecture and celebration reflected growing political tensions. In Prague, despite economic declines, Roman Catholic citizens and institutions continued to raise funds for building projects and public festivities that reinforced a commitment to both nation and faith. Outside the capital, citizens instead used public space to distance themselves from what they viewed as a culturally and economically centralized state. As in earlier years, religious symbols were key vehicles for expressing views on the secular nation.

As Czechoslovak Germans, Slovaks, and Hungarians increasingly distanced themselves from the nation of Hus and Wenceslas, Czech Christians sought to mark the capital with architecture that married religion and nationalism. During this interwar era, the membership of the Czechoslovak National Church and of the Evangelical Church of Czech Brethren also grew, and modernist architects and artists were employed to design houses of worship or to add decorations to the former Catholic Churches bought or leased by these growing sects. The modernist sculptor František Bílek created hundreds of artworks for Czechoslovak Church buildings in Prague and Bohemia.[2] In 1933, the Evangelical Church of Czech Brethren opened the doors of the functionalist Husův Sbor, designed by the renowned modern architect Pavel Janák, in Vinohrady. In 1921, a Czechoslovak Orthodox Church formed; in the 1930s it too opened a newly restored house of worship. Prague's new modern Catholic Churches were particularly remarkable, with church leaders seeking avant garde architects to demonstrate that Catholicism contributed to the new modernist and national landscape in the capital. In Prague, two Roman Catholic churches, each designed by a prominent architect of the era, opened their doors during the Great Depression. Both churches incorporated national elements within the sacred architecture. These Roman Catholic institutions would create a "living cathedral" in Prague's largest public square.

Jože Plečnik's Church of the Sacred Heart in Prague

Art historian Ákos Moravánszky has called the Church of the Sacred Heart "a puzzle that defies attempts at verbal explication."[3] Described variously as neoclassical, neobaroque, monumental, cubist, rondocubist, and purist, the building, a massive brick structure with a giant glass clock, embraces numerous—even opposing—Prague architectural traditions. Yet the Roman Catholic edifice, which opened on May 8, 1932, is remarkable not only for fusing architectural styles, but also for attempting to represent fundamental Czech historical and religious contradictions. It stands in a square named for a Hussite king but honors six Bohemian Catholic saints. Its architect strove to embody a uniquely Czech manner of worship, yet was a Slovene patriot. The church's sponsors wanted the building to reflect a new Czech style, but their architect was educated in Vienna and heavily influenced by Austrian and German architectural theory. Although Jože Plečnik faced criticism as a Slovene with the audacity to propose Czech national stylistic elements, perhaps only a "foreigner" had the distance and perspective to grapple with the manifold influences on Prague interwar culture.

The ironies embedded into the very bricks and columns of the Church of the Sacred Heart reflect several debates prominent among Prague's artists and

intellectuals during the interwar period, debates as to: whether Prague architecture could embrace the international movement called modernism while
celebrating Czech culture and Czechoslovak statehood; whether the role of art
and architecture was to express an individual's spiritual vision or to serve society; whether the new national capital could embody competing narratives of
the city's religious identity; how Czech artists might reconcile anti-Habsburg
sentiment with Vienna's profound and enduring influence.

Just as earlier Czech artists had embraced art nouveau to express the spiritual relationship between modernity and the nation's past, architects in 1920s and
1930s Prague looked to functionalism and especially cubism to develop a nationally oriented modernism. Out of Prague cubist architecture grew rondocubism, a uniquely Czech style fusing folk design elements with cubist structures.
Czech artists differed from other European modernists in their willingness to
consider national influences on their modern designs, and the Slovene architect Plečnik was one of the innovators of this Czech national modernism.[4]

The decision to erect a Roman Catholic church in Vinohrady, the bourgeois
section of Prague behind the National Museum and Wenceslas Square, predated the First Czechoslovak Republic. The affluent residential area, 90 percent
Catholic, did not have a Catholic church until a neo-Gothic edifice opened there

Plečník's Church of the Sacred Heart. Photo by author.

in 1893. Over the next two decades, the population grew from fifteen thousand to fifty thousand, and worshippers used local schools for weekend services.[5] In 1908, Prague's city council approved a second church for Vinohrady, and Catholic organizations began to raise funds. The First World War delayed the project, but the anticlerical mood that followed strengthened Prague Catholics' resolve to mark the city with a modern Catholic building.

In May 1919, the Association for a Second Catholic Church in Vinohrady publicized a competition for an innovative design. As had happened with the numerous monument and architectural projects of the prewar period, the announcement electrified Prague's artistic community. Young professional architects and students from the Academy of Applied Arts submitted several proposals, although most were conceptually traditional; the most original was Jiří Kroha's cubist design.[6] The composition of the art jury demonstrated the national government's willingness to support Roman Catholic projects, as well as the insistence of Prague's modernist art community to oversee additions to the Prague landscape. Representing the national government was Edvard Beneš, who had resided in Vinohrady for much of his youth. Other members included future Prague bishop and art historian Antonín Podlaha, two Vinohrady priests, and several prominent Prague architects.

Although Prague artists promoted modernist architectural innovation, the conservative Vinohrady jury chose a traditional design for the new church. Prague's most prominent architects revolted, decrying the selection of what they termed a mundane historicist building. Twenty-nine architects, including renowned innovators Josef Gočár, Pavel Janák, and Josef Chochol, implored Plečnik, a professor at the School of Decorative Arts, to submit, even late, a design: "Our Association has arrived at the conviction that this competition could produce nothing better and more authentic than a work created by you. We have long been hoping that Prague would one day be enriched with a work of your hands, a work that we are certain would constitute one of its greatest jewels."[7]

Choosing Plečnik to design the Vinohrady church, however, presented an obstacle for the jury, who asked whether a native Slovene could reflect Czech sensibility. Prague Catholic leaders insisted that the project must have a national dimension, and the jury reflected a widely held belief in an inherent (almost mystical) character to Czech artistic expression that only a Czech could embody. Ironically, it was Masaryk, a devout Protestant, who convinced the jury to hire the Slovenian Catholic architect. Not long before, when Masaryk had commissioned Plečnik to renovate Prague Castle for the Czechoslovak government, nationalist circles angrily decried this appointment; the Prague press criticized the president's decision to hire a "foreigner," and several newspapers published angry editorials. Yet, when Plečnik began his work, the Prague public quickly

warmed to the pioneering designer. His castle gardens and courtyards won numerous awards, and artists and public praised his ability to evolve a medieval
and baroque castle into an inviting, dynamic gathering place for the citizenry.
His admirers at *Volné směry* (published by the Mánes Association) featured a
twelve-page spread of photographs and analysis by architect and theorist Pavel
Janák (who would later succeed Plečnik as the castle's architect); the article celebrated Plečnik's "remarkable comprehension of the people's soul and environment" and his "independence and freedom . . . that has given birth to powerful
departures."[8]

Ironically, in his work at Prague Castle and the Church of the Sacred Heart,
Plečnik was more willing to embody Czech national character in his design
than were many Czech architects. He had, in fact, embraced Czech national
culture early in his career.

At the turn of the century, Plečnik had been a successful student of Otto
Wagner, Vienna's leading voice of modern architecture. Yet Plečnik was frustrated with the city's Germanic culture, which did not reflect the empire's diversity. His friendship with fellow Wagner protégé Jan Kotěra then gave Plečnik
tremendous respect for Czech artistic innovations; he thought Prague unpar-
alleled in the empire for blending disparate architectural and artistic styles
and philosophies into a unified composition. Further, Prague's creation of a
national culture in the late nineteenth century led him to regard the Czechs as
natural leaders of a cultural pan-Slavism. Meanwhile, the Czech artistic community watched Plečnik's career with interest. Kotěra, who had returned from
Vienna to lead the Prague secession, introduced Plečnik to the Czech public in
his 1900 *Volné směry* manifesto, "On the New Art."[9] In 1902, Kotěra devoted an
eight-page article to Plečnik's work, which he praised as a unique monumental
style that fused designs from antiquity and folk art. Kotěra particularly admired
Plečnik's "cautioned and skeptical" relationship to modernism, his "spiritual,
meditative nature." Thus Kotěra concluded that Plečnik was truly modern, "a
model for all of us."[10] In 1911, Kotěra brought his old friend and schoolmate
Plečnik to Prague as a fellow professor at the city's School of Decorative Arts.

Although Plečnik would remain in Prague for most of the next two decades, he always felt himself a foreigner in the city. Where he differed from
many Czech nationalists was in his deep commitment to Catholicism. In fact,
after idealizing the Czechs while in Vienna, he found himself disengaged from
Prague's liberal anticlericalism of the prewar years. He was fascinated by the
Hus cult, entered the 1913 competition to design a memorial to Jan Žižka, and
in 1916 designed, along with Palacký Monument sculptor Stanislav Sucharda,
a Hus Memorial for another section of Prague. Yet he was also disturbed that a
city with a 90 percent Catholic population had such a cool religious climate. The

brother of a priest, Plečnik believed his own calling was in sacred architecture, and saw church architecture as a way to fuse modernism's emphasis on utility with the architectural innovation he found lacking in current trends. He questioned Viennese art historian Alois Riegl's theory that classical and renaissance monumentalism did not have intrinsic artistic value, but was only admired for its age by Riegl's contemporary Central Europeans.[11] Plečnik believed instead that he could fuse artistic innovation with modern interpretations of historic forms; in sacred architecture, in particular, he could unite artistry with a deep historical and spiritual tradition.

Plečnik's 1913 Church of the Holy Spirit in Vienna attracted considerable international attention for combining innovation and classicism. This work in particular convinced the Vinohrady jury to hire him. However, he at first declined the Prague commission, claiming unfamiliarity with the Czech religious character. He thought that architecture could express national identity and understood this as a goal for the new church; sensitive to the criticism of his new position as architect of the presidential palace, he was not eager to become embroiled in another nationalist debate.

His desire to create modern settings for worship, and the enthusiasm of fellow Prague architects nonetheless convinced him to undertake the project. After accepting the Vinohrady commission, however, he expressed dismay over Prague's religious climate. He considered the city's priests worldly and passionless, and did not understand the lack of spiritual enthusiasm for a new church. After meeting Father František Škarda, who was heading the Vinohrady building committee, Plečnik wrote of his disgust that the priest had a novel, not the breviary, open on his desk.[12] Perhaps, Plečník may have thought, his church could reinvigorate Prague's spirituality.

Despite his reservations, Plečnik set to work on schemes for *Náměstí Jiřího z Poděbrad* (Jiří of Poděbrady Square). Originally, he recommended expanding a property on the square's periphery, but the Committee for the Building of a Second Church in Vinohrady insisted that the building become the centerpiece of the park-like square. Soon, Plečnik and the committee faced challenges from the Prague City Council: for the first half of the 1920s, the council blocked the committee's proposals, insisting that *Náměstí Jiřího z Poděbrad* remain an open park. Behind the council's reasoning was a thinly veiled anticlericalism, characteristic of this council since the nineteenth century. In response, Father Alexander Titl, the committee's Catholic chaplain, led a tireless campaign to persuade the city council to change its vote.[13] The situation was only resolved when Masaryk, who wanted to placate Catholics as Czechoslovakia moved toward its modus vivendi with the papacy, again stepped in. Masaryk employed the Prague Faculty of Law, which designated a section of the park for the church. The final site and design was not approved until May 1928, nine years after the

Committee for the Building of a Second Church in Vinohrady had announced ⌇
its competition.

Finally able to begin construction, Prague Catholics wanted to demonstrate again that they embraced Czechoslovak nationalism. Therefore, the church committee chose October 28, 1928, the tenth anniversary of Czechoslovak independence, to lay the foundation stone. While Prague citizens joyfully watched parades and fireworks, Bishop Podlaha blessed the cornerstone in a dignified ceremony.[14] For the groundbreaking a year later, a small crowd huddled under umbrellas as two enormous banners, Czechoslovak and Bohemian, obscured a small crucifix on the ceremonial dais.[15]

In addition to the ceremonies' symbolic patriotism, the church's design featured purportedly national elements. Plečnik designed statues of six Bohemian Catholic saints to adorn the altar. Sculpted according to the architect's specifications by Damian Pešan, these statues—icons of St. Wenceslas, his grandmother St. Ludmila, St. Procopius, St. Adalbert (first Czech Bishop of Prague), St. Agnes (daughter of Czech King Přemysl Otakar I), and St. Jan Nepomucký—reminded worshippers of the long history of Bohemian Catholicism.

Although the Church of the Sacred Heart opened in 1932, the sculptures on the altar were added throughout the 1930s. The last, the icon of St. Wenceslas, was donated by the church's chaplain, Alexander Titl.

Plečnik insisted on using only Czech materials in construction. Although he continued to receive criticism for his design and his foreignness, he received praise for such decisions. In Titl's essay for the church's commemorative volume, he spotlighted this use of Czech materials, such as "marble from the Šumava mountains."[16] In 1931, a *Stavitelské listy* review noted, "Plečnik used only carefully processed Czech materials. Even a simple piece of matter is a gift from God. . . . Even in the smallest details we feel the effort of a strong creative spirit."[17]

Plečnik also used dark brick, "the native Slavic language [of] medieval monastic architecture of orthodox Christianity in Serbia and Greece."[18] As in his native Slovenia, Plečnik created "national" designs purposely compatible with international histories and trends. The Western Christianity of the Czechs and Slovenes could still celebrate pan-Slavism and demonstrate that nationalism was inclusive.

Plečnik's Roman Catholic church was also symbolically linked to Prague's Protestant heritage. The church would stand on *Náměstí Jiřího z Poděbrad*, named for the Hussite Protestant king who reigned from 1458 to 1471. The first king freely elected by the Bohemian noble estates, Jiří was known for leading the land during the later years of the Hussite Wars, but also for authoring a peace proposal for Central Europe. Plečnik admired the Czechs' Hussite heritage, while simultaneously wanting to bolster Catholicism; he thus sought to evoke a regal image on the church's exterior to honor the Bohemian royal tradition already acknowledged by both the name of the square and the name of the church; in addition, the cross on the massive clock tower sat atop a copper orb, which evoked both Bohemian history and Jesus's Sacred Heart with its crown of thorns. Plečník's design also reflected Bohemia's more humble traditions. With his interlocking arches on the clock tower, he acknowledged Czech rondocubism, that unique modern style that incorporated Slavic peasant folk motifs in a cubist form.

Plečník turned to the theories of nineteenth-century German architect Gottfried Semper, who took European architecture to the brink of modernism by focusing on a building's elemental skeleton, which is then "dressed." Plečník had grown disenchanted with Wagner's rejection, later in his career, of the façade;[19] along with Janák, the foremost theorist of Czech cubist architecture, he wanted to revive the focus on a building's exterior. As Janák had argued, a building's façade provides "a focal point of energy," through which spiritual meaning would emerge;[20] Plečník believed a façade could create spiritual, national, and historic connection. The deep brown brickwork punctuated with granite, then, symbolized "a regal ermine robe worn over a white garment,"[21] evoking Prague's royal heritage and demonstrating that "the most Sacred Heart rules in Bohemia."[22]

Plečník's classical approach originated with his teacher Wagner. Monumental neoclassical buildings were prominent throughout Europe during the interwar period, yet Plečník, as well as other Prague artists, considered neoclassicism a particularly appropriate "Czech" approach. Plečník believed that the Slavic peoples descended from the ancient Etruscans, and he admired Czechoslovakia's fledgling democracy, Greek civilization's greatest legacy. His design owed more to ancient Greek temple architecture than to Roman Catholic traditions. At Prague Castle and the Church of the Sacred Heart, his classical elements, such as marble decorations, columns, and obelisks, celebrated Czechoslovak democracy. As at Prague Castle, in the church he incorporated ancient architectural motifs, such as obelisks on either side of the clock tower. He added a central column, meant to represent humanity's central position in the universe, and incorporated Renaissance structural design for the external walls. Though he was hoping to convey Christianity's relevance for modern society, ironically the most prominent feature of his building was a huge glass clock, marking time rather than celebrating God's timelessness.

Plečník incorporated modernism's call for functional architecture: a building reflects its purpose. Since he admired Bohemia's long tradition of sacred choral music, he designed the spacious interior of the church to inspire the congregation's participation in liturgical music. Since Plečník's personal mission was to "rejuvenate Christianity" in the modern era, he sought to balance secular and ecclesiastical characteristics in the church interior.[23] In developing what later art historians would call the church's post-Vatican-II feel (with its sense of openness and lack of side chapels and aisles), he participated in the interwar trend in Central European church design that linked Catholic modernism's discussion of liturgical form with modernism's demand for art reflecting a social function; contemporary churches, such as the Roman Catholic Corpus Christi in Aachen, Germany, which also broke ground in 1928, similarly featured open, airy interiors to encourage worshippers' full liturgical participation. As Titl explained to his Vinohrady parishioners, Sacred Heart would reflect "modern collective sensibilities," while taking its main inspiration from the "ancient Christian basilicas of . . . Egypt and Greece."[24]

In 1931, Masaryk commended his friend's innovative design as reflecting a modern concept of worship that honored Christian tradition: "How should a church with its internal arrangement express the main idea of religion. . . I accept Christianity according to Jesus Christ's teachings and that is why I would picture the church as a space for the Sermon on the Mount: a spatial (non-Gothic) hall, with a slightly raised podium which would signify the mountain from which the priest would preach, in this way being seen and heard everywhere by everybody, and not standing on a column near a wall . . . Your church is spacious, airy, and I like that."[25]

Despite the president's lauds, Plečnik would leave Prague for good only three years after Sacred Heart was unveiled. Throughout the 1930s, a resurgence of nationalism in Czechoslovakia revived the attacks on this "foreign" architect, and in 1935, when the Club on Behalf of Old Prague printed a vitriolic letter submitted by 245 Czech women who resented the Slovene's appointment as castle architect, Plečník decided to return to his native Ljubljana.

The women's petition highlighted the revival of a more exclusive Czech nationalism in First Republic Prague: "We have so many excellent Czech architects who would lovingly and patriotically take charge of the necessary adaptations without harming the monument left to us by our ancestors. We are now allowing a foreign architect, using a foreign style, and with neither love nor sensitivity for our historical monuments, to do what the former hostile government did not do. The women of the Czech Republic beg of you: Save our Castle."[26]

The women referred to a "Czech Republic," not a "Czechoslovak Republic," reflecting a prevailing attitude that Czechs were the true heirs of the state and capital, and reinforcing the Czechs' symbolic and real domination of Czechoslovak government and culture. The letter reflects the popular belief, dating as far back as Herder's eighteenth-century advocacy of the *Volksgeist,* that unique national cultures and styles exist and can only be intuited by members of the national group.

Plečnik wanted to celebrate Prague's eclectic character in his Sacred Heart Church. He blended opposing architectural styles—classicism, modernism, and cubism—and acknowledged Bohemia's dual Christian legacies. Yet, in the 1930s, much of Czechoslovakia's diverse citizenry, far from embracing a pluralist culture, resented other national and religious groups.

Indeed, Plečnik's linking of Christian symbolism with civic culture subtly suggested that Jews, for example, could never participate fully in national life. In the case of Prague's Church of the Sacred Heart, even the architect was never fully accepted as a citizen of a city he had inhabited for twenty-four years. Plečnik contributed a distinctive design to Prague's landscape, but he could not overcome the increasingly narrow delineation of national and civic space.

Josef Gočár's Church of St. Wenceslas

Adjacent to Vinohrady lies Vršovice, another residential neighborhood south of the city center. Here, too, the landscape was changed to incorporate experimental modern church architecture. Influential modernist Josef Gočár designed a Roman Catholic church to dominate the growing quarter of Vršovice: Gočár's St. Wenceslas Church stands as one of the most important works of interwar Czech constructivism. Less attention (then and now) has been paid to this church than to Plečnik's Sacred Heart. Gočár's building was less controversial—designed by a Czech and stylistically recognizable; nonetheless, it was an important contribution to Prague Catholicism's assertion of patriotism.

By the 1930s, Gočár had long established his reputation as one of the foremost modern architects in Czechoslovakia. A student of the same Kotěra with whom Jože Plečnik studied in Wagner's Vienna studio, Gočár was an originator of cubist architecture and incorporated Bohemian folk elements into his designs of the House at the Black Madonna (1912) and the Legiobank (1921–1923). He believed that modern architecture should not abandon the national, historical narrative. By the time Gočár received the church commission, he had embraced constructivism, an architectural movement of clean shapes and simple construction, which argued that buildings must reflect their social purpose.

Although a less complicated building than Plečnik's church, Gočár's Saint Wenceslas church shared many features with it. Like Sacred Heart, Gočár's church was dominated by a clock tower, though one significantly narrower and taller, rising to eighty meters. Both buildings featured national elements, from statues or stained glass depictions of national saints to more subtle elements in architectural details. Like other patriotic artists, Gočár sought inspiration from the land; his design followed the natural contours of the site, with a semicircular presbytery on the Vršovice hill. In the interior, stained glass windows

by the artist Josef Kaplický depicted the lives of native Bohemian saints. Most ⌇〜
significantly, Gočár inscribed, in large letters dominating the front of the build-   149
ing, the traditional prayer to Saint Wenceslas, "Guide us to our Future." This
ancient prayer inscribed beneath a ticking on a modern functionalist tower
might seem contradictory, yet, like Czech artists before him, Gočár was convinced that modern art could at once embody the historical memory of the
nation and inspire the nation to strive toward a better future. Although the
church was consecrated in 1931, the peak of the Great Depression, and he was
not a religious man, Gočár still felt his design could lead Czechs to look toward
prosperity.

Many persons, however, felt that the constructivists of the 1930s had lost
the artistry that had imbued Prague's architecture with an emotional and spiritual connection to past and future. Fellow modernist Vít Obrtel responded
to Gočár's Saint Wenceslas Church with: "Constructivists gave people a solid
foundation for creative architecture; they forgot, however, that people don't
only work, they also sing".[27]

Czechoslovak Nationalism at Prague's 1935 Catholic Congress

Perhaps Gočár's modern church did not convey the human passion Obrtel
desired, but other Roman Catholic uses of public space were more emotive. In
June 1935, a quarter million Czechoslovak Catholics gathered on Wenceslas
Square to proclaim their faith. The archbishop of Paris, Jean Verdier, celebrated
mass and delivered a papal greeting to the citizenry, and Czechoslovak Catholics responded by publicly renewing their baptismal promises. However, this
declaration of faith on Prague's central square was not merely a part of religious
celebration, but was also an attempt by Catholics to reassert their central place
in Czechoslovakia's contested national identity. Once more they sought to demonstrate that they were the true Czechoslovak patriots, and that Prague was a
Catholic city.

In the spring of 1935, *Právo lidu,* the Social Democratic daily, sharply
criticized a recent vote by the city council. In a split decision, the council had
granted a permit to Czechoslovak Catholics to erect an enormous illuminated
crucifix on Wenceslas Square for the Catholic Congress. The nation's Catholic
leadership sought to demonstrate that their icons could compete with powerful national symbols such as Prague's National Museum. Prague's political
Left asked, "Will the cross erected on Wenceslas Square stand higher than the
museum?"[28]

The church hierarchy's decision to hold the Catholic congress in Prague
was key in planning the event. The Moravian archbishop of Olomouc, Leopold

Gočár's St. Wenceslas Church. Photo by author.

Prečan, who headed the congress's steering committee (comprising members of the church hierarchy and the Czechoslovak People's Party), announced in 1933 that the festivities would take place in Prague—not in Moravia, where Catholicism and populism enjoyed more support than in Bohemia. On the one hand, Prečan was a moderate, an antifascist, and a close associate of People's Party leader Monsignor Jan Šrámek. He was pro-state and sympathized with Czech nationalism. On the other hand, many Bohemian Czech Catholics, led by Prague archbishop Karel Kašpar, were more conservative and vocal in their distaste for Hussite elements in Czech nationalism and in the leadership of Tomáš Masaryk and Edvard Beneš.

The decision to host the event in Prague thus allowed the city's church hierarchy to assert a Catholic identity for this capital so generally associated with Hussite nationalists (including Masaryk and Baxa). In addition, it was important to Catholics that the seat of Czechoslovak government would host the papal representative a month after the final agreement of the modus vivendi between Czechoslovakia and the papacy had been signed. Catholic leaders were determined to show the nation, the papacy, and the world, that Czechoslovakia was indeed a Catholic country and that Prague was a Catholic city. The enormous cross—a 45-meter-high modern glass and iron sculpture with red and blue lights—towering on Wenceslas Square would palpably assert this claim. Further, by illuminating the cross in the national colors of red, white, and blue, the Catholics were obviously adding a patriotic message to their religious symbol, and the crucifix's modern appearance connoted the church's desire to appear progressive.

The Left in Prague disparaged the garish symbol. *Právo lidu*, the Socialist paper, called the structure a "pretentious illuminated billboard," and likened it to "the other illuminated billboards of bars and cinemas on Wenceslas Square." The church, claimed the Socialists, was no different from the capitalist advertisers: "The advertisements of the clerics' 'shop of holy religion' mix together with the advertisements of various firms and shops." Further, the ostentation belied the spiritual atmosphere of a religious festival: "The place they have chosen is not suitable for true believers who would want to stop and reflect and pray."[29]

Prague's Left feared that Catholics planned to use the festival to attack Socialism and Communism.[30] Social Democrats, Communists, and Czechoslovak Socialists believed that the Catholic Church chose the June dates of its congress to boost the appeal of the People's Party before the autumn parliamentary elections. The Catholic and Socialist parties traditionally competed for the lower-class vote, and competition between the Center–Right and the Left had increased with the Great Depression. Unfortunately for Catholic politicians, well after their congress was planned for the summer, the elections were moved to the spring of 1935. Catholic parties fared poorly, particularly in Prague; indeed, the lack of electoral support for populism in Prague led the Socialist press to proclaim, "This has never been and never will be a Catholic City."[31]

Although the Left decried the city council's decision to allow the cross on

Wenceslas Square, construction went as planned over the course of June 1935. On the day before the congress convened, *Národní listy* vividly described the transformation: "The monumental cross, erected behind the statue of St. Wenceslas on Wenceslas Square, leaves a unique impression. The blue body of the cross is lined in red and is reflected onto a white wall. The top of the cross protrudes above the statue, and is placed on the axis of Wenceslas Square. If you look from the middle of the square, the top of the cross nearly reaches the dome of the National Museum."

Unlike the Socialist newspaper, the conservative and patriotic *Národní listy* did not criticize the grandiose decoration of the square: "The cross is secured on all sides. There is no fear that this 45-meter high Christian symbol would fall. Its base is embedded and secured. The project is the work of architect Chomutovský and engineer Čulín. It's a surprising creation of modern technological construction and lighting. It was built with unusual care."

Still, the article emphasized the slippage of, and competition between, national and religious symbols. "Christian Symbol *above* the St. Wenceslas Statue," headlined the article, with the author expressing fear that the cross impeded views of the National Museum.[32]

Prague's fascist tabloid press capitalized on the potential conflict between the Left and the Catholics. Jiří Stříbrný, ousted from Czechoslovak Socialist Party in 1926, was an extreme right-wing politician who enjoyed stirring up political intrigue. Days before the Catholic Congress began, *Polední list,* Stříbrný's tabloid, warned of plans to tear down the cross. The paper claimed that police had received threats that the cross would be vandalized or removed; the paper warned that the cross could meet the fate of Prague's Marian Column.

The moderate Catholic Prague daily, *Lidové listy,* refuted the claims, assuring its readers that the cross was well guarded, and that the police had received no such warnings. Dismissing the newspaper as sensationalist and the report as "fully fabricated," *Lidové listy* stated that Stříbrný's tactics could not frighten Catholics into canceling their festivities. The paper reminded readers, "We do not live in the era when the Marian Column on Old Town Square was torn down." Catholics would stand together and declare a "nation-wide manifesto" of faith in a city that welcomed them. *Lidové listy* was particularly upset about the story about its beloved city: since the "whole Catholic world" would be watching the capital during the congress, sensationalist reports did a disservice to the Prague public. "Foreign guests should not get the impression that they were visiting an unpeaceful and stormy capital city."[33]

The disagreement between Stříbrný's paper and *Lidové listy* highlights the complexity of right-wing politics in the 1930s. Many Catholic leaders, such as

Lidové listy's editor Jan Scheinost, had flirted with fascism. Corporatism attract- ✧
ed members of the church hierarchy, the Catholic nobility, and the populist   153
Right. Scheinost, for example, had joined the National Fascist Party of Rudolf
Gajda, but returned to the People's Party when it was clear that the fascist leadership did not welcome his vision of Christian nationalism. Although the Right
swayed some Catholic politicians, church leaders did not want political conflicts to interfere with the upcoming congress.

Despite the sensationalism in the rightwing and left-wing press, the days
leading up to the festival passed without incident. *Lidové listy* correctly asserted that this was a "different era" from the revolutionary mood of 1918 when
hundreds of citizens could be incited to anticlerical vandalism. The majority
of Prague's citizens seemed to take the Catholic Congress in stride, if anything,
viewing the influx of visitors as a boost to local businesses suffering during the
Depression. This "different era" allowed the continued reclamation of Prague's
Catholic heritage and of Catholicism's role in the symbols of the capital and the
state.

Like the cross, the other decorations for the festival combined civic, national,
and religious symbols. On the first day of the Congress, June 27, 1935, Catholic
women's and girls' organizations covered the altar with flowers, wreaths, and
banners of various Catholic voluntary organizations. Throughout the square,
flags flew in both the Czechoslovak state colors and the papal colors, and two
large papal banners hung on the stairway to the National Museum. Throughout
the city, there were also museum exhibitions of Gothic art and architecture, emphasizing the long history of Catholicism in the city. Even the National Theatre
flew papal flags, and *Lidové listy* commented on the "surprising number" of papal
flags that hung throughout the city. Jan Scheinost commented on the successful
integration of national and Catholic symbols throughout the city: "The heart of
the nation and the Catholic heart found each other and flew together."[34]

Lidové listy remarked, "The great cross and altar at the St. Wenceslas memorial turned Wenceslas Square into an improvised cathedral,"[35] and this was the
effect the congress's organizers wanted. Of course an outdoor location would
accommodate more participants; yet, creating an organic cathedral in the city's
center aided the efforts to claim Prague's public space as Catholic. Cathedrals
and churches did not merely dot the landscape of Prague. The heart of the city
itself was sacred space.

Claiming Prague's civic identity for Catholics was one goal of the congress,
but broader was the church's hope to assert its stake in redefining the state's
national identity. It was important for festival organizers to show that Prague
was not just the Czech capital but served the whole Czechoslovak state. As

Scheinost wrote in *Lidové listy*, "All Catholics, irrespective of language, felt that Prague was their home."[36]

The 1935 congress was not the first time a Catholic mass on Wenceslas Square had been linked to nationalism. On June 12, 1848, Prague students, angered by Austrian general Alfred Windischgratz's displays of military presence in Prague, had organized a Catholic mass at the foot of the St. Wenceslas statue, to demonstrate the unity of Prague residents, regardless of social class, against Austria. Approximately 2,500 participants had attended the mass, following this with spontaneous cries of "Let's march past Windischgratz!" Students and workers had then marched to the military headquarters, where they clashed violently with soldiers. Soon barricades had risen on the streets of Prague and six days of street fighting had begun.[37] Although ultimately unsuccessful, 1848 was still alive in Czech national memory. In fact, the Catholic press reminded its readers that the 1935 festival mass was not unprecedented and that Catholicism, not solely Hussitism, played a role in the 1848 revolution.

The 1848 mass had aroused Czech national consciousness; the organizers of the 1935 congress hoped to ignite an even broader Czechoslovak nationalism: *Czechoslovakism* would unite the country's national groups while honoring their differences. The June 27 mass was carefully orchestrated for this dual purpose.

The evening ceremony began with a procession into the square. After ten thousand leaders of Catholic voluntary organizations, carrying the banners of their clubs, entered the square, groups of Catholics from throughout the country arrived according to nationality. Throughout the parade, participants sang Slavic hymns. First, Greek Catholics (Uniates) from Ruthenia arrived with their flags; next, the Slovaks marched with banners of their dioceses and parishes. The parade continued with Czechoslovak Germans, Hungarians, Poles, and Moravians; Bohemian Catholics from the various dioceses arrived last. By the time the procession ended, at 7:30 p.m., with the entrance of Archbishop Verdier and his entourage, a quarter of a million participants had crowded the square.

The primary message of the festival was the ability of the church, more than any other organization, to offer a model for Czechoslovak unity. The highlight of the mass was the recitation of the creed in the six languages of Czechoslovakia: Czech, Slovak, German, Polish, Hungarian, and Ruthenian. Catholic newspapers emphasized the multiple languages to assert that Catholics did not privilege one national group (namely, Czechs) in the multiethnic Czechoslovakia.

Although the festival organizers emphasized the equality of national groups in Czechoslovakia, they did single out German Czechoslovaks for a special German mass. The event was held in front of the industrial palace, an art nouveau building that had housed the crown jewels during the Wenceslas Millennium, and the site was decorated with eight crosses and an elevated altar. Clearly, the festival organizers wanted to indicate to disgruntled Czechoslovak Germans, who felt ostracized by Czech-oriented nationalism, that their culture had a place in the church's Czechoslovakism.

Also important to broad appeal was the large number of government officials attending the mass. Several representatives of the National Assembly took their places alongside cabinet members Moric Hruban, minister of social services, Jan Šrámek, minister of state unification, and Jan Dostalech, minister of public works. Although all three were members of the Czechoslovak People's Party, their presence seemed to add national sanction to the festivities. In addition, high-ranking army officers, Prague's chief of police, and the rector of Charles University attended. Diplomats from several countries, and representatives from the French army, attended, as well. Notably absent were Masaryk, Beneš, Prime Minister Malýpetr, and Baxa; however, these leaders did meet separately with Archbishop Verdier, and all reports indicated warm, cordial meetings. Masaryk hosted Verdier at the presidential retreat, Lany, and Baxa met with the archbishop at Old Town Hall. Beneš also publicly thanked Verdier, stressing the Catholic Church's role in assuring world peace, given the rising tide of fascism in Europe. Verdier returned the compliments, publicly thanking both Masaryk and Baxa at the concluding mass at Strahov stadium.

In covering the congress, the Catholic press emphasized the Catholic Church's unique ability to foster Czechoslovakism. A week after the congress ended, *Lidové listy* sharply criticized a gathering of Czechoslovak legionnaires in Prague, saying the legionnaires' attachment to Hus automatically ostracized most citizens. The legionnaires' connected "nation and state building to Hus's national thoughts. They link[ed] only the Czech heart with the correct direction of the nation and the state. . . . The legionnaires' 'Hussite' thinking does not succeed in uniting our whole nation into one element."

On the other hand, argued *Lidové listy*, "the Catholic concept gathered to Prague Catholics of all nations, who came in peace and Christian idealism, to spend several days in the spirit of true union of religion and state." The festival was unique, according to the newspaper, in demonstrating a unified populace while simultaneously arranging the participants according to national groups, whereas other manifestations of nationalism within Czechoslovakia had promoted a single ethnic group.

In addition to claiming this creation of a new nationalism for multiethnic Czechoslovakia, the Catholic press claimed a more correct reading of national memory. A letter to *Lidové listy* from a non-Catholic Prague resident explained "The festival showed that the roots of our nation reach farther and deeper than the Hussite era. That the nation lives also in pre-Hussite Catholic culture." Further, "In the few days of the festival, you did a big piece of the necessary work of our state. Catholic Slovaks stood next to Catholic Czechs, and showed Slovaks that Czechs are not enemies of their religious and cultural orientation. It showed Hungarians and Germans that they have a place in the side of democratic Czechoslovakia. Your congress was universal, but also, however, nationally Czechoslovak."[38]

The Festival, The Catholic Right, and European Politics

In addition to Catholics' continuing struggle to redefine Czechoslovakia's national symbols loomed the question of fascism's influence in Catholic politics. Slovakia's political Catholicism moved increasingly to the Right during the 1930s. In Bohemia and Moravia, as the Czechoslovakian People's Party lost ground in national elections under Šrámek's moderate leadership, Right-leaning leaders of the party, as well as more conservative members of the church hierarchy, gained influence. Jan Scheinost, who wrote extensively about the congress in the Catholic press, had returned to the Czechoslovak People's Party after serving as secretary for Gajda's National Union of Fascists. *Lidové listy*, which had long represented the centrist view of the People's Party, shifted rightward under Scheinost's leadership. And Kašpar, the conservative archbishop of Prague, made no secret of his distaste for Šrámek's pro-state policies. Another influential Right-leaning constituency at the congress was the country's nobility. Stripped of their titles and political influence, many heads of these leading families distrusted Masaryk's Left-leaning government and sought out the Right wing of the People's Party. František Schwarzenberg, from one of the most prominent noble families, took a leading organizational role in the congress; in addition, a reported 270 nobles attended, meaning that the congress attracted more representatives of the nobility than any other event of the interwar period.[39]

The festival's most prominent foreign guests, besides Paris's Archbishop Verdier, were Archbishop Innitzer of Vienna and Cardinal Hlond from Poland. It is not surprising that church leaders from Czechoslovakia's neighbors attended, but was political significance to these choices. The break with Austria, and border disputes with Poland had marked the first years of the Czechoslovak Republic; again, the Catholic Church wanted to cast itself as a peacemaker both within and outside of Czechoslovakia's borders, and inviting the Polish and Austrian church leaders to Czechoslovakia demonstrated that hard feelings toward these neighbors had been put aside. Yet this choice also implied a worrisome link between the Catholic Church and the growing Right in Europe.

Poland's authoritarian regime, and especially Austria's far-right dictatorship under Engelbert Dolfuss, alarmed many in Czechoslovakia.

The liberal news magazine *Přítomnost* wondered what the church's role in the resurgence of the Right might be. In an article about preparations for the Catholic Congress, *Přítomnost* complimented the current Pope Pius IX for dealing wisely and cautiously with Mussolini and using moral sway against Hitler. Yet the magazine questioned how sincere the prodemocratic center of the Czechoslovak People's Party was, emphasizing the interest in fascism of many members. At the festival itself, Catholic leaders downplayed international politics in favor of national issues; except for a celebration of improved relations between Czechoslovakia and the papacy after the modus vivendi, and brief mentions of the threat of international communism, the global context was absent.

Catholic leaders did seem to want to distance themselves from the anti-Semitism of the European Right. The papal representative and the Czechoslovak hierarchy sent a letter to Prague's Jewish leaders, acknowledging the Jews' importance in the city's history. The letter also recognized that Catholics and Jews shared a common heritage in the "old laws."

Nevertheless, attempts to acknowledge Prague's Jewish community during the congress seem hollow, in retrospect. During the festivities, the speakers did not take advantage of the public setting to decry Hitler's increasingly aggressive anti-Semitic rhetoric in Germany, or to denounce similar sentiments at home. Czechoslovak Catholics can be credited for attempting to celebrate a multiethnic patriotism, yet their stance did not embrace multiple faiths or multiple readings of the national past. Throughout the interwar period, Czechoslovak populism would remain a centrist movement with little real fascist power (David Kelly credits Šrámek and his followers for maintaining the Czechoslovak People's Party's moderate stand and loyalty to Masaryk and the state);[40] however, as war approached Central Europe, more virulent forms of nationalism would infect Czechoslovak Catholics and the nation's ethnic minorities.

Chapter 9

National Heroes and Nazi Rule

"The destruction of the Column of the Virgin Mary
has not been atoned for."

Jaroslav Durych, Catholic writer

R ECENT books on Prague during World War II carry titles such as *Prague in Black* and *Prague in Danger.*[1] This was a dark time indeed in the city's history, as citizens witnessed the partition and occupation of their state. The religious issue that dominated politics during this era was, of course, the deportation and annihilation of the Jewish population. In Bohemia and Moravia, over 70,000 Jews lost their lives; the names of 77,297 victims are inscribed on the walls of Prague's Pinkas Synagogue.[2]

Despite the gravity of the occupation and deportation of citizens, however, many politicians remained focused on the question of Czech national identity. The nationalist politics that pitted Catholic and Protestant versions of Czech history against each other remained in the discourse during the war years, 1938–1945. Even during this era of German occupation, harsh and conflicting feelings about nationalism did not disappear. Discussions of historical memory, national heroes, and religious identity were often more subdued, as censorship restricted discourse and laws against public demonstrations prevented nationalist events. Still, Czechs continued to debate the meaning of their national–religious pantheon: Catholics embraced patron saint Wenceslas and recalled the memory of the fallen Marian Column; for anticlerical nationalists, Jan Hus remained a symbol of defiance against authoritarianism. And, when the Czech resistance committed its ultimate act of defiance—the assassination of *Reichsprotektor* Reinhard Heydrich—a church named for the saints who brought Christianity to the Bohemian lands became a refuge for the assassins.

Czechoslovakia on the Eve of War

Throughout the First Republic, Prague had hosted dozens of national festivals, from the celebrations of Hus's and Wenceslas's memories to the enormous celebration of the Czechoslovak Republic's tenth anniversary in 1928. It was sadly fitting, then, that the interwar period's final public national outpouring was the funeral of Masaryk, who died on September 14, 1937, less than two years after resigning the presidency in December 1935 due to failing health. Public festivals created the temporary equivalent of a monument; a liberal journalist and chronicler of the First Republic, Ferdinand Peroutka, wrote of the funeral, "I don't know how many theories there are about what a nation is and how it arises, but I know that in the last few days we've seen the nation, that we've seen it as clearly as one can see a material object."[3] Renditions of the Hussite and Wenceslas Chorales, which followed a speech by Edvard Beneš, connected Masaryk to both streams of religious nationalism. The Catholic journal *Obnova* praised the decision to use both hymns as an indication of "a certain reconciliation between two historical traditions, and the necessity of cooperation between advocates of these traditions in building and defending today's state."[4] The carefully orchestrated funeral procession, attended by enormous crowds characterized in the press as "solemn" and "silent," passed by numerous Prague sites of remembrance in order to join Masaryk's memory to the sacred spaces created for the nation over the past century.[5]

Although the Prague press emphasized the unity of the nation behind the imposing memory of the "liberator president," Czechoslovakia was far from united in the last years of the First Republic. The international Depression led many citizens to extreme dissatisfaction toward the government. The 1933 victory of Hitler in Germany panicked many Czechoslovaks, and the increasing shift toward right-wing politics in Central and Eastern Europe encroached on the usually moderate political temperament in the state. Slovak politics moved in a reactionary direction, particularly after 1933, when a state festival in Nitra to commemorate the eleven hundredth anniversary of the first Christian Church in Slovakia was usurped by the right-wing politician Father Andrej Hlinka, demanding autonomy for his people. German National Socialism began to invade the German communities in Bohemia and Moravia. Throughout the interwar period, the culture of Prague, as the center of Czechoslovak politics and the Czech nation, dominated the national discourse; however, in the 1930s, citizens in the provinces began to challenge the center's authority.

As many Czechoslovak Germans became influenced by radical politics in Germany, right-wing activists began to assert demands for autonomy and to voice their dissatisfaction with Czech rule. In the late 1930s, rightist Germans expressed their anger toward Czechs by attacking the symbol of Jan Hus. In the German-dominated border regions, members of Konrad Henlein's fascist Sudeten German Party attacked statues of Hus and refused to acknowledge Hus Day by closing their businesses.

The Prague office of the Ministry of the Interior carefully cataloged the numerous police reports of attacks on Hus statues and interference in Hus celebrations in German regions. In Osek u Duchcova, vandals attacked a statue of Hus and tore down trees that surrounded the monument.[6] In Horní Litvín, the German paper *Bruexer Zeitung* encouraged its readers to defy the law that shops must close on Hus Day, and to keep their businesses open in protest of the government's support of a national hero in a multinational state; this entreaty was part of a movement throughout the German-speaking regions to encourage Germans to "agitate against the state holiday" on July 6 for Hus.[7] Cities and towns with large German populations, such as Liberec, Cheb, Jablonec nad Nisou, Karlovy Vary, Mariánské Lázně, and Ustí nad Labem, all participated in this campaign of protest.

A few majority-German towns witnessed minor acts of violence during the 1935 Hus commemorations. In Litoměrice, two Germans, Friedrich Schaeffer and Frank Zoefert, attacked a Czech who was honoring Hus in a Social Democrat procession of approximately eighty workers. During the Socialists' parade, the two Germans broke marcher František Hejduk's nose. At the subsequent Hus ceremony, in which one thousand to twelve hundred Czechs participated, protesters heckled the crowd, calling out "Heil Hitler!" and "Heil Henlein!"

In fact, as Konrad Henlein, the Nazi Party leader in the Sudetenland, gained popularity, right-leaning Germans in Bohemia and Moravia began to unify politically to oppose the Czechoslovak state. The national celebrations of Hus Day in the mid-1930s provided excellent opportunities for Germans to unite against the state and institute symbolic boycotts of its symbols. In Prague, most Catholics remained committed to displaying support of the Czechoslovak state, but the late 1930s witnessed increasing dissatisfaction outside the capital.

Second Republic Prague and the Cult of St. Wenceslas

In September 1938, France and Britain acquiesced to Hitler's demands to cede the German-populated Sudetenland of Czechoslovakia to the Third Reich. The treaty, known as the Munich Agreement—or the Munich Betrayal (*zrada*), among many Czechs and Slovaks—destroyed First Republic Czechoslovakia. The agreement, signed by Adolph Hitler, Benito Mussolini, British Prime Minister Neville Chamberlain, and French Premier Eduard Daladier, granted the German-speaking border regions to Germany, and also awarded Hungary the border region in Southern Slovakia. Subcarpathian Rus was granted autonomy. President Beneš resigned in protest and fled to London, where he established a government in exile. Šrámek, too, left Czechoslovakia and served as prime minster of Beneš's London government from 1940–1945. The Second Czechoslovak Republic was founded, under the presidency of Emil Hácha.

Hácha was chosen as Beneš's successor by the National Assembly. Since he was a conservative and deeply faithful Catholic, Czechoslovakia's remaining political leadership hoped he would appeal to the political Right, thus quelling tensions in the state. Educated as a lawyer, Hácha had been a member of the Austro-Hungarian civil service and became a judge in independent Czechoslovakia. In 1925, the highly respected legal scholar became chief justice of Czechoslovakia's supreme court, appointed to the position by Masaryk.

The short-lived Second Republic, ruled by the newly formed National Unity Party, ended with Germany's invasion in March 1939. Hácha, already quite ill when he was appointed president, and suffering emotionally from his recent widowhood, signed the country over to Hitler at a meeting in Berlin. Urging citizens to remain calm, Hácha reported in a radio address that he had signed an agreement that "confidently placed the fate of the Czech people and country in the hands of the Fuehrer and German Reich."[8] The Second Republic became the Protectorate of Bohemia and Moravia, and Slovakia became an autonomous satellite state of the Third Reich. Hácha retained his position, though with even more limited authority, under the protectorate and held the title "State President" until the end of the war.

Following the establishment of the protectorate, Hácha defended his actions as the only way to safeguard his beloved nation. A complex figure, he challenged threats to national sovereignty, such as the dismantling of the Czechoslovak army and the introduction of the Gestapo, while welcoming the limits placed on democratic institutions, which he had long distrusted. Like many Catholic-oriented Czech politicians who stayed in Prague during the war, Hácha was anti-Semitic and did not interfere with legislation against Jews. With moderates like Šrámek serving in the London government, many Catholic politicians abandoned the inclusive patriotism of the Plečnik church or the 1935 Catholic Congress and turned to fascism or deepened right-wing beliefs in authoritarian government.

Moving toward the Right did not signal an abandonment of self-perceived patriotism, however. In an interview with Czech writer Karel Horský, Hácha characterized himself as a martyr who had saved Prague: "And still, as you know, [the statue of] Saint Wenceslas is still standing in its place. Charles Bridge is standing, too, the Castle district was not blown 'into the air' and hundreds of thousands of our young people are still breathing and living."[9]

As they did for Hácha, Prague's sacred spaces continued to function as signs of hope for the leaders and citizens of the capital. Indeed, frequently leaders who capitulated to Hitler told their constituency that they had saved Prague. It is not surprising that Hácha focused on Saint Wenceslas in these comments to Horský. The patron saint was the most convenient national symbol for the Hácha government, having after all combined patriotic characteristics with a legacy of compromise with Germany. To justify collaboration with the Nazi occupiers, Hácha told the Czechoslovak cabinet: "The Czechoslovak statesmen should take the national saint, Duke Wenceslas, as their model. . . . [He] fought for German–Czech understanding, although initially he did not find understanding with his own people."[10]

In calling upon Wenceslas's memory, Hácha echoed the words of the Prague archbishop Karel Kašpar, who issued a long pastoral letter on October 11, 1938, just over a week after the signing of the Munich agreement. Although he considered Munich a "catastrophe," Kašpar blamed the divisive nationalist discourse of the First Republic for much of the crisis: "How offended God had been, beginning with the collapse of the Memorial Column to the Virgin Mary in the middle of the Main Square of Prague. . . . The belief in St. Wenceslas had already so often united our people, whereas Hussitism, . . . the Protestantism of White Mountain, the Godlessness of our new era brought on today's catastrophe."[11]

Thus Catholic leaders posited Wenceslas as a unifying figure, who allowed Czechs to express their patriotism but signalled to Germans that their Slavic neighbors were willing to compromise.[12] Indeed, the Second Republic's choice of Wenceslas as a national martyr resurrected the Habsburg-era and interwar debate between Masaryk and Catholic historian Josef Pekař about the very meaning of Czech history.[13] These two scholars vehemently disagreed over Palacký's premise that Czech–German conflict characterized Bohemian history, and Pekař accused Masaryk of glorifying Hussite history and dismissing Roman Catholic contributions to the region's culture. During the Second Republic, the Wenceslas myth enabled Masaryk's critics to argue that the president's early ideas about history had interfered with his ability to govern. For example, Jaroslav Durych, the Catholic essayist and poet, wrote that Masaryk's "catastrophic anti-Catholic philosophy did not belong among the foundation stones of the Second Republic."[14]

In December 1938, Hácha officially celebrated his inauguration with a mass in St. Wenceslas Chapel of St. Vitus Cathedral, the location of the saint's remains. At the mass, Kašpar spoke about the imperative of beginning the new era in the "spirit of Saint Wenceslas."[15] Unlike Masaryk, who in 1929 did not participate in the Wenceslas celebrations inside Prague Cathedral, Hácha soon officially attended a memorial mass in recognition of the saint's feast day: on

September 28, 1939, a day shy of the one-year anniversary of Munich, Hácha, along with fellow politicians and church leaders, staged a Wenceslas celebration for Prague. After the morning mass at St. Vitus, at Prague Castle, religious leaders carried Wenceslas's remains through the streets of Prague. They followed what was known as the "royal route," walking from the cathedral, across Charles Bridge, through the Old Town, and finally to Wenceslas Square. Their procession mimicked parades of the First Republic and Habsburg era by which leaders and citizens had marked the city for their national cause. More than ten thousand citizens watched the 1939 procession.[16]

Not all Prague residents wanted commemoration of Wenceslas to serve as a sign of compromise with Germany, however. Rather than support the procession, many citizens throughout the day quietly laid wreaths at Wenceslas Memorial in front of the National Musuem. In the evening, five women stood at the memorial and sang the medieval hymn to Saint Wenceslas; the gathering crowd answered with the Czechoslovak national anthem, a clear act of defiance. The police responded by continually silencing the crowd, until they finally dispersed the gathering and arrested five men whom they held for five days. Four were described as "of Czech nationality" and one as a Jew.[17] Early in the protectorate, carefully staged and organized events were tolerated, but any spontaneous displays of Czech patriotism were, as in this case, quickly subdued.

In general, though, the German authorities responded well to the attempt by Hácha to use Wenceslas as a national symbol of compromise with Germany. The Reich propaganda ministry also contributed to the developing iconography, issuing a statement in 1941 that the German and Czech culture shared many attributes that could be found in such cultural institutions as the Saint Wenceslas tradition and the Bohemian baroque.[18]

Even Reinhard Heydrich participated in a ceremony to honor the memory of St. Wenceslas. Appointed *Reichsprotektor* in September 1941, Heydrich was charged with tightening Nazi rule in Bohemia and Moravia and quelling the passive resistance of Czech workers. Still, he saw value in allowing some demonstrations of Czech identity, especially when they conformed with German intentions in the region. In a memorandum to Martin Bormann, head of the Nazi Party chancellery, Heydrich remarked on his participation in the festival for the inspection of the Wenceslas crown and insignia, during which he symbolically handed the seven keys of the Wenceslas Shrine in St. Vitus Cathedral to Hácha. Heydrich informed Bormann that the act symbolized "a covenant of acceptance of the Wenceslas tradition in its loyalty to the Reich."[19]

In thus adapting the memory of Wenceslas, Hácha and other Catholic leaders accomplished a key goal: to preserve some vestige of Czech patriotism through the difficult years of German occupation. However, their willingness to share the symbol with the Nazi regime signalled the deep failure of the era. To stand at the Wenceslas Reliquary in St. Vitus Cathedral with a lead architect of the Final Solution, yet to stand by as the city's Jews were exiled to ghettos, concentration camps, and eventual death, exemplified Hácha's inability to lead the nation.

The Marian Column

Like Kašpar, the archbishop of Prague, who viewed the Marian Column's destruction as the first sign of First Republic Czechoslovakia's ultimate failure, other Catholic leaders used the new regime to redress the wound of the column's loss. In May 1939, only two months after the establishment of the protectorate, Durych, who in the 1920s had decried the use of Jan Hus as a symbol of Czechoslovakia, petitioned Hácha to support the column's rebuilding: "The destruction of the Column of the Virgin Mary has not been atoned for."[20] Much as a decade earlier, Durych did not suggest abandoning Czech nationalism, but instead suggested that the column could symbolize a new form of this nationalism. Durych appealed to Hácha as a fellow believer as well as a leader who wanted to portray himself as a true Czech. Durych wrote that Mary was and had always been the "national mother, queen, and protector of the country."[21] The Czechs brought shame upon their nation by abandoning Mary as their symbol, he said, while neighboring countries continued to call her *Regina*. He assured Hácha that he only needed his approval for the project; voluntary associations would raise the necessary funds. The presidential chancellery responded, promising Durych that his request would be carefully considered. During the tumultuous protectorate and Second World War, however, the resurrection of the Marian Column never came to fruition; the column did not rise again, but the era allowed the voices of its supporters to rise in a way they never could during the First Republic.

Hus during the War

Hus had stood for Czech nationalists' revolutionary goals since his memory was reinvented in the nineteenth century. In the early years of the occupation, journalists occasionally and cautiously used Hus's memory to criticize the occupying regime. On Jan Hus Day, July 6, in 1939, editorials in several newspapers reminded readers that Hus did not tolerate repression, and stood for freedom of speech. Without directly addressing the political atmosphere of the new protectorate, the articles used Hus's legacy to express dismay at the recent loss of freedoms. *Lidové noviny* promoted a day of "quiet reflection," encouraging citizens to think about Hus's importance in a time of war.[22]

However, other writers took the opportunity of the anniversary to critique the First Republic's inequities. Bohumil Švanda, writing in the Agrarian daily newspaper, *Venkov,* condemned the anti-Catholicism he believed Hus celebrations promoted,[23] and argued that Czechs should understand Hussite history in its own right, not from contemporary political motives. Švanda encouraged his readers to embrace, instead, the historic memory of Wenceslas—but, in writing this, he betrayed his own political allegiance to Hácha's circle: Švanda's column displayed a complete reversal from the party's policy under Švehla, who had defended Hus's memory and demonstrated that it did not conflict with his own Catholicism. But Švehla had died in 1933, and Švanda had distanced his party from Hus's legacy. Several leaders in the Agrarian Party saw compromise with the Germans as the only way to maintain some Czechoslovak independence, and Švehla's successor to the Agrarian Party leadership, Rudolf Beran, served as Hácha's prime minister during the Second Republic. (Ultimately, the Agrarians' cooperation with the Second Republic and protectorate led to the party's demise: the compromising collaboration of some of the Agrarian Party leadership led the National Front Coalition to disband the party after the war's end.)

There were numerous editorials in Prague's remaining newspapers and several public commemorations of Jan Hus in July 1939. Prague's mayor laid a wreath at the Hus Memorial, and the university organized a lecture by historian Karel Vojtíšek. St. Nicholas and St. Salvator, in the Old Town, also organized services in Hus's memory. Although both edifices dated from the Jesuit counter-reformation and represented the Bohemian baroque style lauded by the Nazi propagandists, both were Protestant churches: during the First Republic, the Czechoslovak National Church and the Evangelical Church of Czech Brethren had purchased the buildings for their congregations, despite the symbolic incongruity of the architecture. After the 1939 Hus Day religious services, congregants met up with Czech legionnaires, members of several Prague voluntary associations, and girls in Czech national costume; a Hussite minister read from Psalms and the gatherers sang the Hussite hymn, "Ye, who are God's Warriors."[24]

As the German occupation wore on, there were increasingly fewer opportunities for such displays of national feeling. The universities were closed in November 1939 following student demonstrations, and the protectorate government abolished all large-scale public gatherings. The war economy of course halted any plans to erect buildings or monuments. Work on the National Monument on Vítkov Hill, for example, came to a standstill during the war, and the large building there was used to store German armaments.

A Sanctuary in Prague

Another site that reflected Prague's complex religious history became inexorably linked to the tragic war years. The church of Sts. Cyril and Methodius provided sanctuary for members of the Czech Resistance, who assassinated Nazi *Reichsprotektor* Reinhardt Heydrich in 1942. Its crypt was the scene of a pitched battle between seven Czech parachutists and Nazi soldiers.

The small Czechoslovak orthodox community purchased the eighteenth-century baroque church from Prague Technical University in 1933 and dedicated the building on Saint Wenceslas's feast day, September 28, 1935. Designed by famed architect Kilian Ignaz Dientzenhofer, the church was one of many baroque edifices that now housed non–Roman Catholic denominations. The church board named the church after Cyril and Methodius, the ninth-century Thessalonian evangelists who brought Christianity to the Slavs and who, in feuds over Czech identity, were often offered as compromise symbols.[25]

During the German occupation, the church of Sts. Cyril and Methodius became a headquarters of the small Czech resistance movement. From the beginning of the war, Vladimír Petřek, the church's patriotic chaplain, hid persecuted individuals and obtained false baptismal certificates for Jews. The bishop of the Czechoslovak Orthodox Church, Matěj Gorazd, a former Roman Catholic priest who broke from the church during World War I, also worked closely with the Czech resistance.

Although there were resistance activists like Petřek and Gorazd, the protectorate's citizens became known for their complacency under occupation. This partly stemmed from Hitler's 1941 appointment of Heydrich—among the most brutal of Nazi leaders—as *Reichsprotektor* of Bohemia and Moravia. Since 1931, Heydrich had been a member of the SS (*Schutzstaffel*); he was responsible for creating the SD (the *Sicherheitdienst*, the intelligence wing of the SS), for founding the *Einsatzgruppen* (the Nazis' mobile killing units in Poland), and for masterminding much of the Final Solution. Hitler feared Heydrich's ambition and, by his appointment, sought to remove him from Berlin while simultaneously gaining a suitable replacement for the lenient Baron Konstantin von Neurath.

In Prague, Heydrich fancied himself a patron of the arts and decided that the city would be the cultural center of the new Reich. Of course, unlike Czech nationalists who had spent the previous century insisting on Prague's Slavic nature, Heydrich revived the city's German heritage, sponsoring operas and orchestral performances of Mozart and Beethoven. Important to his program was the outlawing of all Czech cultural groups and celebrations, thus banning any public acknowledgment of the Hussite heritage. Occasionally, however, as with the 1941 Wenceslas festivities, Heydrich tolerated carefully orchestrated events such as remembrances of the Bohemian king who had compromised with German princes.

Heydrich swiftly won the title "the Butcher of Prague," by ordering the public hanging of two hundred Czechs suspected of resistance activities and the transport of thousands of Jews from Terezín (in German, Theresienstadt) in Northern Bohemia to the death camps in the East. Heydrich's method has been characterized as a "carrot and stick" approach: while enforcing reprisals against any potential Czech national demonstration, Heydrich worked to stabilize the economy and employ the citizens. As a result, the Czechs never did establish the extensive resistance movement such as existed in Poland or even Slovakia.

Yet the most famous act of Czech resistance directly involved Heydrich. In London, the Czech government-in-exile worked with British commandos to plot the assassination of the *Reichsprotektor*. In May 1942, two Czechs, Jan Kubiš and Josef Gabčík, parachuted into Bohemia, met up with fellow resisters, and plotted an attack on Heydrich's convoy. On May 27, Heydrich was severely wounded by a grenade that Kubiš launched at his car, and the *Reichsprotektor* died ten days later.[26]

Kubiš and Gabčík escaped, and took refuge at Sts. Cyril and Methodius, where Petřek, his family, and several congregants protected them despite Hácha's warning that anyone "who works against the Reich in the slightest way will be destroyed."[27] On June 18, 1942, however, eight hundred Gestapo soldiers surrounded the building. Three of the Czech assassination team were killed; the remaining four committed suicide. For aiding and protecting the rebellion, Bishop Gorazd, Petřek, another priest, and ten congregants were killed by a German firing squad. The Czechoslovak Orthodox Church was disbanded and its property confiscated. The Nazi government then decided to take severe action against Bohemia, and razed the small town of Lidice, said to have connections to the assassins. The entire adult male population was shot, the women were deported to concentration camps, and most of the children were removed for adoption into German families.

In 1947, a memorial plaque was placed on the bullet-ridden walls of Sts. Cyril and Methodius Church. Yet during the Communist era, little was done to commemorate this chapter in Prague's wartime history. The Communist government could not afford to remind its population of a Czechoslovak resistance, since its own identity rested on the nation's debt to the heroic Red Army of the Soviet Union. Not until 1995, on the sixtieth anniversary of the church's rededication, was this history fully acknowledged, again on the feast day of patron saint Wenceslas.

The End of the War, the Return of Hus

After the deadly reprisals following Heydrich's assassination, there was little organized resistance in the protectorate. On May 5, 1945, with German defeat

Memorial to Heydrich's assassins and the victims of the Nazi reprisal. Exterior wall of Sts. Cyril and Methodius Church riddled with bullet holes. Photo by author.

assured, Prague residents finally took to the streets to fight their occupiers. For three days, Prague citizens built barricades throughout the city, and for the first time in the war, the German army attacked Prague landmarks. Most notably, the section of Old Town Hall nearest the Jan Hus Memorial was burned and destroyed. The postwar state would decide not to rebuild it, in part so its ruins might stand as a reminder of the suffering of the city during the war. Over sixteen hundred Czechs were killed in skirmishes throughout the city, and the places of their deaths are marked as small "sites of memory."[28]

On May 10, 1945, two days after the uprising ended, Edvard Beneš and his exile government returned to Prague. The members of Hácha's puppet government resigned, and Hácha died in prison only weeks later, as a result of his severe diabetes. Most remember Hácha as a pathetic figure, who arrogantly believed he could save his nation by martyring himself and capitulating to German demands. However, his willingness, even eagerness, to support anti-Semitic policies demonstrated the narrow, exclusionary nationalism advocated by the Czech Right during the war.

Beneš's government quickly reinstituted the familiar symbols of nationalism from the First Republic, particularly the figure of Jan Hus. Left-wing parties, which supported the revolutionary legacy of the Hussite tradition, dominated the National Front coalition that came to power in the April 1945 Košice Program. Four groups of intellectuals—Communists, nationally oriented Socialists, Protestants, and Roman Catholics—dominated the political-national discourse in the immediate postwar period (as Bradley Abrams has shown); of these, only the Catholics did not extol the virtues of modern Hussitism. Further, Protestant intellectuals of the Czechoslovak Church and the Church of Evangelical Czech Brethren moved increasingly to the Left, for several reasons: the oppression of their leaders under German occupation, a belief in the revolutionary message of Hussite history, and an opportunism that predicted the ultimate victory of Communism.[29] In the years after the war, the desire of Czechoslovakia's Third Republic to link with the legacy of the First thus combined with the strong assertion of the militaristic and revolutionary history of the Hussite movement.

The Third Republic commemorated Jan Hus Day in each year of its existence, from 1945 to 1947. The flexible memory of the martyr appealed to the Communist and Czechoslovak Socialist leaders who spoke at these ceremonies. Communists emphasized Hus's revolutionary message and linked Hussite warriors to the Red Army liberators who had freed most of Czechoslovakia. Socialists recalled Hus's anti-German statements, and emphasized the link between the Hussite wars and the Slavic-German battles of the Second World War.[30] The citizenry seemed ready to embrace Hus's memory again, as well; in 1946 a survey found that the public considered the Hussite era the "most glorious" in Czech history.[31] By the time of the Communist Party's seizure of power in February 1948, Hus's memory had been fully reabsorbed into the national discourse.

Chapter 10

God's Warriors on Vítkov Hill

"Let's be like Hus and Gottwald—strong and brave."

Josef Macek, Prague historian

L IKE the nation's previous governments, that of the Czechoslovak Communist party invested major resources in symbols of its power. From red stars affixed to all state buildings to statues of fallen heroes of the Second World War, new emblems marked public space for the party that declared itself the exclusive ruler of postwar Czechoslovakia. Unsurprisingly, the Communist ideology of the postwar period emphasized rebirth and renewal. Weary Europe looked to the Left for the promise of a better future. Modernity, technology, and equality would replace the brutality and selfishness of capitalism and fascism. In Czechoslovakia, as in almost all European countries, scores of citizens joined the Communist Party and longed for the new.

Yet, even in the postwar march toward the future, Czechoslovakia's Communist leaders sought connection to the past. A bond with history legitimated the party's place in the national trajectory. Marxism, of course, necessitated the ability to demonstrate that the country had indeed arrived at the Communist utopia, having successfully passed through previous stages of economic and political development; so, though the Communist movement was so often associated with internationalism, individual parties developed national ideologies and celebrated select moments of a particular nation's past. They appropriated public spaces, rather than destroy all and build anew.

Thus an incomplete project from the First Republic became the most sacred space in Communist Prague, housing the remains of deceased leaders, and works by leading Czechoslovak socialist realist artists. Vítkov Hill, the site of Hussite general Jan Žižka's victorious 1420 battle, had been intended as a site for a national monument since the late nineteenth century. The hill loomed over Žižkov, Prague's working-class district, the center of left-wing politics since the Habsburg period. It was in Žižkov pubs that František Kysela-Sauer had recruited workers to help tear down the Marian Column in 1918, and in 1946 the district had strongly supported Communist politicians in the parliamentary elections. Žižkov's residents were a major factor in the party's success in this election, during which the Communist Party received 38 percent of the national vote, more than any other individual party.

Czech Socialists with national sympathies, from several leftist interwar parties, had long looked to the revolutionary warrior as its hero, and scores of working-class voluntary organizations were named for the blind military genius. Thus, it was not particularly surprising when the party decided to complete the memorial. When the Nazis had invaded Czechoslovakia in 1939, much of the structure was already finished, and sculptor Bohumil Kafka's equestrian statue of Žižka was ready to be cast in bronze. Yet, during the first years of Communist rule, embracing Žižka as a party hero treaded on dangerous territory, religion. Of course, the official position of the party was atheism, but the history of the Bohemian reformation seemed too rich not to be mined: party leaders did not stray from the First Republic's original intention, to honor and create a cult of death around the handful of Bohemian military successes in history; they merely expanded the tribute to include their great Slavic brothers in the Red Army and to situate Communism in the arc of Czech history.[1]

At the time the Communists took over the country and the monument, the site had already had a long, but not illustrious, history. In the late nineteenth century, the Austrian government had denied Czech nationalists' efforts to erect a monument to Žižka's memory, and when a memorial design contest was finally held in 1913, the art jury found no entry worthy of selection. Originally planned simply as a monument to Žižka, the site took on broader dimensions after the declaration of independent Czechoslovakia, when nationalists proclaimed the need for a memorial in Prague of national liberation. This project was led mainly by the Czechoslovak legionnaires, who declared themselves the modern inheritors of Žižka's legacy and juxtaposed their military exploits with medieval martial history.

So, too, was the cult of death infused into the structure. The building was designed to house the cremated remains of legionnaires and of President Tomáš Masaryk, who however would decline the offer to occupy the black marble sarcophagus intended for him.[2] Although the government willingly supported the creation of the monument, this task was a low priority for the new Czechoslovak state. In fact, the entire process of conceiving and constructing the monument was disorganized, and another failed design contest occurred in 1923.

Finally, in 1925, the very year Czechoslovakia clashed with the papacy over Jan Hus commemorations, a third design competition yielded a winner. Jan Zázvorka's complicated proposal—which included an enormous gathering hall with a pipe organ and seating, smaller meeting rooms, substantial mausoleum space, and a military museum devoted to the legionnaires—was chosen, but not without outcry from the art community. Most notably, in 1927, art critic Karel Teige added the building plans to a list of "dada absurdities."[3] The building, as art historian Matthew Witkovsky would later remark, embraced functionalism but ignored functionalism's aim, to provide society with useful, practical, and well-designed structures: "Zázvorska's work travesties functionalist arguments for structures of pure utility; his heavy, static design marries the look of modernism to the layout of a Gothic cathedral."[4] Despite the criticism of intellectuals and the public's lack of interest, however, Czechoslovakia's interwar leaders participated in the monument's construction. In 1928 Masaryk laid the foundation stone, and Beneš gave a speech at the site.

This site gained more symbolic importance during World War II. The Nazi occupation forced the state to halt construction of the building, and the huge equestrian statue of Žižka was not completed. The building's inauguration, scheduled to coincide with the state's twentieth-anniversary celebrations in October 1938, obviously did not take place; during the war, the German occupiers used the giant structure to store munitions. After 1945, clearing German weapons from the site and replacing them with patriotic art became symbolic of the Communists' leading role in the liberation of Eastern Europe, a concretization of the relationship between Žižka's medieval heroics and modern struggles against tyranny. Žižka had long appealed to left-leaning nationalists, who viewed the communal living at the Southern Bohemia Tábor encampment as an early form of socialism: the Taborites, led by Žižka, had been the most radical of Hus's followers, and had given up their earthly possessions before moving with their families to Tábor.

Nonetheless, drawing comparisons between Communist and Hussite warriors still required juxtaposing Christian and Communist imagery; some artworks from the Communist era even featured Hussite preachers alongside modern soldiers. As completed in the 1950s by the Communist government, the building created a new sacred space for an atheist regime. Along with the city's Bethlehem Chapel, the National Memorial was to serve as a visual reminder of national history as well as a public gathering place. With these two structures, the new government simultaneously commemorated and re-created the past, and sought to create new traditions. What cannot be ignored about both sites is that they functioned as—and looked like—churches. They were the sites of wakes, funerals, and interments for the most revered leaders—places to pay homage to the state, the nation, and the party.

A National Memorial for the Postwar Era

Almost immediately after peace was declared, the voluntary association guiding the project renewed its efforts to complete the monument.[5] In 1947, during the period of power sharing among Czechoslovak political parties, the building was inaugurated with an exhibition, in its eastern portion. This display paid homage to soldiers who died during the Second World War, thus setting a precedent for associating the monument with the struggle against Nazism.

The building's next official use occurred after the February 1948 seizure of power by the Communist Party, but did not commemorate the party or the Red Army's achievements: in September 1948, the main gathering hall housed the remains of Czechoslovakia's second president, Edvard Beneš. In May 1945, President Beneš had been welcomed home to Prague as a national hero. After the humiliating Nazi annexation in March 1939, Beneš had fled to the United States and then to London. There he had led the Czechoslovak government-in-exile and continued to develop Czechoslovak foreign policy, his main role in the country since 1918. The Munich Accords had caused him to lose faith in the Western powers, and he had begun to look to the Soviet Union as a diplomatic partner, despite frequent warnings by his British hosts. Retaining optimism about his small nation's place in Europe, Beneš had believed that Czechoslovakia could become a bridge between East and West; beyond such idealism, he had also realized the impossibility of avoiding Soviet influence, knowing that a group of powerful Czechoslovak Communists, exiled in Moscow, were training for postwar leadership, and that the Red Army was likely to participate, or lead, the eventual liberation of his country.

After the war, few non-Communist politicians seemed to grasp the Communist Party's plan for total domination of the state. A power-sharing agreement in 1945 gave all the prewar parties, save the recently disbanded Agrarians, a place in the National Front, which would lead until elections in 1946. In 1946, the increasingly popular Communist Party won 38 percent of the popular vote, thus electing former Moscow exile Klement Gottwald prime minister in a coalition government. Once Gottwald gained leadership of the governing coalition, the Communist Party—with support from its Soviet counterpart—began work toward overthrowing its ruling partners. By 1947, Beneš began to understand Stalin's plan to bring Czechoslovakia under Soviet domination, but his failing health and despondency prevented real action. In February 1948, the leaders of the other government parties resigned from the cabinet, believing that Beneš would refuse to accept the resignations, causing the government to fall and ensuring new elections. But Beneš did not stand up to the Communists, and instead accepted the ministers' resignations; swiftly, the Communist Party filled the vacant cabinet positions with its own leaders. After a series of strokes, Beneš resigned in June and died on September 3, 1948.

Beneš's death worked to the Communists' advantage. Rather than dismissing him as a class enemy, they could celebrate this president's achievements, particularly emphasizing his embrace of the Soviet Union during the war. By granting Beneš an elaborate, official funeral and laying his body in state at the National Memorial in Vítkov Hill, the party emphasized the continuity of Czechoslovak government. Thus the new President Gottwald paid respect to his predecessor.

Although the funeral took place at the National Museum on Wenceslas Square, and the private burial occurred in Southern Bohemia near Tábor, the public visited Beneš's remains in the National Memorial's cavernous main hall. *Rude právo* published a public manifesto that emphasized Beneš's connections to Vítkov:

> Honorable President!
> During these days all the people of Prague bid you farewell with this manifesto. We wander aimlessly at the Memorial on Vítkov hill, because we stand before you for the last time and bow before you for the last time and sorrowfully express our love, respect and gratitude to you for the last time.
> On Vítkov hill, the site of the most celebrated battle in the history of the Czech people—fought by the ancestors of today's democratic order—you symbolize the culmination of this centuries-long national struggle, not only as a spiritual leader, but also as an intrepid warrior. [You fought] . . . for all that is holy in the Czechoslovak nation and for the triumph of an independent Czechoslovak state.[6]

How sincere the Communists were in their tribute is difficult to gauge. Certainly, Beneš's sympathy for socialism (he was a member of the Czechoslovak Socialists), his idealism about Czechoslovakia's place in Europe, and ultimately his weakness paved an easier road for a Communist victory. Many Czechoslovak Communists with nationalist sympathies probably saw Beneš as a bridge between capitalism and socialism in Czechoslovakia's historical-materialist arc. Of course, it was also politically wise to hail the fallen president. Despite his

feeble resistance to the Nazis in 1938 and to the Communists in 1948, Beneš remained hugely popular with the Czechoslovak people. Praising him cost little,
while disparaging the former leader would win the Party few friends.

Art and the Monument

Just as Beneš's second presidency was a transition to Communism, his
placement at Vítkov Hill represented a transition in the history of the monument. The Communist government planned to replace or add to the artwork
already housed there; in 1951 the Ministry for Information and Enlightenment
created a commission to oversee the monument's technical and artistic aspects.
Representatives from the Prague and national government joined artists and
scholars to create a new aesthetic for the memorial. The commission oversaw
design competitions for artistic pieces, and made judgments on saving or de-
stroying the art already present.[7]

During the interwar period, some of Czechoslovakia's leading artists had
contributed work to the building's interior. The structure modeled a Gothic
cathedral, with several individually decorated "side chapels." The interwar masterpiece of the edifice consisted of Max Švabinský's mosaics in the chapel designed to hold the cremated remains of Czechoslovak legionnaires. Švabinský,
one of the leading Czech artists of the twentieth century, worked on the mosaics from 1935 to 1939. The large-scale work, comprising four wall panels and
two ceiling panels, represented the heavenly rewards the legionnaires would
receive in the afterlife.

The detailed mosaic juxtaposed symbolic figures from different historical
eras on a deep turquoise background. On the first panel, men dressed as Roman senators hold palms and laurel wreaths. Above them, Czech peasants float
in the clouds carrying fruits, wheat, and farming implements. In the next panel, a French revolutionary sansculottes grips the French tricolor flag, leading
World War I soldiers, who emerge from clouds with the flags of the countries
that fought Germany and Austria-Hungary. Below the soldiers an angel floats
downward, bringing a crown to a woman seated on a throne, who weeps as she
stares at a World War I helmet on her lap. Beside the throne a humble blue-
garbed woman stands with a golden-haired boy. Both women on this panel represent alternate depictions of the Virgin Mary: a young mother and the queen
of heaven.

In the third panel, a feminine seated figure represents justice. Above her
a lifeless man is being carried to the heavens on a dark blue cloud. A weep-
ing woman reaches her hand toward him and two soldiers, one carrying a flag

with the Bohemian lion emblem, help lift him. Depicted like Christ after the crucifixion, he is naked except for a flowing cloth draped over his lap. In the fourth panel, an old bearded man—perhaps Saint Peter or God—sits on clouds in front of a Russian Orthodox Church as he writes in a book with a feather pen. Below him stand five crying women, dressed as medieval saints.

Thus, Švabinský's work, reminiscent of romantic era nationalist art, connected legionnaires to a larger revolutionary political tradition as well as to Christian symbolism.[8] Švabinský finished the chapel just as the German army completed its absorption of Bohemia and Moravia into the Reich.

After the war, even though the apolitical Švabinský was heralded by the Communists as a national artist, his work in the National Memorial won little attention. The artist, who considered the mosaics among his finest works, was bitterly disappointed that his masterwork and contribution to the monument went unrecognized and unpublicized by the state. Perhaps the religious imagery did not sit well with party officials, yet the Communists were certainly not strangers to secularizing religious imagery. Their major objection to the mosaics was the glorification of Czechoslovak legionnaires. The state sought to displace the legionnaires' memory with that of the Red Army. Certainly, the legionnaires, many of whom had joined the Whites in the Russian Civil War, were not welcomed in the Czechoslovak Communist pantheon; however, rather than destroy a valuable piece of art by a living artist whose realistic style of portraiture could prove beneficial, the state renamed the legionnaires' chapel the "Hall of the Fallen Soldiers" and placarded the room with signs and poetry celebrating the Red Army.[9] The Czechoslovak Communist Party did not at all hold the legionnaire mosaics against Švabinský, later commissioning him to paint important official portraits, most notably the Second World War hero Julius Fučík. His artwork appeared on banknotes and on dozens of stamps; nevertheless, during the Communist era, his grand mosaics remained unacknowledged.

The "ideological inconsistencies" in the Communist Party (to use the term employed by historian Jan Galandauer and others) saved another important work from the interwar period that might have otherwise been destroyed. Karel Pokorný's marble reliefs of the Czechoslovak legionnaires' heroism were slated for destruction until Prime Minister Antonín Zapotocký decided that the sculptures were too valuable and that removing them might destroy the integrity of the building. Pokorný's theme certainly did not fit the Communists' new aims for the monuments: the four reliefs—*Charge, Defend, Agony, and Death*—celebrated the martyrdom of Czechoslovak legionnaires in Italy, Albania, Serbia, and France.[10] Yet, curiously, the style of the monuments suited the Communist aesthetic; a 1937 art review of Pokorný's work exclaimed: "And the . . . style? It is superfluous, even pedantic . . . poised between realistic and gratuitous form."[11] But such a combination of classical realism with celebration of the nation's heroism practically defines Soviet socialist realism as laid out by Zhdanov in the 1930s; according to Zhdanov, art should have socialist and nationalist form and content, and must provide clear messages to instruct the masses on the meaning of the new society; indeed, the Soviet Union's postwar cultural leaders ordered the new Communist satellites to study the realist tradition in Russian art as work reflecting both anguish and triumph. Thus, in many ways, Pokorný's work prefigured the postwar trends in socialist realism. Viewing it from from afar, a visitor might easily imagine that Pokorný's was indeed a contemporary work commemorating the Second, rather than the First, World War.[12]

Of course, the Communist government also planned to place its own art in and around the monument site. In addition to commissioning scores of local artists to design fountains, plaques, and an outdoor lighting system, the technical–artistic administration held design competitions for distinctive works. A few pieces selected were typical of prewar socialist art. A competition specifically for a sculpture of a worker and a peasant yielded a winner whose entry was "realistic, serious . . . [yet] optimistic."[13] The aesthetics of the monument were complicated, however; the new artistic contributions had to reflect socialist realist philosophy while simultaneously reflecting the somber and spiritual nature of the place.

Socialist realist work after World War II in fact often adapted prewar optimism to reflect the noble suffering of Red Army soldiers. One important work of this era was Vladimir Sychra's 1953 mosaic series installed in the Hall of the Red Army, another side chapel in the National Memorial. This hall paid homage to the Soviet soldiers who lost their lives liberating Eastern Europe, and featured a symbolic marble sarcophagus representing the fallen heroes. The sarcophagus was designed by none other than that Karel Pokorný whose legionnaire friezes had nearly met an untimely fate. The eight panels feature soldiers from different branches of the Soviet military. One, for example, "Artillery Soldier," depicted a young, defiant Red Army soldier, hand on hip, one foot forward. His massive form and stalwart countenance fit well into socialist realist confines, yet his physique and manner did not rival those of 1930s Soviet art. An article in *Vytvarné umĕni* (Decorative arts) explicitly commented upon the mosaics' humility: "The author thus understands that his soldiers are like tranquil guards for our dead heroes. They are not pictured in action, but standing peacefully, as are those lying below."[14] Another review commented that the viewer and the mosaic soldiers stood face to face, as if the soldiers were speaking directly to the onlooker; these soldiers were not aloof heroes but normal people—"young, old, middle-aged."[15]

The art that most directly connected Bohemian religious history with Czechoslovak political development was Josef Malejkovský's bronze friezes for the Vítkov Hill monument's main doors. The three-dimensional detailed panels juxtapose scenes from the Hussite Wars with the Red Army liberation of Prague. But Malejkovský did not avoid the religious aspects of the Hussite struggle. The first of the twelve panels features a preacher, perhaps Hus, instructing a crowd of followers. In the next plate a priest stands behind a pulpit holding a chalice high in the air, and a group of believers stands below eager to partake in the sacramental wine denied the masses by the Catholic Church. Three subsequent tiles portray details of medieval Hussite battles—armored soldiers brandishing swords and maces. Another shows a gentle Žižka sitting among a group of children, in a pose not dissimilar to those found in children's bibles.

Even the doors' style reinforces the monument's appearance—and function—as a modern cathedral. The bronze friezes are reminiscent of the Renaissance panels added to Gothic cathedrals throughout Europe, such as the Baptistery doors in Florence. This architectural feature had regained popularity in the twentieth century, and similar friezes can be found on the 1929 exterior of St. Vitus Cathedral. Like the Florentine masterpiece, Malejkovský's doors place detailed figures in the foreground, while architectural details in the distance, such as Prague Castle or a factory complex, give depth and context.

The remaining six panels, exhibited on the right-hand door, depict modern scenes. Like the medieval theme, the modern story traces the roots of socialism through its recent triumph. In the first panel, nineteenth-century workers carrying a flag look askance as a bourgeois man in a top hat tries to lecture the young men. Next, an armed man on horseback strikes a kneeling worker. Paralleling the Hussite narrative, the noble Red Army defends its beliefs in battle against the oppressor class. In one panel Red Army soldiers sit atop a tank festooned with Communist stars and flowers handed to them by adoring women; Prague Castle looms above the crowd. In the next scene, the soldiers hand a rifle to an eager woman in a babushka; workers line up behind her awaiting weapons so they too may defend their city.

The last two panels connect the two historical periods, the Hussite and the modern. The figures in these scenes look beyond the action in their own panel. One grouping depicts soldiers gathered around a fallen comrade; they look across toward the left-hand, or Hussite, doors. So does the group of workers represented on the last panel: assembled in front of a factory, the three male and single female worker crane their necks to the outside of their frame to gaze

at the medieval scenes on the adjacent door. Here, the artist connects the two
struggles, waged five hundred years apart. The gathered workers view the arc of
history and sacrifice that has given them newfound power in their new Czechoslovakia. The triumph of these workers began not in the demonstrations of the
nineteenth century, but in the demand for sacramental wine by their forebear-
ers. Malejkovský thus connected socialist and Hussite history in the placement
of his sculpted scenes. Indeed, in the top row, a Hussite preacher lifts his right
arm and directly faces a Red Army soldier who lifts his left arm. These two
men, framing the door, convey strength, courage, and defiance.

Although the Communist inheritors of the National Memorial had to counter prewar symbolism with their own aesthetic and political vision, some works
already planned for the monument better suited the Communists' purposes.
Most important was the statue of Hussite military leader Jan Žižka. On July 14,
1950, an elaborate festival on Vítkov Hill celebrated the unveiling of Bohumil
Kafka's long-awaited Žižka Monument. The equestrian statue of the blind general stands in front of the imposing memorial building. Žižka (were he alive and
not blind and marble) would have had one of the best views in Prague, facing
Prague Castle hill and looking down on the Vltava River valley and hundreds of
towers and church spires. The statue itself was as impressive as its view: celebrated proudly as the largest equestrian statue in the world, it was noted to stand 9
meters tall, 9.6 meters long, and 5 meters wide, with a weight of 16.5 tons. The
sculptor modeled his work after Myslbek's St. Wenceslas Memorial, but vastly
increased the dimensions so that the Žižka statue could be seen from the central
Prague it overlooked. Like Švabinský's mosaics, Kafka's statue was delayed by the
German occupation. The sculptor worked on the piece until 1941, but died the
following year, leaving the work uncompleted. In 1948, the Communist government acquired the statue and commissioned sculptors to finish it. Kafka's plaster
model was transferred to sculptor Karel Mašek's workshop, where a bronze replica was cast. Ironically, Kafka's statue had been sharply criticized in the 1930s
for failing to capture Žižka's revolutionary character. The Agrarian Party politi-

Top row of Malejkovský's doors. Photo by author.

cian and former minister of defense František Udržal chastised the artist for Žižka's peaceful expression and the horse's placid stance; and demanded Kafka change his design to have Žižka brandishing a mace upon a rearing horse; the artist and the politician carried on a public and fierce debate until Udržal's death in 1938. With Kafka's subsequent death only minor changes on Žižka's expression and in the angle of his head were made. In the case of this monument, it was the interwar Agrarian Party rather than the postwar Communists that echoed socialist realist art criticism;[16] Udržal had insisted that the statue portray the revolutionary who helped create a new Europe, but the Communist Party was more expeditious. It used a state celebration, rather than the statue's demeanor, to bring out Žižka's revolutionary qualities.

The unveiling and dedication of the statue was an elaborate Communist Party ritual, presided over by Zápotocký and the cabinet of ministers. The public address was presented by the second most powerful man in Czechoslovakia after Klement Gottwald: Alexej Čepička, minister of national defense. The party used the ceremony to attack the enemies it shared with many medieval Hussites: the Catholic Church and the nobility. At Vítkov Hill, the Communists further took advantage of Žižka's military legacy to attack others, including the First Republic leaders, historians, the petite bourgeoisie, and smallholder farmers.

Čepička's main theme pronounced that the Communists' predecessors did not convey to the citizens the proper lessons about Žižka. "The exploiters . . . did not hesitate to avert our people from the revolutionary legacy of the Hussite warriors. Not only was the Vatican guilty of this diversion, but so were many from previous ages such as the ill famed Pekař, who associated Žižka with banditry and madness and Hussitism with religious fanaticism."[17] Here Čepička was referring to the early twentieth-century conservative historian Josef Pekař, who dueled with Masaryk over their divergent views on the meaning of Hus for modern Czechs.

Čepička did not let Masaryk and his government off the hook, either: "Even the pre-Munich republic, which staked out the slogan 'Tábor is our program'— not just for the Czechoslovak army but for the whole state—was not pure and honest about [its commitment to Žižka's heritage.]" Any government that supported capitalism could not be true followers of Žižka. For decades, strong, committed people from all walks of life had fought against the class leaders, the urban and rural bourgeoisie: "Jan Žižka and the deep philosophy of the Hussite military did not express the aspirations and ideas of the life of Czech nobles and after them capitalists and agrarians."[18]

Čepička blamed Beneš, even more, for tarnishing Žižka's legacy of strength and defiance in the face of adversity: "[the] disgraceful, cowardly pre-Munich capitulation testifie[d] to this."[19] The former president, honored on Vítkov Hill and compared to Žižka only two years earlier, was now accused of betraying

Army exercises in front of the Žižka Monument and National Memorial, 2004. Photo by author.

the national heritage. Whereas the weak First Republic cowered in the face of an enemy, Čepička reminded the crowd, the Soviet Army and the Communist underground in both Moscow and Czechoslovakia stood up to the Nazis. The new Czechoslovak army would never disappoint its nation. "Today, after the overthrow of the government of oppressors, . . . our people's democratic army proclaims Žižka's legacy."[20]

As the minister of national defense, Čepička set a new course, connecting Žižka to a more masculine characterization of Czech history. Whereas the humiliating defeat at White Mountain, so often memorialized in feminine imagery, presaged the state's capitulation to the Nazis, recalling Žižka's legacy would commemorate a Czech victory and boost the self-esteem of a nation that lacked military heroics. After the war, many Czechs were also experiencing survivors' guilt as the suffering of their Polish and Soviet neighbors, and their own Jewish citizens, was revealed: compared to the devastation of neighboring countries, Czechoslovakia had fared remarkably well. With the exceptions of the demolition of part of Old Town Hall, and the destruction, by an American bombing raid, of some statues on Palacký Bridge, Prague was largely unscathed, retaining its memorials and spires. Non-Jewish death tolls in Czechoslovakia were fractions of those of its neighbors.

Čepička's speech, arguing that Žižka's heroics began a centuries-long battle against oppression, was designed to tie Prague citizens more closely with the Marxist historical and revolutionary arc. Not surprisingly, he also used the opportunity to tie contemporary Communist leaders to Žižka's legacy: "This heroic statue of a past Hussite warrior, which overlooks Prague, is also proof, that every great era creates for itself leaders, who . . . in the interest of their people . . . conquer onerous tasks." Since Gottwald modeled his leadership style on Stalin, a cult of personality had swiftly grown around the party leader in the late 1940s; Čepička drew on this comparison: "It is happily true not just for the Soviet people, but for the whole of humanity, that in all people's societies stand that great man, like Stalin, a statesman and a military leader. It is fortunate that for the Czechoslovak people, that in this capacity stands our commander in chief, Klement Gottwald."[21]

Never before had a Czechoslovak leader been so boldly recognized for his military role in the state. Masaryk of course had preferred comparisons to Hus, whose philosophy the president had adopted. Although no stranger to public pageantry, Masaryk had preferred the image of philosopher king to that of military hero. Gottwald was no military leader, either: as a young man from a working-class family, he had served in the Austro-Hungarian Army, deserting toward the end of the war. He had finished his military service in the newly established Czechoslovak army, then swiftly became involved in working-class politics. Despite his lack of military prowess, however, he would be the twentieth-century leader most intimately connected with Žižka's memory.

Gottwald's Death

The pinnacle of the National Memorial's history was the decision to display the remains of Gottwald, the country's first Communist leader, on Vítkov Hill.

Gottwald's death had a certain irony. In December 1952, Gottwald's government presided over the Slanský trial, which condemned eleven high-ranking Communists—nine of them Jews—to be executed under false charges of treason and corruption. Three months later, Gottwald traveled to a frigid early-spring Moscow to attend the funeral of Stalin. There he caught a cold, which swiftly developed into pneumonia. He returned to Prague a dying man and succumbed to his illness on March 14, 1953.

Czechoslovak newspapers hailed their fallen leader, and associated his image with Stalin's. As Gottwald was among the "Moscow generation" that had spent the Second World War in the Soviet Union, he was seen as Stalin's protégé and another great liberator of the Slavic people. Gottwald's funeral was the first of a major Czechoslovak Communist in the new era, and the party spared no expense to put on an elaborate show.

The decision to inter the president's remains at Vítkov was announced swiftly, and immediately comparisons between Gottwald and Žižka emerged. Elementary schools were asked to contribute verses to a song in Gottwald's honor, and one in Prague contributed this tribute:

> *He followed the Hussite path*
> *along the shining red tracks of the Taborites*
> *He did not bargain at Munich*
> *and he unmasked the traitor in our midst.*[22]

The timing of Gottwald's death coincided with his unpopularity following the brutal Slanský trial and executions. The party hoped that Gottwald's death so coincidentally close to Stalin's could restore the Czech leader's link to wartime heroism rather than to his image of a ruthless dictator who oversaw the deaths of his own party comrades.

Party newspapers thus linked Gottwald to the Hussite legacy. A tribute in *Rudé právo* by Josef Macek was headlined "Let's be like Hus and Gottwald—strong and brave."[23] Macek was a leading historian at the Czechoslovak Academy of Sciences, whose career focused on Hussite as well as Italian Renaissance history; his 1952 work *The Hussite Revolutionary Movement* and his subsequent books provided a Marxist framework built on thorough historical research.

Throughout his article, Macek repeated the rallying call from the work's title, giving readers examples of how to be like Hus and Gottwald: "We can follow the Leninist-Stalinist path in work and in the struggle to build a proper and happy society, socialism," for example, and "We can unwaveringly support . . . our people's army." He reminded readers that Žižka fought bravely following Hus's own words, "The truth will prevail!"[24] So, too, did Gottwald, Lenin, and Stalin, he added; indeed, for Macek there was no inconsistency in the "truths" believed by Hus and Žižka versus those proclaimed by Gottwald, since these leaders devoted themselves to the lower classes. Because Žižka was a military, rather than a spiritual, leader (although one with a strong faith), Macek and other Communist theorists could link the general to their movement without explicitly discussing religion. Nonetheless, Macek did not stray away from religious themes; he mentioned the "revolutionary preachers" who spoke to the soldiers every day, and emphasized a comment from the "Roman Pope . . . who wrote . . . [that] a poor old lady in Tábor understands the Bible better than quite a few Italian bishops."[25] Although the Communist interpretation focused on the old woman's poverty, there was certainly no denial that Hus's message had been based in the Christian faith and in a personal relationship with the Bible.

Gottwald's funeral took place on Letná Plain, the large open park overlooking the Vltava River flowing through central Prague. Two years later, an enormous statue of Stalin would occupy the site, but in March 1953 Letná Plain was given over to Gottwald. After the public service, a hearse carried the president's body to the National Memorial on Vítkov Hill. Here Gottwald's connection to Žižka was reinforced through music. A parade of workers carried the casket up the steps to the National Memorial; they paused at the statue of Žižka, while singers performed the Hussite Chorale, "You who are God's warriors." (The newspaper referred to it as merely the Hussite Chorale to avoid the contentious word "God.") The body was then carried inside. As *Rudé právo* reported, "From the silent hall of the national monument rose the melody from Smetana's symphonic poem *Tábor.*" The nineteenth-century romantic musical piece about Žižka's encampment in South Bohemia was followed by a slow rendition of the Communist "International." According to the party newspaper, the stirring music enabled "every son and daughter of our land [to find] the Taborite strength to bid farewell to Klement Gottwald."[26]

At the time of Gottwald's death, the party leaders decided that the first Communist president's body should be on permanent display at Vítkov Hill. During the nine months following his death, the central committee of the Communist Party and the Prague chapter of the National Front prepared a mausoleum within the National Memorial complex. On December 5, 1953, at three in the afternoon, the mausoleum opened for party dignitaries, including members of the senate and representatives from the embassies of "people's democracies." Gottwald was laid out in a blue military uniform and hailed as a warrior in the heroic fight for socialism. The public was invited to view the body on Wednesday, Friday, or Sunday afternoons, and many Prague elementary schools took advantage of the new attraction by making it an annual class trip.

During the 1950s, numerous party commemorations took place on Vítkov Hill. In May 1955, ten years after the defeat of Germany, the Czechoslovak

Communists honored their Soviet brothers by ceremoniously opening the Hall of the Red Army in the Vítkov Hill complex. As in the dedication of the Žižka monument, Čepicka gave the keynote address, with the ubiquitous connection of Communist struggles with the Žižka heritage. Naturally, Čepicka focused on the sacrifices of Soviet soldiers in World War II, but he added: "Here, at the Vítkov Memorial, 535 years ago the Hussites fought under their leader Jan Žižka to triumph over the European feudal reaction. Here in the mausoleum lie the great son of our nation Klement Gottwald and his fellow warriors who led our working class to victory over capitalism . . . Here in this memorial hall, we remember all of our awakeners and teachers and advisors in our first steps towards a free life: the Soviet heroes."[27]

Two years later, Gottwald's successor, Antonín Zapotocký, died, and his cremated remains were placed in an urn next to Gottwald's sarcophagus. Like other objects in the Vítkov monument, Zapotocký's memorial was designed by a leading Czechoslovak artist. Karel Stipl, a professor of decorative arts who had participated in the aborted 1923 National Memorial design competition, was hired by the State Memorial Commission to create artwork for Zapotocký's shrine, a stylized bronze and gold wreath and an inscribed plaque in the central hall of the monument. Following the funeral, the National Memorial Committee continued to discuss how to maintain public interest in a site that Zapotocký, who had served on the committee, had cared deeply about. The committee carefully considered proposals to landscape the surrounding hill into a community recreational facility. There were ideas for tennis courts and playgrounds to entice families to Vítkov; others proposed musical concerts on the premises; some committee members considered having the monument function as an art gallery, and urged the state to purchase appropriate paintings by living and deceased Czechoslovak artists. However, the late 1950s was the end of the Communists' intense interest in the National Memorial; Vítkov remained a popular destination for elementary school children, who could pay homage to the father of the nation, but the site never became popular for family outings or workers' picnics.

Gottwald's Decay

As the National Memorial's popularity began to deteriorate, so too did Gottwald's remains. The president's death had caused little rupture in the Communist Party. His successors, Zapotocký as party leader and Antonín Novotný as president, were nearly as hard-line as he. Nikita Khrushchev's famous speech to the Twentieth Party Congress in Moscow, which condemned Stalin's crimes and cult of personality, caused only a ripple in Czechoslovakia, whereas it launched large-scale opposition movements in Hungary, East Germany, and Poland: the Prague Stalinists maintained control of the party and had little interest in allowing reform. Khrushchev had too much on his hands in the other Warsaw Pact countries to chastise the Prague leaders, and the hard line was maintained. A few policy changes occurred: some Communist leaders, like future President Gustav Husák, were rehabilitated and freed from prison. Yet other illegal show trials continued, and the nationalization of small farmers' property intensified.

Nonetheless, there were cracks in the Stalinists' hard wall. In 1956, the Union of Czechoslovak Writers condemned abuses by Stalin and Gottwald, and workers in Pilsen (Plzeň) and other industrial regions held strikes to protest rising prices and the unavailability of consumer goods. And, up on Vítkov hill, pieces of Klement Gottwald's body began to melt away. The president's body had never been properly embalmed, but party leaders believed that exceptional climate control at the memorial would prevent decay. In the decade following Gottwald's death, over seventy doctors and cosmetologists were employed to care for the body while hundreds of engineers and technicians tried to secure the memorial's interior environment. An operating room was set up in the basement for the frequent adjustments to the president's remains—but all to no avail: the body continued to deteriorate. Pieces of the president's face were replaced by wax prostheses, and in 1958 the memorial was closed for forty days. When Gottwald returned, he was no longer wearing his general's uniform, which had been replaced by an ordinary suit. Rumors spread through Prague that the entire body was now a wax dummy.[28]

A second wave of de-Stalinization in the Soviet Union put more demands on the Czechoslovak hard-liners to denounce the crimes of their predecessors. Zapotocký was now gone, but Novotný sought to hold his waning power. Khrushchev's October 1961 speech to the twenty-second party congress was more forceful than the one five years earlier, and was publicly broadcast throughout the Warsaw Pact. In Moscow, Stalin's own embalmed remains were removed from the mausoleum, and any remaining monuments to the leader were removed. The triple pressures of a rapidly decaying body, a growing reform movement in the Czechoslovak Party, and an anti-Stalinist Soviet Union led the party to abandon finally its cult of personality surrounding Gottwald. In December 1962, exactly nine years after Gottwald's body was first publicly displayed, the remains were taken away and cremated. A marble sarcophagus holding the former president's ashes remained, but Vítkov Hill was no longer the place for elementary school children to honor their revolutionary father.

In the following years, little attention was paid to Vítkov Hill. During the period of "normalization" that followed the Prague Spring reform movement,

Karel Lidický's *New Life* sculpture at the National Memorial. Photo by author.

some attempt was made to reinvigorate the monument. Karel Lidický's late-1970s sculpture *New Life* harkened back to the optimism of early socialist realism and featured a robust, happy family of three; the mother thrusts the baby forward to face Prague. In fact, an article in *Husitský tábor,* a journal of the

Czechoslovak church, referred to the work as "the socialist family."[29] The image of the national mother, used in the Habsburg period to promote a gentler version of patriotism, had returned. Just as the seated nursing mother had offered stability to the dizzying Hus memorial, the socialist national mother represented a nonmilitary symbol in a city occupied by Soviet tanks. The National Memorial on Vítkov Hill created masculine images for Prague, but by the 1970s the state was seeking to soften the militaristic messages with feminine imagery.

In 1979, a military ceremony did take place on Vítkov Hill. General Ludvík Svoboda, a controversial figure in Czechoslovak history, was cremated and placed alongside Gottwald's and Zapotocký's urns. Svoboda had been a military hero during the Second World War, commanded the Czechoslovak army, and served as president during the Prague Spring movement. He supported party leader Alexander Dubček's reforms—until a trip to Moscow in August 1968 and the subsequent Warsaw Pact invasion of Czechoslovakia changed his attitude toward the movement. Svoboda's war experience had created great loyalty to the Soviet Union and Red Army, and he believed Czechoslovakia must remain dependent on its mother country. He consequently became affiliated with the post-invasion "normalization" process that squelched the freedoms gained under Dubček. His love of the Soviet Union and his military background made Vítkov Hill a fitting burial place. But it also reinforced the martial image of the National Memorial, an image that one statue of a National Mother could never overcome. Vítkov Hill continued to be a scar on the Prague landscape, one that reminded citizens of tyranny rather than of revolutionary struggles for freedom.

Chapter 11

Rebuilding Bethlehem Chapel

*"It is clearly high time that this place, this cradle from which
we grew into all we became, stand as a memorial."*
Zdeněk Nejedlý, Czechoslovak Minister of Culture,
Bethlehem Chapel, July 1954

O N the 539th anniversary of Jan Hus's death, the doors opened to the restored building where the martyr had preached. Representatives of the city and national government attended the opening ceremony alongside leaders of local Protestant churches. Czech politicians had been lauding the golden Hussite era since the nineteenth century, yet the leading role of Zdeněk Nejedlý, Czechoslovakia's minister of culture, who in 1954 addressed the congregation from the chapel's pulpit, seemed incongruous in the political climate of 1950s Czechoslovakia. The longtime Communist, a cabinet minister of the still young Czechoslovak Socialist Republic, publicly extolled the virtues of a medieval priest and explained why his Party, ostensibly opposed to organized religion, had built a chapel in central Prague.

As with the National Memorial and the Žižka statue, Czechoslovak Communists were attempting to remake the functions and appearances of Prague's public spaces. Rather than completely supplant religiously themed commemorations with monuments to Socialism, the Czechoslovak Communist Party found tremendous value in continuing the Hussite cultural program of the First Republic. Although Communist leaders disparaged Masaryk's "bourgeois" interpretations of Hussitism, they relied on a remarkably similar vision of Czech national memory to legitimate their leadership in Czechoslovakia. However, it was simpler for the party to emphasize Žižka and his radical warriors who fought pope and emperor, especially as the communal lifestyle of Žižka's Táborites suited the Communist economic and social messages; to rebuild a

Rebuilding Bethlehem Chapel

religious edifice and celebrate the legacy of a priest, however, required more historical manipulation.

As had liberals earlier, Communists denied the religious symbolism of the Hussite legacy, but their rhetoric belied that claim; adopting Hussitism necessitated Christian historical references and symbols. Rather than limiting religious discourse in hopes of ending the long debate on whether Hus could be a purely secular figure, the Communists added their own complex response. This in turn led to another surprising reaction: secular dissidents began to look to Catholic symbols, such as the Marian Column, to challenge the regime.

What the Communist Party hoped to gain from such an endeavor has numerous answers. Like the nationalists in the Habsburg and early Republic periods, Czech Communists could use the Hussite heritage to wrest cultural power from the Catholic Church. They could also link themselves to the national discourse of the prewar period, thus legitimating their current rule. They could mark the capital with a "new" building with historic significance, in the perpetual quest to remake Prague. And they could create a gathering space for the new society they were creating.

Yet these reasons were fraught with contradictions. Continuing the First Republic's Hussitism linked the Communist Party with the bourgeois government it frequently decried. And, like the nationalists before them, the Communists found it difficult to excise completely the religious meaning of the Hus legend; no matter how many times Czech leaders insisted that Hus had become a secular figure, it remained impossible to ignore that this man had been a Roman Catholic priest, who died proclaiming his Christian faith. No matter how vigorously the state's leaders insisted that the Bethlehem Chapel was not a religious edifice, they could not remove religious connotations from a building so named.

In this era, Christians connected with the Hus tradition fared better than Czech Catholics. During the years that government committees focused on the process of rebuilding the chapel, the state led a campaign to break the infrastructure of the Roman Catholic Church in Czechoslovakia. Already weaker than its neighbors in Poland and Hungary, the church had little success combating the party's anticlericalism. The constitution of 1948 technically granted freedom of religion to all citizens. Article 17 stated, "Everyone is free to practice his religion, or to be without confession. The practicing of this must however not be in discord with public order or with good morals."[1] It was this caveat that enabled the party to imprison hundreds of church leaders, priests, and nuns in jails or work camps. It allowed the state to nationalize religious schools and to ban or severely censor Catholic publications, pastoral letters, and writings by Catholic intellectuals. Church property was, of course, liquidated, and priests' salaries were paid by the state. Seemingly another contradiction in policy, controlling salaries actually enabled the government to choose which priests it deemed loyal. Priests who joined the newly formed and state-sponsored Communist group Catholic Action were treated generously; other priests received little state compensation. The archbishop of Prague, Josef Beran, who led Czechoslovak Catholic leaders in the protests against these state actions, was placed under house arrest, and a 1950 show trial found nine members of Roman Catholic religious orders guilty of conspiring with foreign powers to overthrow the state.

As in the interwar period when the papal nuncio angrily left Prague during the 1925 Hus celebrations, relations between Communist Czechoslovakia and the Vatican were cut off, this time at the demand of the Communist state. After the Church excommunicated all Communists worldwide in 1949, the party retaliated by expelling the papal representative in Prague to Rome. Yet it allowed the People's Party, under the leadership of collaborator priest Josef Plojhar, to exist in the illusory multiparty coalition. (Šrámek had resigned as party chair during the February 1948 coup and died in Prague in 1956.)

Although some Catholic leaders attempted to coexist with the Communist state, this was not an official policy of the church. However, several Protestant churches—some genuinely committed, others acting out of self-preservation—embraced the new government. The Czechoslovak National Church, which in 1948 had reached a membership of one million, espoused radical politics and anti-Catholic views.[2] The Evangelical Church of Czech Brethren, led by the prominent leftist intellectual and theologian Josef Lukl Hromádka, was more cautious, but still subscribed to a doctrine of socialist Christianity and welcomed the Communist government. Both churches appreciated the Czechoslovak Communist ideology, which, as Bradley Abrams has commented, "largely muted its atheist rhetoric."[3]

Considering itself the true descendant of the Hussite Movement, the Evangelical Church joyfully announced in March 1950 the state's project to rebuild the Bethlehem Chapel. A month later, the church published in its journal its formal resolution of loyalty to the new state, citing in particular the government's commitment to rebuild the chapel, as a sign of "good will" toward Protestants.[4] However, the party's motivations were rather to legitimate Communism's place in the stream of Czechoslovak history; ensuring the loyalty of small groups of Protestant citizens was only a fringe benefit. Further, although the Evangelical Church enthusiastically supported the project, it played very little role in the actual rebuilding and rededication; the project remained firmly in the hands of the Communist Party.

Bethlehem Chapel in Czechoslovak Collective Memory

For a Communist Party to rebuild a church—indeed, to designate large sums of public funds rebuild it—there must have been something important about it. The building in question was the late-fourteenth-century Bethlehem Chapel, a Catholic church where leaders of the Czech proto-reformation had preached five centuries earlier. Little of the edifice remained by the twentieth century. The spot where the chapel had stood contained a private multifamily home, which certain architects and archaeologists claimed retained some original windows, doors, and part of a wall from the original chapel.

The Communist government was not the first to consider rebuilding this chapel, but it was the first to give itself the power to carry out the project. When the interwar government had discussed the possibility of renovating the chapel in the 1920s, the idea had been quickly dismissed because the site contained private property. That the Communists were in the business of nationalizing property did not mean that the process of acquiring and razing private homes was without conflict. Contract negotiations and feuds with property holders on Bethlehem Square engaged several government offices, from 1948 until the 1960s. The building process, too, was arduous. Archeological examinations and excavations were made on the chapel site, hundreds of workers were employed to raze and rebuild, and government committees formed to oversee the design, engineering, architecture, and the cultural heritage of the site.

History of the Bethlehem Chapel

The Bethlehem Chapel was a symbolic center of the early church reform movements in Bohemia. The church was founded in 1391 by burgher Jan Kříž and courtier Hanuš of Mulheim. Kříž was a Prague shopkeeper who donated his 800-square-meter garden for the building and a cottage and cellar for the preacher and custodian. The charter of May 24, 1391, stipulated that the chapel was being founded as a place where Prague residents could hear sermons in the Czech language. Bethlehem Chapel was never a parish church (a fact the Communists would make much of centuries later). When built, it was the largest indoor meeting space in Prague, holding up to three thousand people. Bethlehem Chapel soon became associated with Prague University and developed a reputation as a radical church community and a place for public debate. In addition to reform-minded priests and scholars, ordinary Prague citizens and even Queen Sophie, wife of Bohemian King Wenceslas IV, attended services there.[5]

As a scholar at the Prague university, Jan Hus was among several priests who preached at Bethlehem Chapel. He first spoke there in 1402, and remained a popular orator for the decade until he was forced to leave Prague for his heresy trial at Constance. After Hus's arrest, the chapel gained more historical significance when, in 1412, one Hussite follower, the Utraquist priest Jakoubek of Stříbro, introduced communion in both forms, body and blood, to the congregation. The tradition of offering lay worshippers the wine normally reserved for priests continued in the chapel until 1662, the height of the counterreformation, when the Prague university transferred the chapel to the Jesuits. When the Jesuits' order was suppressed by Pope Clement XIV in 1773, the chapel became the property of the Austrian state, and, a decade later, the chapel was made a branch of the nearby St. Giles' church and parish.

Even during the Habsburg era, the building remained associated with education. In 1786, the First Technical University was founded there, in the St. Wenceslas Seminar room, which the Jesuits had built during their custody. However, soon after the founding, an architectural study found that the building had dangerous structural issues. The vaults were beginning to collapse, and some walls contained numerous cracks. Little by little, the chapel was dismantled, as structural repairs were determined impossible. By the early nineteenth century, the destruction of the Bethlehem Chapel was complete, and a residential block was erected in its place.

The existence of Bethlehem Chapel might have been forgotten completely, but, as Hus's memory became intricately tied to the historical work of František Palacký and the revived cultural life of Czech-speaking Bohemians, the demolished chapel reemerged in the 1860s as a focal point of the national movement. As architectural historian Alois Kubiček wrote in his commemorative volume: "It is not possible to comprehend what the eventful 1860s meant for our nation. At Solferino Austrian absolutism was buried, and at Hradec Králové (Königgrätz) Austrian power in the German government was ended. It meant the salvation of Hungarian Rights, for which the Hungarians had been fighting since 1848. But attempts to secure the rights of the Czech nation, the westernmost Slavic territory on the map of Europe, were in vain. . . . But finally, the year 1868 . . . was marked by memorable and singular success."[6]

Kubiček focused on three key events from the summer of 1868: the laying of the cornerstone of the National Theater in May; the June celebration of Palacký's seventieth birthday; and the first modern commemoration of Hus's death. The last event was an international celebration held in Constance, but Prague citizens also held an observance. Czechs, who were beginning to reassert their political leadership in the "Germanized" city, gathered at the former site of Bethlehem Chapel, filling Bethlehem Square, which was decorated with wreaths, flowers, and a bust of Hus. Private homes on the square were festooned with banners; House No. 255, which stood on the spot of the former chapel, displayed a decorated statue of Hus in a large ground-floor window. The police tried to break up the celebrations, but did not know whom to target in the large crowd. A police report commented on a large gathering of "workers, women, children and servants" in Bethlehem Square. Two months later, on Saturday, September 5, 1868, the square was again the center of a Hus celebration. A banner depicting Bethlehem Chapel hung on House No. 255, and a flag with Hus's motto, "Truth is victorious," swayed in the breeze. Commemorative plaques exclaiming "Here lived Master Jan Hus" or "Here stood Bethlehem Chapel" were placed on the homes that stood upon these sites. The large crowd gathered on the square far into the night, then began the long procession to Husinec in Southern Bohemia, where Jan Hus had been born five hundred years earlier. Famous personalities of the day, including Giuseppe Garibaldi, Victor Hugo, George Sand, John Stuart Mill, and Prague writer Jan Neruda, commented on these events as a manifestation of the cultural nationalism sweeping Europe in that century, echoing Kubiček's assessment that "Celebrating Jan Hus was an important step in our political life."[7]

Bethlehem Square was the natural site for commemorating Jan Hus. As the place where Hus had famously challenged the Roman Catholic hierarchy, the square embodied the historic memory of the emerging national consciousness. However, this site soon gave way to more prominent Prague locations. Many on the steering committee for the Jan Hus Memorial considered Bethlehem Chapel too remote for so important a monument. Although located in the Old Town, the square was tucked away from the "Royal Route"; nor was it on a main shopping district thoroughfare as was Wenceslas Square. Thus Old Town Square became the center of rivalry, and the plans for a new monument seemed more important than the site of a razed building. Nor did a church building suit the needs of secular nationalists seeking to distance themselves from Hus's religious meaning. The memory of the chapel dwindled as the unveiling of the Hus Memorial, the toppling of the Marian Column, and the 1925 national Hus celebrations cemented Old Town Square as the center of Prague's Czech—and Hussite—identity.

Nonetheless, a small group of scholars remained intrigued by the history of the Bethlehem Chapel's former site. In preparation for the subdued 1915 commemorations of Hus's death, V. Vojtíšek wrote an article, "O konči kaple Betlémské" [Regarding the End of the Bethlehem Chapel], the first known publication to raise the possibility of building a likeness of the original building. During the same year, Josef Teige, the city's archivist, published an article, "The Foundations of the Old Topography of Prague," which included rich seventeenth-century archival materials about Bethlehem Chapel and the surrounding homes. The following year, an article in the *Časopis společnosti přátel starožitnosti českých* (Society of Friends of Bohemian Antiquities) offered skepticism that the last remains of the chapel had been completely destroyed in 1855.[8]

These publications inspired Kubiček, who came to a new "more hopeful conclusion" about the ultimate fate of the chapel. The protocol of the magistrate's building commission from February 27, 1836, contained information on a contemporary renovation to House No. 255. The report indicated that the home would use existing brick and stonework up to the second floor, and that the third floor would be newly built. In the tense atmosphere of Prague during World War I, Kubiček kept his theory to himself. But in October 1919, he brought the findings to the leadership of *Společnost Husova musea* (Association of the Hus Museum), a loose-knit group of university professors and other intellectuals who shared a common interest in the Hussite period. This impressive group included Ferdinand Hrejša, a Protestant theologian and historian, and Zdeněk Nejedlý, a music historian who would later serve as minister of education in the Communist government. With their support, Kubiček conducted structural research on House No. 255. In March 1920, he concluded that two of its perimeter walls, the east and west, were original to Bethlehem Chapel. Much of the original north wall also remained; the southern wall had been completely destroyed. The investigation uncovered exciting evidence, including demarcations of three original windows and two entrances to the chapel, excerpts of Gothic writing on the western wall, an artesian well, and the base of a pillar.

Immediately after these discoveries, Zdeněk Wirth, Prague's leading architectural historian, located the 1783 architectural plans of Bethlehem Chapel and its surroundings, and Ferdinand Hrejša discovered plans from 1661. Wirth, who had been involved in several building preservation projects in Prague, presented reproductions of the plans and photographs to the State Archeological Memorials Committee in 1922. That same year, *Společnost Husova Musea* (Society of the Hus Museum) published a book titled *Bethlehem Chapel: Its History and the Preservation of Its Remnants.* The book included a historical overview by F. M. Bartoš and this pronouncement from Hrejša: "Our people will certainly heed the call to preserve the remnants of the chapel . . . just as today we know we must preserve the life and spirit of Hus."[9]

Indeed, the group had reason for hope, as Masaryk's government tied itself to Hussite lore. Beginning almost immediately after the foundation of Czechoslovakia, the Society of the Hus Museum, as well as individual citizens, lobbied several branches of the government to purchase the houses numbered 254, 255, and 256 in order to rebuild the chapel. In 1919, the society contacted the Ministry of Education, and in 1920 a petition was sent to the newly formed

Czechoslovak parliament.[10] In 1930, Kubiček wrote directly to the presidential chancellery, and throughout the 1930s a flurry of letters reached the Ministry of Education and the Ministerial Council.[11] Each letter reported on new architecutral findings and reminded government leaders that the chapel was "a monument of great importance."[12] One letter even remarked on the age of a "Dr. Mayer," who owned House No. 255, and suggested that the Ministerial Council make preparations to purchase the house upon the inevitable passing of this "tottering" man of "quite advanced age" who "constantly complained" about his health. Clearly, the Bethlehem Chapel supporters had investigated not only the archeology of the site but also the status of its occupants. In a later reflection, Kubiček emphasized the "German background" of House No. 255's owner, reinforcing the notion that this landmark of the Czech past had been destroyed by enemies of the state.[13]

Despite these successes and the optimism of the time, Prague institutions responded unevenly to the proposed project. The Memorial Committee of the City of Prague, and the Club for Old Prague continually renewed the plea for the chapel, but Charles University refused to support them. This was an important loss, as the university could claim the strongest historical connection to the building. Thus, as Kubiček later put it, "It was not for this generation to renew the Bethlehem Chapel."[14]

Architect of an Idea

After the devastation of the Second World War and the Communist coup in February 1948, few Prague citizens could have imagined that *their* generation would watch the Bethlehem Chapel rise. Yet, it was the Communist Party leadership that sanctioned and planned the renovation of the historic site. Much of the reliance on Jan Hus as a source for Communist nationalism in Czechoslovakia can be attributed to Zdeněk Nejedlý, who served Communist Czechoslovakia as minister of education, science, and arts from 1948 to 1953. When he was appointed to the multiparty cabinet in 1945, Nejedlý was already a respected elder scholar, well known in intellectual circles. Among left-leaning intellectuals, he was at the forefront in developing an ideology that could fuse socialist ideals with a Czech national trajectory.

Born in 1878, Nejedlý spent his childhood in Litomyšl, a town in East Bohemia. Hailing from this hometown of Bedřich Smetana, the young Nejedlý was surrounded by the romantic music of the nationalist composer, who popularized Czech folk songs and stories in such operas as the *Libuše* and *The Bartered Bride* and such orchestral pieces as *Má vlast* (My Country). Nejedlý's father was a schoolteacher and also a composer, who taught music to his eager son. The

young Nejedlý must also have been aware of the nineteenth-century national-   ⚉
ist writers Alois Jirásek and Božena Němcová, who had lived for a time in this   197
medieval town.

Nejedlý left Litomyšl to attend university in Prague, where he studied under
Jaroslav Goll. Among the most prominent Bohemian historians of the era, Goll
passed to this top pupil his dedication to Czech history and his commitment
to positivism. Goll frequently disagreed on historical questions with Tomáš
Masaryk, advocating a factual, as opposed to a spiritual, approach to national history. Yet even Goll was not immune to the nationalist passions in the
Prague academy; in 1875, the young historian wrote that he "could not imagine
a Czech of any religious denomination or political party 'who when speaking
about the consequences of the White Mountain could remain entirely calm and
cool and could content himself simply with an explanation of how these events
came to pass.'"[15]

Although Goll and Nejedlý quarreled with Masaryk's idealized reading of the
Czech past, they could not avoid the infectiousness of Czech cultural patriotism.
Nejedlý's early work adhered to Goll's positivism, but reflected an admiration for
the achievements of both the Hussite era and the nineteenth-century national
revival. In 1904, while only twenty-six, he published his first book, *The History of
Pre-Hussite Song in Bohemia*. Three years later, he followed this with *The Origins
of Hussite Song,* and in 1913 with *The History of Hussite Song during the Hussite
Wars*. The prolific historian continued to publish after the foundation of Czechoslovakia; his opus included a four-volume work on Smetana's life and music.
Nejedlý wrote not only about music, however, but also about fellow Litomyšl
residents, the nineteenth-century writers Němcová and Jirásek. But even while
writing his scholarly works, Nejedlý continued to develop strong leftist political beliefs, and he contributed to Communist journals throughout the interwar
period. He also devoted himself to a four-volume critique of the president's philosophy, *T. G. Masaryk 1930–1937*, though the opus remained unfinished.

It was not until after 1945 and Nejedlý's return from the Soviet Union, where
he had illegally fled following the Nazi takeover, that he thoroughly fused his
academic interests in Hussite music and nineteenth-century literature, with his
Communist ideology. While in Moscow, Nejedlý had worked as a professor and
researcher at the Historical Institute of the Soviet Academy of Sciences. Like
Klement Gottwald, the first Communist president, others, including Nejedlý,
who lived in the Soviet Union during the war became the first leaders of the
new Communist Czechoslovakia. In 1946, after returning to Czechoslovakia,
he published *Komunisté—dědici velkých tradic českého národa* (Communists—
The Heirs of the Great Traditions of the Czech Nation).[16] This book laid out the
philosophy Nejedlý would use to guide the postwar nation's cultural life.

Nejedlý certainly did not invent the connections between the Hussite tradition and Socialism; already in 1903, Socialists were decrying the Hus Monument committee's interpretations, which did not emphasize the Hussite warriors' communal living. But Nejedlý was the person who articulated these links most clearly, and he was the first in Czechoslovakia to have the power to implement this version of the Hus legacy.

The Communists' reasons for promoting Hussite links were manifold. Of course, Hus's iniquitous treatment by the Roman Catholic Church served the party's strong anticlericalism. Yet Communist Hussitism went deeper than anti-Catholic politics. In particular, the historian Nejedlý understood the centrality of history to Czech politics, since much of the Czech national movement was founded by historians and historical linguists attempting to distinguish their small nation's identity from the surrounding German culture. Anti-Germanism was a key link among the Hussite period, the national renaissance, and the new Communist era. Not unlike politicians in earlier eras, when Czech nationalists cast the Hussite-era disputes as between the Czech-speaking and the German-speaking Prague citizens, and between Bohemian Czechs and the surrounding German population, the Communists emphasized the national character of the conflict. During Hus's era, German-speakers in Prague had begun to feel at a tremendous disadvantage to their Czech neighbors; particularly hard-hit by the plague in the 1380s, German townspeople had feared the popularity and power of the Czech-speaking renegade priest. In the 1409 Kutná Hora decrees, frequently cited by Communist intellectuals like Nejedlý, King Wenceslas IV had given power to Hus's followers at Prague University, causing an uproar among two hundred German-speaking scholars and students, who then left Prague to found Leipzig University. The Germans' unwillingness to support Hus's teaching, according to the Communist intellectuals, had been a precursor to the long-standing conflicts between Czechs and Germans, described by Palacký in the nineteenth century. According to Nejedlý and others, the conflicts with Germany culminated with the viciousness of the Second World War. And, naturally, it was the Communists, led by the Red Army, who defended Slavdom from German aggression and cruelty. In their rhetoric, the Communist leaders emphasized the Pan-Slavic orientation of Hus: his linguistic work improved the West Slavic writing system; his preaching in a Slavic tongue signaled his pro-Eastern feelings.

Communist intellectuals also focused on the social, rather than the religious, aspect of Hus's reforms. The changes Hus made to church services served the poorer classes, since they were not required to know a second language to understand the sermon. Promoting the vernacular aided the medieval working class, according to Nejedlý. Hus also preached against the secular wealth of the church, and criticized such practices as selling indulgences and excessive tith-ing. Each of these actions presaged Marxist understanding of the exploitation of the lower classes by rich institutions such as the church and the nobility. (Of course, Hus also found tremendous support among the Bohemian nobility.) The legacy of Hus's life work, including the Hussite Wars, was, like his religious reforms, interpreted along class lines.

Nejedlý's rhetoric was not entirely disingenuous. He possessed remarkable knowledge of Bohemian history and culture, and interpreted these through his Marxist lens. To be sure, Nejedlý was also a master of politics and rhetoric, but he used these gifts to promote his analysis of the national past. As a dialec-tic thinker, he believed that the Czech lands had reached the culmination of a history of class conflicts, often symbolized by national and religious discord. Rather than dismissing national history as simply aristocratic and bourgeois, he looked to create a parallel working-class narrative. That his interpretations often glossed over details that did not fit his political needs does not mean that he only used Hus's legacy from political expediency. A scholar who had devoted much of his career to researching remote sources on medieval music, Nejedlý loved the past he investigated as well as the future utopia he believed his party could create.

Reconstructing Bethlehem Chapel

The plan to rebuild the chapel was launched at a meeting of the state's cabi-net ministers in July 1948. This meeting was only the ninth gathering of min-isters in the five months since the Communist Party had consolidated power in the February 1948 coup. July was a landmark month for the Czechoslovak Communists, as they forcibly folded the Social Democrats into the Communist Party and replaced the leadership of the handful of remaining non-Communist parties with puppet bosses.

Yet the state ministers still found time to add the Bethlehem Chapel to their meeting agenda of July 30, 1948. Earlier that month, on July 13, Nejedlý had sent a memo to his fellow ministers to consider allocating funds for the chapel renovation. He informed them that the homes at numbers 254, 255, and 256 Bethlehem Square would have to be at least partially destroyed, as they stood on the chapel's former site. And, though the party's program of class warfare against the bourgeoisie included confiscation of property, Nejedlý warned his colleagues that the state should tread lightly in this case. In many instances, Czechoslovak families whose homes were nationalized were permitted to stay in them; private homes were converted to multifamily dwellings, but the origi-nal family often could remain in one of the divisions. However, since the living spaces on Bethlehem Square were to be razed, the owners could not remain. Nejedlý must have realized that confiscating these properties and dismissing the owners would not benefit public relations about his project. The cabinet ministers agreed that the state would, therefore, *purchase* the homes from the current owners, and the Ministry of Finance agreed to allocate twelve million crowns to begin the project, with more funds available when construction was under way.[17]

Although Nejedlý seemed to understand that caution was necessary, the acquisition of the buildings on Bethlehem Square was anything but smooth. The process would occupy several branches the government for over a decade, and negotiations on the financial settlements continued into the 1960s. Many assume that the Communist Party forcibly and brutally seized the property of its citizens, and there were certainly such cases, but the more common scenario was a combination of financial compensation, legal action through the courts and government hearing boards, as well as threats and intimidation. The state was inconsistent in how it responded to the complaints of displaced residents, but did have in place a bureaucracy to assess property and compensate owners. What is remarkable about the individual cases in the case of Bethlehem Square was how far the Communist government was willing to work to justify and carry out this controversial project.

The first site to be nationalized was number 255, a plot which housed several buildings with multiple owners: an auto school and several garages owned by Josef Němec (whose name, government documents revealed, translates as Josef "German"), a small shop owned by a Mr. Červinka, and an apartment building. The chapel extended into other properties, but number 255 was centered on the former location of Hus's church. The building committee of the renovation project also planned to use the property's courtyard for the preparatory engineering and construction work. Notices were therefore sent to the owner of the auto school that his property was confiscated and that he needed to evacuate the garages, which were scheduled to be torn down immediately. A professor of archeology at Charles University, Antonín Frinta, was appointed national manager of the property; engineers, architects, and archeological researchers immediately occupied the courtyard, and the Committee for the Renovation of Bethlehem Chapel took over several rooms in the main building for meeting and office space.

Frinta clearly felt uncomfortable with the role he was asked to play. He believed that as the appointed manager, he might be able to prevent the destruction of some persons' property. In late 1948, he informed the building committee that he did not think that it was necessary to tear down the garages immediately, particularly since an architectural plan had not yet been finalized. His recommendations were overturned by the state economic commission, which cited the building committee's need for the entire courtyard area; the garages were destroyed in early 1949, but the small shop and apartment remained on the property site.[18]

While contributing to the archeological research on the chapel, Frinta continued to advocate for the owners and residents of plot 255. On June 18, 1949, Frinta wrote to the Ministry of Education, expressing his dismay that a bureau devoted to culture and learning was acting in such a high-handed manner. He informed the ministry that Červinka, the owner of the store, had shut the shop and left the premises. According to Frinta, Červinka was "suffering greatly at [their] unresponsiveness to his correspondences." He also reported that Mrs. Musilová, an elderly resident in the apartment building, had left the premises, in apparent response to the threats of architect Kubiček on behalf of the Committee for the Renovation of the Bethlehem Chapel. According to Frinta, Musilová had never been formally notified that she needed to evacuate the building; she was paid up in her rent through the year, and yet had fearfully left her apartment and many of her belongings. She had retained her keys, but when she had returned to collect her possessions, she told Frinta, several items were missing. Frinta wrote that, as the state-appointed manager, he was ashamed that the new government had acted so carelessly. He complained that there was a lack of supervision at the site and that the residents had been treated with disrespect.[19] In response to his letter, Frinta was dismissed from his post and from all involvement in the chapel renovation.[20]

Next door, at number 256, similar strife took place, within walls that once had housed a portion of the medieval sacristy. Several remnants of Bethlehem Chapel were located at this site, so the state concluded that none of the building could be saved. In 1948, the multifamily dwelling housed the owner, Anna Stipková, and her tenants: a mechanic, a furrier, and several pensioners and widows. On the ground floor was a small meat processing operation. The tenants were informed in late 1948 that they should find other accommodations, and Stipková was permitted to "rent" her apartment from the state temporarily "at a fair and reasonable rate."[21]

Stipková hired Jan Herda, a lawyer, to haggle with the state on financial compensation. She submitted complaints that the archeological research team disturbed her frequently and damaged some of her belongings, and demanded that these grievances be redressed in the settlement. The State Archeological Institute retorted, claiming that Stipková, who was referred to as "the renter" rather than the former owner, was an "old lady . . . with a nervous condition" and that she had imagined her claims.[22] Stipková and her lawyer quibbled with the Ministry of Technology on their settlement until July 1949, when the state threatened to cancel its debt to her altogether. Reminding Stipková that this was an era when ownership itself had been abolished, the state warned that if she made any more demands she would receive no payment. In July 1949, Herda drew up a contract that gave Stipková slightly more than one million crowns and designated the state to pay the taxes on the transaction. Stipková moved in with her son's family, and did not contact the state again.[23]

Another family on the square did not settle its claim nearly so swiftly, and negotiations continued into the 1960s. House No. 254 was not originally slated for complete destruction.[24] In March 1949, the cabinet of ministers approved a report that limited structural changes on 254 to reducing the size of two large apartments and evacuating the smallest of several offices on the ground floor. However, in January 1950, the Koblas family was informed that the entire property was to be nationalized and razed "in the interest of the whole country." According to the District National Committee in Prague, "The public interest in renovating the Bethlehem Chapel is higher than the public interest of saving one residential building." Like Stipková, the Koblas family was told that they could negotiate compensation with the government.[25]

The multifamily House No. 254 was co-owned by Bohumil Koblas, an elderly widower, and his daughter Františka Koblasová, a dentist whose private practice was also in the building. The family hired a lawyer, František Jirsa, who immediately informed the state that the family wanted to amicably settle the question of compensation. In April 1950, the District Committee informed the family that the value of their home was 1,275,000 crowns, noting that the prices for domestic housing had fallen considerably, since property ownership was no longer legal. There was little the family could do to dispute the price, but Františka Koblasová was determined to be compensated for the considerable expenses she had accrued when she had established her dental practice in the building. In December 1950, she presented the Ministry of Technology with a long list of work she had contracted on the physical structure of the building, from thorough cleanings to painting and linoleum-laying to installation of electricity. While Koblasová lobbied the state for further payments, the family did not pay taxes on the settlement they had already won.[26]

Koblasová's campaign continued until her sudden death in 1952. With the death of her father shortly before, the responsibility of the property settlement fell to her brother, also named Bohumil Koblas. In February 1953, the state's legal advisory board received an emotional letter from Koblas, who sought relief from the burdensome tax bills he was receiving; he was, he said, simply unable to afford the continually compounding tax; he was unable to tap into any of the settlement his father and sister had received, for the account that the money should have been in was empty. Koblas informed the board that he was not a property owner and that he worked for a newly formed farm cooperative outside Prague, and held a second job as a coachman. The cooperative had held his pay since the beginning of 1953 as a penalty for the unpaid taxes. Toward the end of the letter, Koblas centered in capital letters on one line the single word, PLEASE.

The state could not be moved by the heartfelt plea.[27] After an additional eight years of hearings with various state agencies, Koblas and his attorney learned that all monies associated with the nationalization of House No. 254 would remain locked in a state bank account.[28] He received no compensation for his family's property.

Architectural Plans

While ministries of the new state contended with the confiscation and evacuation of associated properties, the building committee for the renovation of the Bethlehem Chapel was meeting weekly to plan the project. The committee was chaired by the architect Alois Kubiček, who had conducted much of the interwar research on the site and who later wrote the memoir of the rebuilding of the chapel. Although Nejedlý did not attend committee meetings, his representatives let his tastes and wishes be known to the working group. The design of the project itself was the work of professor and architect Jaroslav Fragner and his colleague Professor B. Hacar.

To discourage future criticism that the work on the chapel was not "authentic," Kubiček frequently remarked on the difficulty of the task his committee undertook. The researchers believed that Bethlehem Chapel had been a unique building even in its own era; the design committee claimed there was no existing building that would indicate the correct structure. The project leaders explained that Bethlehem Chapel could not be compared to medieval cathedrals and castles renovated during the nineteenth century: the interior and exterior of Bethlehem Chapel was altogether different from these structures. In particular, the building committee believed that the roof design was unique among Gothic buildings. According to Kubiček, it was "not possible for the architect to find an existing medieval building with . . . this particular type of gable." A seventeenth-century account convinced the committee that the chapel had, on the façade's south and north sides, two powerful gables, but the details of the design were unknown; in the last good drawing of the chapel, J. D. Huber's from 1769, the gables had already been taken down. The committee, therefore, gave the architect full freedom to create a new solution to the gables and roof; Fragner decided to use wood for the roof's timberwork and beams because it seemed appropriate to such a monument. To support such a roof, new pillars were built in the chapel's interior.

Kubiček further noted that the windows had lost their stone workmanship, and any remaining brickwork of the chapel only filled in parts of the modern construction. The committee's archeologists had searched for small fragments of bricks, stone, and tile, but, he said, for safety reasons the façade and flood walls of the chapel were entirely new. To add more authenticity to the design, the committee insisted that, "for the first time in our new era," the project's artisans were using "methods of the old middle ages." For example, a ceramics firm outside of Prague made tiles using a medieval technique.[29]

Nejedlý was particularly concerned with the decorations in the chapel's interior walls. Medieval accounts indicated the existence of frescoes on the walls, but these had been lost, with one exception: on the rear wall, there was a preserved section of Gothic writing, ostensibly from the fifteenth century. As the renovation moved along, new frescoes were created for each chapel wall according to the ideas of Nejedlý, who submitted proposals for the new décor. Art historians and academic artists from the Academy of Applied Arts designed these frescoes to look like fragments of medieval drawings and colors. They included quotes from the Richenthal Chronicle (a fifteenth-century text that described the Council of Constance), Hussite songs, and the Hussite-era

Detail of Restored Bethlehem Chapel. Photo by author.

Czech Bible. Several frescoes were copies from the Jena Codex, a rare contemporary Hussite work, presented to Czechoslovakia by the president of the German Democratic Republic, Wilhelm Pieck. Illustrations from the Codex were turned into slides that the art academy students projected on the walls and traced onto damp plaster.[30] Above the rough stone section was a medieval-style painting depicting Jan Hus being burned at the stake. Like so many pictures of Hus, this work uncannily resembled a medieval portrait of Christ's crucifixion. In it, Hus stands tied to a stake upon a burning pile of logs, yet he maintains a peaceful countenance. On either side, he is flanked by men and women. Some appear to be his followers; others wear symbols of the Catholic Church, such as a bishop's hat or a monk's hairstyle. The paintings were designed to look like enduring fragments of original work, but indeed were modern.[31]

In the end, despite the efforts of the committees, little of the building appeared genuinely medieval. The exterior and interior were painted bright white, and large windows poured sunlight into the cavernous meeting room. There was little ornamentation, except the occasional colorful fresco upon the white walls. If anything, Bethlehem Chapel looked like a modern church, resembling the Catholic churches of the 1930s more than any medieval building still standing in Prague. However, Nejedlý, the visionary of this renovation project, would firmly deny that the building was a church at all.

The Opening Ceremony

Members of the planning and building committees, as well as craftsworkers and other workers toiled on the project for five years. Finally, on July 5, 1954, members of the government, party, and public, along with representatives from the Soviet embassy, gathered on Bethlehem Square, then processed into the rebuilt Bethlehem Chapel to celebrate a new kind of church-state camaraderie. Representatives from the Protestant Czechoslovak Church and the Church of Czech Brethren walked with the state dignitaries. The large crowd heard old Czech Protestant hymns interspersed with Czechoslovak and Soviet anthems.[32]

Standing at the pulpit of the newly rebuilt Bethlehem Chapel, where Hus had preached more than five hundred years earlier, Nejedlý presented his emotional keynote address, explaining why Hus was the most important symbol for the new Czechoslovakia: Hus and his followers had been revolutionaries who stood up to authority; preaching in the vernacular language had enabled Hus to reach common people; his offer of wine to his lay congregants proved that he had not drawn distinctions among social groups. Although the details of Nejedlý's interpretation did not stray far from earlier nationalist rhetoric about

Wall painting from 1950s renovation, with fragment of original fresco, Bethlehem Chapel interior. Photo by the author.

Hus, his analysis owed more, not only to earlier socialist views of Hus, but to a strict Marxist dialectic. The medieval Prague burghers who had attended Bethlehem Chapel services resisted the imperial authority of the nobility. In turn, Žižka's Táborite followers challenged the more conservative Utraquists, the Táborites eschewing private property and living in community. Thus, a microcosm of Marx's historical dialectic existed within the short history of the Hussite Wars.

Nejedlý's ability to tie the Communist's current goals with Hussite ideology further justified the message that the party was the true heir of Czechoslovak history.

Nejedlý's emphasis on Hus's revolutionary ideology, however, could not obscure the contradictions inherent in Communist interpretations of the Hus legacy. Czechoslovak Communists faced a difficult task, to reconcile an atheist ideology with Hus's unmistakably religious legacy. By continually explaining why Hus was *not* a religious figure, Nejedlý and others actually drew attention to the irony of their choice for a national hero. It was impossible to completely remove religious language and symbolism from Hussite rhetoric, and a close reading shows that religious content was far from absent in Nejedlý's speech of 1954.

Much of this speech called attention to the long history of abuses by the Roman Catholic Church, implying that by continuing the struggle that earlier nationalists led against Catholic Austria, the Communist Party truly embodied the national character. Nejedlý emphasized that the Hussite movement "was a struggle against the church, but not theological or religious, but a struggle against the church as the highest financial power of the middle ages." Further, Hus opposed the influence of the church's highest officials, influence that came from economic, not religious, authority: "Those who wanted to be a bishop or archbishop had to pay."[33] Nejedlý also reviewed the history of Bethlehem Chapel during the counter-reformation, reminding listeners, "It was seized by the Jesuits, who loved to exploit the ideas of good people, construing their own meanings."[34] It is difficult to imagine that some readers of *Rudé právo,* where the speech was reprinted, did not note the irony that the Communist state had precisely seized the buildings on Bethlehem Square to impose its "own meanings" upon Prague's public space.

In condemning the Roman Catholic Church, Nejedlý pointed to the economic power of the institution. Yet, he justified these attacks, not in familiar Marxist rhetoric, but in religious terms. The church was guilty of greed, the "greatest sin"; he quoted Hus's sermons on the immorality of avarice and selfishness. Nejedlý also devoted much of his speech to the Utraquist belief in serving the Eucharist in both forms. He did put an economic spin on the former practice that denied Eucharistic wine to lay believers, arguing that the ordained-versus-lay division was akin to class distinction, but he also quoted what Hus supposedly said while celebrating Mass: "Hus always said, 'This is our bread' and not 'This is my bread.'"[35]

Although Nejedlý frequently referred to religious concepts like sin and the Eucharist, he argued that Hus had used the only platform available in the Middle Ages to speak about social reform. "If Hus were alive today, he would not preach. He would speak neither in a chapel nor a church. . . . Today he would speak to the people at Lucerna Theater or somewhere else we frequent. He would go to a place the people patronize."[36] (Ironically, Lucerna is the posh cinema on Wenceslas Square that was founded and owned by future dissident and subsequent president Václav Havel's wealthy grandfather before the Communist Party nationalized the property.)

Nejedlý also asserted that Bethlehem Chapel was not really a church, anyway. It was not even a chapel. He quoted Hus's writings and medieval songs, which referred to the building merely as "Bethlehem." As Nejedlý explained, "Bethlehem was absolutely not what usually one thinks of when one hears 'chapel.' A chapel is thought to be something small, tiny . . . but here one can fit three thousand people, more than a large church, and so this chapel is something more. . . . It was not a church or a chapel."[37]

Nejedlý cited numerous reasons for not considering Bethlehem a chapel. The site had neither a cemetery nor a rectory, and indeed Bethlehem Square had always been considered part of the parish of Sts. Philip and James, which already had the requisite cemetery and rectory. Further, Nejedlý remarked, archeologists had unearthed the remains of a well where local residents could come for water. And this addition, Nejedlý claimed (pointing to the well, which had been partially reconstructed), made "Bethlehem chapel . . . fully different from a church building . . . or a chapel from this or another era." Rather, "It is a huge rectangle, the first great hall, a gathering place for the people, where it was possible to say something different to the people." The decorations on the walls also reflected the differences between Bethlehem and traditional church buildings, he noted. There were no pictures of saints, but instead "depictions of scenes from the life of high-spirited clergy and also simple people . . . and citations from writings and manuscripts and songs, which for the first time one was free to sing."[38]

Many of Nejedlý's claims about the Hussite tradition echoed what nationalists had been arguing for a century, such as that Hus had preached in Czech to speak to the "little people" in a region heavily Germanized. But Nejedlý also played on modern anti-German sympathies, quoting a fragment of a sixteenth-century song, "in desperation the Germans ran toward Bethlehem."

He used this excerpt to remind his audience subtly of Communist sacrifices during the defeat of Nazi Germany—and to give another example of an early source that did not refer to the building as a chapel. However, he only quoted a small piece of the verse that would be familiar to most of his audience. The song tells that Germans disguised themselves as if followers of Jesus in order to massacre Czechs;[39] thus he, like other Communists, played on the raw anti-German sentiment following the Nazi annexation, much as earlier Czechs had tied their cause to the fight against Austrian-German domination. Yet, to do this, the Communists could not avoid reminding their audience also of the Christian beliefs of Hus's original followers.

Nejedlý's emphasis on Hus's use of the Czech language also reflected the interpretations predominating in the interwar period, but Nejedlý questioned the sincerity of Masaryk's Hussitism, telling the audience that the "bourgeois, capitalist republic" never made plans to renovate Bethlehem Chapel.[40] *Rudé právo* also assailed the First Republic for not rebuilding this church and site of national history.[41] In 1954, the First Republic still represented, for many citizens, the embodiment of the Czechoslovak national character; the Czechoslovak Communists vied for this position. By claiming that the Communist Party was more Hussite than Masaryk's government, Nejedlý was suggesting that Communists were better patriots, too. According to Marxist historical materialism, the Hussite revolution represented the "first great struggle against noble, church, and secular authorities";[42] the "bourgeois, capitalist" First Republic had therefore, Nejedlý, explained, been fully comfortable with the Hussite legacy, knowing that it truly stood for proletarian revolution.

And now that the revolution had been achieved, the Communist Party sought to claim Prague's public spaces. According to Nejedlý, Bethlehem Chapel would become the "cradle of the great people's movement against the exploiters of their era." Unlike nationalists, who had supported crass renovation projects, such as the late-nineteenth-century rebuilding of Charles IV's Karlštejn Castle, this generation knew that the name "Bethlehem Chapel . . . is in the blood of our people"[43] and thus represented the beginning of a revolutionary Czechoslovak architecture. This architecture included the site of the 1912 Prague Conference where Lenin represented the Bolsheviks and Stalin was voted to party leadership, and a future museum to Lenin and Gottwald. Nejedlý told his people that Prague's beauty would be no longer founded in the "arrogance of cathedrals" and "gloom of the baroque style," but in a new Communist avant garde.[44] Words alone could not reverse the effect of centuries of Catholic architecture, however; the spires still dominated the landscape of the city, and Bethlehem Chapel remained tucked away in the Old Town.

Chapter 12

Old Symbols Oppose the New Regime

"I keep thinking that a nation which tears down the monuments it raises in other moods . . . deserves to be blurred."

Ludvík Vaculík, Czech dissident

OF the postwar era in Europe, Pierre Nora has written, "No era has ever been as much a prisoner of its memory."[1] In Czechoslovakia, as in other parts of Eastern Europe, the term "prisoner" seems particularly apt. Citizens were indeed jailed, put under house arrest, or silenced for questioning the official memory of the state.

Nonetheless, opponents of the regime found outlets for remembering alternate visions. During the Prague Spring reform movement and the subsequent Warsaw Pact invasion of Czechoslovakia, protesters used conventional tactics: they co-opted existing memorials, most often of Hus and Wenceslas, to reclaim historical symbols for themselves. They critiqued Communist attempts to create a new national identity through large-scale public art projects that they judged had no artistic merit. In both Prague and Warsaw, for example, the same quip was heard:

"Where can I get the best view of the city?"
"From on top of the new Palace of Culture."
"Why is that?"
"Because from there, you can't see the new Palace of Culture."

In a more serious mode, underground poetry from this era explored the phenomenon of memory under totalitarianism, mistrusting a state that obliterated unwelcome memories. This literature employed an unlikely symbol for this exploration: the fallen Marian Column. During the 1940s and 1950s, Czechoslovak Roman Catholics had again revived interest in the Marian Column. This monument—and its absence—came to represent both hope and despair for the faithful who suffered in the new regime. Unexpectedly, during the years of "normalization" following the Prague Spring, nonreligious intellectuals also began to incorporate the story of the Marian Column into their writing. Major writers, such as the future Nobel laureate Jaroslav Seifert and the dissident writer Ludvík Vaculík, delved the meaning of the absent column in an era publicly devoid of cultural creativity and freedom.

Hus, Wenceslas, and Socialism with a Human Face

Even as the Czechoslovak Communist Party controlled Prague's public space, opponents found creative ways to give these monuments, architecture, and parades alternate meanings. The peak of creative activity occurred, not surprisingly, in 1968 during the Prague Spring. After years of economic and intellectual stagnation, reform-minded party leaders chose the Moscow-educated Slovak Communist Alexander Dubček as first secretary; then, when he took office on January 5, 1968, Dubček declared a new beginning for Czechoslovak Communism, with the slogan "Socialism with a Human Face." Thus commenced months of activity, during which banned writers were rehabilitated and even published, religious groups saw increased freedom, and political reforms were instituted.

The emphasis of the Prague Spring was freedom of expression. Censorship was partially lifted in March; this action led to increased criticism from Czechoslovakia's hard-line neighbors, especially the Soviet Union, Poland, and East Germany. Nonetheless, the wave of reform swelled, and censorship was completely abolished in May. The spring witnessed a proliferation of newspapers, with readership increasing exponentially as they offered a diversity of topics, opinions, and analyses. The Czechoslovak Writers Union published the most influential paper, *Literární listy,* which severely criticized past actions of the party and put forth reform programs. And, while Prague residents reveled in their newfound freedom, Warsaw Pact troops slowly moved toward the eastern and western borders.

In June, seventy writers and other public figures, issued the "2000 words" manifesto to bolster the country's reforms. The writer Ludvík Vaculík penned the document and gathered fellow intellectuals to defend their newly won freedom of expression. Further, the document censured the Czechoslovak Communist Party's corruption and totalitarianism, and called upon reform Communists gathered around Dubček to build a true democracy. Its indirect implication

that Czechoslovakia must extricate itself from dependence on Moscow insti-
gated the wrath of Leonid Brezhnev, who called Dubček to a series of meetings
to rein in the reformers. After a summer of negotiations that resulted in little
compromise, Brezhnev ordered the Warsaw Pact invasion of Czechoslovakia,
which began on August 21, 1968.

As Prague witnessed a week of street fighting between the Soviet and Warsaw Pact soldiers and the Czechoslovak citizens, activists used the Hus and
Wenceslas statues as backdrops for public forums. Prague newspapers reported
that at 8 a.m. on the morning of the invasion, "The Jan Hus monument [was]
surrounded by hundreds of Prague citizens. A Czechoslovak soldier and a civilian have placed a Czechoslovak flag on top of the statue."[2] The Hus Memorial
was used throughout the week as a gathering place, as dissident leaders climbed
upon the statue to lead the national anthem and the old Hussite warrior hymn.
Even at the height of chaos during the invasion, the newspaper *Práce* (Work)
proudly reported, "Flags still flutter over the head of the majestic Hus."[3]

The larger Wenceslas Square was the most popular gathering place for Czech
citizens and the most common site of the fighting. Soviet tanks rolled across
tramway lines, and snipers fired toward the National Museum and Czech Radio
building, a headquarters for Czech fighters. Here, the mounted figure of Saint
Wenceslas became an inspiring sight for the beleaguered Prague citizens. *Rudé
právo,* the official Communist Party paper, which supported the Prague Spring
movement, commented, "The inscription on the statue, which normally is un-
noticed, is endowed today with new and vital meaning: 'Do not let us perish,
nor our heirs!'"[4] The paper's observation affirmed that public monuments—and
even the small words upon them—could take on new and powerful meanings
in times of communal crisis.

The Wenceslas Memorial served also as a platform for speakers and fighters, who climbed upon the equestrian statue to protest the Warsaw Pact invasion. Protesters plastered the monument with handmade signs in Russian and
Czech—for example, "Soldiers, go home! Quickly!" Students used the statue
as a message board to get in touch with fellow street fighters, as well as to encourage hope with signs reading, "Dubček, hurrah," which *Rudé právo* claimed
"expressed the opinion of us all." At other times, that week, weary citizens sat
"dejectedly on the pedestal";[5] behind the statue, citizens watched as the National Museum was damaged with heavy artillery. Five months later, on January
16, 1969, Prague university student Jan Palach immolated himself in front of
the statue, to protest the continued presence of Soviet and Warsaw Pact troops.
Immediately, students made posters comparing Palach's act with Hus's immolation, and hung them at the Hus and Wenceslas Memorials.[6] When Palach died

of his injuries a few days later, the area in front of the Wenceslas Memorial took on yet another meaning, as a place to pay tribute to Palach's sacrifice and to commemorate others, especially students, who had lost their lives from the invasion. Dissidents secretly placed flowers and candles, in remembrance, on this new sacred space.

During the 1970s, the government erected a chain link fence around the Wenceslas Memorial to dissuade activists from using it as a political stage. The metal fence's design featured sharp stylized leaves of the linden, the Czech national tree. Communist Party opportunists, who came to the forefront after the Prague Spring's defeat, hoped the patriotic linden symbol would soften the barbed barrier to freedom of expression. Instead, dissidents quickly saw the fence as a tool of "normalization," the state's program that sought to appease citizens with consumer goods while severely limiting freedom of expression. Dissidents viewed "normalization" as a transparent ruse to distract citizens from the continued state oppression. In fact, this fenced-in area came to be known unofficially as Štrougal's garden, named for "normalization's" chief organizer, Ladislav Štrougal, a politician who had sided with the reformers in 1967 but quickly switched allegiances when he smelled defeat. Indeed, after 1968, as historians Zdeněk Hojda and Jiří Pokorný have written, the Wenceslas statue held contrasting meanings of oppression and revolt. The linden-leaf fence spoke of the government's power, but the dissidents' coded message "To the horse!" still called protesters to Wenceslas Square.[7]

Like many Prague landmarks, this memorial shifted meaning again in the new era although its form remained constant. Considered outdated when it was erected in 1912, the equestrian and regal form by the late 1960s appeared masculine and powerful; by then, too, Wenceslas had shed his association with wartime fascism. Instead, his statue reminded citizens of the possibility of independence; his forging of Bohemia's medieval borders now symbolized Czechoslovaks' desire to protect the violated borders of their state. His horse now lunged forward into what would surely be a better future.

These political uses of the major monuments to Hus and Wenceslas come as little surprise. Not only did the statues represent important figures from Bohemian history, but they were also located in Prague's two most prominent squares, where street fighting took place in August 1968. On the other hand, the persistent appearance of Marian Column references in dissident writing is puzzling. The history of that column continued long after its demolition; just as nationalists had rewritten the statue from a commemoration of Swedish defeat to a symbol of Habsburg repression, dissidents began to conflate its destroyers with the party currently in power.

Building Community and a Column Abroad

Before the symbol of the Marian Column was embraced by secular dissidents, Czechoslovak Catholics had found new meanings for the broken statue. As soon as World War II ended, two Catholic voluntary organizations, Orel (the gymnastics club that rivaled *Sokol*) and Lidová Akademie (People's Academy) had begun to collect money from parish churches and individual donors. The organizations hoped to commission a statue that could be erected by 1950, if not on Old Town Square, then at another location in Prague. Of course, the February coup and the Communist suppression of Catholicism that began in 1948 put an end to any chance this dream could be realized. Not only were private church fund-raising activities banned but also Orel and Lidová Akademie were outlawed in 1950.

Czechoslovak Catholics in exile soon began to identify the Marian Column as a symbol of the oppression they had fled. The empty space on Old Town Square represented their longing for their city: a place that no longer (or perhaps never) existed. Zdeněk Rotrekl, a dissident Catholic poet, sentenced to death in 1949, had entrusted some gold to his emigrating colleague, Emil Petřík, imploring him to donate the gold for the crown of a rebuilt Marian Column. Later in the same year, Petřík announced this dream to Czechoslovak Roman Catholic émigrés in Ludwigsburg, Germany, and Petřík and his colleague Vilém Stanecký contacted other émigrés to plan and design such a project. In 1953, the Czech Benedictine monk and émigré Lev Ondrák spoke to Catholic leaders in New York about religious oppression in Czechoslovakia; he revealed Petřík's efforts and suggested that a Marian Column replica be built to honor victims of religious persecution in Communist states. Moved by Ondrák's stirring speech, the Vatican commissioned a replica of the column's Virgin Mary statue. Czechoslovak immigrants in the United States and Canada contributed to the project, as did Catholics in Czecholovakia, who gave money to friends leaving the country. The Communist government swiftly suppressed a 1955 campaign of Czech university students to raise funds for the project.

The statue was not an exact replica of Prague's. Much would be made later of the "richness" of the American statue as compared to the subtlety of the original.[8] The gold crown on the new Marian sculpture formed the most obvious difference; the broken Prague Virgin had not worn one. Further, the church leaders supporting the project insisted on using marble, rather than the original's sandstone, which they feared would "crumble away in one hundred years."[9] The completed statue was displayed in Rome in 1954 and then sent to St. Procopius Benedictine Monastery in Lisle, Illinois.[10] A large delegation from the Catholic hierarchy welcomed the statue to Lisle, and the unveiling ceremony was led by a fellow Catholic leader in exile, Cardinal Thomas Tien, archbishop of Beijing. Giving Tien this role emphasized the statue's meaning "as a symbol of faith and hope for all exiles."[11]

During the 1960s, Prague archbishop Joseph Beran visited the monastery in Lisle and paid homage to the statue. His experiences were linked to the column's existence: a symbol of faith free only in exile. Beran, whom the Nazis had imprisoned at Dachau and Terezín (Theresienstadt) during the war, had been the leader of the Catholic opposition in Prague immediately following the Communist coup. He had particularly decried the party's establishment of an official shadow church, Catholic Action, and its journal, the *Catholic Gazette*. Beran was arrested in June 1949 for announcing to his congregation at St. Vitus Cathedral that "Catholic Action is not an action by Catholics and the so-called Catholic newspaper, offered to you outside the cathedral, is not a Catholic newspaper."[12] For two years he was held under house arrest in the Archbishop's Palace near Prague Castle. He then spent twelve years in various prisons, followed by another two years under house arrest. In 1965, the state allowed him to visit the Vatican if he promised never to return to Czechoslovakia.

Following his emigration, Beran spent the remaining four years of his life visiting Czech and Slovak communities in Europe and North America, where he emphasized his unwavering Czechoslovak patriotism. Unlike many other Catholics, who criticized the entire history of independent Czechoslovakia for its anticlericalism, Beran gained a reputation for combining his faith in God and his commitment to the nation. He was a member of the international Sokol gymnastics organization and often attributed his survival in prison camps to his Sokol training in strength and discipline. He also proudly told of his grandfather's leadership in the early Sokol movement in Pilsen (Plzeň), Bohemia. Unlike many, he remained associated with this patriotic organization, rather than with its Catholic counterpart, Orel. The cardinal's patriotism, combined with his suffering and resilience under the Nazis and Communists, made him a sympathetic figure for both Catholic and non-Catholic opponents of Communism. His visit to Lisle tied the column to a dream of a free Czechoslovakia and separated it from criticism of the anticlerical First Republic.

A Column of Poetry

In Prague, the faithful had to be secretive to honor the Virgin Mary. Each year, on the anniversary of the column's destruction, Catholics stealthily placed candles and flowers at the site. Not only were they remembering their beloved statue, but these citizens were also calling attention to the Communist suppression of religion. In a post-Communist interview with *The Prague Post*, Prague priest "Father Raymond" (who asked to use an alias, even in 1998) explained that believers had used Old Town Square site as a symbol of anti-Communist defiance. "During Communism, I was watched very closely because I put flowers on the spot every Sunday. But of course they were removed immediately."[13]

Those who quietly adorned the site were calling attention to the statue's absence. Writers viewed the vanished Marian Column as representing the loss of their cultural freedom. The range of authors who employed the column's image is remarkable. Václav Renč's poem from 1957 reflected mystical Catholicism and right-wing politics, whereas Nobel-prize-winning poet Jaroslav Seifert's work told of regrets felt by former ardent Communists like himself. Ludvík Vaculík, a former party member who became one of the most active dissident intellectuals in the country, discussed the column's meaning in the *Czech Dreambook,* his volume of reflections on totalitarianism and creativity.

Catholic poet Václav Renč is the author least surprisingly on this list; his poem *Prague Legend* is important for demonstrating the lasting influence of the 1918 attack on the Marian Column in the collective memory of many Czechoslovak Catholics. Whereas the new Marian Column in Illinois represented Czechoslovak patriotism as well as faith, Renč's poem maintained the Catholic Right's attack on Czechoslovak history.

Indeed, Renč's is a mixed legacy. During the interwar period, he associated with fellow Catholic writers, such as Jaroslav Durych, the longtime champion of the Marian Column. Their work employed naturalism, ruralism, and millenarianism to oppose the modernist, avant-garde literature of the era. After the Munich agreement, these writers attacked the First Republic leaders, Masaryk and Beneš, whom they blamed for the anti-Catholic culture prevalent in interwar Czechoslovakia; to do this, Renč, Durych, and others moved toward the authoritarian Second Republic. Renč became famous for calling Masaryk's close friend, the beloved Czechoslovak writer Karel Čapek, "a national enemy."[14] Čapek died of flu and exhaustion on Christmas Day 1938, after spending months leading an international campaign to decry the Munich Accords. His tireless efforts, which contributed to his death at age forty-eight, contrasted sharply with actions of those Catholic writers who supported the puppet government.

Renč's authoritarian politics during the World War II later made him an easy target for the Communist Party. In the 1950s, the Communists rehabilitated non-Communist Čapek and praised the writer for his anti-Nazi activities; this gave the party even more reason to attack Renč as a fascist danger to society. The poet was imprisoned from 1951 to 1962; his works were banned, and he was not rehabilitated until the 1968 Prague Spring.

While he served his prison sentence, Renč was forbidden to write poetry and was denied paper and pens. He wrote the nineteen-chapter Marian Column poem in his head and frequently recited it to fellow inmates, in order to commit it to memory. During the Prague Spring, the poem circulated in typed copies through the *samízdat* (self-publishing) movement. *Prague Legend* was not officially published until the early 1990s, when the Catholic daily *Katolické listy* "rediscovered" it, printing it in segments spread over several weeks. It was finally released in booklet form in 1994.[15]

Prague Legend tells the anguished story of a young man who participated in the destruction of the Marian Column in 1918. In this tale, Renč did not merely use this destruction as a metaphor for suffering in Communist Czechoslovakia. He viewed the immorality that plagued Prague in the early twentieth century as a cause of the era of Communist terror; the Czechs' fate was one they brought upon themselves, and only grace could save these sinners.

The poem begins with the image of the column's Virgin Mary. She represents purity and modesty, but also love of the Bohemian lands. Whereas the Catholic immigrants to the United States who built the replica column wanted to display Mary's regal character, Renč lauds her for her modesty. The poem begins, "The queen of heavenly hosts / . . . pressed her face not into marble, / but only into the stone of this . . . heretical land. / . . . She did not ask her admirers, their hands in soft sandstone, / for gold jewels for herself." Mary watches over Prague, "the stubborn heart of mountainous Bohemia," and observes the growing licentiousness of her people. She laments the sins of the modern age and the decadence of this city where "the eternal flame on the candle of the Christian nation is wasting away."

Although the poem is often heavy-handed, Renč also displays the lyricism and powerful imagery that made him a foremost poet of his time. The epic's third chapter begins, ". . . war came. The kind of war that renews the face of the world / to its deepest wrinkle. And Prague flew into a rage." Throughout the poem, Prague is personified as a female sinner or a spoiled child. Sexual imagery contrasts sharply with the gentle womanliness of the Marian Column.

> *And Prague in its childish defiance and arrogance about all*
> *that thrived here in the past, is feverishly swept away.*
> *The joy of her past broken into fragments*
> *And joys of the future fallen to powder on the street.*
>
> *And on the little square, on the narrow column,*
> *the maternal face with its eternal smile*
> *knowingly, peacefully and quietly*
> *subdued her glow.*

Renč tells the story of the Marian Column's demise through the experience of a fictional participant. Young Oskar is a "suburban lad" who is swept away by the wave of sin and excess in Prague. Walking through Old Town on the day of the planned attack on the column, he becomes "intoxicated" by the crowd. Renč compares Oskar's frenzy, as he is brought into the mob by the hand of a prostitute, to "building toward an orgasm." Oskar's pleasure "intensifies as he momentarily merges with the crowd." Yet, like a sexual release, Oskar's gratification can last only for an instant. Once the column has fallen, "numb women and embarrassed men" view the destruction. They look for evidence that they have realized their revenge. But, says Renč, "blood does not gush from stone." All that is left for the participants is to disperse and go home.

As the crowd retreats, the broken Mary scolds them. "Do you know me, fools? Do you know me, reckless children? / Do you air your anger well?" She reminds them that she was not guilty for the sins for which they blamed her for when they shouted, "Avenge yourselves, Czechs, for White Mountain." She was not at the battle; she did not cause disease. But no one listened, "not even the gray pigeons on the square." Although distraught, the Holy Virgin reminds Prague citizens that in the end she is always victorious; they cannot make her disappear.

Oskar retreats back into his life, and his participation in the mob gives him no lasting satisfaction. He lives his life "as a smuggler." (One wonders if Renč is making a reference to Kysela-Sauer, since he had smuggled sugar and other consumer goods during the World War I.) Time passes, and both Oskar and the personified Prague reflect. With Oskar, "Prague knelt on the castle steps [near] holy statues." Neither feels "joy and revenge," but rather an "uneasy fear" and yet "hope." Oskar walks the city alone until "one day on the small square . . . a bouquet of fresh flowers was found." Prague residents are no longer gladdened by the destruction; instead they bring flowers to the column's site. It is left unclear who brought the flowers on that day, but Renč implies that it was Oskar, remarking, "It was so comic, sneaking around that small square, looking right and left . . . Oskar, you are getting old. / What weakness compels you to open your eyes now?"

Suddenly, the poem's tone changes. From an angry, bitter tenor, the mood becomes nostalgic and poignant. In the most compelling moment of the poem, Renč repeats the earlier refrain: ". . . war came. The kind of war / that renews the face of the world / to its deepest wrinkle. And Prague flew into a rage." The reader immediately understands the comparison Renč is making between the eras following the two world wars. However, the older Oskar is wiser than the youth of 1918: "That time, Oskar did not join the crowd's wave." As young Communists dance in the square, Oskar cries out, "You, Prague, your easy life is over." From then on, Oskar sees visions of the Virgin Mary everywhere he goes; she materializes in apparitions but also in the faces of young girls and old women met on the street. At the end of the poem, as Death waits in a boat to row Oskar to "the other shore," the forgiven sinner is comforted by the Virgin, who rests her "experienced palm . . . on his cold body." And Mary also appears to other citizens. She wanders the streets, "through Prague, through gardens of bell towers / . . . from home to home, from soul to soul." She is "A mother deer, pursued by all and the silent hunter of all." Even in the modern darkness of her city, the Virgin, "Victorious through the ages, . . . knows she awaits her victory / in the stubborn heart of the Bohemian mountains."

Renč's poem is one of persistent faith in the face of adversity. His belief that his city will return to God and Mary sustained the poet through his long prison term. The comparison between the destruction of the Marian Column and the loss of religious freedom under Communism is understandable; in both eras, practicing Catholics felt persecuted by the state. However, it is curious that Renč seems to feel more hostility for the interwar government, which he harshly criticized during the Second Republic, than for the regime that imprisoned him. It is the birth of the state in 1918 that sets the wheels in motion for the future tyranny. His protagonist cannot control his youthful impulses, just as the young state is unaware it is seeding its own future pain.

Although this latter comparison, in conjunction with the Marian Column image, empowers Renč's poem, it also underscores why many Catholic dissidents had trouble finding allies outside their own circle. In the 1950s, the memory of the First Republic was still strong, and anti-Communists idealized Masaryk, Beneš, and its other leaders. Few citizens were willing to admit any links between the two eras.

The Dissident Vision

Nearly twenty years after Renč wrote his epic, Czechoslovak dissidents did begin to explore the parallels between 1918 and 1948. The 1970s was an era of fierce criticism of the Communist government by intellectuals of all stripes. Following the Prague Spring, writers decried the return of censorship and repression. Many of the harshest critics were former party members who had become disenchanted with a leadership that failed to stand up to the Soviet Union, their supposed "mother country." These dissidents did not necessarily give up their belief in Marxist principles, but they argued that Czechoslovakia's totalitarian regime failed to represent these ideals. Other dissidents came from religious communities. Many Roman Catholics, long targeted by the party, joined the dissident movement, along with leaders of the Evangelical Church, which no longer maintained close ties with the party. Prague archbishop František Cardinal Tomášek cooperated with the state until the election of Pope John Paul II, who firmly advocated the church's support of human rights movements in Eastern Europe. Even though Tomášek initially denounced the 1977 Charter on Human Rights, the document that became the foundation of the Czechoslovak dissident movement, he eventually became a more outspoken advocate of that movement, frequently receiving and blessing its spokespersons.[16]

The party continued to repress Roman Catholic institutions and beliefs, firmly controlling religious education and relations with the Vatican. In 1976, in an effort by the Communist Party to discredit the Nepomucký myth, the state conducted a scientific study of Nepomucký's body, entombed in his baroque silver sarcophagus at St. Vitus Cathedral. The saint's tongue, purported to remain living even after the man's death, was reexamined and was declared a scrap of brain matter that had not decomposed.[17] The absurdity of such attacks on the church exasperated even nonreligious Czechs.

One such Czech was Seifert, the celebrated poet, who had had a complex literary and political career. Born in 1901 in the working-class Žižkov suburb of Prague, Seifert never attended gymnasium (a university preparatory high school) or university. He became involved in working-class politics from a young age, working for the Communist newspaper *Rudé právo* while a teenager. At age nineteen, he published his first volume of poetry, *Město v slzách* (The City in Tears), meant to illuminate the hardships of Prague's working class. Yet his relationship with the Czechoslovak Communist Party was tumultuous, as he was not afraid to criticize its methods or its allegiance to the Soviet Union. In 1929, the party expelled Seifert and six other important writers for signing a manifesto protesting what they called Bolshevik tendencies among Czechoslovak Communist leaders. Seifert joined the Social Democratic Party and remained dedicated to working-class issues. Frequently critical of the liberalism of the First Republic, he nonetheless admired Masaryk and, after the president's death, published a volume of poems in his honor.

Although Seifert had broken with the Czechoslovak Communists two decades earlier, his working-class poetry retained the respect of the Communist government. While Renč was committing his poem to memory in a Communist jail, Seifert was receiving the 1955 state prize for literature. Although ardent Communists often criticized Seifert for writing melancholy poetry rather than optimistic socialist realism, he nonetheless enjoyed the party's favor. This would change, however, following the Prague Spring. During the era of artistic freedom in the mid-1960s, he was named Poet of the Nation; as chair of the Union of Czech Writers, he condemned the Soviet invasion of Czechoslovakia in August 1968; he was then elected by fellow writers to chair the Czechoslovakian Writers' Association. Then, in 1970, unwilling to give up some of the freedoms he and fellow writers had gained during the Prague Spring, he defied a state ban on publishing abroad; the state responded by prohibiting him from publishing at home, as well. During the 1970s, as a result, the esteemed poet's work had to be published in the underground self-publishing network, or *samízdat*. In 1977 Seifert signed the Charter on Human Rights, and in 1978, sixty years after the toppling of the Marian Column, he explored what this single act of vandalism had signified for the nation and for himself. His "Head of the Virgin Mary" appeared in *Piccadilly Umbrella,* a *samízdat* collection of his recent poetry. Not surprisingly, this poem differs from Renč's. It is as light and airy as Renč's is heavy and ponderous. In the tradition of modern Czech literature, it combines bittersweet and melancholic emotion with a sharp, humorous irony. Yet there are remarkable similarities between the two works: both depict the human struggle between faith and doubt; both are rich in religious imagery; and both depict men haunted by a Marian apparition toward the end of their lives.

Seifert's poem begins with the narrator, ostensibly himself, venturing out into Prague on a beautiful fall day. He remarks on the "special moment" when autumn arrives, but then describes the fall as "silky . . . with little drops of blood and a light touch of sadness. This is the time when people's wounds begin to hurt more."[18] If this imagery does not remind the reader of Christ's wounds or the stigmata, Seifert then comments that he is visiting a friend who lives near the Lustatian Seminary—that is, a Roman Catholic edifice.

Seifert's work often incorporated real events and characters; in "The Head of the Virgin Mary," the narrator visits his friend Vladimír Holan, who is ill. Holan was in fact another well-known poet of Seifert's generation, who wrote experimental lyrical poetry for most of his career, but also delved into political writing to decry the Nazi invasion of Czechoslovakia and to celebrate the victory of Communism in the late 1940s. A few years Seifert's junior, Holan had a similar intellectual and political journey. He supported the extreme Left during and after World War II, but became disenchanted by the totalitarian nature of the nation's leftist regime. He dissociated from the party during the Stalinist 1950s and was then unable to publish his poetry for over a decade. He remained allied with Czech writers who felt betrayed by the Left.

Seifert's incorporation of his real friend and colleague into the poem further suggests that the narrator represents Seifert himself. Seifert portrays Holan as a man contemplating the spiritual meaning of his life. "As soon as I had entered / Holan snapped his book shut and asked me almost angrily / if I too believed, / if I believed in life after death / or in something even worse." Holan's words are ambiguous.

But Seifert's narrator does not want to partake in Holan's interrogation.

> *I ignored his words.*
> *On a low cabinet by the door*
> *I caught sight of the cast of a female head.*
> *Good Lord, I've seen this before!*
> *It was lying there, resting upon its face*
> *as if under a guillotine.*
> *It was the head of the Virgin Mary from Old Town Square.*

We do not learn why Holan has this figure, which may be a cast replica Holan has collected out of piety or regret, or may be the actual head—which Holan somehow acquired at the site sixty years ago, or somewhere else more recently. Certainly the placement of the head in the bookcase does not imply a great deal of respect. It is placed low and near the door and lies face down. It is difficult to see; it is out of the way. Yet, something has alerted the narrator to its presence, and he begins to recount the events of November 1918. Then, as Seifert tells of "the pilgrims" who overturned the column as they returned from White Mountain, he comments, "It was nowhere near as high as the Vendôme in Paris." Again, in a mode typical of a twentieth-century Czech writer, Seifert pokes fun of his small city that will never compare to Paris, Berlin, or Moscow. Nor, he adds, does the Czechs' vandalism of a statue compare to the true frenzy of revolution; the French revolutionaries used the guillotine to murder the king, queen, and countless others, but the little Czech nation could only break off the head of a statue in sandstone.

But at this point, Seifert shifts tone again and implores, "May they be forgiven." Just as Renč blames the intoxication of the crowd, Seifert claims the pilgrims "were a little high on the first breath of freedom." And then he admits:

> *I was there with them*
> *And the head from the broken column*
> *rolled over the pavement*
> *near where I was standing.*
> *When it came to a halt*
> *her pious eyes were gazing*
> *upon my dusty boots.*

Like Renč's Oskar, Seifert's narrator is a man haunted by the broken Virgin. The image of the decapitated head staring at the young vandal's boots is unsettling; the reader can imagine the "pious eyes" piercing him. Seifert never refers to Mary as a statue; she is animate and active throughout the poem. Nor does she ever truly disappear. Seifert recounts:

> *Now it came rolling up to me*
> *a second time.*
> *Between those two moments lay*
> *almost an entire human life*
> *that was my own.*
> *I'm not saying it was a happy one*
> *but it is now at an end.*

Like the dying Holan contemplating what lies ahead for him, Seifert's narrator is trying to make meaning of his life. Because of this visit to a fellow poet, the protagonist now finds his adult life bookended by two visions of the Virgin Mary, but, unlike Renč's gentle and wise Mother Mary, Seifert's is a somewhat eerie figure. And, whereas we witness Oskar's redemption, we do not know what Seifert's narrator believes. Seifert's poem ends with ambiguity:

> *—Do tell me again what it was*
> *you asked me as I entered.*
> *And do forgive me.*

Clearly, the narrator is now ready to take his friend's contemplation and doubts more seriously than he had on first arriving. But this does not tell us whom he addresses in the last line or from whom he desires forgiveness? We are not told whether he merely is asking pardon for ignoring his friend, or is speaking to Mary herself, or what he wants forgiveness for. Surely for more than breaking a statue with a crowd of fellow citizens, however. Is Seifert regretting his youthful attachment to the Communist Party, his willingness to work within its system for two decades before it turned upon him? Whatever the answers, Seifert and Renč agree that the formative act of vandalism launched their nation's political independence but continued to haunt their country.

We gain more insight into Seifert's thinking from another dissident's works. Ludvík Vaculík's *Český snář* (Czech Dreambook) also considered the meaning of the Marian Column for contemporary society. Like Seifert, Vaculík was a former Communist Party member who came to regret his former associations. Born in 1926, well after the column's destruction, Vaculík was a full generation younger than Seifert. His attachment to Communism dated to the postwar fervor of the 1940s, but the Stalinist direction of his country came to dishearten the young idealist. During the Prague Spring, Vaculík emerged as one of the

Head of the Virgin Mary
from the original Marian
Column. Lapidarium of
the National Museum of
the Czech Republic. Photo
courtesy of Jan Bradna
and the Society for the
Rebuilding of the Marian
Column.

country's intellectual leaders upon writing the manifesto "2000 Words," published on June 27, 1968, at the height of the period's creative ferment. During the 1970s, after the Soviet invasion, Vaculík became the driving force for these intellectuals' *samízdat* movement. He ran Edice Petlice (Padlock Press), an underground publishing house that reproduced and distributed banned literature. With connections to Czech exiles abroad, Vaculík's organization enabled dissident writers to publish abroad and earn income for their work.

Vaculík, a novelist and essayist, remained a prolific writer while he ran Padlock Press. His most unique contribution to Czech literature of this era was *The Czech Dreambook*, which literary and linguistic scholar Michael Henry Heim called "a hodgepodge of current events, memoirs, political historical and philosophical ruminations, and . . . fiction in diary form." Vaculík himself called it part "hard-boiled documentary" and part "magic fiction."[19]

A short section of the *Dreambook* is devoted to the memory of the Marian Column. Like other dissidents of the era, Vaculík found broad significance in the absent monument, writing, for instance: "I can't understand people who renew their whole selves by continuously casting off older parts of the whole that no longer fit. It bothers me that I . . . did so too. In 1952, during my national service, I mechanically signed a form stating that I agreed to leave the Catholic Church. What an ass I made of myself. If I was no real Catholic to begin with, how could I leave the Church?"

Many sections of *Dreambook* describe Vaculík's observations of contemporary Prague. When the writer learned that a small church in Lhotka, in the Prague suburbs, had installed a new Stations of the Cross, he decided to "have a look." Instead of scenes from Jesus' death, however, in this church the stations were metaphorically represented by historical events such as a slave galley, the Thirty Years War, the atomic bomb, a concentration camp. Vaculík wonders how "so experimental a work [found] its way into a tiny church on the outskirts of Prague." Also in this remarkable church is a shard from the Marian Column, embedded into the altar, and there is a plaque at the church entrance describing the events of November 1918. Vaculík was intrigued by the plaque author's "guarded indignation" as he suggested that the vandalism of Old Town Square "set the tone for [the] development of Czechoslovakia." The *Dreambook* author concurred: "I got a kick out of it, it cheered me up, made me gloat in agreement. I keep thinking that a nation which tears down the monuments it raises in other moods and avoids revamping its character in favor of revamping the record of its character—such a nation deserves to be blurred."[20]

Vaculík's wife, Madla, visited the Lhotka church with him. She located on the commemorative plaque at the back of the church a "delicious bits of gossip," which claimed that "the Virgin Mary punished the perpetrators of the crime." Particularly disturbed, Madla suddenly recalled that Seifert had also written about the column, and exclaimed to her husband, "The head of the Virgin Mary Seifert once saw rolling in Old Town Square is now in Holan's house. That means the two of them were there, too!" Her husband is unimpressed, but Madla retorted, "Well, Holan can't walk at all, and Seifert only barely." Vaculík then exclaimed, "Jesus Christ!" and the reader cannot help but chuckle as Vaculík employs a Christian expletive to chide his wife.[21]

Vaculík ended this chapter with his famous biting humor, yet underneath was a serious message. He wrote about Seifert's "pilgrims" who marched from White Mountain to Old Town Square in 1918: "That's the problem, all right. . . . The sinners can always be counted upon to intone their sins so sublimely that the Lord God simply hasn't a clue what to do with us."[22]

Interestingly, Vaculík placed himself among the "sinners" before his birth. Like fellow dissident Václav Havel, who wrote that the line between collaborator and resister did not lie between people but within each individual, Vaculík wrote often that, in a totalitarian state, there is no "us" and "them": the writer was disappointed in his nation as a whole; thus, he was also to blame. Rather than taking responsibility for its own past, the Czechs blamed the church, the Habsburgs, the Nazis, and the Communists; the sin of the nation was to try to wipe out the past rather than to learn the past's lessons. Nations that tear down reviled monuments would have to realize that beloved memories could also be snatched away.

In *Dreambook,* Vaculík cannot stop thinking about Seifert's poem, so he visits the author. He asks directly about the poem and Seifert's own participation in the destruction of the column. Seifert admits that he watched the toppling, but swears that he did not participate. He further confirms that Holan, at age thirteen, could not have contributed to the event. Still, Seifert seemed to defend the crowd, commenting, "Revolutions have rights of their own, and that was a revolution, of sorts, anyway."[23] Vaculík dances around the issue weighing upon him, whether the curse his wife described truly existed. He finally asks Seifert, "What about Sauer? Didn't he die shortly afterwards? Of something complicated?" But Seifert answers, "Not at all. He lived to a ripe old age and died a nice quiet death." Vaculík, still somewhat haunted, tells the elder poet, "The way I look at it, monuments should be left as they are, all monuments." And Seifert answers, "Naturally."[24]

As dissidents and banned writers, Vaculík and Seifert of course feared any attempt to wipe out history. The Marian Column did not matter to them as a symbol of faith or power; neither felt any allegiance toward the Catholic Church or the Austrian Empire. But the obliteration of anyone's memorial threatened their determination to see freedom of expression return to Czechoslovakia.

Ironically, it is often absence that produces the most powerful meaning. During the 1960s, artists throughout Europe and North America sought to produce respectful yet compelling memorials to Holocaust victims. Surrealist artists argued that the modern culture of monuments stemmed from the extremist political goals of nationalist or totalitarian regimes; copying a traditional monumental form would legitimize the very ideals the artists decried. Thus, many postwar public works of art in Western Europe and the United States featured nonrepresentational forms and blank or blackened areas. The vacant memorials reminded viewers of those who were forever lost.[25] In Eastern Europe, another type of empty space gained power; the absence of a familiar monument was more conspicuous than the multitude of statues that remained or were newly erected. For example, historian F. Gregory Campbell wrote eloquently about the "empty pedestals" that dotted the landscape of Czechoslovakia throughout the Communist period. These had once held statues of Tomáš Masaryk, and the bare platforms reminded citizens that democracy had disappeared along with their beloved founder–president.[26]

The same can be said about the Marian Column of Old Town Square, which still towered in people's memories. Similar statues existed throughout Bohemia and Moravia, including other parts of Prague. But only the missing one captured the imagination of poets and politicians. Another Prague empty space gained tremendous significance during this era. In 1955 the Czechoslovak Communist Party unveiled the largest statue of Stalin in the world; the Soviet leader stood just over 50 feet tall (15.3 meters), gazing down on Prague's Vltava River from Letná Hill. Behind him, a parade of smaller statues representing workers, peasants, and soldiers stood, encouraging Praguers to nickname the aesthetic atrocity "The Meat-Market Queue." In 1962, after Khrushchev had denounced his predecessor and Moscow had ordered such monuments destroyed, the statue was blown up. Thirty years later, shortly after the fall of Communism, a new monument of a giant metronome was erected on the concrete plinth that had held Stalin. Yet, to this day, Czechs call the site "U Stalina" ("At Stalin's") and maintain that the dictator's ghost still haunts the city.[27]

Chapter 13

Religious and National Symbols in Post-Communist Prague

"History again demands to be heard."

Václav Havel, letter to
President Gustav Husák, 1975

Iт was November 17, 1989. The crowd that gathered on Wenceslas Square to protest the dictatorial Communist regime strained to listen to the small man standing on a balcony above. As he began to speak, a chant energized the people, "Havel na hrad! . . . Václav na hrad" ("Havel to the castle, Václav to the castle"), encouraging their new leader to take the helm at Prague Castle, seat of Czechoslovak government. Others began to sing the "St. Wenceslas Chorale." Members of the older generation who had joined the student protesters were surprised that the young people, brought up during the Communist regime, did not know all the words to this religious anthem that had united Praguers in 1848, 1918, and even 1968. Yet the coincidence of their sudden leader's name with the appellation of the Bohemian patron saint was lost on few members of any generation. People on the square began to retell the old Bohemian myth: Saint Wenceslas (Svatý Václav) and his knights wait deep within the earth of Mount Blaník, in northern Bohemia; when the Czech people are at their greatest hour of need, the king will reemerge and come to their rescue. It had begun to seem to people that perhaps this quiet and shy playwright, who had spent much of the 1970s and 1980s imprisoned for his outspokenness on cultural freedoms, could be the Saint Václav for their time. The playwright, too, had traveled from northern Bohemia (from his vacation cottage, rather than from deep within a mountain) to join fellow Praguers in the protests that would finally topple the Communist regime. In the euphoria of 1989, it felt possible that Saint Václav had indeed come back.

In the weeks that followed, the Communist Party of Czechoslovakia gave up its position as sole leader in the government. Havel and a broad coalition of dissidents from intellectual, student, and religious circles founded Civic Forum, and began negotiations with the Communist Party. On November 27, a general stike shut down the country. The party offered a coalition power-sharing government to the dissident leaders, but the revolution had gone too far. By the end of the month, the still Communist legislature selected Havel as the nation's first non-Communist president in 41 years. The chants of "Václav na hrad!" had been answered. In his presidential address, held at a ceremonial hall in the castle on New Year's Day 1990, Havel acknowledged the spiritual symbols that had formed a backdrop for twentieth-century Czech history. Although not traditionally religious, Havel viewed Jesus's teachings as a moral compass for the modern era. He quoted his "most esteemed predecessor," Tomáš Masaryk, who had declared that Czechoslovakia's model would be "Jesus, not Caesar." At the end of the address, Havel again paraphrased Masaryk, who had in 1918 quoted seventeenth-century Hussite philosopher Jan Komenský: "My people, your government has returned to you!"[1]

Soon, November 1989 euphoria gave way to political conflicts that got to the very heart of the question of national identity and belonging. Prague as a capital city had long been a symbol to Slovaks of Czech domination in national politics. As war erupted in Yugoslavia, President Havel vowed that the Czechoslovak state would not resort to violence. Thus ensued the "velvet divorce" of January 1993; the Czech and Slovak Republics were now independent states.

When the Marian Column had been torn down in 1918, Czech politicians had reminded nationalists to be aware of the feelings of our "Slovak brothers," who tended to be more religious than their Bohemian counterparts. The Slovaks' voluntary exit in 1993 might, then, have signaled that the issue of religious symbols in secular Prague would disappear, but the sites of memory continued to reflect a shattered and complex past.

The Marian Column in Post-1989 Prague

In the post-Communist era, few Prague citizens attend church. In fact, the Czech Republic today has the second-lowest church-attending population in Europe, second only to the Netherlands.[2] The Roman Catholic Church lost one-third of its membership, and the size of the Czechoslovak National Church and of the Evangelical Church of Czech Brethren dropped by half, over the course of the 1990s. *The Prague Post* explained that revelations regarding the participation of Christian leaders as secret police informers, and the ugly legal battles over property restitution, had led many Czechs to distance themselves from the traditional Christian churches.[3] In contrast, in neighboring Poland the Catholic Church still dominates the national culture. Similarly, in other former Communist countries, such as Croatia and Lithuania, attending Catholic services has become a mark of nationalist pride, and attendance at Serbian and Russian Orthodox services has exploded.

Despite the secularism of most of the city's citizens, the religious–national monuments scattered throughout Prague remain sites of controversy, conflict, and meaning for a culture that continues to seek its place in the modern world. There is a small but active Catholic cultural life in Prague. Catholic voluntary organizations and parishes sponsor concerts and charities, and some Catholic events—for example, the Christmas Eve Midnight Mass at St. Vitus Cathedral—have become renewed national traditions. The rapid democratization of politics following the fall of Communism (this "post-modern era," as a 1991 Czech art history journal described it) has also, of course, brought back into public life a multitude of opinions about the Marian Column. The Society for the Recovery of the Marian Column, formally established on May 14, 1990, immediately began to raise funds for such a "grassroots" movement.[4] By 1998, the organization had raised four million Czech crowns (approximately one hundred thousand dollars) from private donors, mainly Roman Catholic Czechs who viewed the "empty space" on Old Town Square as a symbol of the religious persecution endured by Catholics in the twentieth century. The city government did not block the society's plans to rebuild the monument, but allocated no public funds for the project.[5]

Jan Bradna, a Prague sculptor and founding member of the Society for the Recovery of the Marian Column, rendered a copy of the Marian statue. He told *The Prague Post*, "Czech people are happy about the return of such a statue."[6] On November 3, 1993, the anniversary of the column's destruction, the society staked its claim on the former site by laying a plaque into the cobblestones. In four languages, the plaque reads "Here did stand and will stand again, The Marian Column of Old Town Square." The society engraved this message in four languages—Czech, German, Latin, and English—to represent a rarely remarked aspect of the column's complex history: Czech supplanted German as the city's dominant language, just as the vernacular eventually replaced Latin as the language of local Catholic discourse. The English acknowledges both the support of Czech Americans, and the heavily American and British tourist base of the city's new economy; further, using this "international" language allows the plaque's message to reach a wider audience.

There was immediate dissent to the laying of the commemorative (and prescriptive) plaque. Within months, vandals attacked it, carving and cementing over the words "will stand again" in each language. A letter to the editor of

Jan Bradna's Prague studio, with replica of Marian Column statue. Photo by M. Sosková. Courtesy of Jan Bradna and the Society for the Rebuilding of the Marian Column.

Lidové demokracie (People's Democracy), a Catholic newspaper, called the vandalism "a barbarous act" that brought "shame to the whole nation."[7]

Other viewpoints were more philosophical. In an opinion piece in a Protestant weekly newspaper, the author, Josef Gebauer, decried the possibility of celebrating "three-hundred years of Habsburg subjugation of the Czech nation."[8] He enumerated Habsburg-era injustices, then asked what would be the "historical purpose" of commemorating this era. In particular, he cited the persecution, executions, and exile of Bohemian Protestants throughout the Habsburg period. Gebauer admitted that the column originally commemorated the Swedish retreat, not the defeat of the Bohemians, but he argued that its meaning had expanded.

Gebauer also questioned the plans for a new column on historicist grounds: "For a restored column to return to the square, we would also have to refinish Old Town Hall, demolish the Hus monument, rearrange Paris Street . . ."[9] His allusion was to the ever-changing appearance of a living city, arguing the impossibility of restoring a site to its original state. His article ended with the reminder that "The pre-White-Mountain square did not have a Marian Column."[10] What he subtly argued was that if the Czech nation was to commemorate any historical period, it ought to be one before the Habsburg victory.

Gebauer was one of many Prague citizens who questioned the philosophy behind reviving the column. Academic and cultural journals also took up the issue. Vít Vlnas, an art historian specializing in the Czech baroque, wrote in the cultural review *Přitomnost* (The Present), "Old Town Square cannot be turned into a museum." Vlnas argued that a "baroque Marian Column cannot be an authentic expression of our era."[11] He suggested instead a modern obelisk dedicated to victims of fascist and Communist dictatorships. Lubomír Sršen of the National Museum agreed: "There is no way to rebuild it exactly as it stood one hundred years ago. I think it should be a modern statue, not a historic copy."[12] However, in the art journal *Umění and řemesla* (Art and Crafts), art historian Ivo Hlobil questioned Vlnas's notion. Many movements in art history revive earlier periods, Hlobil argued, and so historicist art could indeed reflect the philosophy of a present era.[13]

Nonetheless, even some members of the Society for the Recovery of the Marian Column questioned the idea of an "authentic" restoration. In fact, Jan Bradna, the sculptor who had recreated the statue of Mary, noted: "I wanted to do something abstract. Something with a set of hands reaching out to the clock tower and another set mounted by the execution site,"[14] referring to the spot on Old Town Square where twenty-seven Bohemian Protestants had been beheaded a year after the White Mountain defeat. In this way, Bradna explained, this newly conceived sculpture "would represent a bond between modern and past history and help put those souls to rest."[15] Other Praguers also believed the revived column could heal religious wounds. A Prague Roman Catholic priest, Father Raymond, explained, "That column has the potential to form a bond between Protestants, Hussites, and Catholics in Prague. It needs to return to the square."[16]

This logic, however, eluded many Czechs, including the Roman Catholic hierarchy, which surprisingly did not support the project. Prague archbishop Miloslav Vlk issued a statement in 1993: "Restoring the Marian Column on Old Town Square is not an official priority of the church; rather [our goal] is to try to revive spiritual life." Further, Vlk feared that a restored column would increase religious tension in the city: "We do not want to create the impression of rivalry in the arena of ecumenism."[17] Similarly, Petr Ettler, a spokesperson from the archbishop's office, explained that the column represented "the old church."[18] Officially, then, the church leadership indicated it had no interest in returning to the counter-reformation era. The Roman Catholic Church has not donated any funds to the Marian Column project.

In spite of serious opposition within and outside the Society for the Recovery of the Marian Column, this association decided that the statue should indeed be an "authentic" replica of the baroque monument. But, for all the society's tremendous effort, the Prague city government three times rejected proposals for Bradna's replica to reoccupy the column's former site. Finally, sensing defeat, the society reached a compromise: it placed the new statue atop a rich, royal blue pedestal in front of the entrance to Our Lady before Týn Church, off Old Town Square. However, the obscure location greatly disappointed many supporters, and in November 2008, on the ninetieth anniversary of the column's destruction, supporters once again gathered to demand that the column move from Týn to the center of the squre.

Týn is the oft-photographed church whose Gothic towers loom over Old Town Square, yet the building's entrance is tucked behind the square, since a row of Renaissance buildings and an arcade stand between the square and the front of the cathedral. To locate Bradna's statue, a visitor must walk around the corner from the square, enter a narrow alley, and pass an outdoor café before finally seeing the portals of Týn. Yet, clearly, people do find it; lying at the base are, almost always, fresh flowers and other mementos.

Even harder to find is the replica of the Marian Column that had been in Lisle, Illinois, for forty years. In 1993, the Chicago-area abbey donated this statue to a Prague monastery. Reporting on the "Exiled Lady's return home," a Catholic magazine paid tribute to the courage of Rotrekl in the 1950s: "His gold symbolically sparkled on the crown during an era when he himself suffered in a communist jail."[19] Yet few Prague residents even know the column exists, and even if someone knows its whereabouts, it is nearly impossible to find: it stands in a small courtyard in the labyrinthine gardens of Strahov Monastery on Petřín Hill; to access it, a visitor needs to climb a steep, narrow path through the woods, accessed from a walking path below the monastery grounds.

Indeed, the Marian Column stands again, but only for a few to behold.

On Vítkov Hill

If no one knows quite what to do with a missing monument that has its own support group, even fewer have reconciled the National Memorial and accompanying Žižka statue to the post-Communist era. Although its complex history predates the Communist period, today's Prague residents associate it completely with the fallen totalitarian system. As a newspaper columnist explained, "The monument was absorbed by the previous regime" and would have to be "rehabilitated and cleansed" of these negative associations to become popular again.[20] Another writer opined, "After true ideological distortion, which it suffered in the last decades, it is only a symbol of state-imposed tradition."[21]

Not only does the monument retain its sinister symbolisms of the Communist period, but it also has become a source of the farcical humor so popular in Czech culture. In a country whose post-Communist president was an absurdist playwright and whose literary hero is the bumbling, disaster-prone "Good Soldier Švejk," the bizarre history of the monument became rich material for post-Communist newspapers and magazines. A newspaper column on the subject was titled "Smiling at the Absurdities."[22] Prague papers informed a new generation about Gottwald catching his death at Stalin's funeral, and about his rapidly decaying publicly displayed body. The graffiti at the site also indicates a lack of respect for the so-called national monument. One of Malejkovský's doors, for example, was altered by a graffiti writer who added a caption to the image of a soldier observing an old woman receiving a rifle: "Damn! Isn't that the lady whose old man and children were shot in an unfortunate incident?" The caption's meaning is ambiguous, but suggests violence, mistrust, and duplicity within Communist society. The graffiti suggests that the very people arming the old lady were responsible for her husband's death, and echoes the cynicism about history that characterizes the post-Communist era.

Early in this period, Vítkov Hill had swiftly become a symbol of the absurdities of life under Communism and the blunders of Communist leaders, yet the post-Communist society still had to determine what meaning to give the site for the new era. One of the most vexing questions was what to do with the bodily remains of former Czechoslovak Communist presidents. In particular, the new Czechoslovak government wanted to purge Gottwald's memory from

Vítkov Hill. Post-Communist newspapers drew on the history of mishaps at the National Memorial to highlight the first Communist president's incompetence. Articles such as "Gottwald's Death and the End of Stalinism", "Who Is Sitting on Žižka's Horse?" and "Jan Žižka with Fireworks" reported on the dilemma about Gottwald's ashes and recounted the sordid history of the monument.[23] Soon after the revolution, the new national government determined that the ashes of dead Communist leaders should return to their families. Members of the newly freed press gleefully reported that Gottwald's daughter declined the offer to retrieve her parents' remains. And, though the descendents of Antonín Zapotocký and Ludvík Svoboda dutifully obtained these ex-leaders' ashes, Gottwald's descendants reportedly had no interest in claiming their relatives' effects.

Finally, the Communist Party of Bohemia and Moravia took possession of the remains and placed Klement Gottwald's, and his wife Marta Gottwald's, ashes in Olšansky Cemetery. In the post-1989 mood of Prague, however, many more citizens paid tribute to another Olšansky site—the grave of self-martyred student Jan Palach—than to the "first workers' President." *Slovo,* a Social Democratic newspaper, used this story to underscore the Communist Party's continued dissociation from the mood of the country. *Slovo* reported: "Even on November 23, 1989 *Rudé právo* [the Communist daily newspaper] commented, 'There were mistakes and oversights in the young revolution, but this does not have to darken the great socialist transformation or the meaning of Gottwald's personality, which was stamped in many specific ways into the achievements and undertakings of Czechoslovakia.'" *Slovo* pointed out that, though even Gottwald's daughter wanted to distance herself from her father's legacy, the Communist Party newspaper clung to its cult of personality.[24]

Ridding the monument of the past president's earthly remains was only the beginning of another absurd chapter in the site's life. In 1993, puzzled over what to do with the place, the Ministry of Culture leased it to Žižkov millionaire Vratíslav Čekan, a business person who had already bought up most of the surrounding area. Čekan, by some accounts a modern-day "robber baron," used the site to host gala parties for his cronies. Meanwhile, Čekan and architect Zdeněk Deyla began formulating plans to make Vítkov a "center for free time" under the "working title, Magic Mountain." The press immediately seized upon the proposal, dubbing it the Czech Disneyland and adding it to the growing list of absurdities associated with the monument. Although more far-reaching and commercial than early ideas for Vítkov, this was not the first entertainment proposal developed to lure visitors: during the 1950s, the Ministry of Culture had considered building tennis courts and children's playgrounds to encourage families to visit the site. Čekan's far-reaching plans included sports arenas, exhibition areas, gardens, restaurants, and theaters, all with a "beautiful view of Prague," but the plan never got past the working-title stage, and by the mid-1990s the monument was ostensibly abandoned.[25]

A single caretaker looked over the grounds on Vítkov Hill, making sure that young skateboarders and unruly teenagers did not damage the national shrine. The building was kept sealed and seemed destined to fall into oblivion—until the year 2000, when Prague was named a European Culture City by the European Union. Thus encouraged to overhaul the city's sites, the National Museum reconsidered Vítkov Hill. It was an embarrassment to the city that this so-called national monument was closed to visitors and was derided by the press and the public. The National Museum took possession of the monument in 2001 and designated it a branch of its organization. The main goal of the National Museum directors regarding the site became to educate the public more completely on its history. Subsequently, on the first Saturday of each month and on such occasions as Prague's annual Museum Night, the monument has been open, with Stanislav Slavík, the memorial's director, giving a comprehensive tour, during which he emphasizes that the building was nearly complete at the time of the Communist takeover, its history belonging to the Masaryk era as well as to Communist times. Slavík has not avoided the Communist history, either, leading guests to the hall with the marble sarcophagi bearing the names (but no longer the bodies) of the Communist presidents.

The National Museum has also encouraged the public to become involved in deciding the fate of the monument. During Museum Night 2004, guests filled out a survey with questions ranging from "Do you know who Jan Žižka was?" to "Would you attend an organ concert here?" A carefully designed web page begins with a letter from the director asking for suggestions, and maintains a discussion board on the monument's future.[26] The memorial holds organ and choral concerts in the main hall and tries to appeal to a full spectrum of tastes. The avant-garde organ group S.H.O.C.K. performed in 2001, and classical concerts occur regularly.[27] Despite these efforts, however, guests of Vítkov Hill apparently still view the monument as a comical vestige of Communism. During Museum Night 2004, an elderly woman chuckled while reading the inscription of a socialist realist statue inside the building; the statue commemorated the suffering of Red Army soldiers during World War II. "If you want to know about suffering," the woman told the marble soldier, "let me tell you what I went through under you!"

And *Lidové noviny,* the highbrow journal commenting on Czech cultural life, questioned whether this site on the outer ring of Prague's hills was ever a true national memorial: even if it had once been, it had long abandoned that meaning. According to the paper, "Naturally, the symbolic center of all of our contemporary revolutionary events lies on Wenceslas Square, with the statue of Saint Wenceslas (Václav). Even though the [National] memorial has ceased to be a state mausoleum, this fact still shrouds it. Nothing can change that."[28]

Saint Wenceslas Recast

In post-Communist Prague, professional historians, cultural leaders, and politicians have sought to reconcile the familiar national symbols with more responsible scholarship and analysis. Inspired by newer trends in cultural European history, Czech scholars have explored the role of myth-making in their national history, in influential books such as Jiří Rak's *Bývalé Čechové* (Once Upon a Time, the Czechs . . .) and Zdeněk Hojda and Jiří Pokorný's *Pomníky a zapomníky* (Monuments and Forgetting). A popular television program hosted by octogenarian art historian František Dvořák takes viewers on informative tours of Prague's sites, emphasizing multiple interpretations of their meanings.

In particular, Wenceslas's geographical and historical centrality in Prague has drawn public attention to the disparity between the symbolic and historical realities of this patron saint. A May 2000 column in one daily newspaper asked "Was Saint Wenceslas a martyr or a collaborator?"[29] Although myths tell the story of a benevolent leader, murdered by his treacherous brother, and who continues to look after the Czech people even to the present day, the historical facts are more complicated; as historian Dušan Trešník told *Právo,* it is more likely that the two brothers led opposing factions of nobles, and that the king faced serious political opposition.

Even the modern history of Wenceslas as a symbol has been reconsidered since the fall of Communism. In particular, the use of the Wenceslas image by Nazi sympathizers has led some Czechs to ask if the saint's symbolic power has thus been irreparably tarnished. However, few members of the Czech public even know this detail of the Wenceslas myth, and the more recent memory of revolutions in Wenceslas Square provides the most powerful image of the Wenceslas symbol for the present generation of Czechs. As Trešník commented, "The Saint Wenceslas symbol functions strangely. Prague is the center of Bohemia, the center of Prague is Wenceslas Square, and the center of Wenceslas Square is that statue. The outcome of every battle and demonstration, culminating in Palach's week, is determined by who controls that statue, who overpowers the statue of Saint Wenceslas."[30]

If the November 1989 demonstrations on Wenceslas Square, then, allowed Svatý Václav to reoccupy his place as the central icon of the Czech nation, some Czechs did not believe the saint was receiving the respect he deserved. Leading this opinion was "hippie" icon Jaroslav Hutka. This folksinger and 1970s dissident left Czechoslovakia for the Netherlands in the mid-1980s, but returned in time to lead folk songs and ballads on Letná Plain during the 1989 protests. In recent years, Hutka has concentrated his energies on running a failed campaign for a seat in the European parliament, and on remaking the Wenceslas Memorial for a new, democratic era.

In the years following the Prague Spring, Wenceslas Square had acquired a tense and politically charged atmosphere. The statue loomed behind images of the Soviet tanks rolling through town, street fights between Prague citizens and Warsaw Pact soldiers, and Jan Palach's self-immolation. The "normalization" government of Gustav Husák had deterred future protests at the site by installing the metal chain fence of sharp, stylized linden leaves previously noted. After the revolution, the fence remained, as the Prague tourist industry wanted to avoid promoting the city as a place where backpackers might lounge on monument pedestals.

At this point, Jaroslav Hutka and his colleagues in the Balbín Poetic Party led the post-Communist campaign to remove the chains. This party, a loose political organization, was named for the seventeenth-century Jesuit priest Bohuslav Balbín, who wrote in Latin while extolling the beauty of the Czech language and history. Thus, Hutka's group not only chose a Catholic namesake; it focused on a Catholic-associated national symbol. The group has not acknowledged this directly, but Balbín and Wenceslas were two symbols of the Catholic alternative to Hussite-inspired nationalism.[31]

Hutka's reasons for demanding the removal of the fence (in Hutka's terms, "Wenceslas's manacles") were very personal. In a series of newspaper columns, Hutka described the meaning for him of the memorial, his articles creating a series of "postcards"—word pictures about his relationship to it. In the first, he recalled sitting on the steps of the National Museum as a young man; his position, behind the statue of Wenceslas, enabled him to imagine the Good King's view, overlooking his city, and it was this view, "in the beautiful era of the 1960s," that embarked the songwriter on his career. Subsequent postcards, however, show Hutka becoming grimmer as time wore on. He described the period immediately following the Warsaw Pact invasion of August 1968, when the statue was boarded up with immense pieces of wood; the following year, a crowd on Wenceslas Square, celebrating the Czech hockey team's world championship victory over the Soviet Union, ripped down these boards. Then he recounted the day he first saw the linden-leaf chains, the government's more permanent solution to Prague citizens' propensity to use the statue, literally, as a political platform. He called the chain "a Bolshevik substitute for barbed wire, which hangs there to this day."

Hutka's recollections echoed Trešník's comments that the Wenceslas Me-

Stylized linden leaves making up the chain around the Wenceslas Memorial. Photo by author.

morial figured into the great emotional upheavals of the twentieth century. Hutka noted that the site incorporated the memory of Czech leaders Masaryk, Beneš, and Havel, as well as the dictators Hitler and Stalin. The site had been a reminder of both joy and sorrow, but, Hutka believed, there was no reason to emphasize the dark remembrances symbolized by the chain fence.

In 1997, Hutka brought the matter to the attention of Prague's mayor, Jan Koukal. According to Hutka, Koukal assured him that the chains would be removed, but this did not occur. Hutka also claimed that Havel had assured him the matter would be dealt with, but nothing had been done. Then, on June 8, 2003, Hutka's group gathered on Wenceslas Square and wrapped red banners around the chain fence to symbolize that the "red" symbol still remained, in Prague; the following year, Hutka and his associates formally created the Balbín Poetic Party and ran for the European Parliament. According to a Radio Prague commentator, Hutka had no illusions that he would win, but used the publicity to further such causes as artistic freedom and fighting poverty among Roma and Sinti communities. His political campaign posters pictured him with John Lennon spectacles and his long reddish hair, peppered with gray, flowing over his shoulders. The following year, the Balbín poets were back, with Hutka leading Czech folk songs among a small group on Wenceslas Square. A master of publicity, he gave interviews to Prague media to garner support.

Finally in 2005, the Prague city government agreed to Hutka's demands. The mayor, Pavel Bém, stood with members of Balbín and chopped a link of the fence with tremendous metal cutters. Almost every Prague newspaper and radio station covered the event, but the most biting remarks came from Ivan Hoffman of *Radiožurnal*. Noting the irony of the McDonald's restaurant across from the statue of Wenceslas, Hoffman pointed out that the Soviet-era chains were gone, but had only been traded for the American chains of fast food and cultural dominance. The removal of Wenceslas's chains having coincided with the appointment of a new president of McDonald's European division, a president who promised to raise sales throughout the continent, Hoffman commented, "[both] Saint Wenceslas and hamburgers are here to stay."

Perhaps the artist who has captured best the uncertainty of how the heroes of the Czech past can be reconciled to the post-Communist era is David Černý. A young Prague artist, Černý has exhibited internationally and has received acclaim for his surrealist art, most notably the "Pink Tank," a Red Army tank that Černý had painted pink after the revolution. In 1999, Černý created "Horse" for the CZ 99 outdoor art exhibition in Prague; the sculpture stood temporarily at the foot of Wenceslas Square, facing Myslbek's statue at the top of the space. Afterward, in 1999, Černý installed this monument to Saint Wenceslas in the Lucerna Palace, an elaborate theater and shopping center on the square. There, Černý's sculpture today hangs suspended from a stained-glass dome near the entrance. An upside-down dead horse dangles by chains tied around his feet, and Saint Wenceslas sits erect upon the horse's belly. Artistic renderings of horses traditionally represent strength, power, and militarism; Černý has emasculated Wenceslas by seating him on a dead horse. The king seems oblivious to his loss of power—he looks ahead, unaware that he cannot move forward. Černý's statue certainly implies that historical symbols have lost their strength and meaning in the post-Communist era.

The statue, unsurprisingly, has attracted numerous interpretations regarding the absurdity of history and commemoration. The most interesting came from Václav Pinkava, writing in 1999 for *Central European Review*, an English-language journal covering the former Soviet bloc: "To my 'screwy' eyes, [Wenceslas] is very definitely modeled on Václav Klaus himself."[32] Václav Klaus has been called the third of the "Václav triumvirate," along with Havel and the Good King;[33] if Havel represents the philosopher king, the conservative Klaus is known for his pragmatism and often abrasive personality. Although the statue's artist has never acknowledged a resemblance to the third Václav, Černý certainly has not hidden his dislike of Klaus, whose 2003 election as president he said was among "my most horrible dreams."[34] At the time of the 1999 installation, the Social Democratic Party headed the Czech government, and Klaus, prime minister from 1992 to 1997, led the opposition Civic Democratic party. While Černý campaigned for Czech acceptance into the European Union, Klaus, a self-proclaimed "Thatcherite," made disparaging comments about it. Černý has also criticized Klaus for working with the Communist party in coalition governments. In any case, whether or not Černý's sculpture subtly recalls Klaus's visage, what is certain is that the statue demands that onlookers ask the purpose of monuments and heroes in a country trying to remake itself once more.[35]

"I Feel Better than Jan Hus"

Rather than inspiring activism or debate among Prague citizens, the Hus Memorial has come to symbolize a new incarnation for the Czech capital, today a major tourist destination. A country of just over 10 million, the Czech Republic each year hosts about 7.5 million visitors, most of whom stay in Prague. Old Town Square has become the center of tourist activity, as crowds of foreign visitors gather to watch the astrological clock, take a carriage ride, or shop for Bohemian crystal. The statue of Hus is described in guidebooks as the focal point of the Old Town, and it is a meeting spot both for locals and for visitors. As an employee for the Ministry of Regional Development, located on the square, joked to the *Prague Post,* "For my statistics, I just look out the window."[36]

For several years following the revolution, tourists and Charles University students sat on the steps surrounding the monument's base as they chatted and read books. Recently, the city government created a "park atmosphere" by planting low bushes around the base—to prevent people from climbing the statue. Unlike the chains around Wenceslas, this addition seemed to bother very few (except a visitor from Seattle who bemoaned that "the purchasers of the Velvet Revolution have decided that 'loitering' is a threat to the 'marketplace.' With the construction of a cosmetic garden barrier encircling the monument, they have buried the readers and talkers in flowerbeds of marigolds, behind ornate chains."[37] In 2007 and 2008, the monument underwent a major restoration, sponsored by Škoda, the automobile enterprise acquired by Volkswagen shortly after the fall of Communism. With the memorial covered by scaffolding and silk-screened advertisements for Škoda, metal workers have repaired leaks and the gunshot wounds the monument suffered during the pitched battles at the end of the Second World War.

Today, commemorations of Hus are considerably less popular than in the Habsburg, Republican, or Communist periods. In 1999, on an official visit to Prague, Pope John Paul II publicly apologized for Hus's execution and suggested a reappraisal of the medieval priest's teachings. The anniversary of the martyr's death remains a state holiday, and the city often hosts a small event

David Černý's St. Wenceslas Sculpture in Lucerna, Wenceslas Square. Photo by author.

on Old Town Square. Those who attend, though, tend to be tourists passing by when the event is taking place. Prague residents are much more interested in combining the day with the preceding Cyril and Methodius holiday to spend a long July weekend at their summer cottages. Similarly, few Czechs pay attention to the legacy of Jan Nepomucký, who has nonetheless become a favorite of tourists. A legend promises good luck to Prague visitors who touch the representation of the dog in the bronze frieze below the Nepomucký statue on Charles Bridge. Each day, hundreds of visitors from around the world wait to rub the spot, shiny from the touches it has received.

Once a year, Bethlehem Chapel hosts the most elaborate Jan Hus commemorations of the post-Communist era; a standing-room-only crowd gathers to celebrate the national hero's life and death. As happened with the National Monument on Vítkov Hill, the post-Communist government did not know how to reconcile the competing histories of Bethlehem Chapel. In 1993, the government granted the site to the Czech Technical University of Prague—a logical benefactor, as the Jesuit Order founded the university at the chapel, in 1786. The Czech Technical University uses the space as its ceremonial hall, holding graduations and other school services there. For the rest of the year, Bethlehem Chapel is a minor, off the beaten path, tourist site.

Once a year, the chapel is transformed into a functioning church. On July 6, the Czechoslovak Hussite Church (the current name of the Czechoslovak National Church, founded in 1920) hosts an ecumenical service there. Czech Radio and Television broadcast the event live, and the three-thousand-seat building fills to capacity. The procession is led by the male and female ministers of the Hussite Church, who are followed by representatives from many of the city's religious communities, including Roman Catholic, Jewish, and Protestant sects. In a move unthinkable in an earlier era, Catholic bishops from throughout the country (for example, in 1993, the bishops of Pilsen and Brno) attend. The theme of the event is often ecumenism and how the religious leaders can work together.

Although the state plays no official role in the service, representatives of the city and national governments attend. In 1993, Havel sent a letter to be read to the congregation. Like his twentieth-century predecessors, Havel emphasized Hus's beliefs that most aligned with the president's own philosophy: "Hus's legacy is first and foremost the belief in freedom of the soul and the conscience. His whole life was a struggle for freedom of thought in spiritual and religious matters."[38]

Prime Minister Klaus attended several of the Bethlehem Chapel commemorations, and spoke at the 1997 ceremony. Known for realpolitik, Klaus nonetheless understood the political value of creating a sense of national identity. In

Klaus's interpretation, "[Hus's] struggle has in it a highly democratic element." The right-leaning Klaus, who had criticized Havel's concept of civil society as romantic and impractical, focused on what he interpreted as Hus's beliefs of "individualism . . . and equality."

In more recent years, Klaus's presidency has been characterized by his skepticism of the European Union. He has publicly expressed fear that the Czech Republic would be swallowed up by the dominant European countries, most notably the historical enemy, Germany. According to Klaus, Hus's efforts to reform the Czech language have led to the nation's literature becoming "one of the most mature in today's Europe." Hus, according to Klaus, was a true Czech patriot who understood the importance of maintaining the nation's individuality. Klaus's desire for the Czech Republic to be a leader in the new Europe was also reflected in his speech: "His life and work opened the path, which facilitated the defeat of Europe's medieval rigidity and eventually freed people to exercise their individual responsibilities. He put this into the hand of the future, in which we now live."[39]

Although Czech leaders today occasionally refer to Hus's legacy, the emphasis on national memory has waned significantly. The idealism of the interwar period and the forced compliance of Communism have given way to a combination of cynicism and pragmatic political beliefs. Havel's tremendous popularity in 1989, when he was hailed as the new Svatý Václav, diminished rapidly, as the economic realities of a new market system made the philosopher–playwright's idealism seem quaint and unrealistic. Today a handful of Prague citizens—religious citizens keeping the memory of Hus or the Marian Column alive, or dissidents ridding the landscape of Communist symbols—remain involved in the politics of national memory; the majority, however, pay little attention.

Yet, there is little doubt that the collective memory, carefully constructed over two centuries by nationalists and Communists, religious and free thinkers, still influences the consciousness of citizens. The twenty-something generation, who barely remember Communism, still relate to the legacy of the national past. The most notable example was the popularity of the hit song "We Feel Better than Jan Hus," which debuted in 2003. The band Monkey Business, whose members are all in their twenties, included this song on their album *Resistance Is Futile,* which featured on its cover a drawing of the Czech antihero the Good Soldier Švejk. Monkey Business, with Czech, American, and British members, is led by two Czechs who write songs that challenge the growing conformity they see in their society. "We Feel Better than Jan Hus" is performed mainly in English, with the name Jan mispronounced with a hard *J,* in the manner of English speakers. Czech songwriter and band leader Roman Holý has admitted that he feels particularly proud of this song, whose loud, almost screaming re-frain "We feel better than Jan Hus. We feel better than Hus" is interrupted by a spoken section in which Hus's entire history is retold:[40] "1371: Jan Hus is born. 1402: as the people's favorite he is appointed to the newly erected Bethlehem Chapel where he launches a twelve-year crusade against the corrupt practices of the clergy. 1414: Hus is summoned to the Council of Constance by Zikmund Liška Ryšavá. He endures a puppet trial and ordered to recant. At his refusal he is condemned to death and burned at the stake on July 6th, 1415!"[41]

The band has acknowledged the absurdity of the song's premise. As key-board player Ondřej Brousek asked, "How can you feel worse than someone who's just been burned alive?"[42] Yet songwriter Holý clearly sees echoes of Hus's life in his country's more recent history. The song has a single line in German, "Verstehen Sie Spass" ("You understand the joke"), which follows the lead sing-er's cry, "It really burns me, baby." Holý's reference to burning evokes memories of Jan Hus's death and the Holocaust. He also engages the Communist period. His double entendre, "We gotta face the party," suggests that the responsibility to face the Communist past rests with the younger generation; his use of the term "puppet trial" for Hus's hearing reminds his audience that injustice has a long history in his country.

The band's tone is at once challenging, ironic, and idealistic. Clearly, mem-bers admire the historic figure of Hus. As bass guitarist Pavel Mrazek disclosed in an interview, "None of us really knows who Jan Hus was. Maybe he was some normal, greedy bastard, who preached what he was told. Perhaps, but no, he held onto those beliefs up to his immolation. . . . We are sympathetic to that; his approach and ours are close. Hus held on tight to the end and did not falter. We are paying homage to him."[43]

Monkey Business's 2003 national and European performances were called the "We Feel Better than Jan Hus Tour." The band joined the trajectory of dark humor that has long characterized the Bohemian sensibility. From counter-reformation paintings that feature a goose roasting on an open fire (Hus means goose in Czech), to a 1920s political cartoon of the drowning Nepomucký with the burning Hus, to the post-Communist youth culture of Monkey Business, the Czechs have laughed at the irony of a pantheon filled with martyred he-roes.[44] The assassinated King Wenceslas, the martyred Hus and Nepomucký, and the overpowered nobles on White Mountain have created a national mind-set of bemused defeatism.

Epilogue—New Times, New Monuments

Tomáš G. Masaryk once remarked, "We have more serious business than statues."[1] Masaryk's comment can make one question the point of writing about a century of nationalism, genocide, and harsh totalitarian rule by focusing on statues and festivals in one Central European city. Yet the stories of these sites of memory elucidate the centrality of nationalism, the passion that people feel for place, and the role of religion in modern society; they demonstrate how people use public space to create a sense of self and of nation in a modern era often described as alienating and fragmented.

"Becoming national" requires a conscious effort on the part of cultural leaders to "transform a segmented and disunited population into a coherent nationality," as historians Geoff Eley and Ronald Grigor Suny have argued. The greatest contribution to the study of modern nationalism, they assert, has been the understanding that nations are not natural entities, but are "invented," "imagined," "created," and "manipulated,"[2] and therefore nation building constitutes a purposeful effort by political actors to unify a people within a common culture and political structure.

This volume has focused on how Prague's Czech leaders transformed an intellectual concept of their nation into a vibrant national culture, in which public art and rituals created unity but also caused conflict and dissent. It relies on several tools of cultural history analysis—particularly religion, aesthetics, and gender—to study this creation of Czech national identity. Symbols could not be neutral—nationalists insisted that statues, songs, emblems, and flags either supported the nation or dishonored it. Therefore, symbols and statues from earlier historical eras were ascribed nationalist meanings that frequently shifted with new political needs. Prague's religious statues became "monuments against their own will," according to Czech historians Zdeněk Hojda and Jiří Pokorný.[3] Some theorists of nationalism infer that such national identity supplanted religion as the primary way in which modern persons defined themselves, but it is more accurate to say that citizens did not want to give up either religious or national identification, and therefore wrestled with contradictory attributes.

In Prague's modern history, it would have been logical to create secular national symbols that appealed to citizens of different faiths, or shifted focus from religious belief altogether. Yet nationalists, from Podlipný to Masaryk to Nejedlý, insisted on maintaining Jan Hus as the central figure in the national pantheon. In turn, political Catholics challenged Hus with their symbols: the Virgin Mary, Saint Wenceslas, and Saint Jan Nepomucký. Perhaps the choices were not so illogical: religious-oriented art occupies a central place in most human cultures, connecting people to a particular sacred space and set of beliefs. Indeed, defined in this way, religion and nationalism fill similar roles, as they link individuals to a place and a unifying mission. Masaryk believed that religion in general, and the spiritual leader Hus in particular, called upon the Czechoslovak citizenry to create a moral and just society. However, by embracing the memory of Hus, Czech nationalists stubbornly excluded many citizens from feeling represented in the nation. Certainly, the symbol of Hus did not cause the disintegration of Czechoslovakia in 1939 and again in 1993, but less divisive symbols might have created a better sense of national unity. Not only did Slovaks, Germans, Hungarians, Ruthenians, and Poles, as well as many Roman Catholics and Jews, feel excluded from the nationalism advocated by the state, but within the Czech nationalist community itself, politicians spent tremendous energy arguing over statues and festivals.

Although it is easy to criticize Czechoslovak politicians for failing to create a unifying set of symbols, the ongoing debates over national identity can also be seen as evidence of a vibrant democratic society, if one with shortcomings. During the Habsburg and interwar periods, lively debates in the press and in town squares convinced citizens of diverse backgrounds that they did have a stake in the ongoing development of national identity. Although the 1929 Saint Wenceslas festival and 1935 Catholic Congress did not solve the national question, these events demonstrated that compromises were possible. During the Nazi occupation and post-1948 Communist rule, dissidents used the example of the First Republic to challenge the authorities' more monolithic definitions of national symbols. Nationalism became, in the words of Prasenjit Duara, "a battleground" upon which meaning continually shifted to reflect the changing needs of a dynamic society. Religion also functioned as a battleground in the twentieth century, as some insisted on a doctrinaire adherence to faith while others mined religion's emotional content for secular uses.

In nationalist iconography, gendered symbols often function similarly to religious images. The traditional characteristics of male and female forms carry deep emotional meaning in both cases. Nationalism created a belief in a common birth and a spiritual family: gendered symbols invented fathers and mothers for the nation's children. As fathers, Hus, Žižka, and Wenceslas represented differing masculine attributes. Wenceslas, the patriarch, symbolized the founder and the nation's indivisibility. Hus was the wise hero; Žižka represented victory and masculine power. The maternal figures, the Virgin Mary or her secular counterpart, the National Mother, reminded citizens of the nation's nurturing qualities, commanded sacrifice, and celebrated the national language. However, like religious symbols, the gendered icons could be divisive. The nationalist movements of the twentieth century coincided with unprecedented changes in gender relations, particularly as women gained new rights and roles; thus, despite the proliferation of feminine images and the participation of women in their creation and commemoration, these traditional depictions of male and female did not always suit the changing roles of real citizens.

Similarly, the vast range of aesthetic styles available to twentieth century artists made the creation of unifying symbols more difficult. Conflicts between traditional and experimental art circles distracted from the meaning that nationalists hoped their monuments would convey. Many twentieth-century artists rejected the very idea of a public monument, yet politicians sought to employ them to create specific messages for the capital city.

In his work on history and memory, Jacques Le Goff paraphrased philosopher Martin Heidegger's thoughts on history: "The past is not only man's projection of the present onto the past but . . . the projection into the past of a future he has chosen, a fiction-history or reversed desire-history."[4] Political and cultural leaders employed the Czech past—mythologized, modified, and manipulated for use in the present—to lead their people toward new futures.

Today's Czech Republic is the closest approximation of a nation-state that Czech people have ever inhabited. If this book has focused on conflicts within the Czech-speaking community, this has not been to dismiss the importance of other groups, but to demonstrate the narrowness and exclusivity of many nationalist projects. The twentieth-century goal to make Prague a truly Czech capital was accomplished not through new monuments but through genocide, expulsions, and national conflict. The murder of the region's Jews, the expulsion of Germans, and the divorce from Slovakia left the Czechs alone in a nation-state and its national capital. Many citizens have distanced themselves from this narrow national character, and have embraced a new European identity. Havel has encouraged his fellow Czechs to explore their connections to a European trajectory toward democracy, a trajectory temporarily lost after Communism effectively rendered the Czechs cut off from European developments for four decades. In 2004, the Czech Republic joined the European Union, whose flag accompanies the Czech national flag throughout Prague.

Rather than learn from the dark events of the twentieth century, however, some extremists have used national hegemony in the Czech Republic to create new "others" to maintain national passion. For example, anti-Romany (anti-Gypsy) rhetoric has intensified in Czech political discourse, even as the European Union has imposed strict regulations for enforcing minority rights. But, even as the small far Right employs racist rhetoric (such as a recent proposal to send Czech Roma to India), the more common response to the new hegemony of the nation state is *forgetting*. Textbooks, for example, neglect to discuss the history of the country's multiethnic community, focusing only on the Czech contributions to nineteenth-century history.[5]

Politicians often speak of the importance of reasserting an identity for the new Czech Republic (as historian Kieran Williams demonstrated in an analysis of recent Czech neoliberal rhetoric). Václav Klaus likens the Communist period to the *temno* (darkness) that followed White Mountain: "Under the banner of proletarian internationalism, we lost our national (and state) identity"[6] He mines Czech history for evidence of a Western, democratic orientation, and de-emphasizes pan-Slavism, cooperation with Russia, and the revolutionary Hussite tradition. Instead, he looks to his namesake, Wenceslas, for his definition of a Czech national "realism," a neoliberal philosophy that emphasizes "democracy, hard work, commerce and self-reliance."[7] Although he carefully distances his interpretations from the misuses of the Wenceslas cult during World War II, he also emphasizes the *Western* values of Wenceslas, "a prince basically more humane and educated than were his still semi-barbaric surroundings, . . . who felt that from the West come not only attackers and conquerors but also, perhaps primarily, bearers and communicators of values in which the life of the individual and the existence of the state can be reliably anchored. . . . It is a tradition of Czech statehood—I emphasize Czech and I emphasize statehood. It is a Christian tradition that pushes certain values to the fore, such as humaneness and culture. It is a tradition linked with Europe."[8]

In his rhetoric, Klaus employs a mild Czech nationalism, celebrating the nation's long-past achievements. Yet, since the fall of Communism, leaders, historians, and citizens have been forced to grapple with the Czechs' complicity in their own more recent history, particularly during World War II and the Communist era. Havel, for example, formally apologized for the expulsion of the country's Germans, and has addressed its need to take responsibility for complicity in the Holocaust. Prague's small Jewish community has demanded that fellow citizens examine the anti-Semitism in Bohemian history.

Czech nationalists, the focus of the present book's study, often considered Jews outside the national community. Today, much of Prague Jewish history has been pre-digested for tourists, who can follow Franz Kafka's trail and visit the old Jewish Cemetery without confronting issues such as the nineteenth-century razing of the Jewish ghetto, Czech complicity with the German occupation, or the Communist Party purges that targeted Jews. Although Prague is no longer the multiethnic city of past centuries, its diverse history still demands reflection from its citizens and visitors.

Some Prague monuments have begun to reflect a nascent dialogue on the Jewish contribution to the city's landscape. In 2000, for example, the Prague city government agreed to put an explanatory plaque on a Charles Bridge statue of Christ's crucifixion; the statue includes a sign reading "Holy" in Hebrew letters. During the eighteenth century, a Prague Jew, accused of not bowing to the figure of Christ, was forced to purchase the inscription, which contradicted his spiritual beliefs. There is now a smattering of memorials to Holocaust victims, such as the list of names of lost Jewish families that was inscribed in the Pinkas Synagogue in the 1950s and restored in the 1990s. A plaque near the Veletržní palac (Trade Fair Palace) by artist and Holocaust survivor Helga Hosková marks the spot from which Prague Jews were marched and then loaded onto trains bound for Terezín. The figures on the plaque are emaciated, stooped, and disfigured, illustrating the devastation of the deportations on people's bodies and psyches.

A 2004 statue of Franz Kafka in Prague's Jewish Quarter attempts to reconcile some of the city's historical divisions. On the monument, unveiled eighty years after the Jewish writer's death, a diminutive Kafka sits atop a large man's

Helga Hosková's memorial at the site of Jewish deportations during World War II. Photo by author.

suit, which is empty but appears to walk forward, carrying the author. The image comes from Kafka's short story "Description of a Struggle," in which the narrator is carried through the streets of Prague, taking in the city's many landmarks. Yet the theme of emptiness on this statue, so common in postwar Holocaust memorials, also conveys the absence of a community lost to the extremes of twentieth-century racist nationalism.[9] The sculptor Jaroslav Rona noted his satisfaction that the statue stands in front of both a Roman Catholic Church

Franz Kafka
statue. Photo
by author.

and a Jewish synagogue, thus reminding onlookers of the historical tensions as well as the common space shared by two faiths.[10]

The theme of emptiness also characterizes the Memorial to the Victims of Communism, by renowned sculptor Olbram Zoubek, who also created a famous bust of Jan Palach from the death mask of the self-martyred student.[11] Unveiled on Petřín Hill in 2002, the Memorial to the Victims of Communism features several male figures on a staircase. Body parts are missing from each figure, until the last figure seems to disappear altogether, the series representing the psychological and physical devastation faced by Communist-era political prisoners. On the steps of the memorial, bronze plaques give approximate statistics for the numbers of political victims during the Communist regime: 205,486 arrested; 170,938 forced into exile; 4,500 dead in prison; 327 shot trying to escape; and 248 executed.

Like many Prague monuments, the memorial has been a site of controversy. Feminist groups have decried the absence of female figures, an absence that reinforces the representation of the citizen as male. Other groups have objected to the contemporary politics surrounding the monument, a project of the Prague City Council, dominated by the right-of-center Civic Democrats. The council neglected to invite then-president Havel—the most famous Czech political prisoner—to the opening ceremony, until the last minute. Havel then declined the invitation to attend, as did Civic Democratic leader Klaus, who feared the political repercussions of participating in a ceremony that had snubbed Havel. At the ceremony, Stanislav Drobný, chairman of the Confederation of Political Prisoners, the association that had supported the council's efforts to erect the memorial, criticized the still legal Communist Party's influence in the country.

The site's emotional content, addressing a period many Prague residents remember keenly, has invited interaction with the memorial, which has thus become a forum for political statements. In 2003, a bomb blast damaged one of the human figures, but no group or individual came forward to explain the political message of the attack. That year, at approximately the thirty-fifth anniversary of the Soviet invasion of Prague, the monument was covered with red adhesive tape, spelling expletives. A group of artists also held a demonstration at the memorial, decrying its kitschy style and poor taste. Yet many other people have left flowers, candles, and remembrances on the staircase, clearly feeling emotionally drawn to a place that evokes so much recent suffering. Although this monument does not have deliberate religious content, it has in fact become another sacred space, for it draws on the themes of martyrdom, suffering, and remembrance so prevalent in Prague memorials.

At the same time that the "empty pedestals," from which the Communist regime had removed the Masaryk statues, have been filled by new images of

Memorial to the Victims of Communism. Photo by author.

the first Czechoslovak president, other artists strive to depict the voids created in the darkest moments of the twentieth century.[12] Monuments such as the Hosková plaque commemorating the Prague deportations of Jews, the Franz Kafka statue, and the Memorial to the Victims of Communism create sacred space in a different way than do traditional depictions of national heroes. By presenting representations of emptiness, these newer memorials ask onlookers to put themselves directly into the monument's open spaces and join those whose voices have been silenced. These memorials often depict people from relatively recent memory, so that today's citizens see themselves more directly represented in the new public art that continually appears in Prague's living museum.

If the Czech émigré writer Milan Kundera is correct, his nation will continue to preoccupy itself with the past. And the living landscape of Prague will continue to reflect the historical memory, the debates, and the conflicts of its citizens. As Kundera has said: "People are always shouting they want to create a better future. It's not true. The future is an apathetic void of no interest to anyone. The past is full of life, eager to irritate us, provoke and insult us, tempt us to destroy or repaint it. The only reason people want to be masters of the future is to change the past."[13]

Notes

Prague—Panoramas of History

1. Hanebrink, *In Defense of Christian Hungary*, 4. See also Porter, "The Catholic Nation," 259–99.

2. Landres and Stier, "Introduction," in Landres and Stier, eds., *Religion, Violence, Memory and Place*, 8.

3. Important studies such as Jeremy King's examination of the largest city in Southern Bohemia and Nancy Wingfield's exploration of multiple ethnically mixed regions in the Bohemian Lands demonstrate that these debates occurred in the provinces. See Wingfield, *Flag Wars and Stone Saints*, and King, *Budweisers into Czechs and Germans*.

4. Landres and Stier, 7.

5. Friedland and Hecht, "The Powers of Place," in Landres and Stier, 35.

6. Kafka, *Briefe 1900–1912*. From a letter to Kafka's friend and schoolmate, Oskar Pollak, dated Prague, December 20, 1902. Kafka refers to Prague as *dieses Mütterchen*. In English it is alternatively translated as "this little mother" or "this old crone." In early twentieth-century German, *Mütterchen* had derogatory overtones but also connoted "motherhood"; thus I am choosing to translate it as "old mother."

7. Norberg-Schulz, *Genius Loci*, 6

8. Confino, "Collective Memory and Cultural History," 1389.

9. Norberg-Schulz, 82.

10. On Czech-German relations as they relate to commemorative practice, see especially Wingfield, *Flag Wars and Stone Saints*. On nationalism, literary movements, and the theater see Spector, *Prague Territories*. A now classic work on this topic is Kimball, *Czech Nationalism*.

11. Nora, *Lieux de Memoire*.

12. Czech scholars who have worked on these issues since the end of Communism include Hojda and Pokorný, *Pomníky a zapomníky*; Macura, *Masarykové boty a jiné semi (o) fejetony*; Rak, *Bývali Čechové*; and Holý, *Little Czech and the Great Czech Nation*. Other recent scholarship on commemoration in Central Europe include Bucur and Wingfield, eds., *Staging the Past*; Unowsky, *Pomp and Politics of Patriotism*; and Dabrowski, *Commemorations and the Shaping of Modern Poland*.

13. Boyer, *City of Collective Memory*, 45–46.

14. Havel, "Power of the Powerlesss," in *Open Letters*, 141–42.

15. Friedland and Hecht, "The Powers of Place," in Landres and Stier, 30.

16. Giustino, *Tearing Down Prague's Jewish Town*.

17. Cohen, *Politics of Ethnic Survival,* and Spector, *Prague Territories.*

18. Gellner, *Nations and Nationalism,* 7.

19. Duara, *Rescuing History from the Nation,* 8.

20. Benedict Anderson, *Imagined Communities.*

21. See Brubaker, *Nationalism Reframed,* and King, *Budweisers into Czechs and Germans.*

22. Hobsbawm, "Introduction: Inventing Traditions," in Hobsbawm and Ranger, *Invention of Tradition,* 1.

23. Gillis, ed., *Commemorations,* 7.

24. Renan, "What Is a Nation?" in Eley and Suny, eds., *Becoming National,* 42–56.

25. Baron, "The Construction of National Honour in Egypt," 245.

26. Wechsberg, *Prague the Mystical City,* 1. The author dedicates this book to "Prague, my love."

27. Seifert, "Introduction," in Plicka, *Prague the Golden City,* 15. Seifert wrote the introduction to this collection of Prague photographer Plicka's black-and-white photography.

28. Hojda and Pokorný, *Pomníky a zapomníky,* 79.

29. Demetz, *Prague in Black and Gold.*

30. Kovaly, *Life under a Cruel Star.*

31. Calvino, *Invisible Cities,* 10.

32. Ibid., 11.

Chapter 1. Preserving the National Past for the Future

Epigraph: Forman, *Dějiny spolku pro vystávení pomníku Mistra Jana Husi v Praze,* 5. This source is the official, self-published history of the Club for the Building of the Jan Hus Memorial in Prague. Carton 13. SZPH, AHMP.

1. Quoted in Forman, *Dějiny spolku,* 1.

2. On the Schwarzenberg family, and their views on Czech nationalism, see Glassheim, *Noble Nationalists,* 28–40.

3. Sucharda, *Historie pomníku Fr. Palackého v Praze k slavnosti odhalení,* 4.

4. Cohen, *Politics of Ethnic Survival,* 10.

5. Ibid., 20.

6. Ibid., 91.

7. Quoted in Forman, *Dějiny spolku,* 6.

8. Rieger approved of the delineation of Kreise and Bezirke along national lines. Only twenty-six out of forty-five judges on the supreme court needed to know both Czech and German; fifteen were not required to know Czech. In addition, the Bohemian Landeskulturamt and Landesschulart were to be divided into national sections, thus limiting the possibilities that Czechs could lead the entire region of Bohemia, where they constituted a majority. The only compromise made by the Germans was that, in communities with minority populations, forty students could have a school in their language providing their parents had lived in the community for five years; if there were eighty minority students, the parents only had to have resided in the town for three years.

9. Spinka, *John Hus: A Biography,* 7.

10. Ibid., 55.

11. Quoted in ibid., 65.

12. Anderson, *Imagined Communities*.

13. On the earliest manifestations of intellectual nationalism, see especially Agnew, *The Czech National Renascence*.

14. Erben, ed., "Výklad desatera," in *Mistra Jana Husa* 1: 133–34. Quoted in Spinka, *John Hus: A Biography*, 77.

15. Quoted in Agnew, *Czech National Renascence*, 64.

16. Szporluk, *Political Thought of Thomas G. Masaryk*, 84.

17. Masaryk, *Meaning of Czech History*, 10.

18. Wellek, "Introduction," in Masaryk, *Meaning of Czech History*, xiv.

19. Forman, *Dějiny spolku*, 9.

20. Ibid., 7.

21. Ibid., 17.

22. Ibid., 18.

23. Quoted in ibid., 21.

24. Forman, *Dějiny spolku*, 25.

25. Nolte explores the rhetorical phrase "every Czech" in her "'Every Czech a Sokol!'" 79–100.

26. "Kniha zápisu," Notebook 1, 1890–1907. SZPH. AHMP.

27. Correspondence. Carton 2, no. 44, 1903. SZPH. AHMP.

28. Garver, *Young Czech Party*, 118.

29. Letter from Sokol v Nepomuku to SZPH, no. 44/19 (May 8, 1908). AHMP.

30. Nolte, "Every Czech," and Garver, *Young Czech Party*, 117.

31. Letter from Ústřední výbor Národní jednoty českožidovské v Praze to Spolek pro zbudování Pomník Husova, no. 44/32, May 21, 1903; letter from Kroužek česko-židovského Dorostu v Praze to Spolek, no. 44/63, June 5, 1903; and letter from Spolek českých akademíku Židu v Praze to Spolek, no. 44/130, June 16, 1903. Correspondence. Carton 2, no. 44, 1903. SZPH. AHMP.

32. See Rachamimov, "Between Czechs and Germans." However, Rachamimov has argued that the Association was not able to reach into German Jewish communities to "convert" these Jews to a Czech identity, and that the Association remained small, with approximately one hundred members.

33. Letter from Spolek českých akademiku Židu v Praze to Spolek, no. 44/130, June 16, 1903. Correspondence. Carton 2, no. 44, 1903. SZPH. AHMP.

34. Forman, *Dějiny spolku*, 15.

35. Cohen, *Politics of Ethnic Survival*, 238.

36. See Pech, *Czech Revolution of 1848*, for an analysis of the early years of the Czech nationalist women's movement.

37. See, for example, Freeze, "Medical Education for Women in Austria," in *Women, State, and Party in Eastern Europe*, ed. Wolchik and Meyer, 51–63.

38. Letter from Anna Ziegloserová, editor of *Ženský obzor*, to SZPH. Correspondence. Carton 2, no. 44/40, May 23, 1903. See also "Husův fond," *Ženský obzor* 4, nos. 2–3: 41. SZPH. AHMP.

39. Nolte, "'Every Czech a Sokol!,'" and Pech, *Czech Revolution of 1848*, chapter 12.

40. Garver, *Young Czech Party,* 295–98.

41. Forman, *Dějiny spolku,* 41.

42. *In Memoriam Aloise Simonidesa,* 34–36.

43. Garver, *Young Czech Party,* 295.

44. Kelly, "Czech Radical Nationalism," 105–6.

45. Mosse, *Nationalization of the Masses,* 89.

46. Forman, *Dějiny spolku,* 42.

47. The various names of Prague's university reflects the city's complex history. Established in 1348 by Charles IV, it was usually known simply as Prague University in Hus's day. In 1366, Charles College, the Carolinum, was founded as a branch of the university. At the start of the Hussite Wars, in 1419, Utraquist Hussites founded a Protestant Academy. Then in 1562, Emperor Ferdinand III called the Jesuits to Prague to found an academy, which became known as the Clementinum. In 1622, the entire university was given to the Jesuits, who controlled it until the disbanding of their order in 1783. In 1882, the university—renamed Charles-Ferdinand University—was officially divided into Czech and German branches. In 1920, the Czech branch was officially renamed Charles University. The German branch was closed in 1945. Throughout the book, I refer to the university by the name it was called at the time, although multiple names refer to the same institution.

48. "Jednatelská zpráva o činnost spolku pro zbudování pomníku Husova v Praze za rok 1903," no. 198: 6. Carton 14. SZPH. AHMP.

49. Sen, "Motherhood and Mothercraft," 231.

50. De Groot, "Dialectics of Gender," 263.

51. Varikas, "Gender and National Identity in *fin de siècle* Greece," 280.

52. Speech reprinted in *Věstník sokolský 17* (1903): 504–5.

53. Šnajdaufová-Čadová, "O Mistru Janu Husovi a jeho významu" reprinted in *Ženský svět* : 154–60. The Festival program lists the speech title of the speech as "On Master Jan Hus and His Meaning *for Czech Women.*"

54. Šnajdaufová-Čadová, 154.

55. Ibid., 158.

56. Ibid., 160.

57. Ibid., 155.

58. Ibid., 160.

59. Garver, *Young Czech Party,* 71.

60. Čech, "Hus," 1–3.

61. For a more thorough gendered analysis of the festival, see Paces, "Rotating Spheres."

62. "Husova oslava," *Katolické listy,* July 6, 1903.

63. "Oslava Husova proti Husovi," *Právo lidu,* July 6, 1903.

64. "Po oslavě Husově," *Právo lidu,* July 8, 1903.

65. "Městacká oslava Husova," *Právo lidu,* July 6, 1903.

66. "Husovy slavnosti," *Ženský obzor* 3–4, no. 2–3: 41.

67. Ibid., 42.

68. *Věstník sokolský* 17 (1903): 505. See also Nolte, *Sokol in the Czech Lands*, 156.

69. Nolte, ibid., 157.

Chapter 2. Art Meets Politics

Epigraph: Šaloun, L. *Šalouna Husův pomník v Hořicích.*

1. Šaloun, L. *Šalouna Husův pomník v Hořicích.*

2. See Wittlich, *Česká secese*, and Wittlich, *Prague, Fin de Siècle*.

3. Quoted in Mosse, *Nationalization of the Masses,* 47.

4. Minutes of the meeting of the Club for the Building of the Jan Hus Memorial in Prague, July 3, 1890. Notebook 1. SZPH. AHMP.

5. Giustino, *Tearing Down Prague's Jewish Town*, 7.

6. Mádl, "Husův pomník," 50–69.

7. See photograph in Mádl, "Husův pomník," 54.

8. Carl Schorske elaborates the shift from historicism to naturalism to expressionism in *Fin-de-Siècle Vienna*. Petr Wittlich discusses the effect of these pan-European trends in *Prague, Fin de Siècle*.

9. Mosse, *Nationalization of the Masses,* chapter 3, *passim*.

10. Wittlich, *Prague, Fin de Siècle,* 58.

11. Ibid., 165.

12. Ibid., 46.

13. Wittlich, "Secesní Orfeus," 26–49.

14. Minutes of the Meeting of the Club for the Building of the Jan Hus Memorial in Prague, July 3, 1890. Notebook 1. SZPH. AHMP.

15. Mádl, "Husův Pomník," 66.

16. Minutes of the meeting of the Club for the Building of the Jan Hus Memorial in Prague, July 3, 1890. Notebook 1, SZPH. AHMP.

17. Wittlich, *Prague, Fin de Siècle,* 165.

18. Šaloun, *Dva návrhy na pomník. M. Jana Husi v Praze* contains photographs of the sculptor's updated ideas for the Hus Memorial.

19. Šaloun, *Husův pomník v Hořicích.*

20. Ibid.

21. Šaloun, *Dva návrhy.*

22. Šaloun, "Z duševní dílny umělcovy," 83.

23. Šaloun, *Dva návrhy.*

24. Ibid.

25. Smlouva, August 26, 1905. Carton 8. SZPH. AHMP.

26. Wittlich, *České sochařství,* 52.

27. Smlouva, August 26, 1905. Carton 8. SZPH. AHMP.

28. Karo, "Feuilleton. Pomník Husův," *Národní listy.* Clipping, from Carton 12, no. 158/102, no date (most likely July 1903). SZPH. AHMP.

29. Quoted in Forman, *Dějiny spolku,* 36.

30. Quoted in Heymann, *John Žižka and the Hussite Revolution.* Lawrence of Březová, a contemporary, acquaintance, and admirer of the blind military genius Žižka, wrote what historians believe the most reliable account of the Hussite wars.

31. Pelikan, *Mary through the Centuries,* 174.

32. "Ladislav Šaloun, o svém Husovi," Reprinted newspaper article from unacknowledged source, no date (most likely 1903). Notebook 1. SZPH. AHMP.

33. Kristeva, "Stabat Mater," in *Female Body in Western Culture,* ed. Rubin.

34. For an analysis of gender imagery in Prague, see Witkovsky, "Envisaging the Gendered Center."

35. Forman, *Dějiny spolku,* 36.

36. "Úvodem k vlastnímu časopisu," *Za starou Prahu: Věstník klubu za starou Prahu,* vol. 1, no. 1 (January 28, 1910).

37. Letter to Prague City Council from *Klub za starou Prahu.* Carton 5, no. 61/35. SZPH. AHMP.

38. "Husův pomník v dnešní formě nepatří na Staroměst. Náměstí," *Za starou Prahu* 2, no. 3–4 (May 8, 1911).

39. "Husův pomník se nehodí na Staroměstské Náměstí," *Za starou Prahu* 2, no. 1–2 (March 24, 1911).

40. "Kaple Božího Těla," *Za starou Prahu* 2, no. 1–2 (March 24, 1911).

41. "O umístění Husova pomníku," from *Samostatnost,* as quoted in *Za starou Prahu* 2, no. 1–2 (March 24, 1911).

42. "Činnost klubu v březnu a dubnu 1911," *Za starou Prahu* 2, no. 3–4 (May 8, 1911): 24.

43. Ibid. See also *Věstník královského města Prahy* (April 1911).

44. Letter from the Club for the Building of the Jan Hus Memorial to the Prague City Council. Carton 5. SZPH. AHMP.

Chapter 3. Generational Approaches to National Monuments

Epigraph: Sucharda, *Historie pomníku Fr. Palackého v Praze k slavnosti odhalení,* 4–5.

1. Hojda and Pokorný, *Pomníky a zapomníky,* 79.

2. Hobsbawm and Ranger, *Invention of Tradition,* 263–307.

3. Katherine David-Fox, "Prague-Vienna, Prague-Berlin," 735–60.

4. On the patronage by Zemská Banka, see Howard, *Art Nouveau,* 80.

5. Letter from Emperor Francis Josef Bohemian Academy of Arts, Humanities, and Sciences to Prague City Council, July 5, 1891. Item no. 3/28/18, Folder: Pomník sv. Václava, 1891–1894. Praesidium. AHMP.

6. Ibid.

7. Palacký, *Dějiny národu českého.*

8. Quoted in Pynsent, *Questions of Identity,* 196.

9. Letter from the Czech Academy to the Prague municipal government, July 5, 1891. Item no. B/28/18, Folder: Pomník sv. Václava na Václavském Nám. 1891–1894. Praesidium. AHMP.

10. Quoted in Plaschka, "The Political Significance of Frantisek Palacky," 49.

11. Web site of the National Museum in Prague, http://www.nm.cz/english/historie .php.

12. See especially Kimball, *Czech nationalism.*

13. See Garver, *Young Czech Party,* 142.

14. David-Fox, "Prague-Vienna, Prague-Berlin."

15. Wittlich, *Prague, Fin de Siècle,* 38.

16. Quoted in Spinka, *Jan Hus: A Biography,* 76.

17. "K soutěži na pomník palackého," *Volné směry* 9, no. 2 (July 1898): 406–36.

18. Wittlich, *Prague, Fin de Siècle,* 25.

19. Ibid., 157.

20. Sucharda, *Pomník,* 9.

21. Zyka, "Slavnost," in *Památník sletu slovanského Sokolstva roku 1912 v Praze,* ed. Ocenawek, 312.

22. Sucharda, *Pomník,* 9.

23. Zyka, "Slavnost," 313.

24. Wood and Greenhalgh, "Symbols of the Sacred and Profane," in Greenhalgh, ed., *Art Nouveau,* 86.

25. Sucharda, *Pomník,* 10.

26. Ibid., 10.

27. Ibid., 11.

28. Wood and Greenhalgh, "Symbols of the Sacred and Profane," in Greenhalgh, ed., *Art Nouveau,* 85.

29. Zyka, "Slavnost," 311.

30. Nolte, *Sokol,* 175.

31. For a thorough discussion of the 1912 Slet, see Nolte, *Sokol,* 174–78.

32. *Věstnik spolku pro zbudování Žižkova Pomniku na Žižkově* 1, no. 3 (January 1908): 2.

33. Riegl, "Modern Cult of Monuments," in *Oppositions Reader,* ed. Hays, 621–51.

34. *Věstnik spolku pro zbudování Žižkova Pomniku na Žižkově* 1, no. 3 (January 1908): 4.

35. "Žižkuv pomník?" in *Narodní politika,* May 21, 1913.

36. Hojda and Pokorný, *Pomníky a zapomníky,* 151.

37. See especially Greenhalgh, *Art Nouveau,* and Lane, *National Romanticism and Modern Architecture.*

38. Wittlich, *Prague, Fin de Siècle,* 17.

39. On the 1913 contest, see especially Witkovsky, "Truly Blank," 42–60, and Wittlich, *Prague, Fin de Siècle,* 240–42.

40. Wittlich, *Prague, Fin de Siècle,* 239.

41. Witkovsky, "Truly Blank," and Wittlich, *Prague, Fin de Siècle,* 240–42.

Chapter 4. World War I and the Jan Hus Jubilee

Epigraph: "Tichý den velkého jubilea," *Večerník Právu lidu*, July 6, 1915.

1. Minutes of the Steering Committee Meeting, March 24, 1915. Notebook 2. SZHP. AHMP.

2. See the July 6 and 7 editions of *Večerník Práva lidu, Právo lidu, Národní politika, Národní listy, Večer, Venkov, Naše hlasy* (Český Brod), *Jihozápadní morava* (Trebice), *Čas, Naše slovo.*

3. See, for example, "M. Jan Hus a česká universita," *Národní listy*, July 6, 1915; "Hus a Slovensko," *Národní listy*, July 6, 1915; "Mistr Jan Hus po 500 letech!" *Čas,* July 6, 1915; "Hus a válka," *Národní listy,* July 4, 1915; and "Ženské hnutí. Co chtěl Hus a chceme my, Ženy," *Národní listy,* July 4, 1915.

4. "Tichý den," *Večerník Právu lidu,* July 6, 1915.

5. Seton-Watson, *History of the Czechs and Slovaks*, 285.

6. Huebner, "Multi-national 'Nation-State,' " 24.

7. Ibid., 26.

8. On the Czech Maffia (Czech spelling), see Paulová, *Dějiny Maffie.*

9. Macartney, *Habsburg Empire*, 813.

10. "Valná hromada Spolku pro postavení Husova pomníku," *Národní politika,* May 3, 1915.

11. Records of the renovation of Hus's birthplace are held in the Okresní Archiv Prachatice (Regional Archives of Prachatice); hereafter, OAP.

12. Paulová, *Dějiny Maffie,* 532.

13. Minutes of the Meeting of the Club for the building of the Jan Hus Memorial, March 24, 1915. Notebook 2. SZHP. AHMP. See also Petr Kreuz, *Dějiny spolku pro zbudování Husova pomníku v Praze,* a short essay that accompanies the inventory of the Hus Fond at the Prague City Archives (AHMP).

14. "Husův pomník předán královské Praze," *Národní politika,* July 7, 1915, 5.

15. Letter from Tělocvičná jednota Sokol v Holešově, Moravě to SZPH, July 1, 1915. Correspondence file, 1915, no. 56 (piece 102). Carton 4. SZPH. AHMP.

16. Correspondence file, 1915, no. 56 (pieces 96, 99, 105, 109, 110, 111, 113, 116, 117). Carton 4. SZPH. AHMP.

17. Correspondence file, 1915, no. 56 (pieces 117, 94). Carton 4. SZPH. AHMP.

18. Letter from Presidium rady královského hlavního města Prahy to SZPH. Correspondence file, 1915, no. 56 (piece 91). Carton 4. SZPH. AHMP.

19. Program, "Slavnostní valné hromadě," no. 199. Carton 14. SZPH. AHMP.

20. Letter from Sokol v Žižkově to SZPH. Correspondence file, 1915, no. 56 (piece 108). Carton 4. SZPH. AHMP.

21. "Ženské spolky a Husovy oslavy," *Ženský svět* 19 (1915): 174.

22. Anna Císařová-Kolářová, *Žena v hnutí husitském.*

23. "Ženské spolky," *Ženský svět* 19 (1915): 174.

24. On Brožík's painting of Hus, see, for example, *Václav Brožík und sein Gemaelde,* and Mádl, *Václav Brožík Odsouzení M. Jana Husi.* Both pamphlets can be found in Carton 13. SZHP. AHMP.

25. Jan Galandauer, "Husův národ a most Františka Ferdinanda."

26. Program, "Slavnostní Valné Hromadě." Carton 14, no. 199. SZPH. AHMP.

27. "Jednatelská zpráva za rok 1915." Carton 6, no. 79. SZHP. AHMP.

28. Baxa's speech was reprinted in several Prague newspapers, including, *Národní listy* and *Čas.* I am quoting from the version published in Žipek, ed., *Domov za války,* 7–9.

29. Žipek, ed., *Domov za války,* 9.

30. Paulová, *Dějiny Maffie,* 533.

31. Quoted in Paulová, *Dějiny Maffie*, 534.

32. *Národní listy*, July 7, 1915.

33. Masaryk, *Making of a State*, 84.

34. Ibid., 71.

35. "*Ve jménu Husově pro svobodu národa*," K. 20. *vyročí Masarykova vystoupení ve Švycarsku dne 4. a 6. července 1915*," Prague, 1935.

36. *Neue Freie Presse*, July 7, 1915.

37. Statistics from the 1921 census are presented in Mamatey and Luza, *History of the Czechoslovak Republic*, 40.

38. Miller, *Forging Political Compromise*, 3.

39. Sayer, *Coasts of Bohemia*, 270.

40. Quoted in Witkovsky, "Truly Blank," 59, from Macura, "Pravda vitězí! Jako politické heslo," in Kroupa, ed., *Veritas vincit*, 70–74.

41. Sayer, *Coasts of Bohemia*, 178.

Chapter 5. Toppling Columns, Building a Capital

Epigraph: Quoted in Sauer-Kysela's memoir of the event: Sauer-Kysela, *Naše luza, jesuité a diplomaté*, 8. Also quoted in Peroutka, *Budování státu*, 117, and in the Catholic newspaper *Lidové listy*, November 11, 1923.

1. Quoted in Gottfried, "Kterák socha Marianská byla stržena," 30.

2. See Wingfield, "Conflicting Constructions of Memory."

3. Olin, *Forms of Representation in Alois Riegl's Theory of Art*, 176. See especially Riegl, "Modern Cult of Monuments," in *Oppositions Reader*, ed. Hays, 621–51.

4. Hojda and Pokorný, *Pomníky a zapomníky*, chapter 2.

5. Miller, *Forging Political Compromise*, 5.

6. For further reading, see especially Polišenský, *Thirty Years' War and the Crisis of the Seventeenth Century*, and Parker, *Thirty Years War*.

7. Mamatey, "Battle of the White Mountain as Myth in Czech History," 335–45.

8. Evans, *Habsburg Monarchy*, 68.

9. The term *tábor* was used by both the Young Czechs and the National Socialists for their party rallies. *Tábor* literally means gathering or camp, but the word also evoked the memory of the Hussite era, since Hus's radical followers lived communally in the Southern Bohemian town they named *Tábor*. The word is of Turkish origin, meaning wagons chained together in a circular fashion. It is found in nearly every East European language, but only in Czech did the word acquire historical and political significance. Bruce Garver discusses Young Czech *tábory* or political meetings in *Young Czech Party*, 71. Agnew analyzes nineteenth-century *tábory* in "Demonstrating the Nation," in Reiss, ed, *The Street as Stage*, 85–104.

10. On the relationship between nationalism and crowd behavior, see especially Freifeld, *Nationalism and the Crowd in Liberal Hungary, 1848–1914*.

11. Several articles and books discuss the artistic merit and value of the column. See, for example, "Dějiny pobožností u Marianského sloupu na staroměstském náměstí v Praze," *Časopis katolického duchovenstva* 65 (1924); "Jan Jiří Bendl, Pražký Sochář Časného Baroku," *Památky archeologické* 40 (1934–1935): 55–91; Royt, "Mariánský

Sloup na Staroměstském náměstí," 25–28; and Šorm and Krajša, "Mariánské sloupy v Čechách a na Moravě Příspěvky k studiu barokní kultury."

12. Quoted in Sauer-Kysela's memoir of the event, *Naše luza, jesuité a diplomaté,* in Peroutka, *Budování státu,* and in the Catholic newspaper *Lidové listy* (see note to epigraph). Peroutka was a journalist with connections with the political leaders of the new Czechoslovak state. His four-volume work *Budování státu* is a first-hand account of the political activities surrounding the building of that state and is considered by Czechoslovak historians the best account of the politics of the era.

13. See also Wingfield, *Flag Wars and Stone Saints,* 145–47.

14. T. Mills Kelly, "Czech Radical Nationalism," 211–12, and "Taking It to the Streets," 93–112.

15. The National Socialists had considered uniting with the Social Democrats, but the Socialist Democrats disapproved the merger. Instead, the National Socialists joined forces with the Czech Anarchists, composed mostly of Prague intellectuals and radicalized Czech coal miners from the German areas of North Bohemia. In the fall of 1918, when the Social Democrats reconsidered the merger proposal in order to strengthen socialism, the Czech Socialists, moving further right, refused because Social Democratic leader Bohumír Šmeral had remained loyal to Vienna early in the war. By the time independence was declared in October, the Czech Socialists had become more interested in radical nationalist agitation than in Marxist economic policy. In 1918, a plurality of Czech voters in the historic provinces of Bohemia, Moravia, and Silesia voted for one of the Socialist parties. In local elections in June 1918, the Social Democrats received 30.1 percent of the vote, and the Czechoslovak Socialists obtained 15.6 percent. The Agrarians secured 20.5 percent, the People's Party 9.7 percent, and the National Democrats 8.2 percent. See Huebner, "The Multi-national Nation State," 230.

16. *Lidové listy,* November 8, 1923.

17. Sauer-Kysela, *Naše luza, jesuité a diplomaté.* Since 1989, there has been considerable interest in the history of the Marian Column; see for example, Bobková, "Jak se strhával mariánský sloup," 20.

18. Sauer-Kysela, *Naše luza, jesuité a diplomaté.*

19. "Denní zprávy," *Národní listy,* November 5, 1918, 3.

20. "Znížení Mariánského sloupu!" *Lidové listy,* November 5, 1918, 2.

21. From Moric Hruban, *Z času nedlouho zaslých* (Rome: Křestanská akademie, 1967), 199. Quoted and translated in Frank Joseph Hajek, Catholics and Politics in Czechoslovakia, PhD dissertation, Emory University, 1973, 39.

22. Connerton, *How Societies Remember,* chapter 2.

23. Turner, "Liminality and the Performative Genres," *in Rite, Drama, Festival, Spectacle,* ed. MacAloon, 19–41.

24. In the late nineteenth century, politically oriented Roman Catholics founded political parties. Bohemian Catholics founded the Christian-Social Party in September 1894 in Litomyšl, and the Catholic National Party in Moravia was established in September 1896 in Přerov. In January 1919, following Czechoslovak independence, these parties merged in Prague as the Československá strana lidová (Czechoslovak People's Party). Jan Šrámek was selected as its chairman.

25. Hajek, "Catholics and Politics," 44 and throughout.

26. Sauer-Kysela, *Naše luza, jesuité a diplomaté*, 6.

27. From the official statement by the National Council released on November 4, 1918. The full text of the statement can be found in Peroutka, *Budování státu*, 118, and *Národní listy*, November 5, 1918.

28. On Slovak nationalism, see, for example, Felak, *"At the Price of the Republic"*; Brock, *The Slovak National Awakening*.

29. Peroutka, *Budování státu*, 117.

30. *Sto let Klub za starou Prahu, 1900–2000*, 134–36. Czechoslovakia would not enact a law for state protection of monuments until 1968.

31. Zápis o schuzi rady hlavního města Prahy, November 27, 1918. Fond: Protokoly schuzí rady městské 1918 (hereafter, PSRM), AHMP.

32. Vlnas, *Jan Nepomucký, Česká legenda*.

33. From *Šibensky* (Prague, 1919–1920). Reprinted in Vlnas, *Jan Nepomucký, Česká legenda*, 259.

34. Hojda and Pokorný, *Pomníky a zapomníky*.

35. Peroutka, *Budování státu*, vol. 1, 407–8.

36. For further discussion of attacks on Nepomucký statues, as well as Habsburg Monuments, throughout Bohemia, see Paces and Wingfield, "The Sacred and the Profane," in Judson and Rozenblitt, eds., *Constructing Identities in East Central Europe*, 147–150.

37. Peroutka, *Budováni státu*, vol. 1, 407–8. See also Feinberg, *Elusive Equality*, 43–48, on the marriage law debates.

Chapter 6. Catholic Czech Nationalism in the Early 1920s

Epigraph: Jaroslav Durych, *Lidové listy*, May 10, 1923.

1. Trapl, *Political Catholicism and the Czechoslovak People's Party in Czechoslovakia, 1918–1938*, 9.

2. Ibid., 54.

3. Felak, *"At the Price of the Republic,"* 29.

4. Mamatey and Luza, eds., *History of the Czechoslovak Republic*, 99. For full election results, see Československá akademie věd, *Přehled československých dějin*, vol. 3, 104.

5. Trapl, *Political Catholicism and the Czechoslovak People's Party in Czechoslovakia, 1918–1938*, 16.

6. On the *pětka*, see Mamatey and Luza, eds., *History of the Czechoslovak Republic*, 108–10 and 125–27.

7. Members of the five-man *pětka* had tremendous power, which was extraconstitutional, and was one of the few features of the country's politics to tarnish the image of a purely democratic Czechoslovak state. Still, the *pětka* enabled the state to remain stable and resistant to the extreme politics prevalent in Central Europe during the interwar period.

8. The debate between centralism and provincial autonomy would continue throughout the First Czechoslovak Republic. In May 1918, Tomáš Masaryk drafted the Pittsburgh agreement to gather support among Czech and Slovak Americans for an

independent Czechoslovak state. In this statement, Masaryk wrote that Slovakia would have provincial autonomy, on the model of an American state, but the particulars thereof would be determined by the elected representatives of the new government. When the constitutional assembly met in 1920, however, a centralized system was established. Slovak Agrarians did not believe their province ready for autonomy, and Slovak Social Democrats completely opposed decentralization. Further, many politicians feared Hlinka's intentions when it was learned that he had secretly gone to the Paris Peace Conference. As a compromise, the assembly adopted the Hungarian system of counties (*Župy*) that would have regional administration. Slovak populists, in particular, were angry that the integrity of Slovakia was not recognized in the constitution. They were not appeased by their inclusion as "state people"—that is, as members of the Czechoslovak nation and not as a national minority. By the 1930s, the autonomy question would become one of the most divisive issues in the state.

9. Trapl, *Political Catholicism and the Czechoslovak People's Party in Czechoslovakia, 1918–1938,* 58.

10. Jaroslav Durych, *Lidové listy,* May 10, 1923.

11. Ibid.

12. Ibid.

13. Ibid.

14. The Ministry of Foreign Affairs compiled a clippings folder on this press war of 1923. See Ministry of Foreign Affairs—Cut-out Archive (hereafter, MZV-VA), no. 1220, 1923–1924. Carton 2457. NA.

15. "Nový požadavek lidové strany: Pomník Mistra J. Husa musí byti odstraněn," *Večer,* May 11, 1923.

16. Ibid.

17. "Zpupná urážka českého národa!" *Socialista,* May 10, 1923.

18. "Nový požadavek lidové strany," *Večer,* May 11, 1923.

19. "Zpupná urážka českého národa!" *Socialista,* May 10, 1923.

20. Ibid. The "black" refers to the Catholic parties. Several parties were nicknamed with a color: the Agrarians (green); Socialists and Communists (red); Catholic parties (black).

21. Hajek, "Catholics and Politics in Czechoslovakia," 128. Šrámek also avoided association with international Catholic movements, and thought of his party as a national political movement.

22. "Sloup třidění duchu," *Pražský večerník,* May 12, 1923.

23. Ibid.

24. *Čech,* October 30, 1923.

25. See *Čech* and *Lidové listy* throughout the fall of 1923.

26. "František Sauer ze Žižkov," *Lidové listy,* November 11, 1923.

27. "Zbabétý hrdina," *Čech,* November 8, 1923, and "František Sauer ze Žižkov."

28. Franta Kysela-Sauer, "Kdo strhl mariánský sloup na Staroměstkém náměstí?" *Rudé právo,* November 4, 1923.

29. Ibid.

30. Antonín Šorm, "Co bude státi znovuvybudování Mariánského sloupu v Praze," *Pražský večerník,* November 3, 1918.

31. "Vítězství Jana Nepomuckého v pátém roce republiky," *Večerní rudé právo*, May 16, 1923.

32. "Svatojanské slavnosti v Praze," *Čech*, May 12, 1923, and (May 13, 1923).

33. *Čech*, May 13, 1923.

34. The Ministry of Foreign Affairs compiled a collection of press clippings about the Jan Nepomucký celebrations of 1923. See MZV-VA 1220, 1923–24, Carton 2457, NA.

35. Rudolf Horský, "Národní náš svátek," *Čech*, May 16, 1923. The Western region of Bohemia near the German border had a high German population.

36. "Stav otázky svatojanské," *Právo lidu*, May 16, 1923.

37. Ibid.

38. *Večerní rudé právo*, May 16, 1923.

39. Ibid.

40. *Čech*, May 13, 1923.

41. Ibid.

42. *Čech*, May 12, 1923.

43. Ibid.

44. *Čech*, May 13, 1923.

45. Ibid.

46. "Upozornění veškerému uchovenstvu Velké Prahy," *Čech*, May 13, 1923.

47. *Čech*, May 13, 1923.

48. Horský, "Národní náš svátek."

49. Ibid.

50. As Ernest Gellner has argued in *Nations and Nationalism,* the dream of nationalists is to create a shared high culture and then to incorporate this ideology into a modern state.

51. Mamatey and Luza, *History of the Czechoslovak Republic,* 128.

52. Trapl, *Political Catholicism and the Czechoslovak People's Party in Czechoslovakia, 1918–1938,* 66.

53. Conway, *Catholic Politics in Europe, 1918–1945,* 30.

54. Hajek, "Catholics and Politics," 175.

55. On Joan of Arc, see Wheeler and Wood, eds., *Fresh Verdicts on Joan of Arc,* and Jewkes and Landfield, eds., *Joan of Arc.*

56. Lightbody, *Judgements of Joan,* 18.

Chapter 7. Religious Heroes for a Secular State

Epigraph: "Svátek či pracovní den?" *Tribuna,* July 5, 1922.

1. Quoted in Wingfield, *Flag Wars,* 164.

2. Thomas Carlyle, *On Heroes, Hero-Worship, and Heroic in History.*

3. "Zrušení některých cirkevních svátku," memo from the Ministry of Interior to the Ministry of Education and National Enlightenment, November 6, 1919, No. 54.687/1919. Carton 2941. Ministerstvo školství 1919–49. NA.

4. On Hungary, see Alice Freifeld, "The Cult of March 15: Sustaining the Hungarian Myth of Revolution, 1849–1999," in Wingfield and Bucur, eds., *Staging the Past.*

5. Bucur, "Commemorations of December 1, 1918, and National Identity in Twenti-eth-Century Romania," in Wingfield and Bucur, eds., *Staging the Past,* 292.

6. Zápis o výsledku porady konaní 24. října 1919 v ministerstvu vnitra o zrušení svátku. No. 54687.1919—odd. 1. Carton 2941. MH 1919–49. NA.

7. "Prohlašení dne 6. července občanským svátkem," Presidium ministerské rady, no. 18.941/20, PMV 1919–1924/IV/H/22. NA.

8. "6. červenec svátkem státním—z vůle národa," *České slovo,* June 28, 1922.

9. "Poslanecká sněmovna." Carton 2941. MH 1919–49. NA.

10. "Svátek či pracovní den?" *Tribuna,* July 5, 1922.

11. Report of the Presidium of the Ministers' Council, June 26, 1922. Carton 3304. PMR/741/12. NA.

12. Report of the Ministry of Post and Telegraph to the Presidium of the Council of Ministers, "Úprava služby v den 6. července 1922." Carton 3304. PMR/741/12. NA

13. "Kult Husův jest nebezpečním pro svobodný národ a samostatní stát," *Pražský večerník,* July 5, 1922.

14. Hajek, "Catholics and Politics," 152–53.

15. Zákon o nedělích a svátcích, Carton 415. MH 1918–49. NA.

16. "The Holiday Bill, April 3, 1925," in Nemec, *Church and State in Czechoslovakia,* 135.

17. *Den,* March 4, 1925.

18. The cumbersome glagolitic was replaced by Cyrilic in the Eastern Orthodox region, but Roman Catholic regions, such as Bohemia and Poland, adopted the Latin alphabet.

19. "Za uzákonění Husova dne 6. července státním svátkem," *Večerní národní listy,* February 4, 1924.

20. Hajek, "Catholics and Politics," 153.

21. See especially Masaryk, *Meaning of Czech History.*

22. "Průmyslníci proti Husovi," *České slovo,* July 8, 1925.

23. "Slavnostní předvečer Husova svátku," *Národní listy,* July 4, 1925.

24. "Maďaři také proti Husovi," Memo from Ministry of Authority in Slovakia to the Ministry of the Interior, no. 93006/25, PMV/1925–30/X/H/44–2 (Husovy oslavy), NA.

25. *Odpolední národní politika,* July 4, 1925.

26. "Husitský prápor," *Právo lidu,* July 8, 1925.

27. "Zpráva o událostech politického rázu ze den 6. července. 1925." PMV/1925–30/X/44–2, NA.

28. Legation of the Czechoslovak Republic at the Holy See to the Foreign Ministry. Sign: T 32/21 (část III), no. 311/87 pol. AKPR.

29. "Odjezď apolstolského nuncia Marmaggiho z republiky," *Lidové listy,* July 7, 1925.

30. *Čech,* July 7, 1925.

31. Even pro-Hus Czechs acknowledged that such a Hussite flag probably never ex-isted historically, yet the commemorative decoration had been used since the nineteenth century in Hus celebrations. See K. Z. Klíma, "Poznámky z týdne," *Lidové noviny,* July 13, 1925.

32. Ibid.

33. Quoted in Hajek, "Catholics and Politics," 155–56.

34. "Klerikální fiasko—Důstojné oslavy Husovy. Veliký tábor lidu proti Vatikánu." *Národní osvobození*, July 15, 1925.

35. "Dopisy k posledním dnům," *Večerní české slovo*, July 16, 1925.

36. "Husitský prápor," *Právo lidu*, July 8, 1925.

37. Miller, *Forging Political Compromise*, 140.

38. Legation of the USA (American Minister, Lewis Einstein) to Secretary of State, January 4, 1928, no. 860F.415 H 96/4. General Records of Department of State, Record Group 59. USNA.

39. "Ještě Hus," *České slovo*, July 8, 1925.

40. Hajek, "Catholics and Politics," 163–65.

41. "Přípravy k Husovým oslavám," *České Slovo*, May 23, 1926. See also PMV/X/H/44–2. NA.

42. "Sokolstvo památce Husově," *Tribuna Večer*, July 7, 1926.

43. Ibid.

44. Quoted in Feinberg, *Elusive Equality*, 35.

45. Ibid., 69.

46. Miles, *Art, Space and the City*, 44.

47. Hunt, *Politics, Culture, and Class.*

48. "Pondělní oslavy Mistra Jana Husa," *Tribuna Večer*, July 7, 1926.

49. Pateman, *Disorder of Women.*

50. John Sterret Gittings, Legation of United States of America, to Secretary of State, July 11, 1927. No. 1439, RG 59, USNA.

51. Andrea Orzoff, "'The Literary Organ of Politics.'"

52. See especially Pynsent, *Questions of Identity.*

53. See Macura, *Masarykové boty,* for an analysis of the Masaryk–Wenceslas iconography. An equestrian statue of Masaryk dressed as Wenceslas can also be found on the campus of the University of Chicago; an émigré group in the United States commissioned that work.

54. Fryček, "Dva symboly," *České slovo*, September 28, 1927.

55. "Sv. Václav a mistr Jan Hus," *Čech*, September 27, 1928.

56. Quoted in Skalický, "The Vicissitudes of the Catholic Church," 303.

57. Ibid.

58. Letter from Czechoslovak Church to Presidential Chancellery. No. 6297/37. Sign.: D 7171/38. AKPR.

59. Ibid.

60. Wenceslas Millennium File. No. D6297/37. February 19, 1929. Sign.: D 7171/38. AKPR.

61. "Pamětní spis," Sign.: T 665/21. AKPR.

62. "Pořád jubilejních slavností u příležitosti Svatováclavského millennia v Praze." Carton 241. PMV 1925–30, VI/O/9–2 (oslavy). NA.

63. "Výstava korunovačních klenotů v chrámu sv. Víta v Praze ve dnech 22–29. září 1929." PMV /1925–30 VI/O/9–2 (oslavy). NA.

64. Report from John S. Gittings at U.S. Legation in Czechoslovakia to Secretary of State, September 30, 1929. M 1218.860F.415, St. Wenceslas/6. RG 59, USNA.

65. Ibid.

66. "Pořád jubilejních slavností." Carton 241. PMV 1925–30, VI/O/9–2 (oslavy). NA.

67. Presidium zemského úřad v Praze to PMV. Carton 241. PMV 1925–30 VI/O/9–2 (oslavy). NA.

68. "Svatováclavské oslavy—učást člen vlády." Carton 241. PMV 1925–30 VI/O/9–2 (oslavy). NA.

69. Kapras had been a leader of the Progressive Party before World War I, and rose to prominence in the National Democratic Party during the interwar period. He published numerous books on Czech legal history, and taught at the Law Faculty of Charles University in Prague.

70. "Odpověď' pana presidenta republiky prof. Kaprasovi při odevzdávání standarty jezdeckému pluku č. 8 Knížete Václava." Sign.: D 5814/29. AKPR.

71. Ibid.

72. Ibid.

73. "Svatováclavské oslavy—učást člen vlády." Carton 241. PMV 1925–30 VI/O/9–2 (oslavy). NA.

74. "Pořád jubilejních slavností." Carton 241. PMV 1925–30 VI/O/9–2 (oslavy). NA.

75. "Zprávu pro dra. Scheiszla. 6/9/27." Sign.: D 7171/38, část pod č. j. D 6297/37. AKPR.

76. "Zprávu pro dra. Schenka. 14/9/27." Sign.: D 7171/38, část pod č. j. D 6297/37. AKPR.

77. Ibid.

78. Gittings to Sec. of State, 5.

79. Ibid., 6.

80. Ibid.

81. Ibid.

Chapter 8. Modern Churches, Living Cathedrals

Epigraph: "Bude vztyčen na Václavském náměstí kříž vyšší než museum?" *Právo zlidu*, May 9, 1935.

1. Mamatey and Luza, *History of the Czechoslovak Republic*, 205.

2. Mickulecká, *František Bílek v církve československé husitské*.

3. Moravánszky, *Competing Visions*, 392.

4. A thorough review of early twentieth-century Catholic architecture in Central Europe is Berglund, "Building a Church for a New Age," 225–39.

5. Margolius, *Church of the Sacred Heart*, 8.

6. Švácha, *Architecture of New Prague*, 189.

7. Quoted in Margolis, *Church of the Sacred Heart*, 9.

8. Pavel Janák, "Josef Plečnik v Praze," *Volné směry* 26: 97–108.

9. Jan Kotěra, "O novém umění," *Volné směry* 5 (1900).

10. Jan Kotěra, "Jože Plečnik," *Volné směry* 6 (1901–1902): 91–98.

11. Riegl, *Kunstwerk oder Denkmal?* In his landmark essay, "The Modern Cult of Monuments," Riegl proposes a distinction between a monument's art value and its historic value.

12. Prelovšek, *Jože Plečnik, 1872–1957*, 223.

13. Krečič, *Plečnik, the Complete Works*, 69.

14. *Chrám Nejsvětějšího Srdce Páne v Praze XII na Kralovských Vinohradech* (Prague, 1932). Commemorative booklet of history and photographs of the church in various construction stages, which was sold at the church blessing in 1932.

15. Ibid.

16. Alexandr Titl, "Úvod," in Plečnik, *Chrám Nejsvětějšího Srdce Pane.*

17. Quoted in Margolis, *Church of the Sacred Heart*, 17.

18. Moravánszky, *Competing Visions,* 392.

19. For a historical and cultural analysis of Semper's and Wagner's theories, see Schorske, *Fin-de-Siècle Vienna*, chapter 2 and throughout.

20. "Obnova průčelí," *Umělecký měsičník* 2 (1912–1913): 85–93. See also von Vegesack, ed., *Czech Cubism.*

21. Margolius, *Church of the Sacred Heart*, 16. While designing Sacred Heart, Plečnik was also creating costumes for Orel, a patriotic Catholic gymnastics club that mirrored Sokol. Long inspired by traditional fabric and needlework, Plečnik incorporated his costume designs into his architecture. Dressing the church in an ermine garment again symbolized the historical Bohemian royalty and Christ the King.

22. Prelovšek, *Jože Plečnik, 1872–1957*, 27.

23. Krečič, "Plečnik and the Critics," in Plečnik, *Architecture and the City,* 25.

24. Titl, "Úvod," in Plečnik, *Chrám Nejsvětejšího Srdce Pane.*

25. Quoted in Margolis, *Church of the Sacred Heart*, 17.

26. Vladimir Šlapeta, "Jože Plečnik and Prague," in Burkhardt, Eveno, and Podrecca, eds., *Jože Plečnik,* 92.

27. Quoted in Výrut, *Čtení o Praze 10,* 29.

28. "Bude vztyčen na Václavském náměstí kříž vyšší než museum?" *Právo lidu*, May 9, 1935.

29. Ibid.

30. Trapl, *Political Catholicism,* 98.

31. "Bude vztyčen," *Právo lidu,* May 9, 1935.

32. "Znak křesťanství nad sochou knížete Václava svatého," *Národní listy,* June 26, 1935.

33. "Proč je hlídán sjezdový kříž na Václavské náměstí," *Lidové listy*, June 26, 1935.

34. Jan Scheinost, "Triumf katolíků a státu," *Lidové listy*, July 2, 1935.

35. "Bude Praha místem svetového kongresu eucharistického?" *Lidové listy*, July 3, 1935

36. Jan Scheinost, "Triumf katolíků a státu," *Lidové listy,* July 2, 1935.

37. Pech, *Czech Revolution of 1848*, 144–45.

38. "Nekatolík o katolickém sjezdu," *Lidové listy,* July 4, 1935.

39. Glassheim, *Noble Nationalists,* 136; Nitner, "Gesamtstaatlicher Katholikentag

Prag 1935," 331–46. Glassheim discusses the festival in greater detail in *Crafting a Post-Imperial Identity*, 245–83.

40. David Kelly, *Czech Fascist Movement, 1922–1942*, 9.

Chapter 9. National Heroes and Nazi Rule

Epigraph: Jaroslav Durych to Presidential Chancellery. Sign.: D 7116/39, D 3078/39. AKPR.

1. Bryant, *Prague in Black*, and Demetz, *Prague in Danger*.

2. Mamatey and Luza, *History of the Czechoslovak Republic*, 321. These statistics represent the reduced borders after March 1939. It is estimated that between 250,000 and 277,000 Czechoslovak Jews from within the prewar Czechoslovak borders were murdered.

3. Quoted in Bolton, "Mourning Becomes the Nation," 115–31. (Quote on p. 115.)

4. Bolton, "Mourning Becomes the Nation," 127.

5. Ibid.

6. See Fond PMV, 1936–40/X/H/25 (Husovy oslavy). NA.

7. "Hustag," *Bruexer Zeitung*, July 4, 1935.

8. Quoted in Bryant, *Prague in Black*, 29.

9. Quoted in ibid., 42.

10. As quoted in Mastny, *Czechs under Nazi Rule*, 23.

11. Quoted in Emilia Hrabovec, "Der Heilige Stuhl und die böhmischen Länder 1938–1945," in Zückert and Hölzlwimmer, *Religion in den bömischen Ländern, 1938–1948*, 119.

12. See especially Rataj, *O autoritativní národní stat*. Other resources on the role of Wenceslas in the Second Republic and Protectorate include Krejca, "Český fašismus," 23–24, and Nakonečný, *Vlajka*. Nancy Wingfield discusses how Wenceslas's memory was seen shortly after the end of the war in *Flag Wars and Stone Saints*, 270.

13. For a thorough overview of the historigraphical debate, see especially Havelka, *Spor o smyslu českých dějin, 1895–1938*.

14. Gebhart and Kuklík, *Druhá republika, 1938–1939*, 183 and 277.

15. Hrabovec, "Der Heilige Stuhl," 120.

16. Bryant, *Prague in Black*, 59.

17. Ibid.

18. René Küpper, "Zur Instrumentalisierung der katholischen Kirche für die nationalsozialistische Protektoratspolitik," in Zückert and Hölzlwimmer, eds., *Religion in den bömischen Ländern, 1938–1948*, 160.

19. Ibid., 162.

20. Durych to Presidential Chancellery. Sign.: D 7116/39, D 3078/39. AKPR.

21. Ibid.

22. Quoted in Demetz, *Prague in Danger*, 51.

23. Bohumil Švanda, *Venkov*, July 6, 1939.

24. Ibid.

25. Coincidentally, the feast day of Cyril and Methodius fell on July 5, the day before Hus's anniversary; in 1925, the First Republic chose their feast day as a state holiday to

create a two-day summer vacation for workers while avoiding the controversial Catholic saints Wenceslas and Nepomucký.

26. On the assassination and aftermath, see especially MacDonald, *Killing of SS Obergruppenführer Reinhard Heydrich*; Bryant, *Prague in Black,* 163–73; and Mastny, *Czechs under Nazi Rule,* 207–10.

27. Quoted in Bryant, *Prague in Black,* 170.

28. Roučka, *Skočeno a podepsáno.*

29. Abrams, *Struggle for the Soul of the Nation,* 53–88.

30. Wingfield, *Flag Wars and Stone Saints,* 269–70.

31. Abrams, *Struggle for the Soul of the Nation,* 98–99.

Chapter 10. God's Warriors on Vítkov Hill

Epigraph: "Buďme husitský a gottwaldovský pevní a stateční," *Rudé právo,* March 23, 1953.

1. See also Abrams, *Struggle for the Soul of the Nation,* 98–103.

2. For a comprehensive overview of Vítkov Hill in Czech national memory, see Galandauer, "Česká vojenská tradice v proměnách času," 5–34.

3. Witkovsky, "Truly Blank," 42.

4. Ibid., 43.

5. "Zpráva o 14. radně valné hromadě 1948, Sbor pro Zbudování památníku národního osvobození a pomníku Jana Žižky z trocnova na vrchu žižkově." Carton 5251. MV 6–6725. NA.

6. "Národ se rozloučil s dr. E. Benešem," *Rudé právo,* September 9, 1948, 2.

7. "Nárvrh na nové složení Sboru a technicko-umělecko komise pro dobudováni Národního pamatníku na hoře Vítkově." Carton 157. Ministerstvo informaci a osvěty (MIO) no. 28571/51, MI-D. NA.

8. Orlíková, *Max Švabinský.*

9. "Prelestění mramoru a kamenické práce." Carton 157. No. 62502/1952. MI-D. NA.

10. Galandauer, "Česká vojenská tradice," 21.

11. A. Matějček, "Reliefy Karla Pokorného v mausoleu Památníku národního osvobození," 208.

12. Fowkes, "Monumental Sculpture in Post-War Eastern Europe."

13. "Protokol o schůzi poroty v užších soutěžích," December 16, 1952. Carton 157. MI-D. NA.

14. Jana Hofmeisterová, "Mosaiky pro síň rudé armády v národním památníku na hoře Vítkově," *Výtvarné umění* 4 (1954): 185–88.

15. Jarmila Jindrová, "Síň rudé armády v Národním památníku na Vítkově," *Tvář,* 1955, 162–66.

16. "O pomník Jana Žižky," *Přítomnost,* May 26, 1937, 324–35.

17. Quoted in Galandauer, "Česká vojenská tradice."

18. Quoted in ibid.

19. Ibid.

20. Ibid.

21. Ibid.

22. "Věčně bude žít v písních lidu," *Rudé právo,* March 29, 1953.

23. "Buďme husitsky a gottwaldovsky pevní a stateční," *Rudé právo*, March 23, 1953.

24. Ibid.

25. Ibid.

26. "Československý lid se rozloučil se svým učitelem a vůdcem," *Rudé právo,* March 20, 1953, 4.

27. "Projev soudruha Alexeje Čepicky k otevření síně Sovětská armády na Vítkově," *Rudé právo,* May 8, 1955.

28. "Kdo sedí na Žižkově koní?" *Svobodné slovo*, January 14, 1995, 6–7.

29. Petr Brátka, "Vytvarné řesení národního památníku na Žižkově," *Husitský tábor,* 1981, 233–37.

Chapter 11. Rebuilding Bethlehem Chapel

Epigraph: Zdeněk Nejedlý, *Husův Betlem a náš dnešek.*

1. Cited in Němec, *Church and State in Czechoslovakia*, 239.

2. On the connection between Czech Protestantism and the Communist Party, see Abrams, *Struggle for the Soul of the Nation,* 76–88 and 253–74.

3. Abrams, *Struggle for the soul of the Nation,* 265.

4. "Resoluce," *Kostnické jiskry,* April 27, 1950, 1.

5. On the history of the chapel, see Vávra, *Betlémská kaple*; Bartoš, *Z dějin kaple Betlémské*; *Betlémská kaple*; and Kubiček, *Betlémská kaple.*

6. Kubiček, *Betlémská kaple,* 7–8.

7. Ibid., 14.

8. Ibid., 15.

9. Ibid., 19.

10. Folder *Betlémská kaple.* Carton 3186. Nos. 45752/4957 and 156628/30. MŠ. NA.

11. Kubiček to Kancelář presidenta republiky. No. D11 701/30, 30.10.1930 MŠ. NA.

12. Památkového sboru hl města Prahy to MŠ. No. 13.562/1937. MŠ. NA.

13. Kubiček, *Betlémská kaple,* 19.

14. Ibid., 19.

15. Josef Petráň and Lydia Petráňová, "The White Mountain as a Symbol in Modern Czech History," in Mikuláš Teich, ed., *Bohemia in History,* 143.

16. Nejedlý, *Komunisté.*

17. "Vypis z usnesení 9. schůze paté vlady, konané 30. července 1948, o obnově BK." Carton 731. Folder: Spisy Min. Techniky o Betlémské kapli (hereafter, BK); subfolder 1948. SPS. NA.

18. "Dům 255 odstranění garaži." Ministerstvo Technicky (hereafter, MT). No. 640/11 VI/6–1948 BK. SPS. NA.

19. Letter from Dr. A. Frinta to MŠ, oddělení památkové re: čp 255. BK. SPS. NA.

20. "Dům 255." MT no. 640/90/VI/6/1949. BK. SPS. NA.

21. Narodní kulturní komise, dům 256, Anna Stipková, najemné. No. 6581/50. SPS. NA.

22. Ibid.

23. Correspondence from J. Herda to MT, 1949. BK. SPS. NA.

24. "Informace pro pana ministra technicky (Obnova BK, Ziskaní dům 254, 256, 238." BK. SPS. NA.

25. Obvodní nár. výbor v Praze I to Koblasovi čj. 2b 146 991/3/49–1-XI–L/Bun. BK. SPS. NA.

26. Letter from Františka Koblasová to MT. BK. SPS. NA.

27. Letter from Bohumil Koblas to *Advokátní poradna*. BK. SPS. NA.

28. SPS v likvidaci, č. 2415/61 to Statní spořitelna v Praze. Carton 164. Folder: PRAHA—kostely, kláštery, zámky; subfolder: BK. SPS-d. NA.

29. Kubiček, *Betlémská kaple*, 78–79.

30. Svoboda, *Prague*, 127.

31. Kubiček, *Betlémská kaple*, 79.

32. "Betlémská kaple slavnostně předána našemu lidu," *Rudé právo*, July 6, 1954, and "Slavnostní otevření památníku husitství," *Kostnické jiskry*, July 14, 1954, 1.

33. Nejedlý, *Husův Bétlem*, 17.

34. Ibid., 9.

35. Ibid., 18.

36. Ibid., 15.

37. Ibid., 14.

38. Ibid., 16.

39. See Čapek, *Betlémská kaple v české literatuře*, 18.

40. Nejedlý, *Husův Betlém*, 12.

41. *Rudé právo*, July 6, 1954, 1.

42. Nejedlý, *Husův Betlém*, 12.

43. Ibid., 7–8.

44. Ibid., 20–21.

Chapter 12. Old Symbols Oppose the New Regime

Epigraph: From Ludvík Vaculík's *Český snář*. Quotations are taken from the excerpts translated into English by Michael Henry Heim in *Cross Currents: A Yearbook of Central European Culture*, 3 (1984): 80.

1. Nora, *Realms of Memory*, vol. 3, xii.

2. From *Rudé právo*, August 21, 1968, as translated in Littell, ed., *Czech Black Book*, 35. This book is a collection of excerpts from Czechoslovak newspapers from the week of August 20–27, 1968.

3. From *Práce*, 2nd (special) edition, August 21, 1968; quoted in Littell, *Czech Black Book*, 34.

4. From *Rudé právo*, August 22, 1968; quoted in Littell, 50.

5. Ibid.

6. The makeshift memorials to Palach are described in Mastny, ed., *Czechoslovakia*.

7. Hojda and Pokorný, *Pomníky a zapomníky*, 116.

8. Bradna, "Mariánský sloup na Staroměstském Nám. v Praze," 47.

9. Ibid.

10. The monastery, thirty miles southwest of Chicago, was named for one of the

Bohemian saints depicted at the base of Prague's Wenceslas Memorial. Czech and Slovak immigrants and their descendants had founded the monastery in 1885, and after World War II it became a refuge for Eastern European immigrant priests. Lev Ondrák served as abbot after his immigration, and his leadership on the project secured the statue's permanent home.

11. Bradna, "Mariánský sloup na Staroměstském Nám. v Praze," 48.

12. http://www.sokolcanada.org/html/canada/history.htm

13. J. M. Giordano, "Resurrecting Mary: A Controversial Historical Landmark May Soon Rise Again," *Prague Post*, July 22–28, 1998, B12–13.

14. Gebhart and Kuklík, *Druhá republika*, 191.

15. Renč, *Pražská legenda*. All quotations from this poem are taken from this publication. The translations are my own.

16. Ramet, *Nihil Obstat,* 132–33.

17. Vlnas, *Jan Nepomucký, Česká legenda,* 283.

18. Seifert, "Head of the Virgin Mary," in *Poetry of Jaroslav Seifert,* trans. Osers, 133–34. All quotations from the poem are from this translation.

19. From Heim's introduction to his translation of the text.

20. Vaculík, *Český snář,* 80.

21. Ibid., 80.

22. Ibid., 81.

23. Ibid., 83.

24. Ibid., 83.

25. See Michalski, *Public Monuments,* 172–89.

26. Campbell, "Empty Pedestals?" 1–15.

27. See Hana Pichová, "The Lineup for Meat: The Stalin Statue in Prague," *PMLA* 123, no. 3 (May 2008): 614–30; and Steven Erlanger, "Prague Journal: Stalin's Ghost Haunts a Czech Park," *New York Times,* February 24, 2001.

Chapter 13. Religious and National Symbols in Post-Communist Prague
Epigraph: Havel, "Open Letter to Gustav Husák," in *Open Letters,* 50–83.

1. Havel, "New Year's Address, 1990," in *Toward a Civil Society,* 13–21.

2. Vladimír Srb, "Náboženské vyznání a demografické, sociálné, ekonomické a kulturní charakteristiky obyvatelstva České republiky," *Demografie* 39, no. 3 (1997): 190–202.

3. Nate and Leah Steppanen Anderson, "The Czech Church: Not Dead Yet," *Prague Post,* October 5, 2005.

4. Giordano, "Resurrecting Mary," B12.

5. *Výstava 99: Budoucnost a přítomnost Prahy 1* (November 4–11, 1999). No publishing information. This source is a photocopied guide to a small exhibition held in November 1999 in Wenceslas Square. Eagle Glassheim provided me with this source.

6. Giordano, "Resurrecting Mary," B12.

7. P. Antonín Odvárka, "Barbarský čin," *Lidové demokracie,* July 15, 1994, 7.

8. Josef Gebauer, "Na tomto místě stál a opět bude stát," *Evangelický týdeník* 41 (1993).

9. Ibid.

10. Ibid.

11. Vlnas, "Mariánský sloup," *Přítomnost* 2 (1991): 21–22.

12. Giordano, "Resurrecting Mary," B13.

13. Hlobil, "Obnova mariánského sloupu?" 97–98.

14. Giordano, "Resurrecting Mary," B12.

15. Ibid., B12–B13.

16. Ibid., B13.

17. Miroslav Frankovský, Milan Zezula, Jaroslav Skarvada, and Miloslav Vlk, "Mariánský sloup na Staroměstském náměstí v Praze," *Evangelický týdeník* 79, no. 4 (1994): 2.

18. Giordano, "Resurrecting Mary," B13.

19. Ludmila Konopíková, "Paní z exilu vrací domů," *Naše rodina*, no. 33 (1993): 16–17. See also Ludmila Konopíková, "Strahovské (s)vítání," *Naše rodina*, no. 44 (1993): 2–3.

20. "Aburditám se usmívám," *Slovo*, January 14, 1995, 7.

21. Michael Borovička, "Neznámý vojín mimo službu," *Svobodé slovo*, January 14, 1995, 7.

22. "Aburditám se usmívám," 7.

23. "Jan Žižka s ohňostrojem," *Lidové noviny*, June 26, 1993.

24. Jaroslav Šebek, "Gottwaldova smrt a konec stalinismu v Čechách," *Slovo*, March 20, 1998, section 2: 1.

25. "Kdo sedí na Žižkově koní?" 6–7.

26. http://www.pamatnik-vitkov.cz/.

27. Jan Schroth, "Probouzení monumentu na vrchu Vítkově," *Literárné noviny*, October 24, 2001.

28. Stanislav Štefáček, "O žižkovském památníku," *Lidové noviny,* August 1, 1992, 11.

29. Matěj Hušek and Ivana Chilářová, "Byl svatý Václav mučedník, nebo kolaborant?" *Právo,* May 23, 2000, 3.

30. Ibid.

31. See Hutka's personal Web site (http://www.hutka.cz/new/) for all quotations from Hutka's writings and information on his campaign.

32. Václav Pinkava, "Flogging a Dead Horse," *Central European Review* 1, no. 19 (November 1, 1999). May be accessed at www.ce-review.org.

33. Andrew Stroehlein, "Three Václavs," *Central European Review* 1, no. 10 (August 30, 1999).

34. Interview of David Černý by Jan Velinger on radio station *Český rozhlas,* July 1, 2003. Transcript found at http://www.radio.cz/en/article/42509.

35. On Černý's work, see his Web site (in Czech and English): http://www.david cerny.cz/.

36. Jeremie Feinblatt, "Spreading the Wealth," *Prague Post*, December 23, 2004.

37. Mark West, "Remembering November 30: A Tale of Two Cities," *Seattle Union Record*, November 29, 2000.

38. "Pozdravný dopis prezidenta Česke republiky shromáždění v Kapli betlémské dne 6. července 1993," *Český zápas,* August 1, 1993, 1.

39. "Husův odkaz je nepominutelnou součástí českých dějin," *Český zápas,* August 3, 1997, 2.

40. "Slavíka bych fakt chtěl," *Lidové noviny,* October 18, 2003.

41. The full lyrics of the song can be found at http://www.monkeybusiness.cz.

42. "Kapela Monkey Business šlechtí styl," *Mladá fronta dnes,* August 28, 2003.

43. "Monkey Business o vymývání mozků," September 1, 2003, http://Novinky.cz.

44. See Pynsent, *Questions of Identity.*

Epilogue: New Times, New Monuments

1. Wingfield, *Flag Wars and Stone Saints,* 164.

2. Eley and Suny, "Introduction: From the Moment of Social History to the Work of Cultural Representation," in *Becoming National,* 3–38.

3. Hojda and Pokorný, *Pomníky a zapomníky,* chapter 2.

4. Le Goff, *History and Memory,* 111.

5. Williams, "National Myths in the New Czech Liberalism," in Hosking and Schöpflin, eds., *Myths and Nationhood,* 140; Čaněk, *Národ, národnost, menšinz a rasismus.*

6. Williams, "National Myths in the New Czech Liberalism," 136.

7. Ibid., 134.

8. Ibid., 137.

9. See, for example, Young, *Texture of Memory.*

10. Pavla Horáková, "Eighty Years after His Death, Franz Kafka Finally Has a Statue in Prague," *Radio Praha,* September 1, 2004 (http://www.radio.cz/en/article/49259).

11. On the Memorial to the Victims of Communism, see Alena Škodová, "Memorial to the Victims of Communism Unveiled in Prague," *Radio Prague,* May 23, 2002 (http://www.radio.cz/en/article/28266), and Rob Cameron, "Prague Monument to Communist Victims Damaged in Explosion," *Radio Prague,* November 11, 2003 (http://www.radio.cz/en/article/47274).

12. Campbell, "Empty Pedestals."

13. Kundera, *Book of Laughter and Forgetting,* 22.

Selected Bibliography

Archives and Special Collections

AHMP: Archiv hlavního města Prahy, Prague, Czech Republic
    Fond: PMMR: Praesidium magistrátu a městské rady
    Fond: PSRM: Protokoly schuzí rady městské, 1918
    Fond: SZPH: Spolek pro zbudování pomník Husova v Praze
AKPR: Archiv kancelář presidenta republiky, Prague, Czech Republic
    Record Group D
    Record Group T
NA: Národní Archiv, Prague, Czech Republic
    Fond: MIO: Ministerstvo informaci a osvěty
    Fond: MŠ: Ministerstvo školtsví
    Fond: MV: Ministerstvo vnitra
    Fond: MZ: Ministerstvo zahraničné
    Fond: PMR: Presidium ministerská rada
    Fond: PMV: Prasidium ministerstvo vnitra
    Fond: SPS: Statní pamatkový sbor
    Fond: SPS-d: Statní pamatková správa-dodatky
NKČR: Národní knihovna České Republiky, Prague, Czech Republic
OAJ: Okresní archiv jihočeský, Prachatice, Czech Republic
USNA: National Archives of the United States of America, Washington D.C., United
    States
    General Records of Department of State, Record Group 59

Selected Magazines and Newspapers

Bohemia. 1928–1938. Prague.
Brüxer Zeitung. 1935. Most, Czechoslovakia.
Čas. 1915. Prague.
Časopis katolického duchovenstva 65 (1924).
Čech. 1923–1929. Prague.
Central European Review. 1999–present. Online periodical, http://www.ce-review.org.
České slovo. 1907–1945. Prague.
Český rozhlas. 2003. Prague radio station with online archive, http://radio.cz.
Český zápas. 1993. Publication of Czechoslovak Hussite Church, Prague.
Dílo 15 (1920). Prague.

ༀ *Evangelický týdeník* 79, no. 4 (1994). Prague.

280 *Husitský tábor.* 1981. Tábor, Czechoslovakia.

Jihozšpadní morava. 1915. Trebice.

Lidové demokracie. 1994. Prague.

Lidové listy. 1922–1939. Prague.

Lidové noviny. 1883–1945, Brno. 1990–present, Prague.

Magazín RP. 1995. Prague.

MF Dnes (Mladá fronta Dnes). 1945–present. Prague.

Národní listy. 1861–1941. Prague.

Národní osvobození. 1923–1939. Prague.

Národní politika. 1883–1945. Prague.

Naše hlasy. 1915. Český Brod.

Naše rodina. 1993. Prague.

Naše slovo. 1915. Prague.

Neue freie Presse. 1918. Vienna.

New York Times. 1989–present.

Novinky. Internet magazine of *Právo,* http://pravo.novinky.cz.

Odpolední národní politika. 1925. Prague.

Prague Post. 1991–present. Prague.

Právo. 1990–present. Prague.

Právo lidu. 1897–1938. Prague.

Pražský večerník. 1918–1923. Prague.

Přítomnost. 1937; 1991. Prague.

Rudé právo. 1920–1938; 1945–1989. Prague.

Šibensky. 1922. Prague.

Slovo. 1995–1998. Prague.

Socialista. 1923. Prague.

Svobodné slovo. 1995. Prague.

Tribuna. 1922. Prague.

Tribuna večer. 1926. Prague.

Tvár. 1955. Prague.

Umělecký měsičník 2 (1912–1913). Prague.

Umění. 1968; 2001. Published by the Institute for Art History of the Academy of Sciences. Prague.

Umění a řemesla. 1991. Prague.

Večer. 1923. Prague.

Večerní české slovo. 1925. Prague.

Večerní národní listy. 1924. Prague.

Večerní rudé právo. 1923. Prague.

Večerník právu lidu. 1915. Prague.

Venkov. 1906–1939. Prague.

Věstník obecní královského hlavního města Prahy. 1911. Prague.

Věstník sokolský. 1903. Prague.

Věstník spolku pro zbudování Žižkova pomníku na Žižkově. 1908. Žižkov.

Volné směry. 1896–1929. Journal of the Mánes Association of Fine Arts. Prague.

Výtvarné umění. 1954. Prague.

Za starou Prahu: Věstník klubu za starou Prahu. 1910–1920. Prague.

Ženské listy. 1891–1903. Prague.

Ženský svět. 1903–1915. Prague.

Selected Secondary Literature

Abrams, Bradley F. *The Struggle for the Soul of the Nation: Czech Culture and the Rise of Communism.* Lanham: Rowman and Littlefield, 2004.

Agnew, Hugh LeCaine. *Origins of the Czech National Renascence.* Pittsburgh: University of Pittsburgh Press, 1994.

———. *The Czechs and the Lands of the Bohemian Crown.* Stanford: Hoover Institution Press, 2004.

———. "Demonstrating the Nation: Symbol, Ritual, and Political Protest in Bohemia, 1867–1875." In Reiss, ed., *The Street as Stage,* 85–104.

Anderson, Benedict. *Imagined Communities: Reflections on the Origin and Spread of Nationalism.* London: Verso, 1983.

Ash, Timothy Garton. *The Magic Lantern: We the People: The Revolution of '89 Witnessed in Warsaw, Budapest, Berlin, and Prague.* Cambridge: Granta Books, 1990.

Backová, Katerina. *Sto let Klub za Starou Prahu, 1900–2000.* Prague: Klub Za starou Prahu, 2000.

Banac, Ivo, and Frank E. Sysyn, eds. *Concepts of Nationhood in Early Modern Eastern Europe.* Cambridge: Harvard University Ukranian Research Institute, 1986.

Barany, George. "On Truth in Myths." *East European Quarterly* 14, no. 4 (October 1981): 346–54.

Baron, Beth. "The Construction of National Honour in Egypt." *Gender and History* 5, no. 2 (Summer 1993): 244–55.

Bartoš, F. M. *Z dějin kaple Betlémské.* Prague: Blahoslav, 1951.

———. *The Hussite Revolution 1427–1437.* Prepared by John M. Klassen. Boulder: East European Monographs, 1986.

Bečková, Kateřina. "Procházky STAROU PRAHOU: Staroměstské náměstí." Prague: Spektrum pro Muzeum hlavního města Prahy, 1990.

Belina, Pavel, and Jan Vlk. *Dějiny Prahy.* Vols. 1 and 2. Prague: Paseka, 1997–1998.

Beller, Steven. *A Concise History of Austria.* Cambridge: Cambridge University Press, 2006.

Berglund, Bruce R. "Building a Church for a New Age: The Search for a Modern Catholic Art in Turn-of-the-Century Central Europe." *Centropa: A Journal of Central European Architecture and Related Arts* 3, no. 3 (September 2003): 225–39.

Betlémská kaple. Prague: Praha informant služba, 1997.

Blom, Ida, Karen Hagemann, and Catherine Hall. *Gendered Nations: Nationalisms and Gender Order in the Long Nineteenth Century.* Oxford: Berg, 2000.

Bobková, Lenka. "Jak se strhával mariansky sloup." *Magazín RP.* March 25, 1995.

Bolton, Jonathan. "Mourning Becomes the Nation: The Funeral of Tomáš Masaryk in 1937." *Bohemia* 45, no. 1 (2004): 115–31.

Borsody, Stephen. *The Tragedy of Central Europe: Nazi and Soviet Conquest and Aftermath.* New Haven: Yale Concilium on International and Area Studies, 1980.

Bosl, Karl, ed. *Die erste Tschechoslowakische Republik als multinationaler Parteienstaat.* Munich: Collegium Carolinum, 1979.

Boyer, M. Christine. *The City of Collective Memory: Its Historical Imagery and Architectural Entertainments.* Cambridge: MIT Press, 1996.

Bradna, Jan. "Mariánský sloup na Staroměstském Nám. v Praze." Unpublished paper, Seminar on the History of Arts and Esthetics, Philosophical Faculty, Charles University, 1993.

Braunerová, Zdenka. "František Bílek." *Volné směry* 4 (1900): 113–34.

Brock, Peter. *The Political and Social Doctrines of the Unity of the Czech Brethren in the Fifteenth and Early Sixteenth Century.* The Hague: Gravenhage Mouton, 1957.

———. *The Slovak National Awakening.* Toronto: University of Toronto Press, 1976.

Brock, Peter, and H. Gordon Skilling, eds. *The Czech Renascence of the Nineteenth Century.* Toronto: University of Toronto Press, 1976.

Brubaker, Rogers. *Nationalism Reframed.* Cambridge: Cambridge University Press, 1996.

Bruegel, J. W. *Czechoslovakia before Munich.* Cambridge: Cambridge University Press, 1973.

Bryant, Chad. *Prague in Black: Nazi Rule and Czech Nationalism.* Cambridge: Harvard University Press, 2007.

Bucur, Maria, and Nancy M. Wingfield, eds. *Staging the Past: The Politics of Commemoration in Habsburg Central Europe, 1848 to the Present.* West Lafayette: Purdue University Press, 2001.

Burkhardt, Francois, Claude Eveno, and Boris Podrecca, eds. *Jože Plečnik, Architect: 1872–1957.* Cambridge: MIT Press.

Calvino, Italo. *Invisible Cities.* Trans. William Weaver. New York: Harcourt Brace Jovanovich, 1972.

Campbell, F. Gregory. "Empty Pedestals?" *Slavic Review* 44, no. 1 (Spring 1985): 1–15.

Čaněk, David. *Národ, národnost, menšiny a rasismus.* Prague: Instituto pro stredoeuroupsko kulturu a politiku, 1996.

Cannadine, David. "Splendor Out of Court: Royal Spectacle and Pageantry in Modern Britain, c. 1820–1977." In Wilentz, ed., *Rites of Power.*

Čapek, Jan Blahoslav. *Betlémská kaple v české literatuře.* Prague: Kalich, 1952.

Čapek, Karel. *Talks with T. G. Masaryk.* Trans. Dora Round. North Haven: Catbird Press, 1995.

Carlyle, Thomas. *On Heroes, Hero-Worship, and Heroic in History.* Oxford: Oxford University Press, 1904.

Čech, Svatopluk. "Hus." Reprint. In *Pamětní list k slavnost položení základního kamene k husovu pomníku.* Prague: Nákladem Slavnostního výboru, 1903.

Červinka, František. *Český nacionalismus v XIX. století.* Prague: Svobodné slovo, 1965.

Císařová-Kolářová, Anna. *Žena v hnutí husitském.* Prague, 1915.

———. *Žena v Jednotě bratrské.* Prague, 1942.

Clark, Christopher, and Wolfram Kaiser, eds. *Culture Wars: Secular–Catholic Conflict in Nineteenth-Century Europe.* Cambridge: Cambridge University Press, 2003.

Cohen, Gary B. *The Politics of Ethnic Survival: Germans in Prague, 1861–1914*. Princeton: Princeton University Press, 1981.

Confino, Alon. "Collective Memory and Cultural History: Problems of Method." *American Historical Review* 102, no. 5 (December 1997): 1386–1403.

Connerton, Paul. *How Societies Remember*. Cambridge: Cambridge University Press, 1989.

Connor, Walker. "A Nation Is a Nation, Is a State, Is an Ethnic Group, Is a . . ." *Ethnic and Racial Studies* 1, no. 4 (1978): 379–88.

Conway, Martin. *Catholic Politics in Europe, 1918–1945*. New York: Routledge, 1997.

Craciun, Maria, Ovidiu Ghitta, and Graeme Murdock. *Confessional Identity in East-Central Europe*. Hants, England, and Burlington: Ashgate, 2002.

Crampton, Richard J. *Eastern Europe in the Twentieth Century—and After*. New York: Routledge, 1994.

Crampton, Richard J., and Ben Crampton. *Atlas of Eastern Europe in the Twentieth Century*. New York: Routledge, 1996.

Cuhra, Jaroslav. *Církevní politka KSČ a státu v letech 1969–1972*. Sešity Ústav pro soudobé dějiny AV ČR, no. 32 (1999).

Czechoslovak Catholics. London: Catholic Truth Society, 1942.

Czechoslovakia Narodní Shromáždění. *Narodní shromáždění republiky Československé v prvém desítletí*. Prague: Statní tiskárna, 1928.

Dabrowski, Patrice M. *Commemorations and the Shaping of Modern Poland*. Bloomington: Indiana University Press, 2004.

David-Fox, Katherine. "Czech Feminists and Nationalism in the Late Habsburg Monarchy: 'The First in Austria!'" *Journal of Women's History* 3, no. 2 (1991).

———. "Prague-Vienna, Prague-Berlin: The Hidden Geography of Czech Modernism." *Slavic Review* 59, no. 4 (Winter 2000): 735–60.

Davis, Susan G. *Parades and Power: Street Theater in Nineteenth-Century Philadelphia*. Philadelphia: Temple University Press, 1986.

De Groot, Joanna. "The Dialectics of Gender: Women, Men, and Political Discourses in Iran c. 1890–1930." *Gender and History* 5, no. 2 (Summer 1993).

Demetz, Peter. *Prague in Black and Gold: Scenes in the Life of a European City*. New York: Hill and Wang, 1997.

———. *Prague in Danger: The Years of German Occupation, 1939–45: Memories and History, Terror and Resistance, Theater and Jazz, Film and Poetry, Politics and War*. New York: Farrar, Straus and Giroux, 2008.

Doob, Leonard. *Patriotism and Nationalism: Their Psychological Foundations*. New Haven: Yale University Press, 1964.

Duara, Prasenjit. *Rescuing History from the Nation*. Chicago: University of Chicago Press, 1995.

———. "Historicizing National Identity, or Who Imagines What and When." In Eley and Suny, eds., *Becoming National*, 151–78.

Duff, Sheila Grant. *A German Protectorate: The Czechs under Nazi Rule*. London: Frank Cass and Company, 1970.

Eley, Geoff, and Ronald Grigor Suny, eds. *Becoming National*. New York: Oxford University Press, 1996.

Erben, K. J., ed. *Mistra Jana Husa: Sebrané spisy české*. 3 vols. Prague: B. Tempský, 1865.

Evans, R. J. W. *The Making of the Habsburg Monarchy, 1550–1700*. Oxford: Oxford University Press, 1979.

Fajt, Jiří, and L. Sršeň. *Lapidárium národního muzea Praha*. Prague: Národní muzeum v Praze, 1993.

Feinberg, Melissa. *Elusive Equality: Gender, Citizenship, and the Limits of Democracy in Czechoslovakia, 1918–1950*. Pittsburgh: University of Pittsburgh Press, 2006.

Felak, James Ramon. *"At the Price of the Republic": Hlinka's Slovak People's Party, 1929–1938*. Pittsburgh: University of Pittsburgh Press, 1996.

Firth, Raymond. *Symbols Public and Private*. Ithaca: Cornell University Press, 1973.

Forman, Stanislav. *Dějiny spolku pro vystavení pomníku Mistra Jana Husi v Praze*. Prague: Spolek pro vystavení pomníku Mistra Jana Hus v Praze, 1903. Carton 13, SZPH, AHMP.

Fowkes, Reuben. Monumental Sculpture in Post-War Eastern Europe. PhD dissertation, University of Essex, Colchester, United Kingdom, 2002.

Freeze, Karen Johnson. The Young Progressives: The Czech Student Movement, 1887–1897. PhD dissertation, Columbia University, New York, 1974.

———. "Medical Education for Women in Austria: A Study in the Politics of the Czech Women's Movement in the 1890s." In *Women, State, and Party in Eastern Europe*, ed. Wolchik and Meyer, 51–63.

Freifeld, Alice. *Nationalism and the Crowd in Liberal Hungary, 1848–1914*. Baltimore: Johns Hopkins University Press, 2000.

French, Alfred. *Czech Writers and Politics, 1945–1969*. New York: East European Monographs, 1982.

Galandauer, Jan. "Česká vojenská tradice v proměnách času. Vrch Vítkov v české historické paměti." *Historie a vojenství* 43, no. 5 (1994): 5–34.

———. "Husův národ a most Františka Ferdinanda." *Historie a vojenství* 44, no. 4 (1995): 3–20.

Garver, Bruce. *The Young Czech Party, 1874–1910, and the Emergence of a Multi-Party System*. New Haven: Yale University Press, 1978.

———. "Women in the Czechoslovak First Republic." In *Women, State, and Party in Eastern Europe*, ed. Wolchik and Meyer.

Gebhart, Jan, and Jan Kuklík. *Druhá republika 1938–1939: svár demokracie a totality v politckém, společenském a kulturním životě*. Prague: Paseka, 2004.

Geertz, Clifford C. *The Interpretation of Cultures: Selected Essays*. London: Hutchinson, 1973.

Gellner, Ernest. *Nations and Nationalism*. Ithaca: Cornell University Press, 1983.

———. *Encounters with Nationalism*. Cambridge: Blackwell, 1994.

Gillis, John R., ed. *Commemorations: The Politics of National Identity*. Princeton: Princeton University Press, 1994.

Giustino, Cathleen M. *Tearing Down Prague's Jewish Town: Ghetto Clearance and the Legacy of Middle-Class Ethnic Politics around 1900*. Boulder: East European Monographs, 2003.

Selected Bibliography

Glassheim, Eagle. Crafting a Post-Imperial Identity: Nobles and Nationality Politics in Czechoslovakia, 1918–1948. PhD dissertation, Columbia University, New York, 2000.

———. *Noble Nationalists: The Transformation of the Bohemian Aristocracy.* Cambridge: Harvard University Press, 2005.

Gottfried, Libor. "Kterák socha Mariánská byla stržena." *Dějiny a součástnost* 5 (1994): 29–30.

Greenfeld, Liah. *Nationalism: Five Roads to Modernity.* Cambridge: Cambridge University Press, 1992.

Greenhalgh, Paul, ed. *Art Nouveau, 1890–1914.* London: V and A Publications, 2000.

Gutkind, E. A. *Urban Development in East-Central Europe: Poland, Czechoslovakia, and Hungary.* New York: The Free Press, 1972.

Hajek, Frank Joseph. Catholics and Politics in Czechoslovakia: Jan Šrámek and the Czechoslovak People's Party, 1918–1938. PhD dissertation, Emory University, Atlanta, Georgia, 1973.

Halbwachs, Maurice. *On Collective Memory.* Ed. and trans. Lewis A. Coser. Chicago: University of Chicago Press, 1992.

Hanebrink, Paul. *In Defense of Christian Hungary: Religion, Nationalism, and Anti-Semitism, 1890–1944.* Ithaca: Cornell University Press, 2006.

Havel, Václav. *Open Letters: Selected Writings, 1965–1990.* New York: Vintage Books, 1992.

———. *Toward a Civil Society: Selected Speeches and Writings, 1990–1994.* Prague: Lidové noviny, 1995.

Havelka, Miloš. *Spor o smyslu českých dějin, 1895–1938.* Prague: Torst, 1995.

Havránek, Jan. *The Czechs: The Nationality Problem in the Habsburg Monarchy.* Prague: Universita Karlova, 1966.

———. "The Development of Czech Nationalism." *Austrian History Yearbook* 3, pt. 2 (1967): 22–60.

Hays, K. Michael, ed. *Oppositions Reader: Selected Readings from a Journal for Ideas and Criticism in Architecture, 1973–1984.* New York: Princeton Architectural Press, 1985.

Heumos, Peter. "Krise und Hussitisches Ritual." In *Vereinswesen und Geschichtsplege in den böhmischen Ländern.* Munich: R. Oldenbourg Verlag, 1986.

Heymann, Frederick. *John Žižka and the Hussite Revolution.* Princeton: Princeton University Press, 1955.

———. *George of Bohemia: King of Heretics.* Princeton: Princeton University Press, 1965.

Historický ústav. *Přehled československých dějin.* 3 vols. Prague: Nakl. Československé akademie věd, 1958–1960.

Hlobil, Ivo. "Obnova mariánského sloupu?" *Umění a řemesla,* no. 3 (1991): 97–98.

Hník, František Martin. *Duchovní idealy Československé církve.* Prague: Nakladatelství Družstva CČS, 1934.

Hobsbawm, Eric J. *Nations and Nationalism since 1780.* Cambridge: Cambridge University Press, 1990.

Hobsbawm, Eric J., and Terrence Ranger. *The Invention of Tradition.* Cambridge: Cambridge University Press, 1983.

Hojda, Zdeněk, and Jiří Pokorný. *Pomníky a zapomníky*. Prague: Paseka, 1996.

Holý, Ladislav. *The Little Czech and the Great Czech Nation: National Identity and the Post-Communist Social Transformation*. Cambridge: Cambridge University Press, 1996.

Hosking, Geoffrey, and George Schöpflin, eds. *Myths and Nationhood*. New York: Routledge, 1997.

Howard, Jeremy. *Art Nouveau: International and National Styles in Europe*. Manchester: Manchester University Press, 1996.

Hrejša, Ferdinand. *Česká konfese, její vznik, podstata a dějiny*. Prague: Nakladatelství české akademie císaře Františka Josefa pro vědy, slovesnost a umění, 1912.

———. *Česká reformace*. Prague: J. R. Vilímek, 1917.

Hroch, Miroslav. *Social Preconditions of National Revival in Europe*. Cambridge: Cambridge University Press, 1985.

Hruban, Moric. *Z času nedlouho zaslých*. Rome: Křestanská akademie, 1967.

Hrubeš, Josef, and Eva Hrubešová. *Pražské domy vyprávějí*. Vols. 1–4. Prague: Academia, 1999 and 2002.

———. *Ve stínu pražských soch a pomníku*. Prague: Nakladatelství Petrklíč, 2003.

Huebner, Todd Wayne. The Multinational "Nation-State." The Origins and Paradoxes of Czechoslovakia, 1914–1920. PhD dissertation, Columbia University, New York, 1994.

Hunt, Lynn. *Politics, Culture, and Class in the French Revolution*. Berkeley and Los Angeles: University of California Press, 1984.

Hus, Jan. *O Církve*. Prague: Nakladatelství československé akademie věd, 1965.

Iggers, Wilma. "The Flexible National Identities of Bohemian Jewry." *East Central Europe* 7, no. 1 (1980): 39–48.

———. *Women of Prague: Ethnic Diversity and Social Change from the Eighteenth Century to the Present*. Providence: Berghahn Books, 1995.

In Memoriam Aloise Simonidesa. Prague: Nakladatelství Melantrich A.S., 1929.

Innes, Abby. *Czechoslovakia: The Short Goodbye*. New Haven: Yale University Press, 2001.

Janáček, Josef. *Ženy české renesance*. Prague: Československé spisovateli, 1976.

Jászi, Oskár. *The Dissolution of the Habsburg Monarchy*. Chicago: University of Chicago Press, 1929.

Jenks, William A. *Austria under the Iron Ring, 1879–1893*. Charlottesville: University of Virginia Press, 1965.

Jewkes, Wilfred T., and Jerome B. Landfield, eds. *Joan of Arc: Fact, Legend, and Literature*. New York: Harcourt, Brace and World, 1964.

Johnston, William M. *The Austrian Mind: An Intellectual and Social History, 1848–1938*. Berkeley and Los Angeles: University of California Press, 1972.

Judson, Pieter M. *Guardians of the Nation. Activists on the Language Frontiers of Imperial Austria*. Cambridge: Harvard University Press, 2006.

Judson, Pieter M., and Marsha L. Rozenblit. *Constructing Nationalities in East Central Europe*. New York: Berghahn Books, 2005.

Kadlec, Jaroslav. *Přehled církevních českých dějin*. 2 vols. Rome: Christian Academy, 1987.

Kafka, Franz. *Briefe 1900–1912*. Frankfurt am Main: S. Fischer Verlag, 1999. (Copublished with Schocken Books, New York.)

Kaminsky, Howard. *A History of the Hussite Revolution*. Berkeley and Los Angeles: University of California Press, 1967.

Kaňak, Miloslav. *Hus stále živý*. Prague: Edice Blahoslav, 1965.

Kann, Robert A. *The Habsburg Empire: A Study of Integration and Disintegration*. New York: Praeger, 1957.

———. *A History of the Habsburg Empire, 1526–1918*. Berkeley and Los Angeles: University of California Press, 1974.

Kantůrková, Eva. *Jan Hus: Příspěvek k národní identitě*. Prague: Melantrich, 1991.

Kaplan, Karel. *Stát a církev v Československu letech, 1948–1953*. Prague: Doplnek, 1993.

Karo, Ninus. "Feuilleton: Pomník Husův." *Národní listy*. Clipping. From Carton 12, no. 158/102. No date (most likely July 1903). SZPH, AHMP.

Kedourie, Elie. *Nationalism*. 4th revised ed. London: Hutchinson, 1985.

Kelly, David. *The Czech Fascist Movement, 1922–1942*. Boulder: East European Monographs, 1995.

Kelly, Theodore Mills. Czech Radical Nationalism in the Era of Universal Manhood Suffrage, 1907–1914. PhD dissertation, George Washington University, Washington, D.C., 1996.

———. "Taking It to the Streets: Czech National Socialists in 1908." *Austrian History Yearbook* 29 (1998): 93–112.

———. *Without Remorse: Czech National Socialism in Late-Habsburg Austri*a. Boulder: East European Monographs, 2006.

Kerber, Linda. *Women of the Republic: Intellect and Ideology in Revolutionary America*. Chapel Hill: University of North Carolina Press, 1980.

Kerner, Robert J. *Bohemia in the Eighteenth Century*. New York: Macmilliam, 1932.

Kieval, Hillel. "In the Image of Hus: Refashioning Czech Judaism in Post-Emancipatory Prague." *Modern Judaism* 5, no. 2, Gershom Scholem Memorial Issue (May 1985): 141–57.

———. *The Making of Czech Jewry: National Conflict and Jewish Society in Bohemia, 1870–1918*. New York: Oxford University Press, 1988.

———. *Languages of Community: The Jewish Experience in the Czech Lands*. Berkeley and Los Angeles: University of California Press, 2000.

Kimball, S. B. *Czech Nationalism: A Study of the National Theater Movement*. Urbana: University of Illinois Press, 1964.

King, Jeremy. *Budweisers into Czechs and Germans*. Princeton: Princeton University Press, 2002.

Kogan, Arthur. "The Social Democrats and the Conflict of Nationalities in the Habsburg Monarchy." *Journal of Modern History* 21, no. 3 (September 1949): 204–17.

Kohn, Hans. *The Habsburg Empire, 1804–1918*. New York: Van Nostrand Reinhold Company, 1961.

Kopičková, Božena. *Historické prameny k studiu postavení ženy v české a moravské středověké společností*. Prague: Historický ústav, 1992.

Korbel, Josef. *Twentieth Century Czechoslovakia: The Meaning of Its History*. New York: Columbia University Press, 1977.

Koreček, Jaroslav, Oldřich Stefan, and Ginette Stočesová. *Kniha o Praha 1959*. Prague: Orbis, 1959.

Kotvun, Jiří, and Zdeněk Lukeš. *Pražský Hrad za T. G. Masaryka*. Prague: Pražský hrad, 1995.

Kovaly, Heda Margolius. *Life under a Cruel Star: A Life in Prague, 1941–1968*. New York: Penguin Books, 1989.

Kraus, Michael, and Allison Stanger. *Irreconcilable Differences? Explaining Czechoslovakia's Dissolution*. Lanham: Rowman and Littlefield, 2000.

Krečič, Peter. "Plečnik and the Critics." In Burkhardt, Eveno, and Podrecca, eds., *Jože Plečnik, 1872–1957, Architecture and the City*.

———. *Plečnik, the Complete Works*. New York: Whitney Library of Design, 1993.

Krejca, Otomar. "Český fašismus (1938–1945): Pokus o bilanci." *Soudové dějiny* 11 (2004): 23–24.

Křen, Jan. *Konfliktní společenství: Češi a Němci, 1780–1918*. Prague: Academia, 1990.

Kristeva, Julia. "Stabat Mater." In *Female Body in Western Culture*, ed. Suleiman.

Kroupa, Jiří, ed. *Veritas vincit—Pravda vítězí*. Prague: Koniasch Latin Press, 1995.

Kubiček, Alois. *Betlémská kaple*. Prague: Státní nakladatelství krasné literatury, hudby a umění, 1953.

Kundera, Milan. *The Book of Laughter and Forgetting*. Trans. Michael Henry Heim. New York: Alfred A. Knopf, 1980.

Kysela, Jan L. *Šalouna Husův pomník v Hořícich*. Prague, 1914.

Landres, J. Shawn, and Oren Baruch Stier, eds. *Religion, Violence, Memory, and Place*. Bloomington: Indiana University Press, 2006.

Lane, Barbara Miller. *National romanticism and modern architecture in Germany and the Scandinavian countries*. Cambridge: Cambridge University Press, 2000.

Le Goff, Jacques. *History and Memory*. New York: Columbia University Press, 1992.

Lesnikowski, Wojciech. *East European Modernism: Architecture in Czechoslovakia, Hungary, and Poland between the Wars, 1919–1939*. New York: Rizzoli, 1996.

Lightbody, Charles Wayland. *The Judgements of Joan*. Cambridge: Harvard University Press, 1961.

Liška, Vladimír. *Husitství: Konec jednoho mýtu*. Prague: Fontána, 2000.

Littell, Robert, ed. *The Czech Black Book*. New York: Praeger, 1969.

MacAloon, John J., ed. *Rite, Drama, Festival Spectacle: Rehearsals toward a Theory of Cultural Performance*. Philadelphia: Institute for the Study of Human Issues, 1984.

Macartney, C. A. *The Habsburg Empire, 1790–1918*. New York: Macmillan, 1969.

MacDonald, C. A. *The Killing of SS Obergruppenführer Reinhard Heydrich*. New York: Free Press, 1989.

Macura, Vladimir. *Masarykové boty a jiné semi (o) fejetony*. Prague: Pražská imaginace, 1993.

Mádl, Karel B. *Vácslav Brožík odsouzení M. Jana Husi*. Prague: Sbor pro zakoupení Brožíkova Husa, 1876.

———. "Husův Pomník." *Volné směry* (1901): 50–69.

Magocsi, Paul Robert. *Historical Atlas of East Central Europe*. Seattle: University of Washington Press, 1993.

Mamatey, Victor S. "The Battle of the White Mountain as Myth in Czech History." *East European Quarterly* 14, no. 3 (September 1981): 335–45.

Mamatey, Victor, and Radomir Luza. *A History of the Czechoslovak Republic.* Princeton: Princeton University Press, 1973.

Margolius, Ivan. *Church of the Sacred Heart.* London: Phaidon Press, 1995.

Masaryk, Tomáš Garrigue. *Česká otázka snahy a tužby narodního obrození.* Prague: Nákladem Času, 1895.

———. *Naše nyněší krise pád strany staročeské a počátkové směru nových.* Prague: Nákladem Času, 1895.

———. *Jan Hus: Naše obrození a naše reformace.* Prague: Čas, 1896.

———. *Karel Havlíček: Snahy a tužby politckého probuzení.* Prague: Nákladem Jana Laichtra, 1896.

———. *Palackého idea českého národa.* Prague: Grosman a Svoboda, 1912.

———. *The Making of a State, Memories and Observations, 1914–1918.* London: George Allen and Unwin, 1927.

———. *The Meaning of Czech History.* Ed. René Wellek. Trans. Peter Kussi. Chapel Hill: University of North Carolina Press, 1974.

Mastny, Vojtech. *The Czechs under Nazi Rule: The Failure of National Resistance, 1939–42.* New York: Columbia University Press, 1971.

———, ed. *Czechoslovakia: Crisis in World Communism.* New York: Facts on File, 1972.

Matějček, A. "Reliefy Karla Pokorného v mausoleu Památníku narodního osvobození." *Umění* 12 (1939): 208.

Merhautová, Anežka, ed. *Katedrála sv. Víta v Praze.* Prague: Akademia, 1994.

Michalski, Sergiusz. *Public Monuments: Art in Political Bondage, 1870–1997.* London: Reaktion Books, 1998.

Mickulecká, Milena. *František Bílek v církve československé husitské.* Prague: ÚR CČSH, 2000.

Miles, Malcolm. *Art, Space, and the City: Public Art and Urban Futures.* London and New York: Routledge, 1997.

Miller, Daniel E. *Forging Political Compromise: Antonín Švehla and the Czechoslovak Republican Party, 1918–1933.* Pittsburgh: University of Pittsburgh Press, 1999.

Moravánszky, Ákos. *Competing Visions: Aesthetic Invention and Social Imagination in Central European Architecture, 1867–1918.* Cambridge: MIT Press, 1998.

Mosse, George. *Nationalization of the Masses: Political Symbols and Mass Movements in Germany from the Napoleonic Wars through the Third Reich.* New York: H. Fertig, 1975.

Nakonečný, Milan. *Vlajka: K historii a ideologii českého nacionalismu.* Prague: Chvojkovo nadatelství, 2001.

Nejedlý, Zdeněk. *Husův Betlém a náš dnešek.* Prague: Orbis, 1954.

———. *Komunisté: Dědici velikých tradic českého národa.* Prague: Práce, 1978. Reprint edition.

Němcová, Božena. *Vybranné spisy: Obrázky.* Prague: Jan Laichtner, 1909.

———. *Babička: Obrázy venkovského života.* Prague: Česká grafická unie, 1949.

290

Nemec, Ludvik. *The Czechoslovak Heresy and Schism: The Emergence of a National Czechoslovak Church*. Philadelphia: The American Philosophical Society, 1975.

———. *Church and State in Czechoslovakia*. Cambridge: Cambridge University Press, 1976.

Nitner, Ernst. "Gesamtstaatlicher Katholikentag Prag 1935: Ein fast unbeachtetes Jubiläum." *Bohemia* 26 (1985): 331–46.

Nolte, Claire E. Training for National Maturity: Miroslav Tyrš and the Origins of the Czech Sokol, 1862–1884. PhD dissertation, Columbia University, New York, 1990.

———. "'Every Czech a Sokol!' Feminism and Nationalism in the Czech Sokol Movement." *Austrian History Yearbook* 24 (1993): 79–100.

———. "Ambivalent Patriots: Czech Culture in the Great War." In Roshwald and Stites, eds., *European Culture in the Great War*, 162–75.

———. *The Sokol in the Czech Lands to 1914: Training for the Nation*. New York: Palgrave Macmillan, 2002.

Nora, Pierre. *Lieux de Memoire*. 3 vols. Paris: Gallimard, 1992.

Norberg-Schulz, Christian. *Genius loci: Toward a Phenomenology of Architecture*. New York: Rizzoli, 1980.

Novák, Arne. *Praha Barokní*. Prague: Mánes, 1915.

Ocenawek, A., et al. *Pamatník sletu slovanského Sokolstva roku 1912 v Praze*. Prague: Ceská obec sokolska, n.d.

Olin, Margaret. *Forms of Representation in Alois Riegl's Theory of Art*. State College: Pennsylvania State University Press, 1993.

Olivová, Vera. *The Doomed Democracy: Czechoslovakia in a Disrupted Europe*. London: Sidgwick and Jackson, 1972.

Orel, Dobroslav. *Svatovaclavský sborník na památku 1000. výroci srmti knižete Václava svatého*. 3 vols. Prague: Statní tiskárna, 1934–1937.

Orlíková, Jana. *Max Švabinský: Ráj a mýtus*. Prague: Gallery, 2001.

Orzoff, Andrea. "The Literary Organ of Politics: Tomáš Masaryk and Political Journalism, 1925–1929." *Slavic Review* 63, no. 2 (Summer 2004): 275–300.

Ozouf, Mona. *Festivals of the French Revolution*. Trans. Alan Sheridan. Cambridge: Cambridge University Press, 1988.

Paces, Cynthia Jean. Religious Images and National Symbols in the Creation of Czech Identity, 1890–1938. PhD dissertation, Columbia University, New York, 1998.

———. "The Battle for Prague's Old Town Square: Symbolic Space and the Birth of the Republic." In Ruble and Czaplicka, eds., *Composing Urban History and the Constitution of Civic Identities*, 165–91.

———. "'The Czech Nation Must Be Catholic!' An Alternative Version of Czech Nationalism during the First Republic." *Nationalities Papers* 27 (1999): 407–28.

———. "The Fall and Rise of Prague's Marian Column." *Radical History Review* 79 (Winter 2001): 141–55; and reprinted in Daniel J. Walkowitz, ed., *Memory and the Impact of Political Transformation on Public Space*, 47–64. Durham: Duke University Press, 2004.

———. "Rotating Spheres: Gendered Commemorative Practice at the 1903 Jan Hus Memorial Festival in Prague." *Nationalities Papers* 28, no. 3 (2000): 523–39.

———. "Religious Heroes for a Secular State: Commemorating Jan Hus and Saint Wenceslas in 1920s Czechoslovakia." In Wingfield and Bucur, eds., *Staging the Past,* 199–225.

Paces, Cynthia J., and Nancy M. Wingfield. "The Sacred and the Profane: Religion and Nationalism in the Bohemian Lands, 1890–1920." In Judson and Rozenblit, eds., *Constructing Identities in East Central Europe.*

Palacký, František. *Dějiny národu českého v Čechách a na Moravě, dle puvodních pramenu.* 6 vols. Prague: B. Kocí, 1908.

"Pamětní list vydaný spolkem pro zbudování 'Husova Pomníku' k Slavnost položení základního kamene k Husovu Pomníku na Velkém Staroměstském náměstí v Praze dne 4. a 5. července 1903." Prague: Nákladem slavnostního výboru, 1903.

Parker, Geoffrey, and Simon Adams. *The Thirty Years War.* London and Boston: Routledge and Kegan Paul, 1984.

Pateman, Carol. *The Disorder of Women: Democracy, Feminism, and Political Theory.* Stanford: Stanford University Press, 1994.

Paulová, Milada. *Dějiny Maffie: Odboj Čechu a Jihoslovanu v letech, 1916–1918.* Prague: Československa grafická unie, 1937.

Pavitt, Jane. *The Buildings of Europe: Prague.* Manchester and New York: Manchester University Press, 2000.

Pech, Stanley Z. *The Czech Revolution of 1848.* Chapel Hill: University of North Carolina Press, 1969.

Pekař, Josef. *O smyslu českých dějin.* Prague: Rozmluvy, 1990.

Pelikan, Jaroslav. *Mary through the Centuries.* New Haven: Yale University Press, 1996.

Peroutka, Ferdinand. *Budování státu.* 4 vols. 3rd edition. Prague: Lidové noviny, 1991.

Petišková, Tereza. *Československý socialistický realismus, 1948–1958.* Prague: Gallery, 2002.

Pichová, Hana. "The Lineup for Meat: The Stalin Statue in Prague." *PMLA* 123, no. 3 (May 2008): 614–30.

Plaschka, Richard Georg. "The Political Significance of Frantisek Palacky." *Journal of Contemporary History* 8, no. 3 (July 1973): 35–55.

Plečnik, Joze. *Chrám Nejsvětějšího Srdce Páne v Praze XII na Kralovských Vinohradech.* Prague: Vydáno v Upomníku Svecení Kostela, 1932.

Plička, Karel. *Prague the Golden City.* London: Hamlyn, 1965.

Podiven. *Češi v dějinách nové doby.* Prague: Rozmluvy, 1991.

Polišensky, Josef V. *The Thirty Years' War and the Crisis of the Seventeenth Century.* Berkeley and Los Angeles: University of California Press, 1971.

———. *History of Czechoslovakia in Outline.* Prague: Bohemia International, 1991.

Politický katolicismus v nástupnických státech Rakousko-Uherské monarchie v letech, 1918–1938. Olomouc, Czech Republic: Univerzita Palackého v Olomouci, 2001.

Porter, Brian J. "The Catholic Nation: Religion, Identity, and the Narratives of Polish History." *Slavic and East European Journal* 45, no. 2 (March 2001): 259–99.

Prasek, Ferdinand. *Vznik Ceskovslovenské církve a patriarcha G. A. Prochazka.* Brno: Ústřední rada Čsl. církve, 1932.

Přehled Československých dějin III, 1918–1945. Prague: Nakladatelství Československé Akademie Věd, 1960.

Prelovšek, Damjan Jože. *Plečnik, 1872–1957.* New Haven: Yale University Press.

Procházka, Gustav Adolf. *Křesťanský humanismus a Československá církev.* Prague: Nákladem ústřední rady CČS, 1932.

Prokeš, Jaroslav. *Jan Žižka z Trocnova a jeho doba.* Prague: F. Borový, 1920.

———. *Základní problémy Českých dějin.* Prague: F. S., 1925.

———. *Počátky české společnosti nauk do konce 18. století.* Prague: Jubilejní fond Královske české společnost nauk, 1938.

Pynsent, Robert. *Questions of Identity: Czech and Slovak Ideas of Nationality and Personality.* Budapest: Central European University Press, 1994.

Rachamimov, Alon. "Between Czechs and Germans: Jewish Students in Prague, 1876–1914." Kulka Prize Lecture presented at the Hebrew University in Jerusalem, January 5, 1994.

Radl, Emanuel. *La Question Religieuse en Tchéchoslovaquie.* Prague: Edition de la Gazette de Prague, 1922.

Rak, Jiří. "Boj o duši národa ve filmu 50 let." *Dějiny a současnost* 13, no. 2 (1991): 34–40.

———. *Bývali Čechové: České historické, myty, a stereotypy.* Prague: Nakladatelství H and H, 1994.

Ramet, Sabrina P. *Nihil Obstat: Religion, Politics, and Social Change in East-Central Europe and Russia.* Durham: Duke University Press, 1998.

Rataj, Jan. *O autoritativní národní stat. Ideologické proměny české politiky v druhé republice 1938–1939.* Prague, 1997.

Reiss, Matthias, ed. *The Street as Stage: Protest Marches and Public Rallies since the Nineteenth Century.* Oxford: Oxford University Press, 2007.

Renč, Václav. *Pražská legenda.* Prague: Společnost pro obnovu Mariánské sloupu, 1994.

Riegl, Alois. "The Modern Cult of Monuments: Its Character and Its Origins." In *Oppositions Reader,* ed. Hays, 621–51.

———. *Kunstwerk oder Denkmal? Alois Riegls Schriften zur Denkmalpflege.* Vienna: Böhlau, 1995.

Riley, Denise. *"Am I That Name?" Feminism and the Category of Women in History.* Minneapolis: University of Minnesota Press, 1988.

Ripellino, Angelo Maria. *Magic Prague.* Ed. Michael Henry Heim. Trans. David Newton Marinelli. Berkeley and Los Angeles: University of California Press, 1973.

Roshwald, Aviel, and Richard Stites, eds. *European Culture in the Great War: The Arts, Entertainment, and Propaganda, 1914–1918.* Studies in the Social and Cultural History of Modern Warfare. Cambridge: Cambridge University Press, 2002.

Rothschild, Joseph. *East Central Europe between the Two World Wars.* Seattle: University of Washington Press, 1974.

Roučka, Zdeněk. *Skočeno a podepsáno. Drama pražského povstání.* Pilsen: ZRandT, 2003.

Royt, Jan. "Mariánský sloup na staroměstském náměstí." *Dějiny a současnost* 5 (1994): 25–28.

Rozenblit, Marsha. "Historiographical Essay." *Austrian History Yearbook* 23 (1992).

Ruble, Blair, and John Czaplicka, eds. *Composing Urban History and the Constitution of Civic Identities.* Baltimore: Johns Hopkins University Press, 2003.

Rutrie, Otto. *Sbory Církve Československé.* Prague: Edice Blahoslav, 1953.

———. *Učení církve československé.* Prague: Edice Blahoslav, 1954.

Šaloun, Ladislav. *Dva návrhy na pomník. M. Jana Husi v Praze.* Prague: Mánes, 1903.

———. *L. Šalouna Husův pomník v Hořicích.* Prague: Unie, 1914.

———. *Dilo—realiguje.* Prague: Unie, 1920.

———. "Z duševní dílny umělcovy." *Dílo* 15 (1920): 83.

Sauer-Kysela, František. *Naše luza, jesuité a diplomaté.* Prague: Nákl. vlastním, 1923.

Sayer, Derek. *The Coasts of Bohemia.* Princeton: Princeton University Press, 2000.

Scheufler, Pavel. *Pražský svět.* Prague: Pražský svět vydavatelství, 2000.

Schmid-Egger, Barbara. *Klerus und Politik in Böhmen um 1900: Wissenschaftliche Materialien und Beiträge zur Geschichte und Landeskunde der böhmischen Länder, Heft 21.* Munich: Lerche, 1974.

Schmidt-Hartmann, Eva. *Thomas G. Masaryk's Realism: Origins of a Czech Political Concept.* Munich: R. Oldenbourg Verlag, 1984.

Schorske, Carl. *Fin-de-Siècle Vienna.* New York: Alfred A. Knopf, 1980.

Schultz, April R. *Ethnicity on Parade.* Amherst: University of Massachusetts Press, 1994.

Scott, Joan Wallach. *Gender and the Politics of History.* New York: Columbia University Press, 1988.

Seifert, Jaroslav "The Head of the Virgin Mary." In *The Poetry of Jaroslav Seifert,* trans. Ewald Osers, 133–34. North Haven: Catbird Press, 1998.

———. *Hlava Panny Marie.* Prague: Národní Muzeum, 1998.

Sen, Samita. "Motherhood and Mothercraft: Gender and Nationalism in Bengal." *Gender and History* 5, no. 2 (Summer 1993): 231–43.

Seton-Watson, R. W. *A History of the Czechs and Slovaks.* Hamden, Conn.: Archon Books, 1965.

Shils, Edward. *Tradition.* Chicago: University of Chicago Press, 1981.

Sidor, Karol. *Slovenská politika na podě pražského sněmu.* 2 vols. Bratislava: Nákladom kníhtlciarne "Andreja," 1943.

Skalický, Karel. "The Vicissitudes of the Catholic Church." In Stone and Strouhal, eds., *Czechoslovakia: Crossroads and Crises.*

Sked, Alan. *The Decline and Fall of the Habsburg Empire, 1915–1918.* New York: Longman, 1989.

Skilling, H. Gordon. *T. G. Masaryk: Against the Current, 1882–1914.* University Park: Pennsylvania State University Press, 1994.

Šmahel, František. "The Idea of the Czech Nation in Hussite Bohemia." *Historica* 16 (1969): 143–247.

Šmejkal, František. *Ladislav Šaloun. Drobná plastika a kresby. Katalog vystavy Praha. zaří - řijen 1981.* Prague: Galerie hlavního města Prahy, 1981.

Smith, Anthony D. *The Ethnic Origins of Nations.* Oxford: Basil Blackwell, 1986.

Šorm, Antonín, and Antonín Krajča. *Mariánské sloupy v Čechách a na Moravě: Přispěvky k studiu barokní kultury.* Prague: Tisteno a vydáno u A. Danka, 1939.

Spector, Scott. *Prague Territories: National Conflict and Cultural Innovation in Franz Kafka's Fin de Siècle.* Berkeley and Los Angeles: University of California Press, 2000.

Sperber, Jonathan. "Festivals of National Unity in the German Revolution of 1848–49."

294

Past and Present 136 (August 1992): 114–38.

Spinka, Matthew. *John Hus at the Council of Constance*. New York: Columbia University Press, 1965.

———. *John Hus and the Church Reform*. Hamden: Archon Books, 1966.

———. *John Hus: A Biography*. Princeton: Princeton University Press, 1968.

Stádníková, Jolana, Antonín Vodák, and Michael Trestík. *Sochy v Praze, 1980–2000*. Prague: Agentura Kdo je kdo Praha, 2000.

Statistická ročenka Republiky Československé, 1934. Prague: Statní úřad statický, 1934.

Steffler, Reinhard. *Die neuen Nationalkirche der Tschecho-Slovakei*. Leipzig: Sächsische verlagsgesellschaft, 1931.

Steiner, Eugen. *The Slovak Dilemma*. Cambridge: Harvard University Press, 1973.

Stone, Norman, and Eduard Strouhal, eds. *Czechoslovakia: Crossroads and Crises, 1918–88*. London: Macmillan, 1989.

Sucharda, Stanislav. *Historie pomníku Fr. Palackého v Praze k slavností odhalení*. Prague: SVU Mánes, 1912.

———. *Pomník Františka Palackého v Praze, Jeho Vznik a Význam*. Prague: Jan Štenc, 1912.

Sugar, P. F., and I. J. Lederer, eds. *Nationalism in Eastern Europe*. Seattle: University of Washington Press, 1969.

Suleiman, Susan Rubin, ed. *The Female Body in Western Culture*. Cambridge: Harvard University Press, 1986.

Švácha, Rostislav. *The Architecture of New Prague*. Cambridge: MIT Press, 1995.

Svoboda, Alois. *Prague, An Intimate Guide to Czechoslovakia's Thousand-Year-Old Capital*. Prague: Sportovní a turistické nakladatelství, 1965.

Szporluk, Roman. *The Political Thought of Thomas G. Masaryk*. New York and Boulder: East European Monographs, 1981.

Taylor, A. J. P. *The Habsburg Monarchy, 1809–1918: A History of the Austrian Empire and Austria-Hungary*. New York and Evanston: Harper and Row, 1965.

Teich, Mikuláš, ed. *Bohemia in History*. Cambridge: Cambridge University Press, 1998.

Teichová, Alice. *The Czechoslovak Economy*. New York: Routledge, 1988.

Tobolka, Zdeněk, and Karel Kramář, eds. *Česká Politika*. 5 vols. Prague: J. Laichter, 1932–1937.

Trapl, Miloš. *Politika českého katolicismu na Moravě, 1918–1938*. Prague: Státní pedagogické nakladatelství, 1968.

———. *Political Catholicism and the Czechoslovak People's Party in Czechoslovakia, 1918–1938*. Boulder: Social Science Monographs, 1995.

Tucker, Aviezer. *The Philosophy and Politics of Czech Dissidence from Patočka to Havel*. Pittsburgh: University of Pittsburgh Press, 2000.

Tudor, Henry. *Political Myth*. New York: Praeger, 1972.

Tuma, Jiří. *Na cestě ke komunistické straně*. N.p., 1975.

Turner, Victor, ed. *Celebration: Studies in Festivity and Ritual*. Washington, D.C.: Smithsonian Institution, 1982.

———. "Liminality and the Performative Genres." In *Rite, Drama, Festival Spectacle*, 19–41.

Uhlíř, Lev. *Ladislav Šaloun a jeho dílo.* Prague: Česká grafická unie, 1930.

Unowsky, Daniel. *The Pomp and Politics of Patriotism: Imperial Celebrations in Habsburg Austria, 1848–1916.* West Lafayette: Purdue University Press, 2005.

Urban, Rudolf. *Die Slavischnationalkirchlichen Bestrebungen in der Tchechoslowakei.* Leipzig: Markertund Petters, 1938.

Vácslav Brožík und sein Gemälde: Mag. Johannes Hus vom Constanzer Concile zum tode verurtheilt. Prague: Verlag des ausstellugs-Comites, 1886.

Vaculík, Ludvík. "Český snář (Czech Dreambook)." In *Cross Currents: A Yearbook of Central European Culture* 3 (1984).

Varikas, Eleni. "Gender and National Identity in *Fin de Siècle* Greece." *Gender and History* 5, no. 2 (Summer 1993): 269–83.

Vávra, Jindřich. *Betlemská kaple.* Prague: Olympia, 1968.

Vegesack, Alexander von, ed. *Czech Cubism: Architecture, Furniture, and Decorative Arts, 1910–1925.* Princeton: Princeton Architectural Press, 1992.

Verdery, Katherine. *The Political Lives of Dead Bodies.* New York: Columbia University Press, 2000.

Vitochová, Marie, Jindřich Kejř, and Jiří Vsktecka. *Prague and Art Nouveau.* Trans. Denis Rath and Mark Prescott. Prague: V Ráji, 1995.

Vlnas, Vít. "Mariánsky sloup." *Přítomnost* 2 (1991): 21–22.

———. *Jan Nepomucký, Česká legenda.* Prague: Mladá fronta, 1993.

Volet-Jeanneret, Helena. *La femme bourgeoise à Prague, 1840–1895.* Geneva: Editions Slatkine, 1988.

Výrut, Karel. *Čtení o Praze 10.* Prague: Zdeněk Urban vydavatelství, 1998.

Walkowitz, Daniel J., and Lisa Maya Knauer, eds. *Memory and the Impact of Political Transformation in Public Space.* Durham: Duke University Press, 2004.

Wandycz, Piotr. *The Price of Freedom.* New Haven: Yale University Press, 1994.

Warner, Marina. *Monuments and Maidens. The Allegory of the Female Form.* New York: Atheneum, 1985.

Weber, Eugen. *Peasants into Frenchmen: The Modernization of Rural France, 1870–1914.* Stanford: Stanford University Press, 1976.

Wechsberg, Lawrence. *Prague the Mystical City.* New York: Macmillan, 1971.

Werstadt, Jaroslav. *Ve jménu Husově pro svobodu národa, K. 20. vyročí Masarykova vystoupení ve Švycarsku dne 4. a 6. července 1915.* Prague: Naše revoluce, 1935.

Wheeler, Bonnie, and Charles T. Wood, eds. *Fresh Verdicts on Joan of Arc.* New York: Garland Publishers, 1996.

Wilentz, Sean, ed. *Rites of Power: Symbolism, Ritual, and Politics since the Middle Ages.* Philadelphia: University of Pennsylvania Press, 1985.

Williams, Kieran. "National Myths in the New Czech Liberalism." In Hosking and Schöpflin, eds., *Myths and Nationhood.*

Wimmer, Anderas. *Nationalist Exclusion and Ethnic Conflict: Shadows of Modernity.* Cambridge: Cambridge University Press, 2002.

Wingfield, Nancy Meriwether. "Conflicting Constructions of Memory: Attacks on Statues of Joseph II in the Bohemian Lands after the Great War." *Austrian History Yearbook* 28 (1997).

296

———. *Flag Wars and Stone Saints: How the Bohemian Lands Became Czech.* Cambridge: Harvard University Press, 2007.

Wingfield, Nancy, and Maria Bucur, eds. *Staging the Past: Commemorations in the Habsburg Lands.* West Lafayette: Purdue University Press, 2001.

Winter, Jay. *Sites of Memory, Sites of Mourning: The Great War in European Cultural History.* Cambridge: Cambridge University Press, 1995.

Winters, Stanley, Robert B. Pynsent, and Harry Hanak, eds. *T. G. Masaryk, 1850–1937.* 3 vols. New York: Macmillan Press, 1989.

Wirth, Zdeněk, et al. *Zmizelá Praha.* Vols. 1–5. Prague: Paseka, 2002.

Wiskemann, Elizabeth. *Czechs and Germans: A Study of the Struggle in the Historic Provinces of Bohemia and Moravia.* New York: St. Martin's Press, 1967.

Witkovsky, Matthew S. "Envisaging the Gendered Center: Prague's Municipal Building and the Construction of a 'Czech Nation,' c. 1880–1914." *Umění* 47, no. 3 (1999): 203–20.

———. "Truly Blank: The Monument to National Liberation and Interwar Modernism in Prague." *Umění* 49, no. 1 (2001): 42–60.

Wittlich, Petr. "Secesní Orfeus." *Umění* 16, no. 1 (1968): 26–49.

———. *České sochařství ve 20. Století, 1890–1945.* Prague: Stát. pedagog. nakl., 1978.

———. *Česká secese.* Vols. 1 and 2. Prague: Odeon, 1982.

———. *Umění a život—doba secese.* Prague: Artia, 1987.

———. *Literatura k dějinám umění: vývojový přehled.* Prague: Karolinium, 1992.

———. *Prague Fin de Siècle.* Paris: Flammarion, 1992.

Wolchik, Sharon, and Alfred G. Meyer, eds. *Women, State, and Party in Eastern Europe.* Durham: Duke University Press, 1985.

Young, James E. *Texture of Memory: Holocaust Memorials and Meaning.* New Haven: Yale University Press, 1994.

Yuval-Davis, N., and Flora Anthias. *Woman-Nation-State.* New York: St. Martin's Press, 1989.

Zacek, J. F. *Palacký: The Historian as Scholar and Nationalist.* The Hague: Mouton, 1970.

Žipek, Alois, ed. *Domov za války: svědectví účastníku.* Prague: Pokrok, 1929, 1931.

Zückert, Martin, and Laura Hölzlwimmer. *Religion in den bömischen Ländern, 1938–1948: Diktatur, Krieg, und Gesellschaftswandel als Herausforderungen für religioeses Leben und kirchliche Organisation.* Munich: R. Oldenbourg Verlag, 2007.

Index

Note: Illustrations are indicated by page numbers in *italic* type.

64, 85, 121, 123–25, 127, 182, 195, 209; and national monuments, 26, 38, 39, 96, 115, 246; and Plečnik, 142, 147; as president, 6, 85–86, 157; and religion and politics, 23–24, 126, 138 (*see also* and Catholicism); reputation of, 219; Seifert and, 220; and Slavic epic forgeries, 61; and Slovakia, 265n8; and Vítkov Hill National Monument, 171–72; and Wenceslas, 132, 269n53; and Wenceslas Memorial, 239; and Wenceslas Millennium, 131–38; and women's equality, 129

Masaryková, Alice, 84

masculinity: cultural associations of, 65–66; Hussite legacy and, 34–35; of national heroes, 248

Mašek, Karel, 179

Mattuš, Karel, 79–80

McDonald's, 240

Memorial Committee of the City of Prague, 196

Memorial to the Victims of Communism, 252, 253

memorials. *See* monuments

memory: in Communist Czechoslovakia, 210; Prague and, 4–6, 16; sacred spaces and, 4–5; values and, 5. *See also* collective memory

men. *See* masculinity

Merhaut, Cyril, 134

Methodius, Saint, 58, 119, 125, 243, 272n25

middle class: economic impact of, 9; and Hus commemorations, 122; and monument construction, 56; and nationalism, 31; political impact of, 19

military: Hussite legacy and, 34; Sokol and, 28, 69; women warriors, 46; Žižka's association with, 69, 71. *See also* Red Army

Mill, John Stuart, 194

Miller, Daniel, 88, 105, 127

Ministerial Council, 196

Ministry for Information and Enlightenment, 175

Ministry of Culture, 235

Ministry of Education, 117, 195–96, 201

Ministry of Technology, 201, 202

Ministry of the Interior, 121

minority nationalities: at Catholic Congress, 154–55; and holidays, 117–18, 160; impact of economic depression on, 139; legislation against, 125

Mittelhauser (general), 124

Moderní revue (Modern Review) (journal), 61

modernism: Catholic Church and, 147; Czech artists and, 61, 72, 141; nationalism and, 40, 57, 72–73, 141; secessionist art and, 40. *See also* avant garde

modernity: attitudes toward, 51, 55; Czech nation and, 81–82; Hus and, 81–82; Hus Memorial and, 49, 51; nationalism and, 18, 37, 267n50

Monkey Business, 244–45

monuments: absence of, 226–27; abstraction in postwar, 226; cult/fever of, 14–15, 18, 56, 70; debates about, 7, 9; and imagined/real communities, 12; intentional vs. unintentional, 88; national, 37–38, 56–73; purpose of, 44; styles of, 15, 56–57, 62, 72–73, 248; value of, art vs. historic, 271n11. *See also* sacred spaces

Moravánszky, Ákos, 140

Moravia: annexation of, 3, 6; as Czechoslovakian, 88; nationalism and, 9; Rodin exhibition in, 15; in Second Republic, 161

Mosse, George, 31, 37

motherhood: and Hus Memorial, 46–51; Mary and, 248; nationalism and, 32–34, 47, 188, 248

Mrazek, Pavel, 245

Munich Agreement (1938), 6, 160–61, 173, 216

Mussolini, Benito, 157, 160

Myslbek, Josef Václav, 56–57, 60–62, 64, 65, 71, 73, 179

Náměstí Jiřího z Poděbrad (Jiří of Poděbrady Square), 144–45

Napoleon Bonaparte, 114

Náprstek, Josefina, 32

Náprstek, Vojta, 20, 24, 27, 29

Národní listy (National News) (newspaper), 26, 28, 44, 61, 82, 92–93, 122, 152

Národní osvobození (National Liberation) (newspaper), 126–27

Národní politika (National Politics) (journal), 77

Naše doba (Our Era) (newspaper), 26

nation: defining, 12; invention of, 246

La Nation Tchéque (journal), 83

National Assembly, 120, 124, 155, 161

National Committee, 94

National Council, 69, 87, 90, 95

National Democrats, 91, 100, 114, 270n69

National Fascist Party, 153

National Front, 165, 169, 173, 184

National Memorial, Vítkov Hill: absurdities concerning, 234–37; art of, 175–82, *181*, *187*, 187–88; Communist Party and, 173–88, 236; Gottwald's remains displayed at, 182–86, 234–35; history of, 170–72; in post-Communist period, 234–37; postwar uses of, 173–75, 185; during Second World War, 165, 171, 172, 179

national memory. *See* collective memory

national minorities. *See* minority nationalities

National Museum, 17, 20, 25, 60, 64, 96, 149, 152, 153, 212, 236

National Socialism, 30–31, 76, 90–91, 159, 263n9, 264n15. *See also* Czechoslovak Socialists; Nazi Germany

National Theater, 34, 61, 82, 126, 153